THE UNFINISHED
MEMOIRS

compliments of the Bangladesh
High Commission, Birmingham

SHEIKH MUJIBUR RAHMAN

THE UNFINISHED MEMOIRS

The University Press Limited
Red Crescent House, Level 6
61 Motijheel C/A
Dhaka 1000, Bangladesh
Phones: (+8802) 9565441, 9852189, 9852190
E-mail: info@uplbooks.com.bd
Website: www.uplbooks.com.bd

Fourth impression in Bangladesh 2018
Corrected impression in Bangladesh 2013

First published in Bangladesh in the original Bangla by The University Press Limited 2012
First published in Bangladesh in English by The University Press Limited 2012
First published in India in Viking by Penguin Books India 2012
First published in Pakistan in English by Oxford University Press Pakistan 2012
First published in Pakistan in Urdu by Oxford University Press Pakistan 2012

Translated from the original Bengali by Dr Fakrul Alam

ISBN 978 984 506 110 0

Published by Mohiuddin Ahmed, The University Press Limited, Dhaka. This book has been set in Crimson Text by SÜRYA, New Delhi and produced by Abarton, 354 Dilu Road, New Eskaton, Dhaka. Printed at the Akota Offset Press, 119 Fakirapool, Dhaka, Bangladesh.

CONTENTS

As a man, what
concerns mankind
concerns me. As a
Bengalee, I am deeply
involved in all that
concerns Bengalees.
This abiding
involvement is born of
and nourished by
love, enduring love,
which gives meaning
to my politics and to
my very being.

Sheikh Mujibur Rahman 3.5.73

As a man, what concerns
mankind concerns me.
As a Bangalee, I am
deeply involved in all that
concerns Bangalees. This
abiding involvement is
born of and nourished
by love, enduring love,
which gives meaning to
my Politics and to my
very being.

Sheikh Mujibur Rahman
30.5.73

(An excerpt from the Personal Notebook of
Bangabandhu Sheikh Mujibur Rahman
Prime Minister of the People's Republic of Bangladesh)

PREFACE

My father, Bangabandhu Sheikh Mujibur Rahman, had to spend the most precious parts of his life in prison. As he got involved in various movements to wrest the rights of his people from those who had snatched them away from them, he had to endure solitary confinement again and again. But he would never compromise on his principles. He was not intimidated even by the hangman's noose. Throughout his life, the cause of his people was dearest to his heart. Their sufferings would sadden him. The only vow he ever took was to bring smiles on the faces of Bengal's impoverished people and build a golden Bengal. He believed that by enjoying their basic rights to food, clothing, accommodation, education and health they would be able to lead an honourable life. The one thought that was constant in his mind was freeing them from the shackles of poverty. That is why he gave up all comforts and happiness and fought ceaselessly and selflessly to attain the rights of his people through a continuous campaign till he was able to bring freedom to the Bengali nation. He was able to establish the Bengalis as a heroic race in the eyes of the world and create an independent and sovereign country. He was able to make the dream of freedom that Bengalis had been dreaming for a thousand years come true. Just when he had succeeded in achieving their economic emancipation he was snatched away from his people by the bullets of assassins. He was made to lie down forever in the green grass of Bengal that had been splattered with his blood. The assassins had thereby managed to mark the forehead of the Bengali nation indelibly with the stamp of infamy.

Twenty-nine years after he had passed away, the autobiography that this great leader had written came into my hands. In what he was able to write we have got the opportunity to learn about many incidents of his passage from childhood to adulthood, his family, and the movements he had become a part of since the time he was a student, his struggles, and many hitherto unknown events of his life. We come across the diverse experiences of his remarkable life in the pages that he had written. He articulates in simple and flowing prose what he had seen, felt and observed in politics. The facts that are revealed by his account of his struggles, his steadfastness and his sacrifices will inspire future generations. Those who have been misled by the fictions of people who distort history will now have the opportunity to discover the truth. This work will provide invaluable information and an authentic account of history to researchers and historians.

This autobiography has been written in my father's own hand. How I came across the notebooks in which this autobiography was inscribed is a long story. At one point I had completely given up the hope of publishing this book and presenting it to you all.

Shortly after he had declared independence at midnight on 25 March 1971, the Pakistani army assaulted the Road 32 home (now House No. 10 on Road No. 11) of the Father of the Nation, Bangabandhu Sheikh Mujibur Rahman, arrested him and took him away. After my father was arrested, my mother, Russel, Jamal and everyone else in the house took refuge in the house next door. Our home was raided again the next day and looted. The raiders took away whatever they could, smashed the rest of the things, and took over the house. My mother had stowed away the notebooks, including his autobiography, diaries and travelogues along with her accounts books, with great care in an almirah in the dressing room attached to my father's bedroom. No doubt because there were a large number of these notebooks which by then may have been discoloured over time, the raiders did not consider them worth looting and left them intact. I thus came across these notebooks as they had been kept.

Soon after all the members of our home who were inside it on 15 August 1975 were murdered, the government sealed the house. I myself returned from exile to our country on 17 May 1981. The Zia government had the house sealed even then. They would not allow me to enter it. On 12 June the Sattar government handed over the house to me. I then found my father's memoir, his diaries and the notebooks of his travels in China. However, I did not find the notebooks containing his autobiography. I also found some typed pages which had been destroyed by termites. Only the upper halves of these foolscap pages remained. Reading whatever was still intact in them, I could guess that they were from his autobiography, but since so much was lost, I decided that what was left would not be of any use. Afterwards, I carried out an extensive search for the notebooks but found nothing. I looked for the original notebooks, the typist and for whatever remained with whoever had taken them, but to no avail. At one point I completely gave up hope of finding them.

However, in 2000 we decided to prepare for the publication of Bangabandhu's memoirs, diaries and his China travelogues. Professor Enayetur Rahim of America's Georgetown University had come to the University of Dhaka to do research on him. Professor Rahim's main area of research was the Agartala Conspiracy case. He had come to Dhaka to hold the Bangabandhu Sheikh Mujibur Rahman Chair established by the Mahbubullah-Zebunnesa Trust. In addition to working on the Agartala Conspiracy case for his research, he also began to work on Bangabandhu's life, memoirs and diaries. The journalist Baby Moudud and I assisted Professor Rahim at this time. He started to translate them from Bengali into English. But his untimely death resulted in a great loss as far as this gigantic task was concerned. I had not even dreamed that he would leave us so suddenly.

I began to despair at the turn of events. Professor A.F. Salahuddin Ahmed, Professor Shamsul Huda Harun and Mr Shamsuzzaman Khan gave us valuable advice and assisted us at this juncture. Subsequently, Professor Salahuddin Ahmed and Professor Harun accepted the responsibility of translation. Baby Moudud and I worked with Mr Khan on editing and typesetting and also made the necessary corrections. We compared what had been typeset with the original manuscript again and again. The work proceeded gradually, overcoming all sorts of obstacles along the way. A deadline was now fixed for publication.

When the work on the 'Memoirs' and the 'Diaries' was almost over, I came across four new notebooks in which the autobiography had been written. On 21 August 2004 a political rally organized by the Bangladesh Awami League was targeted by a horrifying grenade attack. It was aimed at killing me. Twenty-four people, including Mrs Ivy Rahman, president of the Women's Awami League, died in the incident. Miraculously, I survived this assassination attempt. But I was overwhelmed by grief, pain and depression. And it was then that my father's invaluable notebooks containing his autobiography came into my possession. What a remarkable turn of events! It was as if a light had suddenly been sparked in the midst of darkness. I had myself come back to life from the jaws of death. It was as if I had been given a new lease of life. One of my cousins handed these notebooks over to me. He had found them in an office drawer of another cousin, Sheikh Fazlul Huq Moni. Moni was the editor of the newspaper *Banglar Bani.* In all probability, my father had handed the notebooks to this cousin so that he could have them typed. Perhaps he was thinking of having them published. Because Sheikh Fazlul Huq Moni too was martyred on 15 August 1975 he was unable to complete this work. The work thus remained unfinished.

When I had the notebooks in my hand I was at a loss for words. The handwriting was a very familiar one. I called my younger sister, Sheikh Rehana. Our eyes were soon awash in tears. We went over the lines our father had written with our hands so that we could touch him again. It was as if our father was blessing us through the notebooks just after I had come back from the dead. I still had work to do for the poor people of our country—the very people my father used to always describe as Bengal's 'suffering poor'. It was as if the notebooks were telling me that the golden Bengal he had dreamed of still needed to be built. As I turned over the pages of the notebooks and caressed his handwritten lines it seemed to me my father was telling me, 'Don't be afraid, dear; I am with you; go ahead, and be resolute.' It seemed to me that God had miraculously sent a message to me to be indomitable. In the midst of all the grief, pain and depression I had found a shaft of sunlight.

Four notebooks in my father's hand! The notebooks had to be handled with great care. Their pages had become yellow, fragile and frayed. In many places the handwriting had become so indistinct that it was difficult to figure out the words. Some pages inside one of the notebooks had become unreadable and deciphering the lines in these cases proved to be extremely difficult. The next day Baby Moudud, Sheikh Rehana and I started work on the notebooks. Rehana would break down every time we tried to read them. There would be no stopping her flow of tears then. When I began work on the memoirs and diaries I too had often broken down in tears in the initial months. However, I gradually decided to steel myself to the task. The first thing we did was photocopy the notebooks. Abdur Rahman (Roma) helped us do this. We had to be very careful in making the copies for if we moved the pages too often they would tear. Then Baby and I took turns reading all the pages of the notebooks while Munirun Nessa Ninu composed them on the computer. This enabled us to work rapidly since it takes much longer to compose directly from a handwritten script. We took this strategy to save time. The writing had faded so much in places that reading often became a very difficult task. In some places we had to deal with torn pages and writing that had become illegible. In such cases we used a magnifying glass to try to decipher the words. All that had been written in the four notebooks was eventually composed on a computer. The entire notebooks had been signed by the jailer who had noted the number of pages in them. His signature also enabled us to discover their dates of composition.

Next, Baby Moudud and I compared what had been composed on the computer with the notebooks. In this manner we finished the first stage of editing and emending the writing. Then Mr Shamsuzzaman Khan worked with the two of us to edit again, proofread, prepare the notes, scan the work done, and choose the illustrations. Sheikh Rehana was part of everything we did and took overall responsibility of the project.

Even after they have been read repeatedly, one feels like reading these notebooks again. They reveal to us how for the sake of the country and its people a man can sacrifice everything, risk his very life, and endure endless torture in prison. We discover a personality who gave up the prospects of happiness, comfort, relaxation, wealth—everything. How he had forsaken all for the sake of ordinary people can be discovered by an analysis of the autobiography. Following the leads contained in these pages will enable us to gather information about much that still remains to be found out about our past. Many unknown stories will come to light. This fact-filled narrative will allow us to learn a lot more about the movement for Pakistan, the language movement, the movement for independence and self-rule, the struggle for democratic rights, and different conspiracies concocted by the Pakistani government. We will get the opportunity to learn about many other incidents and facts of history. In addition, we will find out how Bangabandhu's experience led him to recognize the machinations of self-seekers and the bid to exploit the country by those who pretend to be administering it. The people of Bangladesh are still going through a lot of hardship. I hope that future generations will be inspired to serve the country and will resolve to do so after going through this autobiography.

This book gives us the story of Bangabandhu's life in his own words till 1955. He wrote it while he was all by himself in the central prison from 1966 to 1969 as a state prisoner. We did not have to do much editing of his writing. Only a few words and the language have been occasionally changed to make the narrative more readable. Because he had intended to publish the story of his life he was going to have it typed. Since he has not dedicated the autobiography to anyone there is no 'Dedication' in this book.

Professor Salahuddin Ahmed offered us valuable advice from the inception of this project. The work of translating the autobiography into English has been done sincerely by Professor Fakrul Alam of the University of Dhaka's English department who was able to complete the translation swiftly. I express my gratitude to them both. Without their valuable advice and assistance it would not have been possible to undertake this great task.

I would like to thank everyone else who assisted in the publication of this book.

SHEIKH HASINA

07.08.2007
Subjail
Sher-e-Bangla Nagar
Dhaka

PS: I wrote the Preface to this work when I was imprisoned. I took steps to publish it after I had been released from jail. I would like to thank Mr Mohiuddin Ahmed, the publisher of UPL, and Mr Badiuddin Nazir, Consulting Editor of UPL, for taking up the responsibility of publishing this work at home and abroad. Dhaneswar Das Champak also helped us with computer graphics and scanning.

SHEIKH HASINA

30.07.2010
Ganabhaban
Sher-e-Bangla Nagar
Dhaka

SHEIKH MUJIBUR RAHMAN (1920–75)

A POLITICAL PROFILE

1920
Sheikh Mujibur Rahman was born on 17 March 1920, in Tungipara village under the then Gopalganj subdivision (at present district) of Faridpur district. He was the third child among four daughters and two sons of Sheikh Lutfar Rahman and Sayera Khatun. His parents used to call him Khoka. He spent his childhood in Tungipara.

1927
At the age of seven, Mujib began his schooling at Gimadanga Primary School. At nine, he was admitted to class three at Gopalganj Public School. Subsequently, he was transferred to a local missionary school.

1934
Mujib was forced to stop studying for a while, at the age of fourteen, one of his eyes had to be operated on.

1937
Mujib returned to school after a break of four years, occasioned by the severity of the eye operation.

1938
At eighteen Mujib married Begum Fazilatunnesa. They subsequently became the happy parents of two daughters, Sheikh Hasina and Sheikh Rehana, and three sons, Sheikh Kamal, Sheikh Jamal and Sheikh Russel. All the sons were killed, along with their parents, on 15 August 1975.

1939

Mujib's political career was effectively inaugurated while he was a student of Gopalganj Missionary School when he attracted the affection of Huseyn Shaheed Suhrawardy, later chief minister of Bengal and prime minister of Pakistan, on his visit to Gopalganj along with A.K. Fazlul Huq, chief minister of undivided Bengal.

1940

Mujib passed the Entrance (currently Secondary School Certificate) examinations. He was admitted as an intermediate student in the arts faculty of Calcutta Islamia College, where he had lodgings at Baker Hostel. That same year he became actively involved in the movement for the creation of Pakistan.

1943

Mujib's busy and active political career took off in the literal sense with his election as a councillor of the Muslim League.

1944

Mujib took part in the conference of the All Bengal Muslim Students' League held at Kushtia, where he played a significant role. He was also elected secretary of Faridpur District Association, a Calcutta-based organization of the residents of Faridpur.

1946

Mujib was elected general secretary of Islamia College Students' Union.

1947

Mujib obtained Bachelor of Arts degree from Islamia College under Calcutta University. When communal riots broke out in the wake of the partition of India and the birth of Pakistan, he played an active role in protecting Muslims and containing the violence.

1948

Mujib took admission in the law department of Dhaka University. He founded the Muslim Students' League on 4 January. He rose in spontaneous protest on 23 February when Prime Minister Khawaja Nazimuddin declared at the Legislative Assembly: 'The people of East Pakistan must accept Urdu as their state language.' Khawaja Nazimuddin's remarks led to a storm of protest across the country. Sheikh Mujib immediately plunged into hectic activities to build a strong movement against the Muslim League's move to make Urdu the only state language of Pakistan. He established contacts with students and political leaders. On 2 March, a meeting of the workers of different political parties was held to plan the course of the movement against the Muslim League on the language issue. The meeting held at Fazlul Huq Muslim Hall approved a resolution placed by Sheikh Mujib to form an All-Party State Language Action Committee. The Action Council called for a general strike on 11 March to register its protest against the conspiracy of the Muslim League against the Bengali language. On 11 March, Mujib was arrested along with some colleagues while they were holding a demonstration in front of the Secretariat building. The student community of the country became restive following his arrest. In the face of student protests, the Muslim League government was forced to release Mujib and other student leaders on 15 March. Following his release, the All-Party State Language Action Committee held a public rally at Dhaka University Amtala ground on 16 March. Mujib presided over the rally, which was soon set upon by the police. To protest the police action he immediately announced a countrywide student strike on 17 March. He was arrested again on 11 September for joining the movement against the 'cordon' system at Faridpur.

1949

Mujib was released from jail on 21 January. He extended his support to a strike called by Class Four employees of Dhaka University to press home their various demands. The university authorities imposed a fine on him for leading the movement of the employees. He rejected the unjust order. Mujib was arrested for staging a sit-in strike before the vice chancellor's residence. When the East Pakistan Awami Muslim League was formed on 23 June, he was elected its joint secretary despite his imprisonment. He was released in late June. Immediately after his release, he began organizing a movement against the prevailing food crisis. In September he was detained for violating Section 144. However, he was freed later.

He raised the demand for Chief Minister Nurul Amin's resignation at a meeting of the Awami Muslim League in October.

The Awami Muslim League brought out an anti-famine procession in Dhaka on the occasion of Pakistan's Prime Minister Liaquat Ali Khan's visit to the province. Once again Mujib was arrested and jailed for leading the demonstration.

1952

At a public meeting on 27 January, the Prime Minister of Pakistan, Khawaja Nazimuddin announced that, in terms of the declaration of Mr M.A. Jinnah, Urdu would be the only state language of Pakistan. The students, youth activists and members of the civil society immediately protested just as they had done in 1948. Although Mujib had been incarcerated since October 1949, he had managed to establish close contacts with the politically active leaders and workers and through them he ensured that an All-Party State Language Action Committee was formed. He encouraged them to observe 21 February as a 'State Language Day'. At the same time he had informed the authorities that he was determined to go on an indefinite hunger strike from 16 February in order to protest his incarceration without charge under the Public Security Act. Soon afterwards on 14 February, the authorities moved him from Dhaka jail and sent to Faridpur jail.

On 21 February, the student community violated the prohibitory order under Section 144 and they were fired upon by the police. As a result of their repressive actions, on the following days, Salam, Barkat, Rafique, Jabbar, Shafiur, Abdul Awal and Ohiullah were killed and they are now recognized as martyrs of the 'Language Movement'. Mujib's hunger strike continued for thirteen days and his health began to seriously deteriorate. The authorities were, therefore, compelled to release him from jail on 28 February.

1953

On 9 July, Mujib was elected as the general secretary of the East Pakistan Awami Muslim League at its council meeting. Efforts were made to build unity among Maulana Bhasani, A.K. Fazlul Huq and Shaheed Suhrawardy with the objective of defeating the Muslim League at the ensuing general elections. To achieve this, a special council session of the party was called on 14 November, in which a resolution to form the Jukta Front (United Front) was approved.

1954

The first general elections in East Bengal were held on 10 March. The United Front won 223 seats out of 237. The Awami League was victorious in 143 seats. Mujib won the election for the Gopalganj constituency by a margin of 13,000 votes, defeating the influential Muslim League leader Wahiduzzaman. He took oath on 15 May as minister for agriculture and forest in the new provincial government. The central government arbitrarily dismissed the United Front ministry on 29 May. Mujib was once again arrested when his plane landed at Dhaka airport from Karachi on 30 May. He was released on 23 December.

1955

Mujib was elected as a member of the Constituent Assembly on 5 June. The Awami League held a public meeting at Paltan Maidan (ground) on

17 June. A twenty-one-point programme was put forward demanding autonomy for East Pakistan. On 23 June, the working committee of the Awami League took a decision that the Awami League members of the Legislative Assembly would resign if autonomy was not granted to East Pakistan.

On 25 August, Mujib told the Pakistan Constituent Assembly in Karachi:

> Sir, you will see that they want to use the phrase 'East Pakistan' instead of 'East Bengal'. We have demanded many times that you should use Bengal instead of East Pakistan. The word 'Bengal' has a history and tradition of its own. You can change it only after the people have been consulted. If you want to change it, we have to go back to Bengal and ask them whether they are ready to accept it. So far as the question of one unit is concerned it can be incorporated in the constitution. Why do you want it to be taken up right now? What about the state language, Bengali? We are prepared to consider one unit with all these things. So, I appeal to my friends on that side to allow the people to give their verdict in any way, in the form of referendum or in the form of plebiscite.

On 21 October, Awami Muslim League dropped the word 'Muslim' from its name at a special council meeting to make the party a truly modern and secular one. Mujib was reelected general secretary of the party.

1956

On 3 February, the Awami League leaders, during a meeting with the chief minister, demanded that the subject of provincial autonomy be included in the draft constitution. On 14 July, at a meeting the Awami League adopted a resolution opposing the representation of the military in the administration. The resolution was moved by Mujib. On 4 September, an anti-famine procession was brought out under the leadership of Mujib defying Section 144. At least three persons were killed when police opened fire on the procession in the Chawk Bazar area. On 16 September, he assumed the responsibility of industries, commerce, labour, anti-corruption and village-aid ministry in the coalition government.

1957

On 30 May, in response to a resolution of the party Mujib resigned from the cabinet to strengthen the organization by working full-time. From 24 June to 13 July, he visited China on an official tour.

1958

Pakistan's President, Major General Iskander Mirza, and the chief of Pakistan's army, General Ayub Khan, imposed martial law on 7 October and banned political activities. Mujib was arrested on 11 October. Thereafter, he was continuously harassed in false cases. He was released from prison after fourteen months but was arrested again at the jail gate.

1961
Mujib was released from jail after the high court declared his detention unlawful. After his release from jail he started covert political activities against the martial law regime and Ayub Khan, the dictator. He set up an underground organization called 'Swadhin Bangla Biplobi Parishad' (Revolutionary Council for Independent Bengal) comprising leading student leaders in order to work for the independence of Bangladesh.

1962
Mujib was arrested under the Public Security Act on 6 February. He was freed on 18 June following the withdrawal of the four-year-long martial law on 2 June. On 25 June, Mujib joined other national leaders to protest the unlawful measures introduced by General Ayub Khan. On 5 July he addressed a public rally at Paltan Maidan. He vigorously criticized Ayub Khan in his speech. He went to Lahore on 24 September and joined Shaheed Suhrawardy to form the National Democratic Front, an alliance of opposition parties. He spent the entire month of October travelling across East Pakistan along with Shaheed Suhrawardy to build up public support for the Front.

1963
Mujib went to London for consultations with Suhrawardy, who was there for medical treatment. On 5 December, Suhrawardy died in Beirut.

1964
The Awami League was reactivated on 25 January at a meeting held at Mujib's residence. The meeting adopted a resolution to demand the introduction of parliamentary democracy on the basis of adult franchise in response to public sentiments. The meeting elected Maulana Abdur Rashid Tarkabagish as party president and Mujib as general secretary. On 11 May, an All-Party Action Committee was formed. Mujib led a committee to defuse communal riots. After the riots he launched a vigorous anti-Ayub movement on behalf of his party. Mujib was arrested fourteen days before the presidential election.

1965
The government charged Mujib with sedition and for making objectionable statements. He was sentenced to one-year imprisonment. He was later released by an order of the high court.

1966
On 5 February, a national conference of the opposition parties was held in Lahore. Mujib placed his historic six-point programme before the select committee of the conference. The six-point demand was the charter of freedom of the Bengali nation. On 1 March, Mujib was elected the president of the Awami League. Following his election, he launched a campaign to obtain support for the six-point demand. He travelled around the country. Police arrested and detained him several times at Sylhet, Mymensingh and Dhaka during his campaign; in all, he was arrested eight times in the first quarter of the year. On 8 May, he was arrested after a speech at a rally of jute mill workers at Narayanganj. A countrywide hartal was observed on 7 June to force the government to release Mujib and other political prisoners. Police opened fire on picketers during the hartal and killed a number of workers in Dhaka, Narayanganj and Tongi.

1968
The Pakistani government filed the infamous Agartala Conspiracy Case against Mujib and thirty-four Bengali civil and military officers. He was named as 'accused number one' in the case. The arrested persons were charged with conspiring for the secession of East Pakistan from the rest of Pakistan. Those accused were detained inside Dhaka Cantonment. Demonstrations took place throughout the province, demanding the release of Mujib and the other co-accused in the Agartala Conspiracy case. The trial began on 19 June in Dhaka Cantonment amidst tight security.

1969
The Central Students' Action Council was formed on 5 January to press for the acceptance of the eleven-point programme which included the six-point demand. The council initiated a countrywide student agitation to compel the government to withdraw the Agartala Conspiracy Case and free Mujib. The agitation was gradually transformed into a mass movement. After months of protests, the government imposed a ban on meetings and processions under Section 144 and resorted to curfews and indiscriminate shooting by the police and the East Pakistan Rifles (EPR). Such actions led to a number of casualties, while the movement itself peaked in an unprecedented mass upsurge that forced Ayub Khan to convene a round-table conference of political leaders and announce Mujib's release on parole. Mujib rejected the offer of release on parole. On 22 February, the Pakistan government submitted to the continued mass protests and freed Mujib and the other co-accused. The conspiracy case was withdrawn. The Central Student Action Council arranged a reception in honour of Mujib

on 23 February at the Race Course ground (Suhrawardy Udyan). One million people attended the meeting. Mujib was publicly declared as Bangabandhu (Friend of Bengal) in the meeting. In his speech on the occasion, he pledged his whole-hearted support to the eleven-point demand of the students.

On 10 March, Mujib joined the round-table conference called by Ayub Khan in Rawalpindi. At the conference he placed the six-point demand of his party and the eleven-point demand of the students and said: 'To end people's anger there is no other alternative to the acceptance of the six-point and eleven-point demands and the granting of regional autonomy.' When the Pakistani politicians and rulers discarded his demand he left the conference on 13 March and returned to Dhaka the next day. On 25 March, General Yahya Khan took over and imposed martial law. On 25 October, Mujib went to London on a three-week organizational tour. At a discussion meeting held on 5 December to observe the death anniversary of Shaheed Suhrawardy, Mujib declared that henceforth East Pakistan would be called Bangladesh. He added, 'There was a time when evil efforts were made to wipe out the word "Bangla" from our land and map. The existence of the word "Bangla" was found nowhere except in the Bay of Bengal. I on behalf of the people proclaim today that the eastern province of Pakistan will be called "Bangladesh" instead of "East Pakistan".'

1970

Mujib was re-elected president of the Awami League on 6 January. The Awami League at a meeting of the working committee on 1 April declared that it would take part in the general elections scheduled for later that year. On 7 June, Mujib addressed a public meeting at the Race Course ground and urged the people to elect his party on the basis of the six-point demand. On 17 October, he chose the boat as his party's election symbol and launched his campaign at an election rally at Dhaka's Dholai Khal. On 28 October, he addressed the nation over radio and television and called upon the people to elect his party's candidates to the National Assembly to implement the six-point demand. When a devastating cyclonic storm hit the coastal belt of Bangladesh, killing at least one million people, Mujib suspended his election campaign and rushed to the aid of the helpless people in the affected areas. He condemned the Pakistani rulers for their indifference to the victims. He called upon the international community to help the people affected by the cyclone. In the general elections held on 7 December, the Awami League acquired an absolute majority. The Awami League secured 167 seats out of 169 National Assembly seats in East Pakistan and won 288 out of 300 seats in the Provincial Assembly.

1971

On 3 January, Mujib conducted the oath of the peoples' representatives at a meeting at the Race Course ground. Awami League members took an oath to frame a constitution on the basis of the six-point demand and pledged to remain loyal to the people who had elected them. On 5 January, Zulfikar Ali Bhutto, the leader of the People's Party, the majority party in West Pakistan, announced his readiness to form a coalition government at the centre with the Awami League. Mujib was elected as the leader of the Awami League's Parliamentary Party at a meeting of the members of the National Assembly (MNAs) of his party. On 27 January, Zulfikar Ali Bhutto arrived in Dhaka for talks with Mujib. The talks failed after three days of deliberations. In an announcement on 13 February, President Yahya Khan summoned the National Assembly to sit in Dhaka on 3 March. On 15 February, Bhutto announced that he would boycott the session and demanded that power be handed over to the majority parties in East Pakistan and West Pakistan. In a statement on 16 February, Mujib was critical of Bhutto for putting forward such a demand and declared, 'The demand of Bhutto saheb is totally illogical. Power is to be handed over to the majority party, the Awami League. The power now lies with the people of East Bengal.'

On 1 March, Yahya Khan abruptly postponed the National Assembly session which prompted a storm of protest throughout Bangladesh. Mujib presided over a meeting of the Awami League working committee. The Awami League called a countrywide general strike on 3 March. After the success of the general strike, Mujib demanded that the President immediately transfer power to his party.

On 7 March, Mujib addressed a mammoth public rally at the Race Course ground, where he declared: 'The struggle this time is the struggle for emancipation. The struggle this time is the struggle for independence. Joi Bangla.' In this historic speech, Mujib urged the nation to break the shackles of subjugation and declared, 'Since we have given blood, we will give more blood. By the will of the Almighty God, the people of this land will be liberated . . . turn every house into a fortress. Face (the enemy) with whatever you have.'

Mujib advised the people to prepare themselves for a resistance movement against the enemy. He asked the people to start a non-cooperation movement against the government of Yahya Khan. There were orders from Yahya Khan, on the one hand, and on the other Mujib's directives from Road 32, Dhanmondi. The entire nation carried out Mujib's instructions. Every organization, including government offices, courts, banks, insurance companies, schools, colleges, mills and factories obeyed his orders. The overwhelming response of the people of Bangladesh to his call was unprecedented in the region's history. In reality, he ruled an independent Bangladesh from 7 March to 25 March.

On 16 March, Yahya Khan came to Dhaka for talks with Mujib regarding the transfer of power. Bhutto also came a few days later to Dhaka. The Mujib–Yahya–Bhutto talks continued until 24 March. Yahya Khan left Dhaka secretly in the evening of 25 March. At the dead of the night of 25 March, the Pakistan army cracked down on innocent unarmed Bengalis. They attacked Dhaka University, the Pilkhana Headquarters of the East Pakistan Rifles and the Police Headquarters at Rajarbagh.

Moments after the crackdown began, Mujib declared independence at 12.30 a.m., 26 March. His declaration was transmitted through wireless to every place in the country. He said, 'This may be my last message; from this day onward Bangladesh is independent. I call upon the people of Bangladesh wherever you might be and with whatever you have, to resist the army of occupation to the last. Your struggle must go on until the last soldier of the Pakistan occupation army is expelled from the soil of Bangladesh. Final victory is ours.'

Mujib also sent a message in Bengali, which reads as follows in translation:

> The Pakistani army has suddenly attacked Pilkhana EPR Headquarters, Rajarbagh Police Line [barrack]. Skirmishes are going on all over the streets of the city. I am calling for help to the nations of the world. Our freedom fighters are fighting valiantly against the enemy to liberate our motherland. In the name of Almighty God I order and call upon you to liberate our country. Fight even if you have one drop of blood in you. Ask for help from the police, EPR, Bengal Regiment and Ansars. Ask them to fight side by side with you. Any question of compromise does not arise. Victory will be ours. Drive out the last soldier of the enemy from our sacred land. Pass this message to all Awami League leaders, workers and all compatriots. God bless you. Joi Bangla (Victory to Bengal).'

Mujib's message was immediately disseminated throughout the country under special arrangements. All sections of people, including Bengali military and paramilitary forces, police, government employees, political workers, students, labours and peasants started putting up resistance to the Pakistan army. The Pakistan army arrested Mujib from his Dhanmondi residence at 1.30 a.m., and whisked him away to Dhaka Cantonment. From there he was flown to Pakistan as prisoner three days later. On

26 March, General Yahya Khan, in his speech, banned the Awami League and declared Mujib a traitor.

On 26 March, M.A. Hannan, an Awami League leader in Chittagong, read out Mujib's declaration of independence over Chittagong radio. On 10 April, the Provisional Revolutionary Government of Bangladesh headed by Mujib as its President was formed.

The revolutionary government took the oath of office on 17 April at the Amrakanan of Baidyanathtala in Meherpur, which is now known as Mujibnagar. Mujib was elected President, Syed Nazrul Islam acting president and Tajuddin Ahmed Prime Minister. The Liberation War ended on 16 December when the Pakistani occupation forces surrendered at the historic Race Course ground, conceding defeat in the glorious war led by the revolutionary government-in-exile. Bangladesh was finally free.

Earlier, between August and September of 1971, the Pakistani junta held a secret trial of Mujib inside Faisalabad (Lyallpur) jail in Pakistan. He was sentenced to death. The freedom-loving people of the world demanded security for him. On 27 December, the Bangladesh government sought Mujib's immediate and unconditional release. A number of countries, including India and the Soviet Union, and various international organizations also demanded the release of Mujib. They held that Pakistan had no right to detain Mujib, who was the President of independent Bangladesh.

1972

Bowing to international pressure, the Pakistan government released Mujib on 8 January 1972. Zulfikar Ali Bhutto met Mujib on the same day. Mujib immediately left for London en route to Dhaka. In London, British Prime Minister Edward Heath met him. On his way back to Dhaka from London he stopped in New Delhi. He was received by Indian President V.V. Giri and Prime Minister Indira Gandhi at the airport. An unforgettable reception was accorded to Mujib when the Father of the Nation reached Dhaka on 10 January. From the airport he drove straight to the Race Course ground. He delivered his address before the mammoth gathering. On 12 January, Mujib took over as the prime minister of Bangladesh. On 6 February he visited India at the invitation of the Indian government. After twenty-four years of expulsion the Dhaka University authorities rescinded his earlier expulsion order.

On 1 March, he went to the Soviet Union on an official visit. The allied Indian army left Dhaka on 12 March at Mujib's request. On 1 May, he announced a raise in the salary of Class Three and Four employees of the government. On 30 July, Mujib went to London for medical treatment and from there he went to Geneva. On 10 October, the World Peace Council conferred the Julio Curie award on him. On 4 November, Mujib announced that the first general election in Bangladesh would be held on 7 March 1973. On 15 December, Mujib's government announced that state awards would be given to freedom fighters. On 14 December, he affixed his signature to the draft Constitution. On the first anniversary of the liberation the constitution of the People's Republic of Bangladesh was adopted.

The important achievements of Mujib's government were: the reorganization of the administrative system, framing of the constitution, rehabilitation of one crore people, restoration and development of the communication system, expansion of education, supply of free books to students up to class five and low-priced books to students up to class eight, effective ban on all anti-Islamic and anti-social activities, for example, gambling, horse race, consumption of liquor, establishment of the Islamic Foundation, reorganization of the Madrasa Education Board, establishment of 11,000 primary schools, nationalization of 40,000 primary schools, establishment of a women's rehabilitation centre for the welfare of distressed women in the war of liberation, establishment of the Freedom Fighters' Welfare Trust, tax waiver up to 25 bighas of land, distribution of agricultural inputs among farmers free of cost or at nominal price, nationalization of banks and insurance companies and of 580 industrial units abandoned by the Pakistanis and employment of thousands of workers and employees, construction of the Ghorasal Fertilizer Factory, primary work of the Ashuganj Complex and establishment of new industrial units and reopening of closed industries. Mujib successfully worked on setting up economic infrastructure to lead the country towards progress and prosperity. Another landmark achievement of Mujib's government was to have Bangladesh recognized by a large number of countries of the world in the shortest possible time.

1973

The Awami League secured 293 seats out of the 300 Jatiyo Sangsad (Parliament) seats in the first general elections. On 3 September, the Awami League, the Communist Party of Bangladesh (CPB) and the National Awami Party (NAP) formed the Oikya Front (United Front). On 6 September, Mujib set off to Algeria to attend the Non-Aligned Movement (NAM) summit conference.

1974

The People's Republic of Bangladesh was accorded membership of the United Nations. On 25 September, Sheikh Mujibur Rahman addressed the UN General Assembly in Bengali for the first time in the history of the UN.

1975

On 25 January, the country switched over to the presidential system of government and Mujib took over as the President of the republic. On 24 February, the Bangladesh Krisak Shramik Awami League, comprising all the political parties of the country, was launched. On 25 February, Mujib called upon all political parties and leaders to join the national party. He felt the need to make Bangladesh a self-reliant nation by reducing dependence on foreign aid. He significantly revised economic policies to achieve the goal of self-reliance. He launched a Second Revolution to make independence meaningful and ensure food, clothing, shelter, medicare, education and generate employment for the people. The objectives of the revolution were elimination of corruption, boosting production of mills, factories and fields, population control and establishment of national unity.

Mujib received an unprecedented response to his call to achieve economic freedom by uniting the entire nation. The economy started picking up rapidly. Production increased. The prices of essentials came down. Imbued with hope, people came forward to help extend the benefits of independence to every doorstep.

However, in the pre-dawn hours of 15 August, the noblest and greatest of Bengalis, Sheikh Mujibur Rahman, the architect of Bangladesh and the Father of the Nation, was assassinated by a handful of ambitious and treacherous military officers. On that day, his wife, Begum Fazilatunnesa; his eldest son, Sheikh Kamal; second son, Lieutenant Sheikh Jamal; youngest son, Sheikh Russel; two daughters-in-law, Sultana Kamal and Rosy Jamal; his brother Sheikh Naser; brother-in-law and Agriculture Minister Abdur Rab Serniabat and his daughter Baby Serniabat; son Arif Serniabat, grandson Sukanto Abdullah; and nephew Shahid Serniabat; Mujib's nephew, youth leader and journalist Sheikh Fazlul Huq Moni and his pregnant wife Arzoo Moni; his military secretary Colonel Jamil; and a fourteen-year-old boy Rintoo were killed. Altogether the assassins murdered sixteen persons.

Martial law was imposed in the country after the killing of Sheikh Mujibur Rahman. Democracy was done away with and basic rights were snatched away. Thus began the politics of killing, coups and conspiracy. The people's rights to food and vote were taken away.

There is an international provision to hold trials of killers and to protect human rights throughout the world. But unfortunately in Bangladesh, a law was enacted on 26 September under a martial law ordinance indemnifying the self-proclaimed killers of Mujib from any trial. Having captured power illegally through a military coup d'état, General Ziaur Rahman stained the constitution by incorporating the infamous Indemnity Ordinance in the Fifth Amendment to the Constitution. He rewarded the killers by assigning them to Bangladesh diplomatic missions abroad. The Indemnity Ordinance, which is against basic human rights, had to be repealed and the killers are to be punished to restore rule of law in the country.

After Mujib's daughter Sheikh Hasina came to power at the head of an Awami League government on 23 June 1996, on 2 October a case was filed in the Dhanmondi police station against those involved in the murder of the Father of the Nation, Sheikh Mujibur Rahman and his family members. On 12 November, the Jatiyo Sangsad annulled the Indemnity Ordinance.

The trial began on 1 March 1997 in the court of the Dhaka district and sessions judge. On 8 November 1998, the judge of the court, Kazi Gholam Rasul, delivered a 76-page verdict in which he sentenced fifteen of the accused to death. On 18 November 2000, two judges gave a split judgement. The matter was then referred to a third judge of the High Court who ruled decisively in favour of upholding the death sentence on twelve of the accused. Five of the convicted prisoners then filed a 'leave to appeal' with the appellate division of the court. When the Bangladesh Nationalist Party–Jamat alliance was in power from 2002 to 2006 it dropped the case from the 'cause-list'. A bench was finally formed to hear the case in 2007. On 19 November, 2009 after 29 days of hearings a judicial bench comprising the chief justice and four other judges rejected the appeal. Thereafter on 27 January four judges also dismissed the review petition. The following midnight, that is, on 28 January, five of the assassins were executed. One of the assassins had died while a fugitive from justice overseas and six are still hiding in other countries. However, the demand that the murderers be tried had finally been addressed thirty-four years after the assassination of Mujib and the murder of his family members.

August 15, 1975 is the blackest day in Bangladesh's history. The nation observes it as the National Mourning Day.*

*Excerpted from the album, *Father of the Nation,* 3rd Edition, 2010, published by the Father of the Nation Bangabandhu Sheikh Mujibur Rahman Memorial Trust, Dhaka.

My friends keep telling me, 'Why don't you write your memoirs?' My colleagues keep saying, 'Write down your experience of politics; it will prove to be of use one day.' My wife told me one day while sitting with me in a room within the jail gate, 'Since you are idle, write about your life now.' I told her, 'I can't write, and in any case what have I done that is worth writing about? Will the public benefit from the stories of my life? I haven't been able to achieve anything! I guess all I can say is that I have tried to sacrifice a bit of me for my principles and ideals.'

One evening my jail warden locked my door from outside and left. From inside the small room of Dhaka Central Jail, I looked at the sky. I thought of Mr Suhrawardy[1] then. Of how I came to be acquainted with him. How I had become intimate with him. How he taught me the essentials of political life and how I came to earn his love.

Suddenly it occurred to me: What if I wasn't able to narrate events skilfully? Would it really be awful if I wrote down whatever I could remember? At least I would be able to while away time that way! Often in jail, my eyes would tire from reading books and newspapers all the time. And so I took a notebook and started to write. I found that I could still recollect many things. My memory was serving me well. Perhaps I would get a few dates wrong by a day or two, but I was hopeful of getting the events down more or less accurately. Renu, my wife, had bought me some notebooks and left them for me with my jailers. They had vetted them and then allowed me to keep them. Renu too reminded me once more what I should do with them. And so this day I have started to write my memoir.[2]

~

I was born in Tungipara village of Gopalganj subdivision in Faridpur district.[3] Ours was the last union[4] carved out of the southern part of the district. The Modhumati river flows past it. This river separated Faridpur from Khulna district.

Tungipara's Sheikh family was fairly well known in the region. Now it can be viewed as a middle-class family. From the old people and well-known men of the locality some stories associated with this region and the family can be gathered. I was born into this family. A very religious man named Sheikh Borhanuddin founded it many years ago. That the Sheikh family was once well-established can be deduced from the fact that buildings made from small bricks dating from the Mughal era are part of the family heritage. There were four such buildings once. There was only one entrance door to the compound housing these buildings and during my childhood it was shut from within with the help of a wooden door shutter. A grandfather of mine used to live in one of these buildings. In another an uncle somehow still survives. Another of these buildings has collapsed and now houses poisonous snakes. Most members of our extended family no longer have the wherewithal to keep these buildings standing. Many of them now live in tin-roofed houses surrounding these crumbling buildings. I was born in one of these houses.

From family elders as well as the lyrics of songs sung by local bards I managed to find out how the Sheikh family plummeted in status from being possessors of great wealth to proprietors of ruins. I have no doubt that most of the accounts I gathered of the family's fortunes are true. The Sheikh family, in fact, has lost almost everything and can now only boast of their past glory and deeds of a long time ago.

No one knows exactly where Sheikh Borhanuddin came from and what made him decide to live on the banks of the Modhumati. The buildings in our family compound were over two hundred years old. No records exist of the next three or four generations either. But some information is available about Sheikh Borhanuddin's grandson and about two brothers two generations down the line. Many stories about these two brothers can still be heard in the region. One of them was called Sheikh Qudratullah and the other one was named Sheikh Ekramullah. All of us who now remain are descendants of these two brothers. The Sheikh family was quite well-off even during the lifetime of these brothers. They were landlords and owned big businesses.

Sheikh Qudratullah was a businessman and very much a family man. Sheikh Ekramullah was a leader of men; he dispensed social justice in the locality.

Sheikh Qudratullah was the older of the two brothers. This was the time the East India Company had annexed Bengal and built the Calcutta port. The English began to settle in the region and cultivate indigo. One story about Sheikh Qudratullah still makes the rounds here. It is a true story. In

Alaipur of Khulna district an Englishman called Mr Ryan began to plant indigo and build a cottage. Indeed, the cottage still exists. The Sheikhs had a fleet of boats. These would sail to Calcutta. Mr Ryan would often detain these boats and the boatmen for a long time. He would seize not only the boats of the Sheikhs but also those of other people. If anyone attempted to resist him, he would punish them brutally. Everyone knows how vicious the Englishmen of that period were. The Sheikhs had not yet become weak and powerless. They fought Ryan's men and took them to court on innumerable occasions. The verdict that the court eventually delivered was that Ryan had been unjust in his dealings. The court told Sheikh Qudratullah he could impose any amount of money as penalty on Ryan and declared that the Englishman was bound to pay the amount. That was how justice was dispensed in those days. Sheikh Qudratullah decided that the best way to humiliate Ryan would be to have him pay half a poisha,[5] in other words, half of the coin of the lowest denomination. To this Ryan said, 'I am willing to give you as much money as you want, but don't humiliate me, for then the English will make me an outcast since a blackie managed to fine me only half a poisha'. It is said that the Sheikh replied, 'I don't count my earning, I just weigh my wealth. I don't need money. You have insulted my people and so I have taken revenge.' Sheikh Qudratullah was more commonly known as 'Kodu Sheikh' to the people. Even now the old folks of Khulna and Faridpur narrate this story to others. There are songs too of 'Qudratullah Sheikh's half a poisha fine' that are still sung. Once I had gone to Bagerhat for a meeting. With me was the advocate Zillur Rahman. On my way I met an old man in the train. When he found out who I was, he told me the story. The story is quite popular even in Khulna.

It was one or two generations after the deaths of Sheikh Qudratullah and Ekramullah that the Sheikh dynasty began to decline in importance. Successive turns in their fortune meant that while they continued to be considered aristocrats, their wealth and property gradually diminished. The English used to look at the Muslims suspiciously. The first event of note in this period is that after Rani Rasmoni became a zamindar she immediately waged war against the Sheikhs with the help of the English. Sheikh Asimuddin used to look after the Sheikhs' Calcutta property and trading establishment. There was endless litigation involving land-ownership with Rani Rasmoni's estate. In Sriramkandi village, a place only three miles away from the Sheikh holdings, lived a very formidable man named Tamizuddin. He sided with Rasmoni on the land issue. He was a good fighter. Once the two sides were engaged in a conflict. Rani Rasmoni's forces were defeated in the conflict. Tamizuddin lay injured and was captured by the Sheikhs after which it was believed that he died in custody. A case was filed against them. All the Sheikhs were arrested. They managed to become free again only after they had spent a fortune.

Another unfortunate event happened soon after. The Tungipara Sheikhs' lands bordered the estate of another clan, whose genealogy also went back a long way. They were known as the Kazi dynasty. They were distant relatives of the Sheikhs. But they were constantly involved in clashes with them despite the blood ties. Although the Kazis were no match for the Sheikhs in terms of wealth or property they feuded with them endlessly. One branch of the family, however, was on our side. But the members of another branch were in league with Rani Rasmoni's men. This branch would never accept the primacy of the Sheikhs in the region. In the end they adopted a reprehensible strategy. Although the majority of the Kazis had become one with the Sheikhs a faction of them had decided to fight the Sheikhs. An old man of the Kazi dynasty called Sirajtulla Kazi had three sons and a daughter. The sons got together to strangle their father and grab his property and left the body on the roof of the Sheikh family's barn. The brothers and the sister all knew what had really happened. However, the brothers had frightened their sister into silence. They then went to the police and informed them that there was a dead body in the place. They helped the police retrieve the body. They also persuaded them to arrest all the members of the family. The Sheikhs found themselves in a tight spot once again.

My paternal grandfather's uncle and my wife Renu's paternal great-grandfather eventually declared bankruptcy in Calcutta and returned to the village. The Calcutta property had to be forfeited. As soon as the Sheikh men were jailed, and there was no one to maintain their business interests, boatmen, influential businessmen and traders who did business with the family drowned their boats and assets and fled the scene of the crime. The Sheikhs had already spent a considerable amount on the Tamizuddin murder case. The Sheikh estate was put up for sale and was on the point of being purchased. The case dragged on for a long time. The lower courts sentenced all of them to jail. In the end the case went up to the Calcutta High Court. The lawyer representing our family petitioned the high court to launch a fresh inquiry with the help of the CID [Criminal Investigation Department]. This was because we knew that the charges were all fabricated. The high court too found the case of dubious merit and ordered a new inquiry. An officer went to our village disguised as a mad man and began gathering information. One night Kazi Sirajtulla's three sons were quarrelling over something or the other. In the course of the heated argument, one of them said to another, 'Didn't I say that it wasn't right to kill our father in such a manner and that nothing would be done to the Sheikhs?' The other brother said, 'You killed our father by choking him!' The sister said, 'Abba wanted some water and you wouldn't even let him have that!' The CID officer overheard the conversation since he was hiding in a corner of their house. A few days later the three brothers and the sister were arrested and were made to confess their parts in the death of their father.

The Sheikhs were now released while Sirajtulla's children got life sentences. But while the Sheikhs had become free, they had lost everything in getting themselves acquitted. Their business was gone, the estate all but lost, and all they had left was some land that they owned in and around their homes. As a matter of fact, the land that they owned was not inconsiderable. Still, they managed to cultivate properly whatever was left. Since this was enough to feed the family my great-grandfather and his brother would spend their time playing dice. That and eating and sleeping were their only business. They were equally conversant in Persian and Bengali. Renu's grandfather, my grandfather's first cousin, had written his autobiography in very fine Bengali. Renu managed to inherit a few pages of the work along with the property she and her sister got from her grandfather. Renu's father, who was not only my father-in-law but also my uncle, passed away while his father was alive. According to Muslim law Renu wasn't supposed to inherit the property. But because Renu had no uncles, her grandfather willed his property to the girls. We could have gleaned more information about our family had we been able to recover more pages of the autobiography. But someone or the other must have stowed it away to keep some things in the dark. Renu searched a lot for the remaining pages but to no avail. We have heard some other stories about our ancestors, but it is difficult to determine their authenticity.

Even when the Sheikhs had fallen on hard times, they couldn't stand the English. And because they refused to accept the English or learn their language, they fell behind in society. Also, land owned by Muslim families tends to get fragmented because of Muslim inheritance laws. And so while the family continued to grow, their property continued to be split and their financial situation grew steadily worse. However, a few Sheikhs were relatively better off than the others.

It was from my grandfather's generation that the Sheikhs began to learn English. My grandfather was not well-off since he was one of three brothers who went their own ways. My grandfather's eldest brother was quite wise. In his lifetime, he used to solve local disputes and social matters.

My grandfather died suddenly. My eldest uncle died shortly after he had passed his entrance examination for college and at a time my father was about to sit for the same examination. My father found himself in a tight spot since he had become responsible for his family and its many junior members. My grandfather's eldest brother had no sons but had four daughters. He married off his youngest daughter to my father and gave her all the property. My maternal grandfather's name was Sheikh Abdul Majid while my paternal grandfather was called Sheikh Abdul Hamid. The youngest brother was named Sheikh Abdul Rashid. The English later gave Sheikh Abdul Rashid the title of 'Khan Saheb' and this is what locals used to call him. Even though my father's situation eventually improved he had to bear all the expenses of my uncles' education and my aunts' marriages. In the end he was forced to abandon the idea of studying and left the village looking for a job. In those days Muslims had a tough time finding jobs. Ultimately, he managed to get a position in the Dewani court where he eventually became a sherestedar.[6]

The day I passed my matriculation examination and went to Calcutta's Islamia College was the day my father collected his pension money and returned home.

I need to narrate an event here that will surely astonish many. When I got married I must have been around thirteen years old. After Renu's father died, her grandfather called my father and said, 'You will have to marry off your eldest son to one of my granddaughters. This is because I intend to bequeath all my property to my two granddaughters.' Renu's grandfather was my father's uncle and I had to marry her because of my father's command. The marriage ceremony was confined to an official registration. All I could gather about the event was that I had been married off. I was not able to comprehend the implications of the act. Renu herself was three years old then. When she was five years old her mother died. All she had left in the world was her grandfather. He, too, died when she was only seven. When he died she came to live with us. She was raised with my siblings. Her eldest sister was married off to one of my cousins. They took over my father-in-law's house, since Renu and I didn't need a home to move to. In any case, their house was next to ours. The other events of our married life will be narrated hereafter.

~

I was born on 17 March 1920. My father's name was Sheikh Lutfar Rahman. My grandfather's youngest brother, Khan Saheb Abdul Rashid, had set up a school called M.E. School. This was the only English-language school in our area. Later it became a high school and it still exists. I studied in this school till I completed my third grade. Then I went to Gopalganj to stay with my father and enrolled in Gopalganj Public High School.

My mother's name is Sayera Khatun. She would never stay with my father in town. She would look after our property. She used to say, 'My father gave me his property so that I could stay in our home. If I leave for the city, no candle will light up the house, and we will displease him.'

My maternal and paternal grandfathers' houses were adjacent to each other, and I usually dwelled at my maternal grandfather's. I stayed with my father and began my education with him. I used to sleep with my father. I couldn't fall asleep without holding on to him. Since I was the eldest son, I used to get all his affection. His second brother had no children and his youngest brother had only one son. My cousin was conferred the title of 'Khan Saheb' and became a member of the Provincial Assembly of East Pakistan when General Ayub Khan became president. He was also a member of the District Board. His name is Sheikh Musharraf Hossain.

In 1934, when I was in grade seven, I became gravely ill. As a child I was very naughty. I used to play a lot and sing, and was proficient in brotochari, a kind of folk dance. Afflicted by beriberi, my heart became very weak. My father took me to Calcutta for treatment. He consulted the most famous Calcutta physicians—Shibapada Bhattacharjee, A.K. Roy Chowdhury and others—and followed the treatment regime they had devised for me for over two years.

In 1936 my father was transferred to Madaripur as its sherestedar. Since I was still ill, he had my mother come over to be with us. In 1936 my eyes started to fail me. I was suffering from glaucoma then. At the advice of our local physicians, my father took me to Calcutta once more for treatment. At this time I had enrolled in Madaripur High School and was in grade seven. In Calcutta we consulted Dr T. Ahmed. My sister was staying in Calcutta then, since my brother in-law was working in the office of the Accountant General of Bengal [AGB]. She was the second of my sisters and the mother of Sheikh Fazlul Huq Moni. Moni's father was distantly related to us, and part of the Sheikh family. I used to stay with my sister and had no problems living in Calcutta. The doctor recommended an eye operation, stressing that any delay could make me blind. He had me admitted to Calcutta Medical College Hospital. I was scheduled for surgery at 9 a.m. I was so scared that I tried to run away but did not succeed. I was taken to the operating theatre for surgery on one eye. Within ten days there was another surgery on the other eye. I eventually recovered but had to wear glasses from then on. That is why I have had glasses since 1936. I also had to discontinue studies for a while.

After the eye operation I returned to Madaripur but had nothing much to do for some time. No studies and no sports for me; going to meetings in the evening was the only diversion I had. This was the time of the Swadeshi movement.[7] Madaripur's Purna Das was then terrorizing the British. The Swadeshi movement for self-rule had spread to every part of Madaripur and Gopalganj. It seemed to me that Subhas Bose's party was the most powerful of all the political parties in Madaripur. Boys who were still in their teens flocked to join it. When some of the party people saw me attending their meetings regularly they became interested in me. I began to harbour negative ideas about the British in my mind. The English, I felt, had no right to stay in our country. We had to achieve independence. I too became an admirer of Mr Bose and started to travel back and forth between Gopalganj and Madaripur to attend meetings. I also began to mix with the people in the Swadeshi movement. That the then SDO [subdivisional officer] of Gopalganj had cautioned my paternal grandfather, Khan Saheb, is a story I came to know later.

I resumed studies in 1937. However, I didn't go back to my old school, since my friends there had moved far ahead of me in their studies. My father had me admitted to Gopalganj Mission School. He himself went back to the town. He engaged Kazi Abdul Hamid as my tutor. He even set aside a room in our house for him. My father had built the Gopalganj house himself. My tutor established the Muslim Welfare Association, a society to help poor students in Gopalganj. He enlisted our help to collect alms from all over the Muslim part of town for this cause. We used to go from door to door every Friday for this. He would then sell the rice and with the money collected help students buy books and meet examination and other expenses. He would also search all over town to find houses where these boys could stay, paying for their lodging by tutoring the children in the families. I had to do a lot of work for him. But he died suddenly of tuberculosis. I then took over the society and looked after it for a long time. Another Muslim teacher used to keep track of the money collected. He became the president and I the general secretary of the society. If any Muslim refused to help us, we would join forces to make him pay his share. In some cases, we resorted to having such people's houses pelted with stones at night. My father often punished me for following this policy. However, he would not prevent me from working for the society itself. I used to also play a lot. I especially enjoyed playing football, volleyball and hockey. Although I wasn't very good at these games, I used to play for the school team. At this time I wasn't really active in politics.

My father used to keep many newspapers. He subscribed to *Ananda Bazar*, *Basumati*, *Azad*, the monthly, *Mohammadi* and *Saugat* and other newspapers. I used to read them from an early age. I was older than most boys in my class because of the four years I had lost due to my illness. I was a very obstinate boy. I had my own gang of boys. I would mercilessly punish anyone who offended me. I would fight a lot. If any member of my band was ever insulted we would pounce on the offender. At times my father would become fed up with my aggressive manner. Since we lived in a small town where all my deeds would eventually be reported to him, I was quite scared of my father. I was also scared of Mr Abdul Hakim Mia, another gentleman of the town, who was also my father's close friend as well as his colleague. He would either report our activities to my father or scold us himself. Even if we managed to escape my father's attention we failed to escape Hakim Mia's hawk eyes. We used to live on one side of the town and he on the other. He has passed on, but his children have done well in life. One of them has a good job with the central government and the other one is a Civil Service of Pakistan [CSP] officer. The then Gopalganj MLA [member of the Legislative Assembly] was Khondokar Shamsuddin Ahmed, a famous lawyer. His eldest son Khondokar Mahbubuddin Ahmed, aka Feroz, was my friend. We were very close to each other. Feroz is now an advocate at the high court. We were such great friends that we felt miserable if we failed to meet each other every day. My father and Khondokar Shamsuddin Ahmed were also good friends. Mr Ahmed was a very amiable man. People used to respect and love him. He was a member of the late A.K. Fazlul Huq's Krisak Shramik Party.[8] When Mr Huq became the prime minister of Bengal and joined the Muslim League, Mr Ahmed followed him, even though no party of the period was well-organized. Everything used to depend on personal popularity in those days. The Muslim League existed more on paper than in actuality.

In 1938 a significant event of my life occurred. Mr Huq was then the prime minister of Bengal and Mr Suhrawardy the labour minister. They were scheduled to visit Gopalganj. A huge meeting was to be organized for their visit. It was decided to hold an exhibition on the occasion too. After all, the two eminent leaders of the Muslim community of Bengal would be coming to town and all Muslims of the area were excited at the prospect. I was still in school then. As I noted before, I was older than the boys I used to hang out with and so was given responsibility of the volunteer brigade. I formed the brigade with everyone who was willing to join it regardless of their religion or beliefs. Later, it became apparent that the Hindu boys were leaving the group one by one. Unable to figure out why this was happening, I asked a friend what was going on. He told me that the Congress party had directed them not to participate in the event and had even instructed them to make sure the leaders were not given a grand reception. They were also asked to ensure that shops were made to shut down on that day. In those days Hindus owned 80 per cent of the shops in town. The news surprised me since we didn't treat Hindus and Muslims differently then. I was very friendly with the Hindu boys. We used to play, sing and roam the streets together.

Our leaders said that because Mr Huq had formed the government with the help of the Muslim League, the Hindus were fuming. This information had an electric effect on me. Mr Huq and Mr Suhrawardy were to be given a reception. We had to do everything that was necessary to achieve this. I formed a volunteer brigade with the help of the Muslim boys. Some Scheduled Caste Hindus joined our brigade too. They did so because Mukunda Bihari Mullick was a minister of the cabinet and he was part of Mr Huq's entourage. The Hindus formed a majority of the town's population. People came from the villages, armed with all sorts of weapons, ready to fight if there were any attempts to thwart the event. There was even the possibility of a communal riot breaking out.

Mr Huq and Mr Suhrawardy arrived as scheduled and the meeting was finally held. The exhibition was inaugurated formally. Everything took place peacefully. Mr Huq went to the Public Hall while Mr Suhrawardy went to the Mission School. Since I was a student of the Mission School I welcomed him. He inspected the school and then walked towards the launch and I followed him all the way. He asked me a few questions haltingly in Bengali that I answered as well as I could. He looked at me and asked me my name and wanted to know about my family. A government official told him about my family's origins. He took me by the arm and asked me affectionately, 'Don't you have the Muslim League in your area?' I told him that there was no such organization and that not even the Muslim Students' League was active here. He made no other comment but wrote down my name and address in his notebook. A few days later I got a note from him thanking me and asking me to meet him if I ever went to Calcutta. I replied to his letter. This is how I started to write to him from time to time.

Another noteworthy event occurred at this time. The Hindus and Muslims were somewhat wary of each other. There were a few Hindu villages surrounding Gopalganj town. One or two Muslims were tortured in them. I had a class friend called Abdul Malek who was a kinsman of Khondokar Shamsuddin Ahmed. One evening, probably in March or

April, I was coming home after playing football. Khondokar Shamsul Huq, aka Basu Mia Muktar (later president of the Awami League, Gopalganj subdivision), called me and said that Malek had been forcibly taken to the house of a Hindu Mahasabha leader called Suren Banerjee and beaten up there. Could I look into the matter? He stressed that since Malek was my friend I should try to free him from their clutches. I decided to waste no time. I gathered some students and went to their house and requested them to let Malek go. A gentleman called Ramapada Dutt started to abuse me verbally as soon as he saw me. I protested and immediately sent for the boys of my band. In the meantime Ramapada went to the police to inform them about me. Three policemen arrived. I declared that they would have to let Malek go or I would snatch him away. My uncle, the late Sheikh Serajul Huq, was then a student and used to stay in a hostel. He was the first cousin of both my parents. I had an uncle in Narayanganj called Sheikh Zafar Sadek. His older brother had died soon after he had passed his matriculation examination. When he heard that I had sent for people he came to help me with a group of boys. By this time we were involved in a fight with the Hindus. Both sides were in the thick of action. We managed to break the door and snatch away Malek. The whole town was tense. Nobody dared to say anything to me.

That day was a Sunday and my father was in Tungipara. He was expected back the next day. But the distance he had to cover was almost fourteen miles. My father used to go to Tungipara every Saturday and return on Monday in his boat.

The Hindu leaders huddled together with some Hindu officers and filed a case against me. In it Khondokar Shamsul Huq Muktar was accused of instigating this crime. The charges against me were homicide and of starting a riot and looting. In the morning we found out that my uncle, Muktar; the *muhuri* [clerk] of Khondokar Shamsuddin Ahmed, MLA, Zahur Sheikh; my good friend and neighbour Sheikh Nurul Huq, aka Manik Mia; Syed Ali Khondokar; my class friend Abdul Malek; and a lot of other students were also among the accused. They seemed to have left no sons of distinguished Muslims of the area out of the list. At nine in the morning we learned that my uncle and quite a few other people had been arrested. But how could the police arrest us? The officer at the police station was feeling embarrassed. At ten the police officer stood outside in the field chatting to someone, clearly intending to let me use the opportunity to disappear. Our house was located next to the Town Hall. My cousin was from Madaripur. He told me, 'Why don't you go to the neighbouring house?' I declared, 'I'm not going anywhere! If I do, people will say that I was afraid.' At this point my father had come back from his trip. The police officer followed him into the house. He told my father what had happened. He showed him the warrant for my arrest. My father said, 'Take him!' The police official said, 'Let him eat. I am leaving a policeman behind. He has to be in the police station by 11 a.m. If he delays, it will be difficult to get bail for him.' My father asked me, 'Did you get into a fight?' I kept quiet, indicating thereby that I had.

I took my lunch and then went to the police station. I saw that eight others, including Manik and Syed, had already been arrested and brought to the station. As soon as I came, they rounded us all up and took us to the court. We were not handcuffed but had guards surrounding us. The police officer in the court was a Hindu. When we arrived there he had us shut in the small room in the court jail that was next to the courtroom. As soon as he saw me he exclaimed, 'Mujibur is a violent chap. He has attacked Ramapada with a knife. He shouldn't be given bail under any circumstance.' I retorted, 'Don't talk nonsense, such talk won't do you any good.' Those who were sitting with the police officer said, 'Imagine the cheek of the boy!' The others asked me to keep quiet. Later, I found out that the others had lodged a complaint against me for trying to kill Ramapada with a knife. He was in a bad state and had been admitted to hospital. I had actually fought him with a stick; when he had tried to hit me with it I had grabbed it from him and had hit him instead. In the process I had managed to wound him in the head. The Muslim lawyers appealed to the court for our bail.

However, only Muktar was granted bail. We were to be sent back to the jail. The SDO was a Hindu and wouldn't grant us bail. The court officer attempted to handcuff us. I protested but the others restrained me and so I had to go to jail. It was a subjail and consisted of a single room. One part of it was screened off and had been set aside for women prisoners but since there weren't any we were kept on that side. We were allowed to have food, clothes and bed linen sent to us from our homes. After seven days in prison we were allowed to go. Within ten days all of us had been given bail.

Telegrams were sent to Mr Huq and Mr Suhrawardy. People were sent to Calcutta to contact them too. Gopalganj town was all astir. My father was friendly with the Hindu lawyers of the town. All of them respected him. The two sides met on a number of occasions and finally decided that all proceedings would be withdrawn and the case dismissed. We would have to pay 1500 taka as compensation. All of us pooled in to pay this amount. My father had to pay the most. This was the first time in my life that I had been to jail.

~

In 1939 I went to Calcutta for a visit. I met Mr Suhrawardy there. Mr Abdul Wasek led students at that meeting. We talked to him and invited him to come to Gopalganj. We told Mr Suhrawardy that we would form a Muslim Students' League as well as a Muslim League in our town. By that time Khondokar Shamsuddin, MLA, had joined the Muslim League. He became president of the Muslim Student League and I its general secretary. The Muslim League was formed. One Muktar Saheb was made secretary but I used to do all the work. A Muslim League Defence Committee was also formed. They made me its secretary. And so I gradually got drawn into politics. My father did not prevent me from participating in politics; his only concern was that I should continue to pursue my studies. I was in fact getting interested in my studies then. I had after all lost a few years already because of my illness and was beginning to make up for them.

~

In school I was crazy about sports. However, my father tried to discourage me from playing since my heart wasn't strong. My father himself was a good sportsman. He was secretary of the Officers' Club. I was captain of the Mission School. When my team played father's club people were quite excited. Our school team was quite strong. We used to admit the best players of the region and exempt them from paying tuition fees.

In 1940 my team managed to defeat my father's team in almost every sport. And yet the Officers' Club had no shortage of funds. It would recruit players from outside our area. All of them were big-name players. In the last football match of the season our team drew with father's team for five successive days. We were all students and the eleven of us always played together whereas the Officers' Club always had to hire a fresh set of players for every game. But we had become exhausted from the effort. Father said we would have to play the next morning to come up with a decisive result. He argued that they couldn't keep the players that they had hired in our town forever since it was costing them a lot.

However, I pointed out that we had examinations the next morning and thus wouldn't be able to play at that time. The secretary of Gopalganj Club began to shuttle back and forth between my father and me and after some time gave up in exasperation, declaring, 'This is between you and your father; I can't keep shuttling back and forth as a negotiator between you two forever.'

The headmaster of our school was a man called Roshoranjan Sen Gupta. He used to tutor me at that time. My father summoned him. I took up position along with my players at one goalpost while my father took his stand on the other side. The headmaster urged me to yield to my father's request and play the next morning since they had a real problem on their hands what with their out-of-town players. I told him that the eleven of us were exhausted since we had been playing endlessly all year long. I pointed out to him that our bodies were aching and we needed to rest for at least a couple of days. The alternative would be to have us lose badly. I also stressed that we hadn't lost a game that whole year and this was the final of the prestigious A.Z. Khan Shield Tournament. A.Z. Khan was a SDO who had died in Gopalganj. Among his sons, Amir and Ahmed were my childhood friends. I was especially close to Amir. He now works in Radio Pakistan and is better known as Amiruzzaman Khan. When his family had to leave Gopalganj when Mr Khan died, I was very sad. But to come back to my story, in the end I had to yield to the headmaster's request and so our team played father's team the next morning. We lost the game by one goal.

~

In 1941 I was scheduled to sit for my matriculation examination. That I would pass it appeared to be a sure thing. Mr Roshoranjan was teaching me English while the maths teacher of our school, Mr Monoranjan, was tutoring me in that subject. I was intimidated by maths, since I tended to make mistakes in it. I felt that I wouldn't get a first division because of maths. But the day before the examination started I had high fever and mumps, which left me with a sore throat. In fact I had a 104-degree fever. My father stayed awake the whole night to nurse me. He brought all the physicians of Gopalganj town to treat me. But nothing they did could alleviate the high temperature. In the end my father decided that I wasn't going to sit for the examination. I told him I would try to do my best and even appear for it from my sickbed. The first day the test was on Bengali. I had such high fever in the morning that I found it impossible to lift my head; nevertheless, I wrote as much as I could. In the evening the fever started to recede. I did well in the other subjects. But when the results came out we found that I had got poor grades in maths even though I had received second division grades in all other subjects. I felt shattered.

By this time I had become deeply involved in politics. I had begun to spend a lot of time going to meetings and speaking in them. I lost interest in sports as a result. All I could think of was working for the Muslim League and the Muslim Students' League. I believed that we would have to create Pakistan and that without it Muslims had no future in our part of the world. The one newspaper that I read was the *Azad* and I felt that all I read in it was true. I went to Calcutta soon after my examinations. I began attending meetings there too. I also went to Madaripur and set up a Muslim Students' League there.

I also resumed my studies. After all, I would have to pass my examinations. I often visited Mr Suhrawardy's house. He was very affectionate. And I soon became associated with the Muslim League in Gopalganj.

In the war years the relationship between Mr Fazlul Huq and Mr Jinnah soured. Mr Huq refused to submit to the leadership of Mr Jinnah and formed a coalition government in Bengal with Shyama Prasad Mookerjee. The Muslim League and its workers started a campaign to discredit him. I joined in this campaign whole-heartedly. In this year I passed my matriculation examination and was placed in the second division. I now got myself admitted to Calcutta's Islamia College and stayed in Baker Hostel. In two by-elections in Natore and Balurghat the Muslim League put up candidates against Mr Huq's candidates. I took my followers to both these places and campaigned tirelessly at Mr Suhrawardy's directive.

Something noteworthy happened at this time, though I can't remember the exact dates now. The year, probably, was 1941. Faridpur's Muslim Students' League was organizing a conference. Many distinguished people were invited to it. Among them were the poet Nazrul Islam and the educationists Humayun Kabir and Ibrahim Khan. But we were not allowed to stage the event. Instead Section 144, prohibiting congregations, was imposed on the town. We then held the conference in Mr Humayun Kabir's house. Kazi Nazrul Islam sang his songs on that occasion. We declared that the conference wouldn't discuss political issues and would concentrate on teachers and students and their roles. Nevertheless, the students attending the conference split into two factions. In 1942 I went to Faridpur and managed to bring the feuding factions together and made them all concede that it was important to work unitedly to achieve Pakistan. At that time Mr Mohan Mia was president of the district's Muslim League and [Abdus] Salam Khan was its general secretary.

In 1942 Mr Jinnah was scheduled to visit Bengal to join the conference of the Provincial Muslim League. The conference was to be held in Sirajganj, Pabna. I headed for the conference with a large group of party workers. Most of us were from the Muslim Students' League. The reception committee had its office in Syed Akbar Ali's residence. I preferred to stay close to Mr Suhrawardy on all occasions. Mr Anwar Hossain was one of our leaders. I had come to know him in Calcutta. Mr Suhrawardy liked him a lot.

The students were split into two groups. Chittagong's Fazlul Quader Chowdhury was the leader of one group. He was always squabbling with Mr [Abdul] Wasek. I don't think it will be wrong to characterize Mr Wasek as the father of the League's student faction. He held the post of president of the Muslim Students' League, a position he had occupied for a long time. He had probably completed his studies at least fifteen years ago. And yet he wasn't willing to relinquish his position. If anyone opposed him he would say, 'Who are you to talk? You are neither a councillor nor a member of the Students' League. Get out of the meeting immediately.' At first no one objected to his behaviour out of respect for him. The first major difference surfaced probably either in 1941 or 1942 in the Chuchura conference. Fazlul Quader Chowdhury and our group objected vehemently to his actions. In the end, Mr Suhrawardy had to intervene to resolve the situation. But my group and I left the conference in support of Fazlul Quader Chowdhury's position. At that time Sadekur Rahman—now a high-ranking government official—was the general secretary of the provincial wing of the Muslim Student League. Anwar Hossain succeeded him in this position later. We were present at the Bogra conference but didn't take part in the proceedings since the president of the All India Muslim Student Federation, Raja Saheb of Mahmudabad, pledged to hold an election immediately after electing an ad hoc committee. Such a committee was formed in the end, but it existed only on paper.

Around this time, I became very popular among the students of Islamia College. I managed to nominate a candidate who was even able to defeat the official Students' League candidate. This college was at the heart of the student movement for the freedom of our country. The next year too Mr Anwar's official Students' League candidate lost to us. In the next three years no one attempted to contest the election against us. The student union elections were held but candidates were elected unopposed. I would nominate candidates after consultations with the student leaders and there would be no other nominations. Everyone knew that nobody could get elected if he did not have my backing. Zahiruddin would back me up. He was from Calcutta and he was quite influential among the students. There everyone also respected him since he was a selfless worker. He was fluent in English, Bengali and Urdu. Later, he moved on to study in the university but we continued to be good friends. When he left Calcutta to work for some time in Dhaka Radio I was handicapped by his absence.

In 1943 a terrible famine broke out. Hundreds of thousands of people were dying. At this time I became a member of the Provincial Muslim League Council. Mr Abul Hashim had become the general secretary of the

League. Mr Suhrawardy had nominated him. Mr Khawaja Nazimuddin had nominated Khulna's Mr Abul Kashem but Mr Hashim was able to defeat him and become the general secretary, succeeding Mr Suhrawardy. From this time on, the Muslim League broke into two factions, one of which was progressive and the other reactionary. Under Mr Suhrawardy's leadership we wanted to make the Muslim League the party of the people and make it represent middle-class Bengali aspirations. Up to this time the Muslim League had not become an organization that was rooted in the people. It used to serve the interests of landlords, moneyed men, and Nawabs and Khan Bahadurs. They would prevent anyone else from playing a role in the League. In district after district these people had monopolized the League.

Under Khawaja Nazimuddin's leadership not less than eleven members of his family were elected from Dhaka in 1937. When in 1943 he became prime minister he made his younger brother Khawaja Shahabuddin the minister for industries. We objected to this but he wouldn't listen to us. We then went to Mr Suhrawardy with our objections but he said nothing in our support. He himself had become the minister for civil supplies. By this time the famine had spread. Hundreds of thousands of people were swarming to the cities in search of food. But there was no food or clothing left for them. The British had confiscated all naval vessels for the war effort. They had stockpiled rice and wheat to feed their soldiers. Whatever was left had been appropriated by businessmen. This led to a horrifying situation. Businessmen began to sell rice that would normally sell at ten takas a maund at forty or even fifty takas. Not a day went by without people dying on the city streets. A few of us students went to Mr Suhrawardy and told him, 'There is no way you can save the masses and in turn you will end up being wrongly blamed for everything.' He replied, 'Let me see what I can do. I hope to be able to save at least some lives.'

Overnight, Mr Suhrawardy was able to create a huge civil supplies department. He organized 'Control' shops to sell foodgrain. He gave orders for gruel kitchens to be opened in villages. He went to Delhi to inform the central government of the gravity of the situation in Bengal and asked for aid. He had rice, wheat and flour transported in barges. But the English had given priority to the war effort and for them the people of Bengal came second. As far as they were concerned, precedence would have to be given to the movement of arms. Trains would therefore first allot space to arms and ammunitions. Only the leftover space could be used for moving foodgrain. The English were locked in battle and Bengalis would have to die of hunger as a consequence. And this in a land that was once fabled for its resources! When the East India Company had annexed Bengal following Mir Zafar's betrayal in the eighteenth century, Bengal was so rich that a wealthy businessman of Murshidabad had enough money to buy the city of London. And now I saw what we were reduced to: mothers dying in the streets while their babies still suckled; dogs competing with people for leftovers in garbage dumps; children abandoned by their mothers who had run away or sold them driven by hunger. At times they failed to do even that since there would be no buyers. They would knock on doors and cry out: 'Give us some food, I am dying and can't go on; at the very least give me some of the water that you have strained off the boiled rice.' She would often die even as she uttered these words! What were we to do? We distributed our hostel leftovers among the famished, but how far could that help solve such a massive problem?

It was at this time that Mr Suhrawardy organized gruel kitchens. I too decided to stop studying and joined in the effort to help the distressed. We opened quite a few gruel kitchens. We would try to give the poor at least one meal a day. We opened such kitchens in the Muslim League Central Office in Calcutta and in the city's madrasas and other places. I used to work throughout the day. Finally, at night I would return to the dormitory or go to sleep on a table in the League office.

I had quite a few people working along with me in the famine relief effort. One of them was Pirojpur's Mr Nuruddin, who later became a member of the East Bengal Provincial Assembly. He was a selfless worker. Despite the fact that he was loyal to Mr Anwar's faction of the party that we were feuding with, I liked him a lot. The superintendent of Baker Hostel was Professor Saidur Rahman, who later became principal of Dhaka's Jagannath College. He treated me very affectionately. I had no time then to take part in the hostel's politics or elections. But Professor Rahman would seek my advice. The principal of the college was Dr I.H. Zuberi. He too treated me affectionately. I would go to him directly whenever I had to and talk to him frankly. All the teachers of the college would treat me well. If I deemed it necessary, I would open the doors of the college assembly hall to hold a meeting. The principal would overlook my actions. The Muslim teachers of the college supported the movement for the creation of Pakistan. The Hindu and Christian teachers would keep quiet since all the students were Muslims. A few students were opposed to the idea of Pakistan but because they were in a minority they would not dare say anything in protest.

At around this time I returned to Gopalganj to join in the relief work being carried out there. Gopalganj was surrounded by Jessore district on one side, Khulna on another and Barisal on yet another side. I returned to my home town to find the situation there was appalling. Most people had turned into nothing but skin and bones from the lack of food. Gopalganj's Muslims were business people and the land was fertile. They were usually able to make ends meet. In the face of the current situation many people advised me to hold a conference to which we could invite Mr Suhrawardy and other Muslim League leaders. Seeing the gravity of the situation in our three districts they would perhaps do something to provide relief for our people and save them from death. We sat down with our workers. After much discussion we decided that our region had so far not witnessed a major conference which had as its main agenda the creation of Pakistan. Organizing a conference on the subject would inspire the people of our three districts to support the idea of Pakistan. In other words, we would be able to achieve two goals: popularize the idea of Pakistan as well as bring relief to our people. We invited workers from all parts of our region to attend the conference. After some discussion we decided that we would call the conference 'The South Bengal Conference for Pakistan'. We also resolved to invite people from all three districts. A meeting was scheduled to form a reception committee. A secretary and a chairman would be chosen from among senior leaders of the party. But none of those who were asked agreed to hold these positions since the event would cost a lot of money. The country after all was reeling from the famine and raising funds under these circumstances was a difficult task. In the end everyone made me the chair of the reception committee and a businessman from Jessore named Moulvi Afsaruddin Mollah the secretary.

I left for Calcutta to invite our party leaders. When I went to see Mr Suhrawardy I found Mr Khawaja Shahabuddin with him. Mr Suhrawardy told me, 'As you can see I am terribly busy; nevertheless I will try to come. Request Mr Shahabuddin too and surely he will go.' Reluctantly I invited him and he agreed to attend. Mr Tamizuddin Khan was then the education minister. He too hailed from Faridpur. We invited him and he also agreed to join us. I also invited Maulana Abdur Rashid Tarkabagish and Mr Habibullah Bahar Chowdhury. By this time Mr Moazzem Hossain Chowdhury (Lal Mia) had left the Congress party. He joined the Muslim League and become secretary of the Provincial Muslim League's Relief Committee. I used to work with him in distributing relief and he showed immense faith in me. He had managed to procure a lot of medicines, clothes and money and wanted me to be with him as he distributed them. We would have to send clothes to every subdivision. Booking freight space to send goods during wartime was a difficult task; you would have to spend at least ten days inquiring before you could find space to send some items of clothing. Often we would have to keep accounts. At times I would even have to tie the relief clothes into bundles. However, I never said no to anything that I was asked to do. In any case, when I asked Mr Moazzem to accompany me he agreed readily.

I worked out a schedule for our activities, raised a bit of money from the more affluent people of our community, went to the villages and started our work. My people now became active everywhere. My father took on the onus of catering. The cooking for the conference would be done in a government official's house. But soon people disagreed over the arrangements. When things started to get out of hand it was decided that everything would be done in our Gopalganj house. I constructed a pandal made out of sails. To do so I borrowed sails from those who owned big boats in our locality. I thus managed to construct a pandal where we could seat two thousand people and we were able to do so without incurring too much expense.

Many people tried to prevent the conference from taking place. They sent off telegrams to all the leaders who had been invited dissuading them from coming. With only three days left for the formal inauguration of the conference, Mr Tamizuddin and Mr Shahabuddin telegraphed me inquiring if the conference could be called off. I telegrammed back saying that cancelling the conference was out of the question. Mr Suhrawardy telegrammed to say that he wouldn't be able to attend. Apparently, he had to attend a food conference, probably in Delhi or somewhere else. Everyone kept telling me to make plans to travel to Calcutta since we would be incurring a huge loss if no one turned up at the conference. People were supposed to come to the conference from far-off places. It was originally scheduled to be held for two days but that wasn't going to be possible because of the famine. It was decided that we would have a meeting of delegates in the morning and a public meeting in the evening.

I left for Calcutta after entrusting my duties to my colleagues. Mr Tamizuddin had already left for Khulna en route to the conference. I brought back Mr Shahabuddin, Maulana Tarkabagish and Lal Mia and reached Khulna. When I got on to the launch I asked them all why they had telegrammed me three days ago wanting me to cancel the conference. I found out that Mr Wahiduzzaman, who had joined the League after quitting Mr Huq's party only recently, was incensed at my being the chairman and opposed the idea of a conference being held in Gopalganj. He would have no role to play then! And yet from 1939 to 1943 this man had opposed the Muslim League as well as me. Mr Salam, the district League secretary, was also opposed to the staging of the conference in Gopalganj since he had not been consulted about it, despite his position. He had also sent messages to the leaders urging them to stay away from it.

All the leaders knew me to be a very dedicated worker. All of them used to treat me affectionately. Mr Suhrawardy had told them to attend the conference. They were also aware that not attending the conference would be a snub to me and that the students of Calcutta would become restive if anything was done to upset me. And so I managed to land up in Gopalganj with all the leaders in tow. They were greeted in style. The whole of Gopalganj rang with cries of 'Long Live Pakistan'. The leaders were delighted with the huge turnout. The meeting was going to start as scheduled. But a storm that had struck the town the previous night had destroyed the pandal. The sails had been torn to shreds by the strong winds. The meeting, however, was held on the stage despite the tattered sails.

The leaders left that night. But my plight was quite desperate afterwards. Where would I get the money to pay the bills? The sails had been damaged and no one would give me any money to repair them. The leaders had offered no financial assistance. However, some of the people who had lent me the sails were very fond of me. Many of them were well-off and their sons had joined my team of workers. These people went away, taking their torn sails with them. But a few didn't and, encouraged by the malcontents, refused to accept the torn sails. They wanted money as compensation. What was I to do? I was depressed by the way things had turned out. My mother and my wife had come to Gopalganj from our village home three days ago to look after the guests. Overworked, I had become unwell. In the evening I had high fever. My father asked me why I looked so shaken. He had already spent a lot of money on the conference. But he wasn't a rich man and I couldn't ask him to help me any further. However, he came up with a solution to my problems on his own. The people who had been affected but were not well-off he sent away after giving them some money. But one businessman had lost eight to ten sails and wanted to be paid for all of them. He threatened to sue me if I failed to do so. My father said, 'Take some money and have them repaired. But you will gain nothing by threatening us. Those who have been encouraging you to take action against us don't know that proving in court that we took your sails will be quite difficult.' The man nevertheless asked his lawyer to file a case against me. In the end, though, he decided not to press charges.

Meanwhile, I became very ill. Renu looked after me during my illness.

We had been officially married in our childhood but it was only in 1942 that the marriage ceremony was held publicly with the usual rituals. Slowly I started to get better.

I would have to go to Calcutta again now since I had to sit for my examinations. But I hadn't studied at all for them. I had spent all my time doing relief work. My father said to me at this time, 'Son, I have no objections to you engaging in politics; that you are participating in the movement to attain Pakistan is also a good thing; but please don't neglect your studies. If you don't study you won't become a good human being. And one other thing: if you have sincerity of purpose and honesty of purpose you will never be defeated in life.' I never forgot these words of advice he had for me.

On another occasion, some prominent people of Gopalganj had told my father that the course I had taken would land me in jail sooner or later. They advised him to dissuade me from politics since it would ruin my life. I distinctly remember my father's response: 'He is working for our country. He isn't doing anything wrong, is he? If he has to go to jail in the process, let him. That won't sadden me. And his life won't perhaps be ruined either. I certainly won't interfere. I believe that if we don't attain Pakistan Muslims will be wiped out.' Often my father would discuss political issues with me. He would ask me why it was that I believed in Pakistan. I would try to answer his queries the best I could.

I remember one particular day when my father and I discussed politics till two o'clock in the morning. My father was very impressed with my views. The only advice he had for me was that I should desist from attacking Mr Fazlul Huq personally. This was also what my mother told me another day.

And the fact was Mr Huq hadn't earned the title of 'Tiger of Bengal' for nothing. The people of Bengal had indeed fallen in love with him. Whenever I attempted to say anything to slight him I would be stopped. I remember one day when I was in a meeting that I had organized in our own union. I had raised questions such as: Why had he left the League? Why was he now against the idea of Pakistan? Why had he joined hands with Shyama Prasad Mookerjee to form a cabinet? At one point an old man, someone who held my grandfather in great esteem, who visited our house regularly and had great respect for everyone in our family, stood up and said, 'Say whatever you like. But please don't say anything against Mr Huq. If he doesn't want Pakistan, neither do we! Who is this Jinnah? We know nothing about him! On the other hand, Mr Huq has always cared for poor people like us.'

After his speech I changed my tactics. I decided that I wouldn't blame Mr Huq directly. Instead, I concentrated on explaining to everyone why it was important for us to fight for Pakistan. I should add that whenever we raised a black flag to show our dissatisfaction with Mr Huq, the public would assault us. At times we even had to run away from them or else were beaten up. After we had been beaten up a number of times I decided to change the content of our speeches. Previously I had made the mistake of targeting the man himself when I spoke. The result had always been disastrous for us. Instead of helping our cause such an approach harmed it. When I began to understand that I was hurting the feelings of ordinary people I decided I would have to concentrate on explaining the causes behind our movement for Pakistan. There would be two Pakistans, as envisaged in the Lahore Resolution. One would comprise Bengal and Assam and would be called East Pakistan. It would be an independent and sovereign nation. The other Pakistan would consist of the Punjab, Baluchistan, the Frontier Province and Sind. This would be called West Pakistan and it too would be an independent and sovereign nation. As for Hindustan it would consist of the Hindu-majority areas of India but Muslims would have equal rights there too. I always carried a map of India with me. I would also have Mr Habibullah Bahar's *Pakistan* and Mujibur Rahman Khan's massive book of the same name with me. I knew both books almost by heart. I would also have cuttings from the daily *Azad* in my bag whenever I travelled.

I knew all about the Sepoy Mutiny and the Wahabi movement. I was aware of how the British had snatched away power from the Muslims and how almost overnight Muslims were deprived of their wealth and how Hindus flourished at their expense. I knew too how Muslims were driven out of their estates, businesses, the army and other jobs and how Hindus took their places. Muslims had been rulers of the country and therefore couldn't tolerate the English. They would rebel whenever they found an opportunity to do so. I had read about the way the Wahabi movement was launched by thousands of Bengali Muslim warriors. They had travelled all across India from Bengal and from there had gone all the way on foot to the Frontier Province to take part in a holy war. I would narrate these events and highlight Titu Mir's rebellion and Haji Shariatullah's Faraizi movement and then move on to the history of the movement for creating Pakistan. I would be scathing about the role played by Hindu moneylenders and zamindars.

My speeches would be full of religious sentiments. But there were good reasons for harbouring them. On the one hand we would study, play and hang out with Hindu boys. Many of them were my friends. The local Hindus held my own family in high esteem. And yet when I went to visit some of my Hindu friends they wouldn't invite me into their houses because their families feared I would pollute them.

One particular incident left a deep impression on my mind; in fact, I still remember it vividly. I had a friend called Noni Kumar Das. We used to study together and he lived close by. He used to spend the whole day with us and would secretly eat with us. One day I went to his house. He took me to a room inside their house and made me sit there. He used to stay with his uncle. His aunt used to treat me affectionately. After I returned, Noni came to my house close to tears. I asked, 'Noni, what is the matter?' Noni said, 'Don't come to my house any more. After you left my aunt scolded me a lot for bringing you inside the house. She had the whole floor cleaned with water afterwards and forced me to wash everything.' I told him, 'All right I won't come to your house any more but you can keep coming to my house.' However, I used to go to the home of other Hindu classmates who never said any such thing to me. In fact, many of their parents treated us very well. But experiences like the one I had in Noni's house made many Bengali Muslims resent Hindus for their religious prejudices against them. I saw evidence of this resentment and indignation in the city. The Hindus who would come to our home would always treat us with great respect. There were quite a few Hindu villagers that were retainers of one branch or the other of my family.

However, the Muslims of Bengal were in general smarting under the power wielded by Hindu landlords and moneylenders. They were also bent on not cooperating with the British. They had vowed not to work for the English or speak their language. This policy had left them straggling behind the Hindus. On the other hand, Hindus had learned English and by appeasing the English had moved forward. But when they turned against the English later, many of them did not hesitate to die for their beliefs. Some spent their lives in prison, bent on driving the English out of India. If these selfless freedom-loving and dedicated Hindus had attempted to promote Hindu–Muslim unity while carrying on the movement to drive out the British and had stood up against the rapacious Hindu landlords and moneylenders who were oppressing the Muslims, perhaps the bitterness between the two communities would have been contained. Of the Hindu leaders, only Deshbandhu Chittaranjan Das and Netaji Subhas Bose had understood the importance of such gestures and had often cautioned Hindus against their prejudice. Rabindranath Tagore had also warned the Hindus about their stance through his writings.

But it was also true that Muslim landlords had been treating their Hindu tenants shabbily. However, they oppressed them as their landlords and not because of their religion. At that time one saw that whenever a Muslim leader spoke up for the rights of Muslims many Hindus, including educated ones, and even the brightest of them, would raise their voices in anger. Similarly, even before they spoke for Pakistan Muslim leaders would preface their speeches by abusing Hindus.

Around this time Mr Abul Hashim managed to infuse new vigour into Muslim League workers. He was able to convince them through his arguments that the demand for the creation of Pakistan wasn't directed against the Hindus but was meant to reconcile people of these two religions. It would lead to the two brotherly people coexisting peacefully. He would discuss ideology with some of us in the League and would talk to us in the Muslim League office at night. He used to live in Burdwan and would stay in a room in the Muslim League office when in Calcutta. Mr Suhrawardy had rented the League office. He himself had been paying for the rent up to 1947. Mr Hashim told us we would have to build a library and devote ourselves to studies. He declared that we wouldn't be able to attain Pakistan only by badmouthing Hindus. I was completely devoted to Mr Suhrawardy.

Because Mr Hashim too was devoted to Mr Suhrawardy I used to admire him and listen to his views. Mr Hashim would do nothing without consulting Mr Suhrawardy. The Muslim League's funds and finances all had one source: Mr Suhrawardy's pocket. He had to raise money for the League all the time. I will discuss this point later. Mr Hashim would tell us that we would have to rescue the League from the clutches of reactionaries. He declared that we would have to base our organizational activities in villages. You couldn't build an organization from the top. We would also have to take the organization out of the pockets of zamindars. After consulting with Mr Suhrawardy he embarked on a tour of the whole of Bengal. He was an excellent speaker. He had a good command over the language. He was at ease in both Bengali and English.

At this time students became divided into two powerful factions. I came to Calcutta and found out that I would have to set out for Delhi to participate in the All India Muslim League Conference [1943]. There was great interest in the conference. But anyone wanting to take part in it would have to bear all expenses himself. Mr Anwar Hossain took along some members of his faction. He must have managed to raise the necessary funds. Mir Ashrafuddin, secretary of the Islamia College Union, and I decided that we would go to Delhi on our own. We had already been made delegates to the conference. Mir Ashrafuddin, aka Makhan, came from a village called Kazir Kasba in Munshiganj, Dhaka district. He was my cousin's son. His parents had died when he was still a young boy but had left him a lot of money. His father had been a deputy magistrate.

I told Mr Suhrawardy that we would join the Delhi conference. He said that it was a good idea and that it would enable us to see leading Muslim figures of India. The two of us and some of Mr Anwar Hossain's people boarded different compartments of the same train. We weren't friendly with them. Ashraf and I had managed to bring along enough money to meet our expenses. Whenever I needed money badly I would ask my elder sister for some. She would get the money for me from my father. My father had told her that if I needed help I should go to him. I could also depend on my mother to help me out with money. From time to time Renu also gave me some money. Whenever I went home she would give me whatever she managed to raise so that I could meet my expenses. She would never say no to me and would not spend any money on herself. She used to stay in our village home and save everything for me.

We left for Delhi from Howrah. This was my first trip outside Bengal. I always had a great desire to see Delhi. I had read about its history and heard about it from friends. I therefore wanted to see famous places in Delhi such as the Red Fort, the Jama Masjid, Qutb Minar and so on. I also wanted to visit Nizamuddin Aulia's shrine.

When we arrived in Delhi a group of volunteers working for the Muslim League greeted us and took us to the Anglo-Arabian College. We were to spend the nights in tents erected in the college premises. We were to share a tent with a student from Aligarh and possibly Allahabad. Mr Anwar's faction had been given another tent.

A huge pandal had been erected for the occasion. We went to the meeting with our delegate badges on. We had been assigned separate seats as delegates from Bengal. At the end of the first day of the conference a huge procession came out with Mr Jinnah leading it, seated on an elephant. We followed him. The streets were packed with people. There were arrangements for supplying us all with water everywhere. Otherwise a lot of people would surely have died in the heat. We circled the streets of Old Delhi and then returned to our tents in the evening. The conference sessions resumed at night. One person I can still remember from that night was someone who spoke in Urdu for three hours. He had a sonorous voice and very expressive gestures too. I could understand the Urdu spoken in Calcutta a bit but this speaker's Urdu was quite difficult for me. The speaker, in fact, was Nawab Yar Jung Bahadur. But even though I couldn't understand him properly it was impossible to leave the place without listening to him speak!

However, I was not feeling well. It was hot during the day and yet the nights were cold in Delhi. The next day I just couldn't get out of bed. My whole body was aching. I hadn't had motions for two days by then. My chest, stomach and indeed every part of me was stiff. I lay in bed till the afternoon without eating. Makhan kept me company all the time. I needed to consult a physician but didn't know anyone that I could go to. We tried contacting a volunteer who told me that he could help me later. But he disappeared and that was the last I saw of him. In the evening Makhan became quite worried. I too became frightened. What was going to happen to me in this part of the world where I was a stranger? I didn't have much money with me either. Makhan said, 'Uncle, let me go and see if I can bring a physician who can examine you. If you continue to be sick like this, things might really get bad.' I had no idea where Mr Suhrawardy was then. The leaders we had spoken to had not been of any help. But we were in a place where everyone had to look out for himself. But just as Makhan was going out to get a doctor, Khalilur Rahman came to see me. He, of course, had no idea that I was sick. He was quite close to me. He was also famous for his dedication to the Student League. He used to study in Aleya Madrasa and stay in Eliot Hostel.

Eliot Hostel was next to Baker Hostel. We used to jokingly call it 'Idiot Hostel'. Khalil had come to Delhi a year ago after graduating from Aleya Madrasa to study medicine in Ajmal Khan's Institute for Islamic Alternative Medicine. He took a look at me and exclaimed: 'Good grief! How come you didn't consult anyone?' He told Makhan that he wouldn't have to bother to get a doctor for me and was going to get one himself. In half an hour's time he managed to get a physician for me. The doctor examined me thoroughly and gave me some medicine. Khalil had already briefed him about my situation. He assured me that I didn't have to worry. I would have motions after taking the drug that he had prescribed; he asked me not to take any food that night. I was also to take a pill in the morning. He told me that I would be fine by evening. Fortunately for me things turned out just as he had predicted.

By next morning I was beginning to feel well again. The conference was also going to conclude shortly. Khalil stayed with us for the remaining two days of the conference. He also offered to take us around Delhi.

Something else happened at this time that is worth mentioning. Barisal's Mr Nuruddin Ahmed had quarrelled with Mr Anwar Hossain. Mr Nuruddin had come to us quite upset. All his money was with Mr Hossain. His pockets were absolutely empty. He declared to us that he would rather starve or walk all the way to Calcutta than go to that man again. Makhan had defeated Mr Nuruddin in the Islamia College elections and had become the College Union general secretary. The students were fond of Mr Nuruddin but he was defeated because he belonged to Mr Hossain's faction. Even though I was studying for my intermediate examination I had already become the leader of our faction. We would all stay in the same hostel. I told Mr Nuruddin that he could stay with us and wouldn't have to go back to Mr Hossain. However, we didn't have the money to buy his ticket so that he could go home.

We decided to stay in Delhi for three more days. Khalil took us to see the Red Fort, the Diwan-i-Khas, the Qutb Minar, Nizamuddin Aulia's shrine, and all the sights of New Delhi. We spent all our money in the process!

A quick calculation showed that we didn't have enough money to purchase three tickets. Even if we bought two tickets, we would have to go without food in the train. My only friend in Delhi was Khalil, but he was a student, and had no funds to spare. Nevertheless, we came to the station. We decided to buy one ticket and stay in the 'servant' compartment. If we did get caught for travelling without tickets, we would deal with that problem in Calcutta.

In those days there was a separate compartment for the servants of people who travelled first class. The servants would serve their masters during the journey but stay in this car when their services were not needed. When we were going to Delhi, we had travelled on inter-class tickets. Now that we had run out of money, what else could we do? And so we purchased a third-class ticket to Howrah station. We also bought two platform tickets and went inside the station. Makhan was very good-looking. Nobody would believe that he was a servant. We had come to know that Khan Bahadur Abdul Momen Saheb was travelling on this train. This was what Nuruddin had found out. We figured that if we got into a spot we would deal with it then. Nuruddin knew the Khan Bahadur. He was a member of the Railway Board. We got into the 'servant' compartment that was next to his compartment. We asked Makhan to go to the upper berth as soon as the train started moving. We pointed out to him that his looks would be a giveaway. In all probability no railway official would come to this particular compartment. If anyone did show up, we would let Nuruddin deal with him. Once a ticket checker did come. He asked, 'Who do you work for?' Nuruddin replied promptly, 'Mr Momen.' The man went away satisfied with the answer. Nuruddin brought some fruits from time to time and we survived on them since we didn't have the money to buy either rice or roti.

And so we somehow managed to reach Howrah station. But what were we going to do next? We decided that Makhan would go out with all our bags and then deposit them somewhere. He would then buy three platform tickets and rejoin us. We would then leave the station together.

As soon as the train stopped, Makhan got down. The two of us were wearing clothes that were stinking by now. Nobody would believe that we had travelled from Delhi. I hid my glasses. Makhan came back with three platform tickets. By then most other passengers had left. Only those with excess luggage were still in the station. We kept close to them. As soon as Makhan gave us our platform tickets we went out together. When we had left the station we found out that we had only one taka between the three of us! We got on to a bus with that and managed to reach Baker Hostel. We were famished by this time.

It is from this period onward that Nuruddin and I became close friends. He would have to pay for this friendship later. After martial law was imposed in Pakistan in 1958, almost no leader had the time to listen to the problems of party workers. Only Mr Suhrawardy had the time for them and the inclination to help them whenever he was able to do so. Mr Suhrawardy was very fond of Nuruddin. Later Nuruddin became the temporary general secretary of the All Bengal Muslim League. Mr Anwar contracted tuberculosis and was admitted to Jadavpur Hospital. Mr Suhrawardy paid for all his expenses then.

~

In 1944 it was decided that the Students' League would organize a conference for that year. For a long time, the annual conferences had not been held. I was quite popular in Calcutta—in fact no one would dare oppose me in Islamia College. I would work for both the Muslim League and the Students' League. If we organized a conference in Calcutta no one would speak up against it.

I should add that Mr Suhrawardy was fond of Mr Anwar too. He was almost back to normal health by this time. But people from Dhaka's Student League or from our camp did not like him. Only Shah Azizur Rahman from Dhaka was on Mr Anwar's side. Mr Shah was a wonderful speaker. I had heard him speak first in Bogra. Finding it impossible to organize a conference either in Dhaka or in Calcutta, Mr Shah called a provincial conference in his own district of Kushtia. This was the time Mr Anwar's faction was feuding with Mr Nuruddin's. Mr Anwar sent someone to request me to work with his faction. He also offered me a position if I did so. I told him I wasn't interested in a position and would rather discuss the situation with everyone. On the other hand, Mr Nuruddin's faction also wanted to talk things out with me.

I would have to take sides sooner or later—I was that important in Calcutta at that time. This was because Mr Fazlul Quader Chowdhury had quit his studies by then. Mr Zahir [Zahiruddin] did not care for student politics and was concentrating entirely on the Muslim League.

All the students of Calcutta would visit Mr [Abul] Hashim. I had become friends with everyone who would go to him for classes. Among those who used to work selflessly for the Students' League at that time were Nuruddin, Burdwan's Khondokar Nurul Alam and Sharfuddin, Sylhet's Moazzem Ahmed Chowdhury, Khulna's Ekramul Huq, Chittagong's Mahbub Alam and Nuruddin's cousin S.A. Saleh. In the end I joined this group because we were all fond of Mr Suhrawardy and Mr Hashim. On the other hand, Mr Anwar's faction was devoted to Mr Suhrawardy but couldn't stand Mr Hashim.

When Mr Suhrawardy saw the extent of the difference between the two factions he called us all in a bid to reconcile us. However, he failed in his attempt. This was when I got into an argument with Mr Suhrawardy. He wanted us to give Mr Anwar a prominent position but I declared that this wasn't possible. I pointed out that he was a divisive force in the party and wasn't the type who encouraged good workers. Also, he had never filed a statement of accounts. All of a sudden, Mr Suhrawardy burst out, 'Who are you? You are nobody.' I retorted, 'If I am nobody, then why have you invited me? You have no right to insult me. I will prove that I am somebody. Thank you sir. I will never come to you again.' I walked out of the room, uttering these words at the top of my voice. Nuruddin, Ekram and Nurul Alam joined me in protesting against Mr Suhrawardy. The secretary of Bulbul Academy,[9] Mr Nurul Huda, was very fond of Mr Suhrawardy. He would always stick close to him. All of us used to treat him with respect. He had excellent manners. If anyone was in a spot he would be there to help the distressed person no matter what time of the night it was. Mr Huda was present at that time. While I was storming out of Mr Suhrawardy's house, Mr Suhrawardy asked Mr Huda to bring me back. I was so angry that I had burst into tears. Mr Huda managed to catch up with me. He told me that Mr Suhrawardy was shouting from upstairs asking me to come back. My friends had also been telling me it would be bad manners to ignore Mr Suhrawardy's request. And so I decided to meet Mr Suhrawardy once again. Mr Suhrawardy told everyone present, 'Go and work for the elections. Don't fight each other.' Then he called me affectionately to his own room. He said, 'You are being sentimental. I wouldn't have said these words to anybody else. Because I care for you and treat you like my own I felt I could say such things to you.' He then rubbed my forehead affectionately. And that he really meant what he said and loved me and cared for me I knew through all his subsequent actions and in everything he did for me till his dying day. Now when I think of him in jail I remember what he had told me then. Even in twenty years he never veered from what he said that day. Indeed, from that day, every day of my life I was blessed with his love. In all these years no one could take me away from him and I didn't let anyone deprive me of his affection.

When the two factions failed to reconcile their differences even after the meeting at Mr Suhrawardy's house, elections were the only way out. Mr Fazlul Quader Chowdhury managed to grab control of the Chittagong branch of the Muslim League with the help of Student League workers. The Khan Bahadurs began to lose their hold over district Muslim League offices. From 1943 I have been friendly with the Chittagong people. In Chittagong men like M.A. Aziz, Zahur Ahmad Chowdhury, Azizur Rahman, Dr Sultan Ahmed, Abul Khair Chowdhury and some others became leaders of the Muslim League and the Student League. Some of the workers of course were cut adrift. But Aziz and Zahur are still active politically. Zahur is in the Workers' League now and is also president of the City Awami League. M.A. Aziz (now general secretary of Chittagong District Awami League) was jailed several times in Pakistan and had to stay there for long periods. Mr Fazlul Quader Chowdhury was their leader for a long time. Later he switched to the Muslim League. Aziz and Zahur joined the Awami League. Mr Chowdhury became very self-centred and obstinate. This was why those who had elected him leader of the Chittagong branch later abandoned him.

I telegrammed the Chittagong group to send delegates to the Kushtia Students' League meeting. I sent people to all other districts. Nuruddin, Ekram, Sharfuddin, Khondokar Nurul Alam and I worked with all our other colleagues night and day for the conference. We were hard up since Mr Hashim had no money to give us. However, Mr Suhrawardy was able to give us something. We raised some money from donations and then our group arrived in Kushtia. We had with us two hard-working colleagues named Q.J. Azmeri and Hamid Ali. Azmeri was a hot-tempered person. He used to get into fights at the slightest provocation. He was also quite strong and courageous too. He was related to Mr Hashim. It should be pointed out here that Kushtia neighbours Faridpur district.

Faridpur's delegates were split into two factions. One of them was on my side and the other with Mr Mohan Mia. Mr Mia himself was in

Mr Anwar's faction. When we reached Kushtia it was obvious that of the delegates that had already assembled there 70 per cent were our supporters. The leaders of the two factions decided to negotiate to find if they could sort out their differences. Bogra's Fazlul Bari, now a member of East Bengal's Governor Abdul Monem Khan's cabinet, was made the chairman of the session. But words lead to quarrels and quarrels lead to fights. Mr Shah Azizur Rahman had already recruited many thugs in anticipation. We told him that if his men resorted to force we wouldn't ever let him stay in Calcutta. But in the end no compromise was possible. The Comilla Students' League leaders had been staying with us. But in the morning we heard that they had become part of Mr Anwar's faction because they had been offered three positions. Mr Rafiqul Islam had become councillor in Calcutta because we had nominated him to the position. He used to be part of all our deliberations. Mr Shafikul Islam used to stay in Baker Hostel. He had always been on our side when we opposed Mr Anwar. Mr Hakim was a good friend of mine. We had been together for a long time now. And yet they too had deserted our side that morning. Nevertheless, we were still dominant. We were confident that Mr Anwar's faction would be defeated.

The council meeting was to be held in a cinema hall. Mr Hamoodur Rahman, who is now a judge of the high court, assumed the role of the chair. He was a member of the ad hoc committee. We demanded that he chair the session on behalf of the All India Muslim Students' Federation. When we entered the hall we saw that it was full of outsiders. We pointed this out to the chair. On our behalf Ekramul Huq raised the question of the right of these people to stay in the session. He declared that every one of them would have to vacate the hall. Two doors would then be opened through which only delegates would enter after two representatives of each faction had checked their credentials at each gate.

Meanwhile, many students who had come from outside to witness the event were crowding the veranda upstairs. One student who was in shorts was saying in a loud voice, 'I know that many of these people aren't students and are outsiders. Shah Aziz [ur Rahman] has managed to get them inside the hall to swell his faction.' In a while I found out that this was Kamruzzaman (later president of the East Pakistan Students' League and a member of the East Bengal Assembly who was to be elected on an Awami League ticket).

Mr Hamoodur Rahman ignored our demands and began proceedings. Whereas twenty students were supposed to be co-opted only after the conference began, he gave them the right to vote immediately. We repeated our demand that outsiders should be ejected from the hall. People started to shout at the top of their voices. We realized that we could end up in a fight. A few of us reviewed the situation and after talking things over decided to leave the meeting with our supporters. If we had wanted to we could have established another organization. After all, we had our supporters in all districts. However, we decided to refrain from such a course. On the other hand, we also stuck to our resolution of not allowing these people to hold any more meetings in Calcutta. The All Bengal leaders would not find a place there where they could carry out their activities unchallenged.

No more elections were held by these people till 1947. Both the Muslim League and the Students' League split into two factions from then on. One faction was identified with the names of Mr Suhrawardy and Mr Hashim. The other faction was associated with Mr Khawaja Nazimuddin and Maulana Akram Khan. All of us held Maulana Akram Khan in high esteem. As a matter of fact, we had no quarrels with him.

It was at this time that something else happened that created a sensation. After consulting Mr Suhrawardy, Mr Hashim brought out a draft manifesto for the Muslim League. It noted that the Muslim League was a political organization and therefore should involve itself with political issues. It would have to indicate what kind of economic structure Pakistan should have once the nation had been created. It suggested that the zamindari system should be abolished. It included many other such radical statements. Inevitably, there was an outcry as soon as Mr Hashim's manifesto was published. Those among us who were young or were students or were progressive-minded took up these points and began to speak out on them. We needed to realize Pakistan and it was important to spell out what kind of economic and political framework Pakistan would have once it was created. Mr Hashim would spend hours indoctrinating us on these issues. He would come to Dhaka for a few days at a time and would sit down with party workers to discuss these issues. He would also spend a lot of time in the Calcutta Muslim League office for similar meetings. He would always keep in touch with party workers. I accompanied him to many such meetings.

It would be wrong of me not to mention a prominent student leader of the time in my narrative since he did not belong to any faction and did not tolerate wrongdoing. Indeed, everyone knew him to be outspoken in the interest of truth. All the leaders treated him affectionately. Everyone now knows him as Judge Abu Sayeed Chowdhury of the Dhaka High Court. He tried his best to reconcile the two factions. Mr Suhrawardy would pay heed to whatever advice Mr Chowdhury had to give him.

Two other men who are judges now but were also prominent at that time are worth mentioning too. One of them is Mr Abdul Hakim. He was then the vice-president of Taylor Hostel and was actively involved in student politics. On the other hand, Justice Muksumul Hakim was not involved in student politics when he was in Calcutta. He was a good student and always focused on his studies.

At this time and after Mr Nazir Ahmed was killed, Mr Shamsul Huq led the Dhaka students along with Mr Shamsuddin Ahmed, the late Mr Aziz Ahmed (of Noakhali), Khondokar Mushtaq Ahmed and a few others. All of them were devoted to Mr Suhrawardy. Afterwards they also became followers of Mr Hashim. All of them felt that in addition to working for the Students' League they would have to get involved in the activities of the Muslim League to prevent it from being manipulated by coteries. Mr Hashim opened a branch of the Provincial League in 150 Mughaltuli, Dhaka. Many of them worked as full-time workers, just as was the case with Communist Party workers. Mr Shamsul Huq was in charge of this office. We, on the other hand, were full-time workers at the Calcutta office. Although I had a room in the hostel, I used to spend most of my time in the Muslim League office. I would study at night. From time to time I attended classes in college to ensure that I fulfilled attendance rules. But what would be the point of studying if we didn't achieve Pakistan? Many of us had this question in our minds.

The two factions were to confront each other again when the Muslim League was about to hold its next council meeting. We decided that we would elect Mr Hashim general secretary and would have his manifesto adopted by the party. On the other hand, our opponents had resolved that they would not allow Mr Hashim to be secretary. Many leaders were supporters of Mr Suhrawardy. But while they followed him they could not stand Mr Hashim. In the end Maulana Akram Khan, Mr Suhrawardy and Mr Nazimuddin met to select a panel. They resolved that Mr Hashim would be the secretary but that his manifesto would not be adopted. A subcommittee was formed to report on the manifesto. If I remember correctly, this was what they had decided. However, I cannot recall what else they had agreed upon. In any case, Mr Suhrawardy declared that this wasn't the time to get involved in fights over such issues since our real goal was to achieve Pakistan. If we confronted each other now on other issues the movement for creating Pakistan would take a back seat.

~

At this time the Muslim League government of Bengal was dissolved. The governor of Bengal took the administration of the province in his own hands. Mr Suhrawardy noted that in the wartime situation businessmen had begun to stock clothes to sell them in the black market later. On the one hand, the food situation was deteriorating although Mr Suhrawardy was working day and night to bring things under control. On the other hand, unscrupulous businessmen were playing with the lives of ordinary people for their selfish reasons. Mr Suhrawardy ordered his staff to surround the warehouses of the Marwari businessmen in Barabazar. The whole of Barabazar was encircled accordingly. Thousands of yards of cloth that had been stockpiled were discovered. It was found out that all the buildings had warehouses that were hidden from public view. Similar instructions were sent to uncover stockpiled foodgrain throughout the city. But the Marwari businessmen were not to be defeated so easily. They now spent a lot of money and managed to buy off quite a few members of the legislature so that they could have the government dissolved. The result was that the government lost a motion against it by just one vote. Fortunately, this was not a vote of no confidence. Mr Khawaja Nazimuddin declared that he would call for such a vote the next day. If he failed to win the motion, he was willing to resign. The speaker of the house was Mr Nowsher Ali. The next day he ruled that a vote of no confidence had already been passed against the government and so there would be no need to have a formal vote of no confidence one more time.

I was present with a few students in the assembly at that time. When the news spread outside that the League ministry had been dissolved the Marwaris began to celebrate their victory. I found the situation so intolerable that I assaulted some of them. Some of our workers began to beat up the Marwaris until they fled the scene. Mr Mohammad Ali rushed out and tried to restrain us all. Hindu leaders came out in protest. In any case, after some time things cooled down and we left the area. The Muslim League government had been in office for around one and a half years, although the governor had retained ultimate control of the province in his hands.

I knew that Mr Suhrawardy was a member of the Calcutta Club. Whenever he was in Calcutta he would try to spend an hour or two there. However, from the time he became minister of civil supplies he would never find the time to go to the club. He would work in his office till midnight. Nuruddin and I would often go to his house after midnight to meet him and to discuss the political situation since he never had the time to do so during the day. He had instructed us to meet him then.

Till that time, I had no idea that members of the Legislative Assembly were capable of being bribed in such a manner. These were the people who were representing the province and the masses! I remember that we had been given the task of guarding a few members so that they could not desert the party. I do not want to name them since many of them are dead now. One of these MLAs was confined to the Muslim League office. He tried to leave it again and again but failed to do so because of our vigilance. After a while he told us, 'Let me go; don't worry. The opposition is offering us some money and if I make some money this way why should it bother you all? For, in any case I will vote for the Muslim League.' I looked at him incredulously. He was an old man and looked impressive and was educated—how could such a man say such things to us? He would accept money from a party that wasn't his own and yet not vote for it despite being bribed to do so. To what depths had the people of our society sunk! We had to drag this gentleman into the office from the street. All the time he had been looking for an opportunity to switch over to another party!

~

One day Mr Fazlur Rahman called me to his office. He was the chief whip of the party then. He said, 'You will have to take the twelve o'clock train and go to Rangpur. You will have to bring a member of the Muslim League who is an MLA and also a Khan Bahadur back with you. I have telegrammed him and even sent a messenger to him and yet he hasn't shown up here. Only you will be able to persuade him to return. Mr Suhrawardy wants you to go on this mission. Your ticket has been bought already.' He gave me a few letters along with the ticket. I went back to Baker Hostel, collected my bag, filled it with a few clothes and then headed straight for the station. I did not even have the time to eat. It was wartime and it was difficult to eat outside the house. I got on the train. Trains did not run to schedule then since they had to adjust their schedules to military troop movements.

Although the train was scheduled to reach Rangpur at eight in the evening we reached the town at two in the morning. I hadn't managed to eat anything en route and the train had been very crowded all the way. I had never been to Rangpur before. I learned that the station was three miles away from the town. After a lot of effort I managed to get a rickshaw to take me there. The rickshaw puller knew where the Khan Bahadur lived and was able to take me to his house. I managed to wake him up eventually and handed over the letter to him. He knew me well. He told me that he would go to Calcutta the next day since he didn't want to take the next train that was supposed to leave Rangpur at five-thirty in the morning. I told him that in that case he should send a letter with me and I would return on the five-thirty train. He thought that was a good idea. He didn't inquire if I'd had anything to eat on my way and if I would like to eat anything now. The only thing he asked me was if I needed a bed to sleep in since it was three o'clock already. I said that there would be no need for that since I would be able to spend the time left easily. In fact, I knew that if I went to bed I wouldn't be able to get up in time since I was feeling exhausted. But my stomach was growling and I knew no place in Rangpur where I could get food at that time of the night. The last time I had had food was in Baker Hostel over twenty-four hours ago. I told him that it would be nice of him to send me a glass of water. He made sure that I would be able to go back to the station by five o' clock on a rickshaw run by someone he knew. And so I returned to the railway station to catch the train to Calcutta that morning.

I reached Calcutta in the evening. This time I managed to have some tea and biscuits on the train. When I arrived at the hostel I finally managed to eat a proper meal. It was tough to have stayed without proper food for such a long time and I was pretty upset because of this. I told Mr Fazlur Rahman that he should never again send me on such a mission to anyone remotely resembling this Khan Bahadur.

The Khan Bahadur did show up the next day as promised. Guards were posted to ensure that he stayed loyal to us. But in the end he managed to give us the slip. Even though we searched for him he was nowhere to be found. We were still students who loved our country very much and it pained us to see such opportunism and such meanness. Of course we would see a lot more of such behaviour but this was the first time I had come across someone so small-minded. Somehow it seemed impossible to us to believe that such men would help us in achieving Pakistan and making our country independent and free from British rule. The Muslim League was previously a party belonging to landlords and people who had been given titles by the British because of their loyalty to the Raj. Their accomplices were moneylenders and profiteers. Such people would have never created Pakistan. If Mr Suhrawardy and Mr Hashim hadn't made the Muslim League popular among Bengali youths and students and if they hadn't attracted Bengali Muslim intellectuals to the party, the movement for Pakistan would never have become popular among the people of Bengal who came mostly from the peasant class. We did try to obstruct these selfish people from playing a prominent part in the party but we couldn't control them completely. Thus no sooner was Pakistan created than these opportunist Khan Bahadurs and British titleholders grabbed power. What events contributed to their success will be made clear in the following passage.

~

After Mr Suhrawardy had ceased to be a minister he concentrated on establishing the Muslim League on a sound footing. Having managed to tackle the initial assault on them, the British were able to change the tide of the war. This was the time the Congress had succeeded in popularizing the Quit India movement throughout India. Mr Suhrawardy and Mr Hashim too had managed to make the Pakistan movement a popular one. It was Mr Hashim who had taught us to believe that we would have to take up arms against the British. We too had an inborn hatred of the English. We were no supporters of Hitler's Nazis and yet we took delight in every news item about reverses faced by the English in the war. This was the period when Netaji Subhas Bose had formed the Azad Hind Fauj by recruiting both Hindu and Muslim Indians to fight the British. It almost seemed at times that the Japanese were closer to us than the British. But then again it occurred to me that having the English replaced by the Japanese would not bring us any closer to freedom. We were also hurt by the Japanese invasion of China. When we listened to Subhas Bose addressing us on the radio from Singapore we used to get excited. It seemed to us then that if he managed to land his troops in Bengal it would be easy for us to oust the English. But then again it occurred to us that having him in Bengal would not bring us any nearer to Pakistan. And what would happen to the millions of Muslims of the country then? But then again I thought that someone who could leave everything in his country to spearhead a movement for its independence could never be parochial in his outlook. In my mind, my respect for Subhas Bose continued to grow.

I used to believe with my heart and soul that Muslims would be wiped out in an undivided India. Why were the Hindu leaders so upset about the idea of Pakistan? Both Hindus and Muslims could live side by side in India. Both communities could be given equal rights. Hindus could live as citizens in Pakistan just as Muslims could live freely in India. The Muslims of Pakistan would embrace the Hindus who lived with them as brothers just as the Hindus of India would with the Muslims who lived amidst them. This was the period when we began to change the tone of our public speeches. We would discuss these issues with our Hindu friends for hours. Nothing would induce them to accept our point of view. During 1944 and 1945 Hindus and Muslims would argue these issues everywhere, including on trains and steamers. At times they would switch from verbal arguments to fisticuffs. By this time Muslim youths were no longer divided over the issue. They were all united in the belief that they would have to achieve Pakistan.

One day Mr Fazlul Huq invited some students from Islamia College to have dinner with him. We could not decide whether to go or not. In the end I said, 'Why shouldn't we go? We will request him to return to the Muslim League. If we believed that our principles were so weak that merely going to him would be betraying the idea of Pakistan then we shouldn't be in the Pakistan movement at all.' I took along Mr Ekramul Huq of Khulna even though he wasn't a student of Islamia College, since he was quite influential. He used to treat me with great affection and respect. In fact there were six or seven of us who decided to go in the end. Mr Fazlul Huq sat down to have lunch with us. He said, 'Have I quit the Muslim League? Or did they expel me from it? Mr Jinnah can't stand me and is upset by my popularity. He will never be able to do in his lifetime what I have already done for the Muslims of Bengal. Bengalis aren't given their rightful place anywhere. What they have been trying to do is to leave me out and make Mr Nazimuddin their sole leader.'

We took the opportunity to present our point of view. Ekramul Huq said, 'If you stay within the fold of the Muslim League and if you support the movement for Pakistan, Bengali Muslim students can only support you. And what would happen to us Muslims if we fail to achieve Pakistan?' He replied, 'Who was responsible for the Lahore Resolution of 1940? I was! Who knew Jinnah then?' We renewed our invitation to him to join us and departed from his house. We had covered a lot of issues while we were there though now I can't remember them all. All I am presenting here are the parts I can still recall. I had met him previously only once in Gopalganj in 1938 and that too for only a few moments. On that day I considered myself fortunate that I had finally got the opportunity to talk to him face to face for a while.

Meanwhile, the Muslim League office as well as Mr Suhrawardy had come to know of our visit to Mr Huq's house. They began to fear that we would desert them for Mr Huq. A few days later when I went to meet Mr Suhrawardy he told me with a smile, 'So you seem to be visiting Mr Huq quite often nowadays; do you get to dine sumptuously there?' I told him that I had gone there only once. I also informed him about the things we had talked about. He said, 'You did all right. After all, why won't you go if he invites you?' I said, 'We have requested him to join the Muslim League.' Mr Suhrawardy said, 'It will be great if he does so. But he won't come and won't be allowed to do so either. He has a few people with him who won't be accepted anywhere and they are the ones who are trying to keep him outside the Muslim League.'

Mr Suhrawardy was a liberal. He had no mean streak in him at all. But some other leaders of the Muslim League kept making fun of us for visiting Mr Huq for some time. Because I was quick-tempered and obstinate I would answer back whenever they said anything to me on the subject. I didn't really care about anyone and always had my say. I would do whatever work was given to me diligently. I would never try to evade responsibility. I was the type who could work very hard. That was why even if I had a sharp tongue nobody would say anything in response. I would always support the students whenever they needed me. I would be there whenever a student was in trouble or when he couldn't find accommodation in the hostel or when he needed a free seat there. As soon as anyone approached me for help I would talk to the principal, Dr Zuberi. However, I would not take up any cause that was unjust. This was why our teachers always listened to what I had to say. Students in general were fond of me. The hostel superintendent Mr Saidur Rahman knew that I had a lot of visitors. When student leaders from different districts came to town we had to put them up somewhere or the other and someone would therefore always stay with me. This was inevitable since my room was open for them until they got secure lodgings elsewhere. One day I told Dr Zuberi, 'Sir, please let me have the room assigned for sick students since it is big and can accommodate ten to fifteen people.' This room also had an electric fan. I of course wanted to retain my own room too. He said, 'All right. Take over the room. But make sure that no students object to the move.' I declared, 'Even if one or two of the students might be opposed to the idea, no one will dare oppose me.'

Baker Hostel had a number of free rooms for poor students. In those days only those who were genuinely needy would get to stay in these rooms. This is in contrast to the situation nowadays where calls are made on the telephone demanding that rooms be given to certain students. Islamia College also had a fund to help poor students. Mr Narayan, who was a teacher of the sciences, was in charge of administering this fund. Even though I was a student of the arts faculty, Mr Narayan used to like me a lot. This, despite his knowledge that I was working for the cause of Pakistan almost all the time. All the students of the college were Muslims. Why was a Hindu teacher given such a responsibility? The answer is that he was the model teacher. To him whether one was a Hindu or a Muslim was irrelevant. He would not only help students with the money he received from student fees and the government but also from funds he had himself raised from philanthropic Hindus and Muslims. I have rarely come across teachers who are as large-hearted as he was.

It was at this time that I was forced to accept the position of general secretary of the Islamia College Students' Union as the unanimous choice of all. But despite all my efforts I failed to reconcile the two groups. Both groups had insisted then that either I should become the general secretary or they should be allowed to contest each other in an election. In fact, I worked as general secretary in this way for two successive years. Now the two groups were clamouring for elections but if they were allowed to contest each other this process would become an irreversible one. A lot of money and study time would be wasted in the process and we would be fighting each other all the time. However, I had to give in to their demands and told them that I would stay on as general secretary only for three more months since the issue of Pakistan was coming to a vote and I would have to work for the cause outside the college endlessly. I knew I would not be able to spend any time in the college any more. I therefore resigned from my position as general secretary and handed over charge to someone else.

The election issue began to gather momentum from the beginning of 1945. Elections would be held in March 1946 and Muslims all over India would vote in a referendum on whether they wanted Pakistan or not. This was because of the Congress's claim that it represented Muslims as well as Hindus of India. They pointed out that Maulana Abul Kalam Azad was their president. They emphasized that in a united India Hindus would not be able to dominate hundred million Muslims unfairly. Moreover, Muslims were in the majority in quite a few provinces of the country. What is more, if the country became two states, the Muslims in India would be wiped out. On the other hand, the Muslim League made it clear that Hindus in Pakistan would have equal rights. They also demanded the same treatment for Muslims in India. The Lahore Resolution states the Muslim League's position clearly as we can see from the following extract:

1. While approving and endorsing the action taken by the Council and the Working Committee of the All-India Muslim League as indicated in their resolutions dated the 27th of August, 17th & 18th of September and 22nd of October 1939, and 3rd of February 1940 on the constitutional issue, this session of the All-India Muslim League emphatically reiterates that the scheme of Federation embodied in the

Government of India Act, 1935 is totally unsuited to and unworkable in the peculiar conditions of this country and is altogether unacceptable to Muslims of India.

2. It further records its emphatic view that while the declaration dated the 18th of October 1939, made by the Viceroy on behalf of His Majesty's Government is reassuring in so far as it declares that the policy and plan on which the Government of India Act, 1935 is based will be reconsidered in consultation with the various parties, interests and communities in India, Muslims in India will not be satisfied unless the whole constitutional plan is reconsidered de novo, and that no revised plan would be acceptable to the Muslims unless it is framed with their approval and consent.
3. Resolved that it is the considered view of this session of the All-India Muslim League that no constitutional plan would be workable in the country or acceptable to the Muslims unless it is designed on the following basic principles, viz., that geographically contiguous units are demarcated into regions which should be so constituted with such territorial readjustments as may be necessary that the areas in which the Muslims are numerically in a majority as in the north-western and eastern zones of India should be grouped to constitute 'independent states' in which the constituent units shall be autonomous and sovereign.
4. That adequate, effective and mandatory safeguards should be specifically provided in the constitution for the minorities in the units and in the regions for the protection of their religious, cultural, economic, political, administrative and other rights and interests in consultation with them.
5. This session further authorises the Working Committee to frame a scheme of constitution in accordance with these basic principles, providing for the assumption finally by the respective regions of all powers such as defence, external affairs, communications, customs and such others matters as may be necessary.

The daily *Azad* was the only Bengali paper that supported the Muslim League and the movement for the creation of Pakistan. The founder and owner of this newspaper was Maulana Akram Khan. He was president of the Provincial Muslim League. He couldn't stand Mr Abul Hashim. He was angry with Mr Suhrawardy for supporting Mr Hashim. He was also angry with us for the same reason. That is why his paper would rarely report any of our activities. If on the few occasions it did so it was because of Mr Mohammad Modabber. Later Mr Sirajuddin Hossain (now the news editor of the daily *Ittefaq*) and a couple of friends got jobs in the daily *Azad* office. They would try to sneak in a story or two of our activities whenever they got the opportunity to do so. How the [Calcutta-based] *Morning News* treated us isn't even worth commenting on. Even though the paper supported the movement for Pakistan completely, it was a paper owned by a group that could only be described as representing the ruling class. It would never want to publish anything about us. It also disapproved of everything that Mr Hashim did. But because the Students' League and Muslim League had a few workers who supported him it would be forced to occasionally publish a report on his activities.

I realized that we would have to bring out at the very least a weekly newspaper, especially to circulate our ideas among party workers who had joined us recently. It was difficult for Mr Hashim to publish a newspaper on his own since he was hard up. On the other hand, Mr Suhrawardy had resumed his work at the Calcutta High Court. He had a good income and was well known in Calcutta as a very good barrister. Not only did the poor people of Calcutta love him, the rich people of the city also listened to whatever he asked them to do. I had never seen him inconvenienced because of lack of money. Mr Hashim proposed to Mr Suhrawardy that a paper be brought out. He declared that if he was given some seed money to launch the venture he would be able to raise the rest himself. Many people felt that Mr Nuruddin and I would be able to persuade Mr Suhrawardy to agree to our proposal about publishing a newspaper.

And so the two of us called on Mr Suhrawardy one day. We tried to convince him that we wouldn't need a lot of money for the venture since the newspaper was to be a weekly one. We had some pretty good writers among us who would be willing to write for the paper for very little money. A few in fact wouldn't have to be paid at all. Mr Suhrawardy agreed to our proposal after we had met him a couple of times to impress on him the importance of the project.

There were quite a few rooms vacant in the ground floor of the building where the Muslim League was housed. There was therefore no problem in finding space for the newspaper office. Mr Hashim himself became the editor and started to bring out the weekly regularly. Many of us in the Muslim League began to sell the paper in the streets. Mr Kazi Mohammad Idris took over the responsibility of publishing it. He had already acquired a good name as a journalist. He was an amiable man. We had representatives all over Bengal. They began to contribute to the weekly. The paper was a hit with the intellectuals. Many Hindus also began to read it regularly. The paper was titled *Millat*.

The other group began a campaign to label Mr Hashim a communist even though he was really a follower of Maulana Azad Sobhani, who had quite a reputation as a philosopher. Mr Hashim invited him to come to

Calcutta. When he came he took classes with us. My colleagues would attend his classes till late in the evening. But it was impossible for me to sit still for a long time. I would join in Maulana Sobhani's classes for a while and then leave. I would tell my friends, 'Go ahead and become pundits. I have too much work to do. Let me first work to attain Pakistan and then I will be able to sit down to discuss other issues.' I was lucky that I was able to leave these sessions without offending Mr Hashim; his eyesight was so bad by then that he couldn't see me leave. However, he would catch me once in a while. When this happened he would want to find out the next day why I had left the class the night before. I would reply, 'But I had so much work!' And it was true that I had a lot of work to do for the sake of the party, especially amongst students.

~

The election schedules were announced. A Parliamentary Board was to be formed for the Muslim League. A meeting of the council was scheduled in Calcutta's Muslim Institute. The Muslim League Parliamentary Board was supposed to have nine members. Two of them were to be ex-officio members. One would be nominated from the Muslim League Parliamentary Party and the other would be appointed from among the MLAs. The council would elect the remaining five members. The party had already split into two factions. However, since the elections were to be on the issue of Pakistan all of us knew that it would be best not to fight each other at this time. All appreciated the fact that four of the members would be the president of the Provincial Muslim League, Maulana Akram Khan; the leader of the Muslim League Parliamentary Party, Mr Khawaja Nazimuddin; a representative of the Parliamentary Party; and a Muslim League member elected from the Upper House. Because Mr Nazimuddin was the leader of the Parliamentary Party, he had the loyalty of the majority of the MLAs and members of the Legislative Council [MLCs]. Even though Mr Suhrawardy was the deputy leader Mr Nazimuddin decided to nominate Mr Fazlur Rahman instead of Mr Suhrawardy. He therefore confronted Mr Nazimuddin and asked him what the point in electing Mr Rahman was since he could become a board member after a council election. We had made Mr Fazlur Rahman a member since he would not be able to be one on his own. Mr Nurul Amin was probably chosen a member from the Upper House of the Muslim League. In this manner four out of the nine members ended up being from his faction. It was entirely possible that he would be able to get one more member on his side through elections. The possibility alone led to infighting. We protested and inquired why Mr Suhrawardy would not be chosen to represent the MLAs. We declared that he had been slighted since he was the deputy leader of the Muslim League parliamentary party and deserved to be selected. This was a conspiracy! Mr Suhrawardy tried to dissuade us from getting into a confrontation by telling us that our protests would be to no avail. But I pointed out to him that he had been too giving. I said, 'Mr Nazimuddin should have remembered that he had become the leader of the Muslim League and MLA only because of your generosity. Mr Fazlul Huq had almost driven Mr Nazimuddin out of politics by defeating him in the election held in Patuakhali. He would never be able to win any elections in East Bengal if his opponent was Mr Huq. He had been elected only because Mr Suhrawardy had resigned from one of his seats and allowed him to contest from it. And even Mr Suhrawardy himself wouldn't have managed to get elected outside Calcutta.'

In 1937 Mr Suhrawardy had been elected a member of the Legislative Assembly from two seats in Calcutta. Mr Nazimuddin had to return empty-handed after being defeated in Patuakhali. He had no option then except to quit politics. Mr Suhrawardy threw a challenge to Mr Huq and declared that he would have Mr Nazimuddin elected in a by-election from one of the two seats that he would vacate. He said that he was aware that Mr Huq would do his utmost to defeat him in the election through one of his stooges. Mr Huq took up the challenge and had one of his men contest the election. However, Mr Nazimuddin won in the end thanks to Mr Suhrawardy's backing. And now it was this very man who had insulted him! We decided we would try to get five of our people elected to the council and would not let anyone nominated by Mr Nazimuddin get elected. We were confident we had the majority of the votes in the council.

Maulana Akram Khan tried to reconcile the two factions. Mr Suhrawardy and the Maulana discussed the situation in the latter's house. I could see at one point that Mr Suhrawardy was relenting. The Maulana said, 'We are now in a struggle to achieve Pakistan. Why fight each other at this time? It's best to settle the issue peacefully.' We pointed out that the Maulana and Mr Nazimuddin had already been elected. Why did they then choose one more of their own and not you? We would never agree to this.

I can't remember the exact day when all this happened but clearly remember the incident itself. It had been decided that in the evening there would be an attempt to arrive at a compromise in the party room of the Calcutta Assembly where MLAs, MLCs and League leaders would all be present. We decided to spring into action as soon as we heard this. We managed to gather two to three hundred students from Baker Hostel and other hostels and then move to the scene of the meeting. This was going on behind closed doors. I knocked on the door and told them that we demanded to be heard. In the end the leaders agreed to give us a hearing. They opened the doors. The students went inside.

I was the first speaker and spoke for almost half an hour. I told Mr Suhrawardy, 'You have no right to agree to a compromise. We do not want to compromise with the feudal Khawaja. When Mr Nazimuddin became the prime minister in 1942 he made his own brother a minister. He had made eleven of his family members MLAs. Didn't this country have people outside his own kinsmen? We won't allow the Muslim League to be a party run by a coterie. We have already demonstrated against Mr Huq and if necessary we will demonstrate against you as well.' We forced Mr Suhrawardy to leave the meeting. After we had left Mr Fazlul Quader Chowdhury and Faridpur's Lal Mia also gave speeches in our support. We had our own meeting at night. We spent almost the whole night with Mr Suhrawardy. Mr Nazimuddin contacted him at one point on the phone and wanted to find out whether we would be ready to compromise. We were, however, aware of the conversation that had taken place between them. Mr Suhrawardy had told Mr Nazimuddin that he would let them know by nine next morning what he intended to do. He asked us to gather in his house by 8 a.m. the next day. This was a time when Nuruddin, Ekram, Nurul Alam, Sharfuddin, Zahir and a few of us would stick to each other all day long. Fazlul Quader Chowdhury had also come to Calcutta with his followers. He was very popular among the students of Chittagong.

In the morning we reached Mr Suhrawardy's house exactly at eight. He had talked to quite a few people during the night. He sat with us, and we stuck to him. He told us that he wasn't sure whether we would be able to get all five seats. I said, 'Trust us; we will win. God willing, there is no reason on earth why we should lose.' I handed the telephone to him and said, 'Tell Mr Nazimuddin that we want the elections to be held.' Mr Suhrawardy did exactly that. He told Mr Nazimuddin, 'Whatever happens will happen through elections. The Muslim League belongs to everyone and so why should a solution be imposed from up above?' Mr Nazimuddin said something or the other to evade the issue. I could hear Mr Suhrawardy say, 'No, it's too late for that. You didn't behave properly with us.'

We said goodbye and came away. At night the representatives from the districts showed up. One whose presence I can still recall is Mr Mujibur Rahman Muktar, secretary of the Noakhali District Muslim League. He gave a very eloquent speech to the leaders of his district. All the Noakhali district representatives admired Mr Suhrawardy. Mr Hashim had taken the helm of our office ably and it was running quite smoothly. We had kept people in the two railway stations of Calcutta, Sealdah and Howrah, to receive the councillors and arrange for their accommodation. The student volunteers had left their hostels to meet the representatives of their districts. For two days we worked very, very hard. Maulana Ragib Ahsan and Mr Osman were at that time leaders of the Calcutta Muslim League. All the members of the Calcutta Muslim League were devoted to Mr Suhrawardy. They too had taken to the streets with their cars and their followers to campaign on his behalf. The day of the meeting thus saw hundreds of our workers show up. Those of us who were members of the council went inside the hall while the workers stood outside and kept on campaigning on Mr Suhrawardy's behalf. The whole auditorium rang with shouts of 'Long live Mr Suhrawardy' and 'Long Live Mr Hashim'.

After some deliberations, Mr Suhrawardy and Mr Hashim came up with five names: Huseyn Shaheed Suhrawardy; Abul Hashim; Maulana Ragib Ahsan; Ahmed Hussein; Lal Mia. Lal Mia proposed these names on our behalf while Mr Nazimuddin did so for his faction. At this point Mr Fazlul Quader Chowdhury became all worked up and began canvassing to nominate himself as a candidate to the Parliamentary Board. I too lobbied on his behalf. Mr Suhrawardy was on the point of agreeing to have him nominated. By this time they hadn't decided on taking Fazlul Quader Chowdhury at Lal Mia's expense. It was then that Mr Chowdhury met Mr Nazimuddin and proposed joining his faction along with his Chittagong delegates. When Mr Suhrawardy heard this he said, 'Under no circumstance should he be nominated since he has proved himself to be so greedy even at this age.' Meanwhile, Mr Nazimuddin also decided not to nominate him from his faction. In the end Mr Chowdhury ended up voting for Mr Suhrawardy. Everyone in his group admired Mr Suhrawardy. M.A. Aziz, Zahur Ahmad Chowdhury, Abul Khair Siddique and Azizur Rahman Chowdhury were all admirers of Mr Suhrawardy. They had been somewhat hurt at what Mr Chowdhury had attempted to do. They were all my friends too.

When the council meeting began, Maulana Akram Khan spoke for a while. Next, Mr Abul Hashim began to speak as secretary of our organization. But no sooner did he start speaking than a few of Mr Nazimuddin's followers began to heckle him. We objected to this approach and the result was chaos in the meeting. Almost all the young delegates were on Mr Suhrawardy's side, so how could they stop us? Nobody said anything to Mr Nazimuddin. All the members of his faction got their share of insults. My friend Aziz and I noticed that Mr Shah Azizur Rahman had lined up after Mr Nazimuddin with the files of the Muslim Student League in his hand. The two of us decided that we would snatch away the files since having them in our possession would help us in our organizational work. When Mr Nazimuddin was about to leave, with Mr Shah Azizur Rahman following him, Aziz grabbed Mr Rahman. I took the files away from him saying, 'Don't talk; just leave!' Nowadays when I meet Mr Shah Azizur Rahman and we chat I always smile remembering that scene. Mr Shah Azizur Rahman, I should point out, joined the Awami League in 1964 and became the leader of the Awami League in the National Assembly and the deputy leader of the opposition. We continued to be enemies till martial law was imposed in 1958 and it was later that we become allies.

Maulana Akram Khan decided to adjourn the meeting till the next day. He declared that voting would take place at 10 a.m. Ballots were prepared. A box was placed in the next room. Each delegate would have five votes. I was canvassing inside and someone or the other complained to the Maulana. He came and said, 'What do you think you are doing, young man?' I replied, 'I am a member and not just a young man.' The Maulana laughed at this and went away.

Vote counting went on till evening the next day. All five members nominated by Mr Suhrawardy won the election. I had brought some garlands along and so had many others. When I garlanded Mr Suhrawardy he told me affectionately, 'You were right. We were really worried about Lal Mia's chances of winning.' I had personally appealed to many delegates so that he could win. Mr Suhrawardy managed to get only a few votes from the Faridpur district delegates. Lal Mia and I were among those few voters. The rest went to Mr Nazimuddin at the instigation of Mr Tamizuddin, Mohan Mia and Mr Salam. But I had managed to get a few Faridpur votes for Lal Mia. Although Lal Mia and Mohan Mia were brothers they had opposed each other.

It is pertinent to point out here a funny thing about the relationship between the two brothers. After he became a member of the Parliamentary Board, Lal Mia worked for his brother's nomination. He did not agree to having someone from our faction being nominated then. We managed to get two of the six Faridpur seats only after many arguments with them. The two men from our faction who were chosen were Rajbari's Khan Bahadur Yusuf Hussein Chowdhury and Madaripur's Iskandar Ali. Mohan Mia lost to Dattpara's Shamsuddin Ahmed Chowdhury alias Badshah Mia. As soon as the results were announced, Badshah Mia declared, 'My victory is the Muslim League's victory; it is Pakistan's victory.' Lal Mia and Mohan Mia were always in different camps. At first Lal Mia worked for the Congress and Mohan Mia for the Muslim League. When the two of them joined the Muslim League one brother became part of Suhrawardy's faction while the other sided with Nazimuddin. And when Ayub Khan declared martial law in Pakistan, one brother joined Ayub Khan's party while the other one became part of the opposition. This meant that no matter who was in power one of them would always be in the ruling party. I saw the two brothers playing this unique game throughout our lives. No matter what happened during the day, at night the two brothers were on the same side and they were always united in their own interests.

At around this time we received orders from the Muslim League to go to different districts to take charge of the election offices set up there. It had been decided that election offices and camps to train workers would be set up in every district and subdivision. In each district, capable people would be put in charge of these camps. I can remember the set-ups in some of the districts even now. Kamruddin was given the responsibility for Dhaka, Shamsul Huq for Mymensingh, Khondokar Mushtaq Ahmed for Comilla and Ekramul Huq for Khulna. I was put in charge of Faridpur district. We left for our district headquarters with bicycles, microphones, horns and relevant papers. The district league was asked to cooperate with us. We were to open a camp to train workers in each thana and subdivision of the district. I had to leave my college and come to Faridpur.

I had visited Faridpur on previous occasions but had never stayed there for more than a day. When I was given the charge of Faridpur district Mohan Mia was upset. He made it known to everyone that I shouldn't be given a place to stay in town. He was president of the District Muslim League and he did not want me around. I sent all that I had brought along with me with Mr Abdul Hamid Chowdhury and Mollah Jalaluddin to Faridpur. Hamid and Jalal were students at Faridpur College and they had to leave their studies for the time being. Nobody in Faridpur town agreed to rent a house to me. In the end I was forced to put up in a two-storeyed house owned by a distant relative that was located a little away from town.

And so we had an office of our own. We arranged training sessions for our workers. I began to tour the entire district. I had offices opened in Madaripur, Gopalganj and Rajbari and work started for the elections everywhere. I soon had offices at the thana level too. At this point I had to go to Calcutta from time to time. Mr Suhrawardy and Mr Hashim had visited Gopalganj a few days ago. There was a huge meeting on that occasion. Mr Salam's faction refused to host them since they had come to the town at my request. They stressed that I was a mere member of the Muslim League and nothing more. There was a lot of debate on the issue in Gopalganj. Just two days before Mr Suhrawardy was supposed to come I let it be known that I had been entirely responsible for the birth of the Gopalganj Muslim League. Mr Suhrawardy was scheduled to come to the town and I was bent on receiving him; if anybody had other ideas they would have to deal with me.

I had my people ready the night before they came. By the afternoon of his arrival a few thousand people showed up, armed with shafts, spears and other indigenous weapons. Mr Salam also showed up with his men. However, they made no move to oppose my supporters. When he stood up to give a speech after Mr Suhrawardy, Mr Hashim and Lal Mia had delivered their speeches, his men attempted to chant, 'Long live Salam!' At this point my men began to heckle them. The two sides shouted at each other. In the end Salam's people were forced to leave the meeting. My men began chasing them. Mr Suhrawardy went out of the meeting and positioned himself between the two factions. Both factions had men armed with swords, shields and other weapons and chances of people getting killed were very high. But both factions were amazed at the way Mr Suhrawardy managed to place himself between them. Mr Hashim had left for my house by this time. Later, Mr Suhrawardy and Mr Hashim became very angry with Mr Salam because of the stand he had taken.

Afterwards, Mr Suhrawardy sent his people to Gopalganj and Madaripur to gauge the extent of our popularity. Quite a few people wanted nominations, but it was important to find out who had the best chances of getting elected. The incumbent MLA Shamsuddin Ahmed had already joined the Muslim League. Then there was the retired deputy police commissioner Khan Bahadur Shamsuddoha, Mr Abdus Salam Khan and one or two other men of some standing. Mr Salam was very popular in Gopalganj and without a doubt 80 per cent of the people of the town wanted him to be their representative. When Mr Suhrawardy inquired about the extent of Mr Salam's popularity from my father, he replied that the people wanted Mr Salam as their candidate. However, Mr Khondokar Shamsuddin was as eligible as he was in other ways. Mr Suhrawardy told me that he believed that the people wanted Mr Salam, and this was confirmed to him by my father. I said, 'You must go by the wants of the people; I certainly won't object to that decision.' I had already had a talk with Mr Salam on the subject. However, Mr Hashim didn't want him. I had no idea why he took this position. I tried to persuade him till the end to nominate Mr Salam. But the only result of my attempt to do so was that

Mr Hashim became angry with me. Nevertheless Mr Suhrawardy filed a report stating that Mr Salam had the best chance of getting elected and he was ready to nominate him. He talked to Lal Mia and Mr Hashim on the subject. This was a time when a lot of money was being spent on securing nominations. I was informed that this was happening but could find no direct evidence of money being splashed around. In the end it was Khan Bahadur Shamsuddoha who was nominated by the Provincial Parliamentary Board. However, the Central Parliamentary Board struck out the Khan Bahadur's name and nominated Khondokar Shamsuddin Ahmed instead. I imagine that Mr Salam would have been elected in any case if he had chosen to stand on his own but he preferred not to contest against the Muslim League candidate. After all, the issue at stake was Pakistan. But it was wrong to have nominated Khondokar Shamsuddin Ahmed since he had joined the Muslim League only a few months back. The only reason he was nominated was that his cousin had married Khawaja Shahbuddin's daughter. It was Mr Khawaja Nazimuddin who had persuaded Mr Chaudhury Khaliquzzaman to nominate Mr Ahmed for the position.

~

Mr Suhrawardy was a generous man. There was no meanness in him and he wasn't influenced by partisan feelings or prejudices. He did not believe in cliques or coteries and did not try to work through factions. If he found someone eligible he would trust him fully. He had tremendous self-belief. He tried to win men's hearts through his honesty, principles, energy and efficiency. But his personality was also the reason he suffered humiliation and defeat again and again. It is good to be generous but if you are too nice when dealing with mean people both the country and the people will suffer in the end.

We Bengali Muslims have two sides. One is our belief that we are Muslims and the other that we are Bengalis. Instances of envy and treachery can be often found in our history. Surely no other language in the world has the equivalent of the Bengali word for envy. Translated literally, the word would mean 'mortified at another's good fortune'. You will find words such as envy and malice in all languages and these are qualities people all over the world have but only Bengalis are stricken by grief at another's prosperity. They are never happy to see their brothers do well. That is why Bengalis have been oppressed by other races throughout the ages despite being blessed with so many other good qualities. The country is fertile and endowed with plenty. Few countries in the world have the kind of fertile land that we have. And yet we are so poor! The reason is that for ages others have dominated us because of our own fault. We don't know ourselves and till we do and learn to understand our mindset we will not be free. Often it has been seen that an illiterate man who is fair, who wears flowing clothes and has a well-groomed beard and can speak a few words of Arabic or Persian is hailed as a saint soon after coming to Bangladesh. Bengalis spend thousands and thousands of takas to get his blessings. But if you cared to get to the truth of the matter you would find out that the man is really an employee of some fruit shop in Calcutta or perhaps an accused in some murder case! Blind faith and belief in the supernatural are thus other faults of our people.

Initially, Bengalis failed to appreciate Mr Suhrawardy's greatness. By the time they learned to value him they had run out of time. In the elections he raised the fund for the campaign and for organizational work almost wholly on his own. The Central Muslim League did sanction some funds for the purpose but it was Mr Suhrawardy who raised the bulk of the money needed to conduct elections. He purchased hundreds of bicycles with his own money. As far as I know, after the creation of Pakistan he stayed back in Calcutta for a while to clear the debts he had incurred in the process. I have pointed out previously he was the trusting sort. But he was soon in trouble because of this trait. Despite the fact that his faction constituted the majority in the Parliamentary Board he could not nominate his own people in many cases. When Mr Nazimuddin's faction lost the elections they resorted to other measures to have their way. Mr Nazimuddin let it be known that he would not contest the election and that Mr Suhrawardy would henceforth lead the Muslim League. He requested Mr Suhrawardy to nominate people who had been in the Muslim League for a long time and assured him that they would all support him. Since Mr Nazimuddin wasn't going to contest the elections, what did Mr Suhrawardy have to fear? Mr Suhrawardy was persuaded by this line of argument and ended up nominating the old Muslim Leaguers.

I think Bengali Muslims had 119 seats in the Bengal Legislative Assembly then. The ploy that Mr Nazimuddin adopted meant that at least fifty of his men were nominated. On the other hand, his men dominated the Central Muslim League. Mr Liaquat Ali Khan, Khaliquzzaman, Hussein Imam, Mr Chundrigar and others were intimidated by Mr Suhrawardy since they knew he was better than them in all ways. The Central Parliamentary Board did its bit by replacing the candidates nominated by the Provincial Board in thirty seats (although it is true a couple of them were Mr Suhrawardy's supporters).

When the elections were over it was obvious that the League had come out successful in 116 out of 119 seats. I may of course be wrong about the exact number since I can't remember all the details exactly now. But it was clear after the results were posted that Mr Nazimuddin's faction had ended up with the majority. On the surface, they had to acknowledge Mr Suhrawardy as their leader but behind the scenes they continued to intrigue against him. Mr Suhrawardy did not believe in cliques and so he chose ministers on the basis of their qualifications. In fact, he made many members of Mr Nazimuddin's faction parliamentary secretaries and whips. He even made Mr Fazlur Rahman a minister.

~

Mr Churchill had sent the Cripps Mission during the war for negotiations but nothing came of it. When the war ended and Mr Clement Atlee became the prime minister for the Labour Party, he announced that he would be sending the Cabinet Mission to India on 15 March 1946. It would consist of three ministers who would be coming to India for discussions with different parties to try to come to a solution that would lead to India's independence in the shortest possible time. The Viceroy would be consulted to form an interim government consisting of representatives of the major parties as soon as possible. The members of the Cabinet Mission were Lord Pethick-Lawrence, the secretary of state for India; Sir Stafford Cripps, president of the Board of Trade; and Mr A.V. Alexander, First Lord of the Admiralty. They would come to India and meet the Viceroy and leaders of political parties to work out the finer details of independence.

Mr Atlee's speech on the subject did not mention the Muslim demand for Pakistan. Instead, he had slighted the demands of the minority community in it. Let me give a short extract of what Mr Atlee had said in his speech here: 'Minorities cannot be allowed to impede the progress of majorities.' The Congress greeted his speech with satisfaction. However, Mr Muhammad Ali Jinnah was highly critical of it.

The Cabinet Mission reached India on 23 March. The statements they made when they reached India upset us. All of us would go to Mr Suhrawardy whenever we came across their statements and ask him what the outcome of the Cabinet Mission's deliberations was going to be. Mr Suhrawardy would respond calmly and tell us, 'We have nothing to fear; they will have to meet our demand for Pakistan.' We hardly saw him during the daytime and so Nuruddin and I would go to meet him at 11 p.m. By the time we finished our meetings with him it would usually be very late. The two of us would often walk from Theatre Road to Baker Hostel. On a few occasions we ended up sleeping on the chairs in the renovated weekly *Millat* office where they had set up a new press. Mr Hashim used to live there too. Khondokar Nurul Alam was the manager of the press at that time. We, in fact, preferred to use the *Millat* office instead of the Muslim League office. Muslim League MLAs and workers from outside Calcutta would also stay in the office then. Barisal's Formuzul Huq, joint secretary of the Muslim League, also lived in the office with his family. Mr Suhrawardy would pay him his salary month after month.

All of a sudden, we came to know that Mr Jinnah had summoned a convention of all members of the Muslim League's central and provincial councils from all over India [at Delhi, 7–9 April 1946]. In the last election the Muslim League had won by an overwhelming margin in Bengal. In most other provinces where Muslims constituted the majority it had emerged as the largest party. However, in Punjab, Sind and the Frontier Province, the Muslim League had not been able to form a government by itself. It was only in Bengal that the Muslim League led by Mr Suhrawardy could form a government on its own. In Punjab there was a Unionist government led by Khizir Hayat Khan. In the Frontier Province Dr Khan headed a Congress government and in Sind Mr Allah Bux was at the head of a government that was opposed to the Muslim League. Of the four provinces where the Muslims had a majority it was only in Bengal that the Muslim League could form a government by itself. Everywhere else it took its place in the opposition camp. It must be pointed out here that India was then divided into eleven provinces.

Mr Suhrawardy gave orders to make arrangements for a special train to carry Muslim League MLAs from Bengal and Assam to Delhi. The train, named East Pakistan Special, was to leave from Howrah station in Calcutta. Ten to fifteen student workers from Bengal were to go to the convention in it. Mr Suhrawardy gave us permission to do so. The whole train was draped in the Muslim League flag and was decorated with flowers. We set aside two interclass coaches for ourselves. Some of the students naughtily scrawled on the body of one of the coaches 'Reserved for Sheikh Mujib and party'. This was to make sure that no one else boarded that particular coach. They also felt that my name would be enough to ensure Mr Suhrawardy did not protest against our action even though it was Nuruddin who was officially the Students' League leader. Indeed, all of us used to follow his lead.

Two microphones were installed in Mr Suhrawardy's and Mr Hashim's coaches. Arrangements had been made to give receptions to Mr Suhrawardy and his party in almost every station where the train was supposed to stop. The victory of the Muslim League in Bengal had a huge impact on Muslims throughout India. Zahiruddin had been given a place close to Mr Hashim's coach since he would have to give speeches in Urdu all along the way: Zahiruddin was the only one among us who was equally adept at English, Urdu and Bengali. Whenever we had to address any ward in Calcutta I would speak in Bengali and Zahiruddin in Urdu.

Among those who had been authorized to go on the train to Delhi with us and who were ready to do so were Nuruddin, Zahiruddin, Q.J. Azmeri, Anwar Hussein (now a high-ranking official of Eastern Federal Insurance), Shamsul Huq, Khondokar Mushtaq Ahmed, Murshidabad's Kazi Abu Nasser and my uncle Sheikh Zafar Sadek. Many students who had come to the station to see us off at Howrah station decided to join us when they heard that they could accompany us without having to pay for the ticket in this special train even though they had not packed any clothes for a long stay. There were ten such students and we didn't have the heart to say no to them since they were devoted workers of our party. Shouts of 'Praise God', 'Long live the Muslim League', 'Long live Pakistan', 'Long live Muhammad Ali Jinnah' and 'Long live Shaheed Suhrawardy' filled the station as the train started to move.

The entire train had been fitted with loudspeakers. Zahir, Azmeri and I raised slogans most often on the microphone. Our train had to stop at every station along the way even though it wasn't supposed to do so. Thousands of people had assembled at every stop to greet Mr Suhrawardy and the delegates of the Bengal Muslim League. When the train reached Patna in the morning we saw that Patna station was overflowing with people. They were raising slogans such as 'Long live Bengali Muslims', 'Long live Shaheed Suhrawardy', 'Long live Pakistan', 'We will fight our way to Pakistan', etc. The Bihar Muslim League had made arrangements to feed all of us and each of us was garlanded. It soon became obvious that at the rate we were progressing we would not be able to arrive in Delhi in time. Wherever we came across people raising slogans we would stop the train. Mr Suhrawardy got irritated at the frequent stoppages but I kept pointing out to him that these people had been waiting for a long time for the train to pass so that they could get a glimpse of him and that it would therefore be unfair not to stop the train for a minute or so. In any case, this was how it went that night. People crowded the small stations on the way and waited eagerly for our train to stop. At Allahabad station they had our entire train redecorated with flowers. En route many students from Bihar and UP [United Provinces] boarded the train. Many of them became my friends and these friendships continued even after the independence of Pakistan. Some of them would later migrate to Pakistan.

By the time we reached Delhi it was evening, even though we were supposed to be in the city that morning. We were eight hours late in all. Muhammad Ali Jinnah had delayed the convention opening for our arrival. It was supposed to begin at 9 a.m. and so we had to head for the meeting straight from the station. The Delhi Muslim League volunteers took the responsibility of looking after our luggage. We reached the meeting site while raising slogans in Bengali. The delegates who had already taken their seats stood up to greet us. We were given a place to sit right next to Mr Jinnah. Whenever a slogan was raised in Urdu we responded with one in Bengali.

Mr Jinnah stood up to speak. The entire audience listened to his speech intently and in silence. It seemed that everyone present shared the same thought: Pakistan would have to be achieved at any cost. After Mr Jinnah finished speaking a subject committee was formed. On 8 April this committee met for the first time. The resolution that was taken there altered the Lahore Resolution in some ways. Only Mr Hashim and a few others objected when the word 'States' of the previous resolution was replaced with 'State' but they were overruled and the emendation was adopted.[10] Scholars can perhaps decide whether this convention had the right to alter the terms of the resolution adopted in Lahore in 1940. The council was the ultimate authority in the Muslim League. Later we were told that the Lahore Resolution had not been altered and that this resolution was the result of that particular convention. Mr Huseyn Shaheed Suhrawardy requested Mr Muhammad Ali Jinnah to submit the proposal since he was the prime minister of Bengal and in fact the only Muslim League prime minister of India.

The resolution adopted by the council was as follows:

> Whereas in this vast subcontinent of India a hundred million Muslims are the adherents of a faith which regulates every department of their life—educational, social, economic and political—whose code is not confined merely to spiritual doctrines and tenets or rituals and ceremonies and which stands in sharp contrast to the exclusive nature of Hindu Dharma and Philosophy which has fostered and maintained rigid caste system for thousands of years, resulting in the degradation of 60 million human beings to the position of untouchables, creation of unnatural barriers between man and man and superimposition of social and economic inequalities on a large body of the people of this country and which threatens to reduce Muslims, Christians and other minorities to the status of irredeemable helots, socially and economically;

Whereas the Hindu caste system is a direct negation of nationalism, equality, democracy and all the noble ideals that Islam stands for;

Whereas, different historical backgrounds, traditions, cultures social and economic orders of the Hindus and the Muslims made impossible the evolution of a single Indian Nation inspired by common aspirations and ideals and whereas after centuries they still remain two distinct major nations;

Whereas, soon after the introduction by the British of the policy of setting up political institutions in India on the lines of western democracies based on majority rule which means that the majority of the nation or society could impose its will on the minority of the nation or society in spite of their opposition as amply demonstrated during the two and half years' regime of Congress Governments in the Hindu majority provinces under the Government of India Act, 1935, when the Muslims were subjected to untold harassment and oppression as a result of which they were convinced of the futility and ineffectiveness of the so-called safeguards provided in the constitution and in the Instruments of Instructions to the Governors and were driven to the irresistible conclusion that in a United India Federation, if established, the Muslims even in Muslim majority provinces, could meet with no better fate and their rights and interests could never be adequately protected against the perpetual Hindu majority at the centre;

Whereas, the Muslims are convinced that with a view to save Muslim India from the domination of the Hindus and in order to afford them full scope to develop themselves according to their genius, it is necessary to constitute a sovereign independent State comprising Bengal and Assam in the North-East zone and the Punjab, North-West Frontier Province, Sind and Baluchistan in the North-West zone.

This Convention of the Muslim-League Legislators of India. Central and Provincial, after careful consideration hereby declares that the Muslim Nation will never submit to any constitution for a United India and will never participate in any single constitution-making machinery set up for the purpose, and that any formula devised by the British Government for transferring power from the British to the peoples of India, which does not conform to the following just and equitable principles calculated to maintain internal peace and tranquillity in the country, will not contribute to the solution of the Indian problem—

1. That the zones comprising Bengal and Assam in the North-East and the Punjab, North-West Frontier Province, Sind and Baluchistan in the North West of India, namely Pakistan Zones, where the Muslims are in a dominant majority, be constituted into one sovereign independent state and that an unequivocal undertaking be given to implement the establishment of Pakistan without delay.

2. That two separate constitution making bodies be set up by the peoples of Pakistan and Hindustan for the purpose of framing their respective constitutions.
3. That the minorities in Pakistan and Hindustan be provided with safeguards on the line of the All-India Muslim League resolution passed on March 23, 1940 at Lahore.
4. That the acceptance of the Muslim League demand for Pakistan and its implementation without delay are the sine qua non for the Muslim League co-operation and participation in the formation of an interim Government at the centre.

This convention further emphatically declares that any attempt to impose a constitution on a United India basis or to force any interim arrangement at the centre contrary to the Muslim demand, will leave the Muslims no alternative but to resist such imposition by all possible means for their survival and national existence.

After Mr Suhrawardy finished speaking, twenty to twenty-five leaders from different provinces gave speeches in support of the resolution. Mr Abul Hashim delivered a wonderful speech on the occasion. After the resolution was adopted unanimously, Mr Liaquat Ali Khan submitted an oath and all Muslim League leaders of Provincial Legislative Assemblies put their signatures on it.

Once the convention came to an end those who had boarded the train from Howrah station on impulse because they had come there only to see us off found themselves in a fix. How were they going to return to Calcutta? There was no special train to take them back to the city. We just couldn't figure out a way to help them.

We had come prepared to go to the shrine of Khawaja Muinuddin Chisti in Ajmer from Delhi and from Ajmer we were ready to go to Agra to see the Taj Mahal. In 1943 too I had returned from Delhi without seeing the Taj Mahal and so this time I was determined to see it. It was something that I had hoped to do since childhood. However, a few of us went to Mr Suhrawardy and told him about the fix the students who had come from Calcutta were in because they had come without any planning or invitation. Mr Suhrawardy said, 'Someone has already collected some money to help them. He is supposed to consult you and then distribute the money among them.' I replied, 'I have no idea where this person who had been given the money is—he must have left already.' Mr Suhrawardy became very angry. The man he had trusted was not a student. I don't want to divulge his identity now. However, Mr Suhrawardy gave me more money to help the students out. He sanctioned twenty-five taka for each of them, estimating that this would be enough to take them back to Calcutta. Khondokar Nurul Alam and I gave each of them this money and made them sign receipts. They took their leave and headed for Calcutta.

Around ten of us then left for Ajmer along with Mr Fazlul Quader Chowdhury. We knew that we wouldn't face financial problems since Mr Chowdhury was with us. Before we left we toured Delhi extensively. For hundreds of years Muslims had ruled India from Delhi. How could we know then that we would have to give up control over the city? Delhi's Red Fort, Qutb Minar and Jama Masjid continue to testify to the glories of Muslim architecture. When we went visiting Old Delhi and its surrounding areas we saw testimony to the greatness of Mughal rule everywhere.

Our group finally boarded the train to Ajmer. Our elders had told us innumerable stories of the city. 'If you are able to make your request in the right frame of mind, the great saint of the city will fulfil your wish,' we had often been told. When we reached Ajmer we found that many people were waiting to take us to their homes so that we could stay there. I wondered what was happening. Why were these people so eager to host us? We didn't accept any of their invitations though and left all decisions that were to be taken to Mr Chowdhury since he was going to be our leader on this tour. We had already agreed to follow him around. He came down from a first-class compartment of the train with his luggage and told one of the people present so eager to host us: 'Take us to your house.' The gentleman quickly summoned some vehicles and took us with him assuring us that he had enough space to accommodate all of us. We bathed and dined in his house. Later we realized that these people are known as 'khadims'. We discovered that they are very courteous and never set a price on their services. They ensure that the people living with them have places to stay in, enough to eat and escorts to take them around Ajmer. They only ask you to pay for things that you have to pay for because the custom requires you to do so. For the expenses they themselves incurred they will accept whatever you are willing to pay them at the end of your visit. I believe that they have to give a portion of their receipts to the shrine committee since they have to look after the upkeep of the shrine. In the saint's shrine no one is allowed to go hungry. Thus food is continually being cooked in that place and people dine there all the time.

When we arrived at the shrine we were overwhelmed by what we saw. Hundreds of people kept streaming in and out of the shrine endlessly. Many people were praying inside. Some were crying out in grief while others had tears rolling down their faces. All uttered the same prayer, 'Dear saint, reveal yourself to us.' Some people were playing a harmonium and singing beside the saint's grave. Even though I couldn't figure out all the words of the songs I tried to follow them. We prayed in the shrine and then went out and listened to the singers performing. I believe the songs they sang are called qawwali. We paid some money to the singers. I didn't feel like leaving but we had to go at one point. We were to head for Taragarh Mountain where there were a few more shrines of the saint's companions.

Taragarh Mountain is quite high. We were supposed to climb it. How did the Muslim soldiers master this steep ascent to defeat the soldiers of Prithviraj? This was of course in a war when fighter planes hadn't been invented. Students of history know very well why the saint had chosen this place. Our host had given us a guide for the trip and this man narrated the history of the battle to us. Eventually we managed to climb to the top of the mountain. We stayed there for a long time. Stretching before us was a vast desert. On the other side was Ajmer town. By the time we came down from the top it was early evening. We went back to our host's house for lunch and then once more left it to visit Anar Sagar.

This was a huge lake. The town had grown till it had encircled the lake on all sides. Some structures built during the Mughal period are still in evidence on the shores. These are places where the emperor and his wives used to rest. The emperor who has left his mark here most is Shahjahan. The place where he and his wife used to stay in is still intact. It is made of white marble. We spent the entire evening there. When the sun had finally set we headed for the town slowly. We are people from a riverine place and we love our waterbodies. How can I explain how difficult it was for us to leave this lake in a land that was otherwise a desert? One of my friends even said, 'How about spending the night here?' It really was a great idea; however, we didn't have the right to do so. Nobody was allowed to stay here at night. It was therefore not a good idea to try to stay. After all, who would bail us out if the police decided to arrest us and take us to jail in this distant land?

We returned to the saint's shrine at night. We stayed there for a while and then returned to our host's house. Our host had arranged a very good dinner for us. At night we rested contentedly.

We said goodbye to Ajmer's shrine and got on to a train again to go to Agra where Mumtaz Mahal was lying in eternal rest in the Taj Mahal. I had been dreaming of visiting the Taj Mahal for a long time now. It is the greatest monument of Mughal architecture and art. It is a testimony to Emperor Shahjahan's immortal love and one of the seven wonders of the world. We kept on talking about it as we came closer and closer to the monument. Many people from all over the world come to India to see the Taj Mahal. It will be difficult to find people anywhere who are totally ignorant about this famous monument. We were impatient to see it. We even kept thinking that the train was not moving fast enough and delaying us from viewing it. We had no idea that we would be reaching it on a full-moon night. After all, we hadn't consulted a calendar to find out when we could see it best. We thanked the moon and our fates too.

We reached Agra in the morning. We had decided to stay there for two days. We planned on staying in one hotel or the other. There were quite a few of us—about twelve to fourteen people. We would have to spend a lot of money. It would have been better to put up in one of the wayside places built for travellers. But no sooner did we reach Agra than we were besieged by agents from innumerable hotels. One such agent told us, 'You are from Bengal and must stay in our Bengali hotel and will find that convenient.' Mr Chowdhury shot back, 'Does your hotel have a tent? There are quite a few of us.' He replied, 'I can put up one for you.' We decided that we would go to Agra Hotel. Mr Chowdhury took a room and had two tents put up for the rest of us. We were happy to get a bed to sleep in. All we needed, we felt, was enough water for our baths and a toilet. The owner of the hotel was a Bengali and a gentleman and received us cordially. He ordered the manager to look after us well. Mr Chowdhury had settled the amount that we were to pay for our stay and gave him that amount. We didn't have to pay anything.

We left the hotel soon after we had taken our baths since we were all eagerly looking forward to seeing the Taj Mahal. We got up on the tonga. It was very hot outside. But I won't be able to express in words what we saw since I don't have that kind of command over them. All I could think was: how could such a wonderful thing be built? What I saw was much more beautiful and solemn than what I had imagined the monument would be. The best time to see the Taj is when the sun is setting and when the moon is beginning to smile in the sky. We didn't stay for long since we wanted to see Agra Fort and Itimad-ud-dowla's tomb before dusk. We intended to return to the Taj Mahal as the sun started to go down. We kept the tongas with us all the time.

Itimad-ud-dowlah is where Noorjahan's father is buried. We came to Agra Fort. We saw all the sights here—Diwan-i-Am, Moti Masjid, the Mochi building and Nagina Masjid. We also went to see the Diwan-i-Khas and Jasmine Tower. This place has a lot in common with Delhi's Red Fort. Mughal buildings tend to resemble each other, as is obvious as soon as you view them. On the side of the fort facing the Yamuna river were some stone structures. Once upon a time you could look at the Taj through them. Now they aren't there any more. However, there is a glass casing on one of them. You can see the Taj Mahal clearly through it. We saw everything here as well as the Taj and then headed for Shish Mahal. The guide told us a lot of things about the sites. Some of these are true but some appear to be fictitious. One thing was for sure though: after the Mughals had ceased to rule, a lot of their monuments were pillaged. The Jats and the Marathas took some of the stuff away while the English swept almost everything clean and took all they had gathered to England. The loot ended up as the property of the English nobility. Nevertheless, some remnants of Mughal rule can still be found in many places in India and Pakistan.

We had our fill of Itmatuddowlah and eventually returned to the Taj to view it again. It was getting to be evening. We had seen Delhi's Red Fort already and so didn't expect to spend much time at Agra Fort. As the sun was setting we reached the gates of the Taj Mahal. We were to stay there for a long time. The main gates were kept open till 10 p.m. when the guards would ring the bell to announce that visiting hours were over for the day. We would then have to abandon the Taj for the night. Some of us sat down while a few of us selected a place to pray. We heard the call to prayer. On this day many people had come to view the Taj from India as well as overseas. Bengalis, Marathis and Punjabis—in fact people from all over India seemed to be present. We asked the guide if the Taj was always as crowded as we had found it that day. He said, 'Not really. It is during full moon that the Taj overflows with people.' When the sun went down, it seemed that golden light beams were flowing towards us. The Taj appeared to have taken on a completely new look for this occasion. Some time after sunset the moon made its appearance. It burst out of the darkness and with it the Taj seemed to have dropped its veil and taken on a look that was absolutely breathtaking. It was so lovely! Even as I write this account twenty-one years later, the Taj's beauty overwhelms me; I'll never forget its loveliness. We stayed there till the guards shut the main gate of the Taj.

The next day we were to visit Fatehpur Sikri. Mr Chowdhury had already arranged for a bus to take us there. We would have to return in the evening after visiting Fatehpur Sikri and Sikandra and leave that very night for the junction called Tundla. It was through Tundla that the trains from Delhi went as they headed for Calcutta. We would have to take the train that would end up at Howrah junction.

Our bus arrived in the morning. We got ready and boarded it quickly. The bus started moving as soon as Mr Chowdhury got on it. Fatehpur Sikri was only twenty-eight miles away and wasn't supposed to take a long time to reach by road. In fact, our bus reached Fatehpur Sikri even before we could stop talking about the marvels of Mughal architecture. Emperor Akbar had built Fatehpur Sikri as his capital. It really wasn't built any differently from Agra Fort. However, it was much bigger than that structure. The huge field in front of Fatehpur Sikri is called Khanwa. It was here that Emperor Babar defeated Sangram Singh to lay the foundation of the Mughal Empire in India. But it is difficult to figure out why Akbar chose this spot to build Fatehpur Sikri. Historians have different views in this respect.

We crossed the Agra Gate and entered through the main gate of the Fort called Buland Darwaza. After going through this 134-foot-high gate we saw the tomb of Salim Chisti. We prayed for him here and then went inside the fort. We also prayed in the shrine dedicated to the saint. Salim Chisti was the religious guru of Emperor Akbar. The songs and dances being performed here were similar to those we had seen in the Ajmer saint's shrine. But nobody would have dared to sing or dance in this manner in any of the shrines of our own province. Both Khawaja Muinuddin Chisti, the saint of Ajmer, and Salim Chisti were supposed to have been lovers of music. We visited all the main spots—the prayer room, Abul Fazal's house, the Hamamkhana, the guest house, Meena Masjid, Jodhabhai Mahal and Salim Garh. Each of us seemed to be bent on spending some time in every one of these spots. As for myself, I wanted to visit most the famous musician Tansen's house. He lived in a building outside the palace in a small house on a hill. No doubt because he wanted to practise undisturbed, he had opted to stay at a distance from everyone else. I wasn't very happy to see his house though. However, who knows whether he really lived here or not. It all happened so long ago!

Emperor Akbar himself stayed here for only two years even though he had built this palace and fort at such great expense. He had to go back to Agra Fort then. Historians claim that he was forced to return to that fort because this spot ran out of water. Somehow I couldn't convince myself that this was the reason for that decision. I am sure there was some other reason he went back. The emperor had built Fatehpur Sikri, including the palace and the fort, on eight square miles of land. There were 2900 rooms here. Agra Fort, on the other hand, had only 500 rooms. Even after rooms had been found for the emperor's entire retinue Fatehpur Sikri could house 60,000 soldiers. Emperor Akbar had the will and power to do whatever he wanted to. That he couldn't provide enough water for Fatehpur Sikri and had to leave it for this reason is something I find impossible to accept.

We were supposed to catch the evening train. A local train would take us to Tundla from Agra. Next to Fatehpur Sikri was a rest house. We had lunch there and then left for Sikandra, where Emperor Akbar was buried. He had chosen this site for his tomb himself. Starting from Delhi, I had seen the tombs of quite a few emperors and kings but it was Akbar's solemn and simple tomb that I liked most. The whole place was full of plants and fruit-bearing trees. The tomb itself was built of white stone.

We were running out of time. Mr Chowdhury began to remind us that it was time to go back. We got on the train. We gathered our baggage in Agra and headed for Tundla station. Here we met many of our co-workers from Bengal. The station was very crowded. We dumped our baggage in Mr Chowdhury's first-class carriage and headed for our own one. Everybody managed to do so except me. I had to get on a first-class carriage with a friend. We thought we would get down from it at the next station and then shift to another carriage. But though I kept knocking on the door, none of the gentlemen inside would open it. I was forced to hang on to the handle of the carriage while standing on the steps. The train was running at great speed by now and I was afraid that I would lose my grip and fall down. That would be fatal. I held on desperately with both my hands and urged my friend to do so too. This was the kind of train that doesn't stop at every station. We were getting increasingly frantic. If the train kept moving we wouldn't be able to hold on to the handle for long since our hands and legs were stiffening. After a while the train ground to a halt. We got down immediately. I called out loudly for my friend Anwar. He had a ticket for an inter-class car and had my things. He, for his part, was getting quite anxious wondering about us. We managed to enter his car somehow through a window. The train started to move again. We reached Howrah station the next day. All of us had managed to return with all our things intact but somehow I had managed to lose my suitcase on the way and had only my bedding with me when I got down.

~

It occurred to me now that I was back that I should devote myself to studies for a while. I hadn't been able to pay my fees because I had run out of money. I would have to go to our village home to collect the money needed since I had to pay fees for a whole year. I also needed money to buy a new set of clothes. I came home and told Renu about my situation. I would have to talk to my father about the money. When I did so, however, he looked unhappy although he didn't tell me anything. Later, he said to me, 'When you travel abroad you should only take some clothes with you and should be careful.' Then he gave me the money I needed, saying, 'I don't want to hear any excuses from you any more. You'll have to do well in your BA examinations. You've wasted a lot of time. Just because you were working for the movement for Pakistan I had kept quiet all this time. But now you'll have to concentrate on your studies.' I said goodbye to my parents and sisters and brothers and then went to Renu's room. I saw that she had some money in her hands. With great effort she seemed to have held back her tears since it is believed in our part of the world that to shed tears at the moment of parting could bring bad luck. All she said was, 'Once you are in Calcutta you seem to lose all interest in returning. This time you must return home as soon as your college closes.'

As soon as I returned to Calcutta I paid my fees and managed to get hold of some of the books that my friends had taken from me for their studies. When I went to classes now some of my teachers would take note of my presence. One or two of them would even quip, 'You have finally managed to find time to come to college for studies.' I wouldn't respond to them but only smiled, as did my classmates.

But studying wasn't easy even if one intended to be studious. The Cabinet Mission was in India at this time. Both the Congress and the Muslim League were negotiating with the Cabinet Mission. We were bent on accepting Pakistan and nothing else would do for us. In the *Millat* office as well as in the Muslim League office we would discuss these issues animatedly every day. Sometimes meetings were organized and I addressed the people present there. The Congress and the Muslim League were coming close to accepting the Cabinet Mission plan. According to it, defence, foreign office and the ministry of communications would stay with the central government while the remaining ministries would revert to the provinces. Later, however, the Congress reneged on its commitment to the plan. As a result the Cabinet Mission plan had to be abandoned. The way the Cabinet Mission plan was being negotiated by the British it seemed to me that they were eager to hand over power to the Congress and leave India as soon as possible. But Muhammad Ali Jinnah knew the Congress and the British government well and it wasn't easy to deceive someone like him.

On 29 July Mr Jinnah summoned a council meeting of the All India Muslim League in Bombay. I couldn't attend this meeting because I didn't have the funds to do so.

Mr Jinnah declared that 16 August would be 'Direct Action Day'. He issued a statement urging everyone to observe this day peacefully. He wanted to show the British government that the ten crore Muslims of India were determined to achieve Pakistan at any cost. The Congress and Hindu Mahasabha leaders began to issue statements claiming that 'Direct Action Day' was really directed against them.

We were asked to organize events appropriate for the day. Mr Hashim met us to discuss how we could observe it best. He said, 'You'll have to go from neighbourhood to neighbourhood; you must even go to Hindu neighbourhoods. You'll have to tell them that we are struggling not against the Hindus but against the British and so join us as we observe the day regardless of your race or religion.' We fitted loudspeakers to cars and went out on the road. We began to broadcast our message in both Muslim and Hindu neighbourhoods. We focused entirely on our demand for Pakistan. We emphasized that we were not against Hindus but against the British. A few leaders of the Forward Bloc[11] came to our office after they heard us speak and proposed to discuss with us how both Hindus and Muslims could observe the day peacefully. We agreed to talk to them. But we were no match for the propaganda campaign launched by the Hindu Mahasabha and the Congress. They managed to convince the Hindus that we were really against them.

Mr Suhrawardy was the prime minister of Bengal at that time. He asked us to ensure that the day was observed peacefully. He said, 'If there is any violence on the day the Muslim League will get a bad name.' He declared that 16 August would be a government holiday. This infuriated the Congress and the Hindu Mahasabha even more.

We worked out how we would deploy our forces on the day. The meeting was to be held in Calcutta's Garer Math. Processions from different localities would end up at this venue. The students of Calcutta's Islamia College would assemble there at 10 a.m. I was asked to take charge there. However, we would all have to go to Calcutta University at seven in the morning to raise the Muslim League flag. Nuruddin and I biked to the university. We raised the flag. Nobody opposed us. But we came to know later that as soon as we had left the flag was lowered and shred into pieces. We returned from the university to our college via Bowbazar. I had the college gate and the hall door opened. But if we had delayed returning by only half an hour Nuruddin and I would have been murdered and our bodies disposed of. However, we realized that the situation was rapidly getting from bad to worse by the time we had come back. Nuruddin left me in the college and went to the Muslim League office. He said that he would return soon.

By this time only a few workers had gathered in the college premises from Baker Hostel. I opened the assembly room for them and asked them to get things ready for a meeting. A few Muslim girl students came here from Monnu Jan Hostel. They were all workers of the Muslim League. Among them were Hazera Begum (now Hazera Mahmud Ali), Halima Khatun (now Mrs Nuruddin), Joynab Begum (now Mrs Jalil) and Sadeka Begum (now Sadeka Samad).

Within a few minutes of their arrival some students came running to the college. They were all bloodied. Some of them had knife wounds on them while others had been hit in the head. I couldn't figure out what I should do now since we weren't ready for anything like this. The girls stepped forward and told me, 'Send the wounded to us and also arrange for some water.' But where would they get bandages to dress the wounds? They began to cut pieces of cloth from their saris and ornas. I sent news of the situation to the nearby hostels. As soon as some of the injured had had their wounds dressed, I sent them to a physician who lived nearby.

A student told us that the Hindus weren't attacking anyone moving in groups but were targeting anyone walking by himself or people in pairs. We were informed now that the students who had attempted to raise the League flag in Ripon College had also been attacked. Islamia College was next to the Hindu neighbourhoods of Suren Banerjee Road, Dharmatala and Wellington Square. We came to know that the mosque in Wellington Square had also come under attack and that a Hindu mob was heading for the college.

We left behind a few of our boys to be with the girls and then forty or fifty of us walked towards the Dharmatala intersection although we were unarmed. I had no clear idea till now of what a riot was like or what mob violence meant. We saw that hundreds of Hindus were attacking the mosque. The moulvi of the mosque was fleeing towards us, chased by a group of men armed with sticks and swords. Nearby were some Muslim-owned shops. Some men emerged from them with swords in their hands. A few of us immediately cried out, 'Pakistan Zindabad'. In no time at all, our numbers swelled. By this time the Hindu mob had reached us. We had no option but to resist them. We picked up whatever bricks or stones we could find and started to attack them. In total there were about 150 of us. A few men handed over some sticks to us so that we could defend ourselves although we had no idea who they were. Till now the skirmish had been limited to brick-throwing. By this time a huge procession had arrived at the scene. They had been obstructed unsuccessfully in a number of places. All of them had sticks in their hands. They now joined us. For a few minutes the Hindus stopped advancing and so did we. In the meantime, the police had attempted to scatter us by using tear gas. They increased their patrols. The whole of Calcutta had by now turned into a hand-to-hand combat zone. I can vouch though that the Muslims were not at all ready for the riots.

We left for Garer Math. We had lost a lot of time by then. Thousands upon thousands of people had already assembled there. The processions coming from Kalighat, Bhawanipur, Harrison Road and Barabazar had all come under attack. Mr Suhrawardy addressed the gathering and asked the people there to return to their homes. But how would the Muslims living in Hindu-majority areas go back? The Central Muslim League office was full of such people. This was also true of the City Muslim League office. Many people left for Zakaria Street, Wellesley, Park Circus and Beniapukur, areas that could be labelled as Muslim areas.

Countless people had been hurt; we had to send them to Calcutta Medical College and Campbell and Islamic Hospital. We were receiving telephone calls by the minute from people pleading with us to rescue them and telling us that they were trapped and that their children would be murdered before the night had passed. A few of us sat by the telephone, taking down the phone numbers and addresses of the callers. The League office had become a refugee camp. The Islamia College gate was kept open to admit people fleeing from attacks.

We tried to open the Calcutta Madrasa gate for the same purpose, but the guard posted there wouldn't allow us to do so. I ran to the principal to request him to have the gates opened and he ordered the guard to let people in. People from surrounding areas kept informing us of the overall situation in their communities. Baker Hostel and Eliot Hostel were already full. Now we had to worry about saving the boys in Taylor Hostel. We weren't being able to collect any information about them. All we knew was that a few students had left the hostel in the afternoon. Some of them, on the other hand, were trapped there. The building was so designed that it could be entered through one gate only. Hindu houses surrounded it and so any attempt to torch it would have engulfed all the houses of the neighbourhood too. Hindu mobs had tried to break the gate open several times in the night but had failed to do so. I couldn't get through to Mr Suhrawardy. Every time I phoned him I was told that he was in Lalbazar where the police headquarter was located. Nuruddin tried at night to rescue the Taylor Hostel boys with the help of a vehicle and a police escort. There were quite a few Hindus in the Taltola and Wellesley area who had secretly asked us to help them. After a lot of effort, we were able to send some of these Hindu families to Hindu neighbourhoods, even though the process was quite risky. We also managed to save some of the Hindu families living around Baker Hostel. What we had to do was take them across to Suren Banerjee Road.

I myself had a lot to worry about. Of the six of my brothers and sisters, five were in Calcutta and Srirampur then. I didn't have to worry about the third of my sisters because she was in Beniapukur. I had another sister staying with her at that time. My youngest brother, Sheikh Abu Nasser, was studying for his matriculation examination. He was almost a child in some ways and would take turns to stay with any one of us. He was quite spoiled and wouldn't listen to any of us. I assumed he had gone to Garer Math. He hadn't returned to my room. Who knows whether he was still alive! Srirampur was in bad shape. My sister lived in a neighbourhood that had only two Muslim families.

Calcutta city streets seemed to be strewn with dead bodies. Neighbourhood after neighbourhood was in flames. It was a horrible scene! That people could treat each other in this way was too frightening a thought. I tried to find out where my loved ones were. My youngest brother-in-law lived in Harrison Road's Tower Lodge. I took a fire brigade car to his place only to find out that he had gone to Carmichael Hostel. Nasser was neither with my third sister nor with me. When I asked the youngest of my brothers-in-law, Syed Hussain, about him, he said, 'Nasser was with me on 16th August, but though I asked him to stay with me he wouldn't. I didn't insist on his staying either, since this wasn't a safe area and we too would have to flee it.' I wasn't able to trace his movements from here and didn't know how to get about the task.

Arrangements had been made for refugees to stay in Lady Brabourne College. Women would have to stay on the first floor and the men on the ground floor. The workers were divided accordingly. I had to come back here from time to time. I also helped in rescuing stranded Muslims. In one or two places I came under attack while trying to help in this work. We also rescued Hindus wherever possible and had them sent to Hindu localities. It was obvious that people had lost their human sides in the violence and had regressed to their animal selves. On 16 August the Muslims had taken a beating. The next two days the Muslims beat up the Hindus mercilessly. The hospital figures were proof of the fatalities and injuries sustained by both communities on these days.

Meanwhile, the hostels were running out of rice and flour. Shopkeepers weren't opening their shops, afraid that their goods would be looted. I went to Mr Suhrawardy. What could be done? He said, 'Go and meet Nawab Nasrullah [the younger brother of Nawab Habibullah of Dhaka and a very amiable person devoted to Mr Suhrawardy and the deputy chief whip]. I have put him in charge.' We rushed to meet him. He took us to St Xavier's College and said, 'The rice is stocked here and you'll have to make arrangements to take what you want. We don't have any vehicles to transport now. The army has taken all our vehicles away. But if you prefer to wait, we can arrange for some cars.'

We managed to get hold of a pushcart, but who would be pulling it? Nuruddin, Nurul Huda, now an engineer working for the Dhaka Improvement Trust (DIT), and I loaded the rice and started to pull the cart. Nuruddin was extremely thin and didn't have the strength to pull anything. Nevertheless, between the three of us we managed to deliver the rice to Baker Hostel and Eliot Hostel. Now how could we deliver the rice to Carmichael Hostel? It was far away and we would have to go through Hindu neighbourhoods to reach it. It was impossible to use a pushcart to go there. After much effort Nuruddin managed to get a fire engine for the job. The three of us managed to deliver some rice to the hostel and then came back.

I came to know that Srirampur had stayed peaceful, but where could Nasser be? The rioting and pillaging had stopped somewhat by the time I sent someone to Srirampur to find out if anyone had heard anything about him. Later, I found out from that person what had happened to him. Nasser had come to Calcutta on the 16th. He had got into trouble almost immediately when he entered Harrison Road. He had managed to save his life by somehow getting on an ambulance. When he was young Nasser had been afflicted by typhoid and had ended up with a partially paralysed leg. As a result he has to drag his feet while walking. He had managed to attract the attention of the ambulance driver because of his gait. He had stayed inside the ambulance throughout the day. In the evening he had taken the train from Howrah to Srirampur. The journey took three hours. En route, the train had been attacked more than once. He had somehow escaped.

But what must also be said about the whole episode was that many Hindus risked their own lives to save Muslims. Similarly, many Muslims ended up sacrificing their own lives to save their Hindu neighbours and acquaintances. I myself saw proof of this. Of the many calls we had received in the Muslim League office many were from Hindus. They had stowed away their Muslim friends and acquaintances and had called for them to be rescued since they would be killed along with the Muslims they had hidden in their homes if they were found out.

I also saw men who seemed unfazed by the human side of the riots. They had broken into shops and had been looting them, as if they had nothing better to do. I had tried to stop one of these looters and almost got into trouble. He had tried to assault me.

Soon curfew was imposed and people could no longer go out at night. Anyone seen in the streets after dusk would be shot at sight. The army usually would leave the person they had shot on the streets. They would aim their guns at every open window. In the morning we would see many dead people on the road.

One day Sylhet's Moazzem Chowdhury (now an MNA, of the Sylhet Convention Muslim League) and I were given the responsibility of guarding a Muslim slum that was located between Park Circus and Baliganj, since every night Hindu mobs were trying to attack it. The reason for this was that there weren't many of us who could use guns. Both Moazzem and I knew how to use guns since our fathers used to own firearms.

Around evening we got a summons from the *Millat* office to go to the slum. We left as quickly as we could on foot since there was no vehicle available to take us there. We had just managed to cross Lower Circular Road and enter a small lane past it when the curfew began. We started to walk past the graveyard. The moment we heard a car coming we hid ourselves and when it passed we emerged into the street again. With great difficulty we managed to come to the Park Circus ground. Now we had to figure out how we could cross it. After a lot of effort we managed to reach the house of Mr Mohammad Nasiruddin, the owner of Saugat Press and editor of the famous journal of the same name. From here we moved on again and reached a friend's house. But what was to be done now? My friend's parents refused to let us go out and risk our lives since the military was patrolling the streets. They were ready to shoot even at a shadow. We found out that we had no option except to stay put. We spent the night with my friend and failed to reach our destination on this occasion. However, the place we were supposed to guard was untroubled that night. We had managed to cross about one and a half miles in the curfew but could have been shot at any point then.

In Park Circus Justice Siddiqui, Mr Abdur Rashid, Mr Tafazzal Ali (an ex-minister) and some others led the defence. We were volunteers. In Sealdah and Howrah stations separate camps for Hindus and Muslims had been set up to prevent outsiders from entering since if a Muslim entered a Hindu camp or vice versa, the situation would have become incredibly volatile. Among the women of Calcutta, Mr Suhrawardy's daughter Mrs Akhtar Sulaiman; Nawab Nasrullah's daughter, Ifat Nasrullah; Begum Akhtar Atahar Ali, the editor of the weekly *Begum*; Noorjahan Begum; Begum [Zerina] Rashid; Rokeya Kabir; and the girls of Monnu Jan Hostel and Brabourne College worked very hard day and night in the refugee centre to help the women just as we did with the men. Although it was tough on them, I saw Hazera Mahmud Ali, Halima Nuruddin and a few others work throughout the night on occasion.

Calcutta was devastated. Muslims were taking refuge in Muslim neighbourhoods and Hindus were flocking to Hindu ones. The only place where friends could still meet was in Esplanade, or Chowringhee, as we called it.

The state of affairs began to deteriorate even more when one day the calm that had descended for a while ended because a knife fight had broken out over a trivial issue. Mr Suhrawardy had been working hard day and night to control the situation. Out of the 1400 police of Calcutta fifty or sixty were Muslims; Muslim officers were similarly few in number. How would Mr Suhrawardy be able to hold on to power? He tried to recruit 1000 Muslims into the police. However, the English governor of the time objected to his move. Mr Suhrawardy, in turn, threatened to resign over the issue. He managed to have retired army men from the Punjab inducted into the police in large numbers. This led to an outcry, especially from the Congress and Hindu Mahasabha newspapers.

No sooner had the Calcutta riots ended than rioting broke out in Noakhali. The Muslims there had started looting Hindu houses and torching them. Dhaka was witnessing riot after riot. As if in response, Bihar was in flames too. In districts throughout Bihar Muslims were being attacked in a planned way. This resulted in many deaths. Many houses were being destroyed there. Three days after the riots had broken out in Bihar we headed for Patna. Many others had volunteered to be there. Quite a few doctors from Calcutta had also left for Bihar. Mr Yakub, one of my Calcutta colleagues who was also a very good photographer, brought along his camera. He travelled all over the province taking pictures of what was happening. Mr Fazlul Huq also left for the state the day Zahiruddin, Nuruddin and I headed for it.

Mr Suhrawardy had informed the Bihar Muslim League leaders that the Bengal government was ready to assist them in any way they desired. He told the Bihar government the same thing.

When we reached Patna we found that the situation there was alarming. Moreover, we didn't know anyone there. Where should we go? However, Zahir had been to Patna on several occasions. We decided to stay in a hotel called Grand Hotel that was owned by a minister of the Bihar government named Mr Yunus. Here Maulana Ragib Ahsan had opened an office on behalf of the Bengal Muslim League. Mr Abdur Rab Nistar arrived in Patna on the very same day. Nuruddin would leave for Calcutta three days later but Zahir would stay back.

We sat together to work out what we could do to help. Mr Suhrawardy had said that if the Bihar government could load a train full of refugees and send them to Asansol the Bengal government would take care of them. When I communicated this to Mr Akmal, an ICS [Indian Civil Service] officer, he asked me how I could claim to speak on behalf of Mr Suhrawardy. He seemed to have taken a look at me and decided that I was too young to have been taken into confidence by Mr Suhrawardy on so important an issue. I declared that I knew what Mr Suhrawardy had in mind and was ready to speak on his behalf. The people present there looked at me with disbelief. I then gave them Mr Suhrawardy's phone number and asked them to verify my statement by calling him.

We were supposed to sit down with them for further discussions in the morning. Mr Akmal told me, 'We are going to send people to Asansol from this very day.' It was proving impossible to provide accommodation to the people who were coming to the city from rural areas. Places like Anjuman-e-Islamia had been set aside for this purpose and were already full. Many volunteers had arrived by now. Among them were Pir Manki Sharif's followers, and students like my friend Mostafa from Aligarh and Syed Ahmed Ali. Around a thousand volunteers had come from Calcutta and assembled in Patna. They included students, doctors and national guards. The victims were being rescued from villages in far-flung parts of the province. I led a group of about a thousand refugees towards Asansol. The Muslim League leader there, Maulana Yasin, had been informed by telegram of our coming. He was waiting for us at the train station with two trucks and some volunteers. We kept the refugees in the station. Many of them were wounded. Nuruddin informed Mr Suhrawardy of the situation. Word had been sent to him from Patna too. He ordered the district magistrate and the SDO to find accommodation for the refugees and to provide them with food.

Nuruddin sent some doctors and volunteers from Calcutta to assist me. The SDO was an Englishman. He was young and had excellent manners. Mr Suhrawardy had instructed that the refugees should be accommodated in the barracks built during the war to house troops. The government arranged for food supplies. To decide how we would distribute food items, the SDO, Asansol Muslim League leaders and I had a meeting. The first camp was opened in a storehouse called Nigah. This could accommodate about a thousand people. Later, the Kandulia camp was also set up. This could contain about ten thousand people. I named this camp Hizratganj. Maulana Yasin approved this name gladly. The refugees would get down at Asansol and Raniganj stations and be transported by trucks to these camps. Maulana Wahid assisted me throughout. We used to study together. He is now a pir at Shajadpur.

We had made no special arrangements for our own dining. We used to eat with the refugees. There were no shops nearby. Hundreds of refugees were joining the camps every day. We couldn't give them more than one meal a day. We had set up a hospital. Mymensingh's Dr Abdul Hamid and Gafargaon's Dr Hazrat Ali used to run this hospital. Asansol's SDO, Mr Rose, brought along an elderly white woman with him one day to help us run things. She had some experience of running refugee camps since she had worked in a government camp set up for those fleeing the war in Burma. She came up with a plan that was of great help to us.

Seven days later, Mr Salimullah Fahmi of the Bengal government was appointed officer-in-charge of the refugees. He looked for me when he reached Asansol. Later, he came across me in the Moira camp. He made all the camps part of the government's responsibility. However, the Muslim League volunteers continued to assist in the camps' workings. Mr Salimullah and I consulted each other over the appointments of the superintendent, assistant superintendent, ration-in-charge, guards and other staff.

It was proving impossible to cook food for the inmates of all camps at one spot. Ration cards were therefore made and each family was supplied with rice, pepper, onions and other essentials for seven days. Only meat was to be distributed every alternate day. The refugees were very happy with this decision. It took almost a month for us to get everything in order. Mr Zafar Imam came from Bihar to find out how the refugees were being looked after by the Bengalis. He came to meet me in my office. We had an office set up by then and I used to live next to it. Arrangements had been made for my food to be cooked here. When he saw how we had set up things he thanked us profusely. He also met the refugees and inquired of them about the facilities they had received and the problems they were facing.

We opened two more camps at Moira and Madhaiganj. Ten thousand refugees were sent to these camps. Among them were educated people. There was no more space for anyone at Asansol. More camps were then opened at Bishnupur, Andale and Burdwan. We sent fresh batches of refugees to these places. Almost everyone working with me began to fall sick out of sheer exhaustion and lack of sleep and food. I had to send many of my assistants who had worn themselves out thus to Calcutta. Mr Mohammad Ali and A.F.M. Abdur Rahman were ministers in Calcutta at this time. They came to Asansol to visit us along with Begum Sulaiman, Ifat Nasrullah and a few other workers. They had informed me beforehand that they would be coming to see us. I went to Asansol to meet them. We showed them the state of the camps. I had to take leave of everyone and return to Calcutta with them. Begum Sulaiman was astonished to see how worn out I myself had become.

And so I came back to Calcutta after six weeks, feeling quite unwell. By the time I had reached Baker Hostel I felt very sick. My fever just wouldn't go away. When Mr Suhrawardy was informed of my state he remembered to take care of me even though I was really a nobody in the Muslim League set-up. He found a bed for me in the Tropical School of Medicine's European Ward and then sent for me. I stayed in the hospital for fifteen days and he kept inquiring about my health from the principal of the institution all the time. That is why the principal would visit me regularly. Eventually I became well and returned to Baker Hostel.

The things I had learned about management from the English lady in Asansol and the experience I had gathered on my own there became very useful for me later in all the work that I did. I decided at this point of my life that I would have to pass my BA examination. I met Dr Zuberi, our principal. He said, 'I know that you have worked hard for Pakistan. I don't want to stand in your way if you want to take the examination. However, you will have to promise me that you will concentrate on studies for the next few months and will leave Calcutta and go somewhere else to do so and return just before the examinations. Only then will I allow you to sit for them.' By this time the qualifying examination had already taken place. I swore an oath in front of Professor Taher Jamil, Professor Saidur Rahman and Professor Nazir Ahmed to do so. I took permission to take all my books to my friend Sheikh Shahadat Hussein's house in Ultadanga in Howrah. He had already passed the examination in 1946 and was now employed in an office there.

I passed my BA examination successfully. I had returned to Calcutta just before the examination. I had quit the hostel by then. My younger sister's husband, Barisal's Advocate Abdur Rab Serniabat, was living in a rented house in Park Circus at that time. My sister was with him and I joined them. A few days later my wife Renu came to Calcutta too. She had decided that if she kept me company I would be successful in the examination. Sheikh Shahadat Hussein took two months' leave from his job to help me with my studies. Later in life he did me a lot of harm. But I never said anything to him then because of the help he gave me at this point of time. His house was very close to mine.

~

Mr Hashim wanted to be president of the Muslim League since Maulana Akram Khan had resigned from this position. But Mr Suhrawardy was not willing to accept him as the president. He persuaded the Maulana to withdraw his resignation letter. Mr Hashim was so upset at this that he took leave from his position as secretary of the League and went away to Burdwan. When he was in Calcutta he would usually stay in the *Millat* office. But by this time he was no longer as popular with students and young people as he once used to be. Many of us had become disillusioned with him for a number of reasons. For example, when he came to Calcutta he would criticize Mr Suhrawardy openly. This was because instead of making the *Millat* a daily he had brought out the daily *Ittehad* with Nawab Hassan Ali as the publisher and Mr Abul Mansur Ahmed as the editor. Maulana Akram Khan's daily *Azad* had also become quite critical of Mr Suhrawardy because of the same reason—it had been the only Muslim daily till then. Now that another newspaper was being published the Maulana's followers seemed even more upset than he himself!

At the end of 1946 Indian politics found itself faced with a very complicated situation. The British government was determined to hand over power at any cost. The Muslim League had already accepted the Cabinet Mission proposal. The Congress had accepted it initially but backtracked from this position subsequently. Nevertheless, the Viceroy, Lord Wavell, announced the formation of an interim government with the Congress party in it. Because he had not treated the Muslim League well, it decided that it would not be party to any interim government formed by Lord Wavell. Under the leadership of Pandit Nehru, the Congress, on the other hand, decided to join the government. However, Lord Wavell let it be known that five posts of ministers had been set aside for the League and it could join the government whenever it was ready to do so. By not joining the government the Muslim League found itself in a difficult situation. In the end Mr Suhrawardy met Lord Wavell to discuss a way out so that the League could become part of the interim government. Mr Jinnah had authorized him to negotiate on behalf of the League. As a result Mr Jinnah and Lord Wavell met and came to an agreement about the League's role in the government. At the end of October, Liaquat Ali Khan, I.I. Chundrigar, Abdur Rab Nishtar, Raja Ghazanfar Ali Khan and Jogendra Nath Mandol joined the interim government on behalf of the League. If the Muslim League had not taken this decision the Congress would never have agreed to accept its demand for the creation of Pakistan.

In June 1947 a declaration was made to the effect that India would be partitioned. The Congress agreed to this since it had been decided that both the Punjab and Bengal would be split into two. Except for Sylhet, no part of Assam would be part of Pakistan. Calcutta and its surrounding regions would be part of India. Maulana Akram Khan and other Muslim League leaders protested fiercely against the decision to split Bengal. It was all right for us to give up the district of Burdwan but why should we not retain Calcutta? The Congress and the Hindu Mahasabha began to create public opinion in favour of the partition of Bengal. We for our part decided to organize public meetings against this plan.

But how could those of us working at the provincial level know that at the central level both the Congress and the Muslim League had accepted the formula that would lead to the break-up of Bengal? Certainly, the Bengali leaders did not know that Bengal would be split into two. They were under the impression that the whole of Bengal and Assam would become part of Pakistan. Now it was becoming obvious that only one district of Assam would be allowed to join, and that too if it decided to cast its vote for Pakistan in a referendum. In Bengal the Hindu-majority districts would be ceded to India. We became frustrated by this turn of events. The Calcutta and West Bengal League workers would tell us when we met, 'You people will be leaving us; only God knows what our fate will be!' We really began to feel pity for them. Calcutta Muslims had made up their minds that they would not leave the city no matter what happened. The finance minister of Mr Suhrawardy's cabinet, Mr Mohammad Ali, had already announced that Calcutta would remain our capital. We had no way of knowing that it had already been decided at Delhi a long time back that Calcutta would be given up to India. It was a decision that we could never understand.

At this time, Mr Hashim and Mr Suhrawardy on behalf of the Muslim League and Sharat Bose and Kiran Shankar Roy on behalf of the Congress party met to discuss the situation. The subject of their discussion was whether an alternative could be found to the splitting up of Bengal. Mr Suhrawardy went to Delhi to meet Mr Jinnah and with his permission began negotiations to find a way out. The Bengal Congress and Muslim League leaders came up with a formula. The Bengal Muslim League working committee accepted the formula unanimously. As far as I remember it stated clearly that Bengal would be an independent and sovereign nation. The people would elect a Constituent Assembly. That Assembly would decide whether Bengal would join either Hindustan or Pakistan or stay independent. If the majority of the Assembly decided in favour of joining Pakistan, then Bengal would become part of that nation. However, if most people wanted to be part of India, then Bengal would be allowed to join India. And if the people wanted independence they could have that option too. Mr Suhrawardy and Mr Sharat Bose took this formula to Delhi where they intended to meet Jinnah and Gandhi. Mr Bose has left a written testimony to the effect that Jinnah had told him the Muslim League would have no objections if the Congress party was willing to accept this formula. As for the British, they had let it be known that they would accept no new formula that had not been agreed upon by both the Congress and the League. Mr Bose felt insulted when the leaders of the Congress refused him an audience and returned home. Apparently Sardar Vallabhbhai Patel had told him, 'Mr Bose, stop acting crazy; we want Calcutta.' Gandhi and Nehru for their part had said nothing but had referred Mr Bose to Patel. And Patel had been very rude in his dealings with Mr Bose. When he returned to Calcutta Mr Bose issued a written statement making all of this public and admitting that Mr Jinnah had accepted the formula.

Many leaders have tried to cast aspersions on Mr Suhrawardy and us as supporters of a united Bengal. This, despite the fact that some of these leaders were themselves members of the Muslim League working committee where the resolution had been adopted unanimously. In his own lifetime, Mr Jinnah never blamed Mr Suhrawardy in public since nothing could have been approved without his consent in those days. When we were involved in the movement to make both Bengal and Assam part of Pakistan, it is difficult to comprehend what harm could have been done if a united Bengal became one with Pakistan. It was only after the decision to partition Bengal had been taken, with the part that opted to be part of Pakistan being allowed to do so, that people began to badmouth us for their own political ends. But there could be no harm done in asking for more rather than less. Of course we could also be happy with what we had received. Mr Khawaja Nazimuddin had decided on 22 April 1947 that 'a United Bengal would be good for both Hindus and Muslims'. As president of the Muslim League, Maulana Akram Khan had declared, 'Bengal would be split over my dead body. As long as I am alive I will not allow Bengal to be partitioned. The whole of Bengal will become part of Pakistan.' He may not have used these exact words but this was the substance of his statement. One needs only to check the 1947 issues of the daily *Azad*, a newspaper that is still being published, to verify what I have said here.

At this time, the Viceroy, Lord Mountbatten, was helping the Congress covertly in all sorts of ways. He wanted to be Governor General of both India and Pakistan. But Jinnah did not agree to this since he intended to make himself the Governor General of Pakistan. He probably did not think well of Lord Mountbatten. This annoyed Mountbatten so much that he seemed bent on doing harm to the cause of Pakistan. Even though Radcliffe was given the responsibility of demarcating the boundary, many believe that Mountbatten seemed to have secretly worked with the Congress to come up with a map of their own. However, those of us who were young did not want Jinnah to become the Governor General. We hoped that he would first become the prime minister and later the president. I doubt if Lord Mountbatten would have done as much harm to Pakistan if he had become its Governor General. This is what I myself believe. Jinnah was cleverer than us all and only he knew what motives he had in wanting to become the Governor General.

As soon as Pakistan was created, political conspiracy became rife. In particular, a conspiracy against Mr Suhrawardy was hatched in Delhi. This was because what we in East Bengal would get as our share came to more than what the people of the Punjab, Sind, the Frontier Province and Baluchistan would get; after all, our combined population was greater than theirs. Mr Suhrawardy's personality, uncommon political acumen, wisdom and efficiency made many uneasy. This was because these qualities would make him want to be the prime minister of Pakistan in the future and nobody would be able to oppose him. Mr Jinnah himself loved Mr Suhrawardy. These were the reasons the conspirators felt that he would have to be cut down to size immediately. On the one hand, Calcutta was torn apart by communal riots. On the other, the partition council had been convened. The Congress had formed a shadow cabinet in Calcutta.

Behind the scenes people were plotting to remove Mr Suhrawardy from the scene and install Khawaja Nazimuddin in his place. Nobody seemed to think that it was necessary to hold elections in the Punjab even though it too had been partitioned. Although Nawab Mamdot came from East Punjab he was made chief minister of West Punjab. Even though Liaquat Ali Khan was from India he was made prime minister of Pakistan. But because Mr Suhrawardy was from West Bengal he was told that he would be able to stand for elections only in East Pakistan. And yet the MLAs of the whole of Bengal had unanimously made him their leader and he had been their prime minister.

It was in this situation that orders came from Delhi for elections to be held in our part of the subcontinent.[12] What was Mr Suhrawardy supposed to do—govern, protect the Muslims of his region or busy himself with elections? He had to go to Sylhet too for the referendum. He sent thousands of workers like us to Sylhet for this. Moreover, it was he who did most of the fund-raising for this purpose. Mr S.M. Ispahani had given a lot of money as the treasurer of the Bengal Muslim League, something that I can attest to. This was because I was present at the meeting when he discussed the issue with Mr Suhrawardy at 40 Theatre Road. When we went to Sylhet and plunged headlong into the referendum campaign, Mr Suhrawardy accompanied us. I met him at a huge public meeting in Karimganj. I had given a speech on the occasion.

Maulana Tarkabagish, Manik Mia (editor of the daily *Ittefaq*), Fazlul Huq and 500 party workers reached Sylhet in due time. The Sylhet referendum committee did not have to do anything out of the way for us. Its only responsibility was to guide us to where we were supposed to be working and then aid us to reach that destination. Mr Suhrawardy had made all the arrangements to meet our expenses. We didn't have to ask for help from anyone. Mr Shamsul Huq joined us from Dhaka with many of his men. At Mr Suhrawardy's request, the philanthropist R.P. Shaha sent a few launches to Sylhet for us. Muslim League workers were able to use them to campaign on behalf of Pakistan. This was necessary since we needed this particular form of transportation badly. Mr Shaha was Mr Suhrawardy's friend and therefore he could not turn down his request. Mr Shaha is still in Pakistan. He has funded Mirzapur Hospital, Bharateswari Homes Girls' High School, and Kumudini College. Those institutions are thriving because of his patronage.

We returned to Calcutta after winning the Sylhet referendum. We found out then that a faction of the League had decided that Mr Nazimuddin would contest Mr Suhrawardy for the leadership of the Muslim League. The Central Muslim League had given instructions from Delhi that an election should be held for this position. Mr I.I. Chundrigar would preside over the election process on its behalf. But nobody seemed to have noticed that things were heating up over the division of the resources between the two countries. Everyone was too preoccupied with the election. Mr Nazimuddin left the country for London and Delhi after having accepted his nomination. Mr Suhrawardy did all the work for staging the elections and raised the necessary funds. He wasn't able to rest for a day while holding the office of prime minister. He had got involved in everything—the riots in Calcutta, Noakhali and Bihar; Muslim League organizational work; and all the hectic activities going on in Delhi and Calcutta. And to think that when the time came to elect a leader some people would consider someone else—only posterity will be able to judge how unfair this was. Those who were opposing Mr Suhrawardy harped on one theme—he was from West Bengal and so how could he be prime minister of East Pakistan? Mr Suhrawardy had never thought in terms of two factions and had therefore nominated Mr Nazimuddin's supporters and had made them ministers, parliamentary secretaries, the chief whip, the speaker, etc. And yet these people were conspiring all the time to harm his interests. On the other hand, the West Bengal MLAs would not be able to vote for him since they were now part of a different state. And his own party was opposing him through a faction led by Mr Hashim. Mr Hashim said nothing to any of his men openly. But he secretly told many of them not to vote for Mr Suhrawardy and even instructed some of them not to do so. But Mr Suhrawardy was oblivious to all these manoeuvrings. He was not going to do anything to thwart them. He wasn't even going to request anyone to vote for him. If he was requested to do something he would say, 'If they want to they will vote for me and if they don't they won't; what am I supposed to tell them?'

Mohammad Ali, Tafazzal Ali, Dr Malek, Sabur Khan, Anwara Khatun, Faridpur's Badshah Mia and Rangpur's Khairat Hussein were among those working for Mr Suhrawardy. But Mr Mafizuddin Ahmed, the chief whip of his party, was working secretly for Mr Nazimuddin. Mr Shamsuddin Ahmed from Kushtia, a minister in his cabinet, too was trying to work up support for Mr Nazimuddin. Only Mr Fazlur Rahman—also a minister at this time—told Mr Suhrawardy openly that he had no other option except to vote for Mr Nazimuddin. I admired him for being so open about his preference. Nevertheless, despite all of them, there were more votes in favour of Mr Suhrawardy than against him.

However, seventeen of the nineteen MLAs of Sylhet arrived in Calcutta in time for the vote. When Dr Malek had gone to Sylhet to campaign on Mr Suhrawardy's behalf they had asked him, 'What exactly is Mr Suhrawardy's programme?' Dr Malek had told them that the first thing Mr Suhrawardy intended to do was abolish the feudal zamindari system. This had the opposite effect since except for three all Sylhet MLAs were zamindars. They were of course alarmed. They had been accommodated in Hotel Biltmore. We had been to Sealdah station to receive them and had taken them to the hotel. These Sylhet MLAs demanded that Mr Suhrawardy set aside three ministerial positions for them. In reply Mr Suhrawardy said, 'I will make no promises. You will get what you deserve.' On the other hand, those campaigning on behalf of Mr Nazimuddin had made a concrete offer to them. Except for a couple of them, all the Sylhet MLAs voted for Mr Nazimuddin and this led to Mr Suhrawardy's defeat.

At 2 a.m. on the eve of Election Day—I was at Mr Suhrawardy's house and he was lying down in the veranda—Dr Malek came and said, 'We seem to be in bad shape; it might be a good idea to spend some money to alter the situation.' Mr Suhrawardy told him, 'Malek, Pakistan has been achieved and I have no intention of polluting the sacred soil of the country by bribing anyone. I would rather not be a leader of the country by adopting underhand tactics. I have done what I was supposed to do.' Mr Malek said, 'What you say is of course right, sir; we too hate such unfair means.' From that day onward I began to admire Mr Suhrawardy even more. Mr Suhrawardy is dead now but Mr Malek is still alive. Only the three of us were present during that conversation.

I remember that we had informed Mr Suhrawardy in the morning about how they had lured away our MLAs and kept them in Mr Shahabuddin's house. We urged him to inform the Calcutta Muslim League so that we could all force them back since they would not be able to withstand our combined strength. Mr Suhrawardy merely smiled and said, 'There is no need for this. People will laugh. You are a bit too young and don't quite understand the situation.' Calcutta was still experiencing riots. If he wanted to, he could have imposed a curfew and postponed the elections by a few days since he was still the prime minister. But that he didn't do, which is proof that he was not hungry for power. He never believed that he should hold on to his position at any cost. And he certainly didn't believe in the politics of conspiracy. Pakistan's politics, however, began on a murky note. As long as Jinnah was alive nobody dared to indulge in conspiratorial politics openly. But the day he died such politics surfaced in the country.

As soon as Mr Nazimuddin was elected the leader he declared that Dhaka would be the capital and returned to the city along with his men. He didn't think for a moment about the fate of the hapless Muslims of West Bengal. He didn't even bother to pay attention to the things we could claim from Calcutta as our fair share. As a consequence, we didn't get what was ours. Some government officials had got into fights and had claimed their share by force and managed to load some goods on steamers and trains and these constituted all we got as our share. If we had claimed our rightful portion in Calcutta, we wouldn't have lacked anything when we started out. Mr Nazimuddin did not consult the Muslim League or for that matter anyone else in declaring Dhaka the capital city. Doing so implied that we had no claims to Calcutta any more. This left Lord Mountbatten with the problem of deciding what was to be done about Calcutta. His dilemma has been described in the book *Mission with Mountbatten*.[13] The British hadn't yet decided whether Calcutta would be part of Pakistan or remain in India. There was also the option of making it a 'free city' if no solution could be found. The problem issued from the fact that Calcutta's Hindus and Muslims were at daggers drawn. At any time the rioting could take a turn for the worse. Even if Calcutta was going to be part of India there was the possibility that the area till Sealdah station would be part of Pakistan.

The Hindus would be willing to give up a lot to retain Calcutta proper in India.

Mission with Mountbatten also reveals to us that an Englishman did not want to come to Dhaka as the governor of the new province since the city was supposed to be very hot in the summer. In a letter Lord Mountbatten had responded to his decision thus: 'East Pakistan has one of the major hill stations of the world and you will have no problem staying here.' This indicates that Darjeeling was also supposed to be part of our share. But Mr Nazimuddin's declaration put paid to all this. When he found out that there was no possibility of any other disputes Mountbatten took advantage of the situation and demarcated the boundary line so that Jessore's Muslim-majority station of Bongaon would become the south-eastern border of East Pakistan. Even though Muslims constituted a majority in Nadia, he allotted Krishnanagar and Ranaghat Junction to them. Similarly, even though there were more Muslims than Hindus in Murshidabad he gave the entire district to India. In Maldah district there were as many Hindus as there were Muslims and so he divided it into half. But although Dinajpur had a Muslim majority he cut Balurghat into two so that Jalpaiguri and Darjeeling could go to India and Assam could have a direct link with the rest of the country. All these districts really should have come to Pakistan. In the east, even though the referendum had been won in favour of Pakistan, the Muslim-majority subdivision of Karimganj went to India. We had believed that they would have to cede Kachar district in Assam as well as Sylhet but this was not to be. I was especially saddened by the loss of Karimganj since I had spent a lot of time there during the referendum.

The lesson in all this is that if leaders make mistakes the people have to pay! We had given up willingly the Calcutta that had been built with the money derived from the people of East Bengal. I believe that this happened because some people in the Central League wanted Calcutta to go to India. In other words, they had agreed to give the city up even before being asked to do so. They knew that if Mr Suhrawardy had been made the leader this would have been difficult to accomplish and so they achieved their goal by subterfuge. If Calcutta had become part of Pakistan the country would have no other option but to make the city its capital since the people of East Bengal could claim that they constituted the majority and since it was the most important city in the whole of India. Calcutta, after all, had been the capital of the whole of India during the early part of British rule.

Some other incidents happened at this time that are worth recalling. Mr Hashim used to manage Millat Press, which the Muslim League owned.

The future of the press had to be settled now. Mr Hashim had found himself in debt previously and had already sold one of its machines to clear his debts. He summoned Mr Shamsul Huq from Dhaka and told him, 'Many of the workers are going to move to Dhaka but I don't want to move to Pakistan. Take the press with you and keep the team that has been running it so that work can go on as before.' Mr Huq discussed the situation with us and it was decided that the press would be reinstalled in the Muslim League office at 150 Mughaltuli, Dhaka. We would bring out the *Millat* again and each of us would be responsible for running a department of the press. Mr Huq came to Dhaka to work out the details and then returned to Calcutta. But when he returned Mr Hashim was singing a different tune. He now told the Calcutta workers, 'Since you have decided to stay back in Calcutta you will probably need to have the press here. How else are you going to survive in the city? Those who come from the part of Bengal that is now in Pakistan won't need to work in it since that country is now a fact and since they will be returning to it.' The Calcutta workers said, 'Yes, that's right.' When Mr Huq heard them say this he returned to Dhaka without telling them anything. At that time I wasn't seeing Mr Hashim regularly. This was because he didn't trust me since he thought I was too much of a Suhrawardy supporter. For my part, I did not like the way he had behaved with Mr Suhrawardy. As far as I was concerned he had behaved treacherously with him.

One day Mr Nuruddin, Nurul Alam and Kazi Idris asked me to meet them in Bengal Restaurant, which was close to where I lived. I asked them what they were up to. They told me, 'Something unfortunate has happened. Mr Hashim is planning to sell the press. Since we have built it through subscription how can we face the public and tell them what has happened?' I said, 'What can I do?' All of them told me that I would have to oppose him. I said, 'Why should I try to oppose him? I am going back to Pakistan. I have no idea when I will be coming back to Calcutta again. Why should I bother? You all were Mr Hashim's cronies and you all had struck my name off from your list a long time back, so why should I do anything now?' They said in unison, 'If you tell him he won't dare to sell the press.' I told them then, 'Okay, I will request him not to.'

The next day I went to Millat Press to meet Mr Hashim. My colleagues were in the next room, listening intently to our exchange. I began by addressing him gently. I said, 'I believe you are going to sell the press.' He replied, 'What else is there to do? It is running at a loss every month. And in any case who will run it now?' I said, 'Khondokar Nurul Alam has run it all this time as the manager. If you are selling it to try to cut your expenditure how will the workers survive? And how will we be able to show our faces to people again? We raised subscriptions from the whole of Bengal for the press. If we sell it now everyone is going to slander us.' Mr Hashim burst out suddenly, 'I will have to sell it off anyhow for who is going to pay its debts?' I said, 'You sold part of it a few months back. Didn't you get enough then to pay off the debts?' He was angry by this time but I was angry too. When I left him I told him that I would thwart any attempt of his to sell the press and would ensure that no one came up with an offer to buy it. Mr Hashim was really upset at this. The next day my friends in the press came and told me, 'Mr Hashim has stopped eating. The only thing he keeps saying is, "Mujib has insulted me." Please go and meet him again and tell him that he should do what he feels is right.' I told them, 'Are you joking?'

I was meeting Mr Suhrawardy regularly then. Sometimes I would accompany him to meetings, especially the ones organized to restore communal harmony. I narrated to him one day everything that had happened between Mr Hashim and me. He became upset. Why had I been rude to Mr Hashim? This shows how forgiving a man he was. I went back to Mr Hashim and apologized to him. I said I shouldn't have talked to him the way I did. I told him, 'Do what you feel is best. I really shouldn't be saying anything.' Mr Hashim was going to stay back in India while I was going away to Pakistan where my home is in any case. Mr Hashim was pleased because I had apologized to him. I might have had a difference of opinion with him but it was difficult for me to forget that he had taught me the basics of politics. If I have been mistaken or if I have done wrong I have never had difficulty in acknowledging my mistake and expressing my regret. If I knew that I had made a mistake I would correct it. After all, we all make mistakes. I had another flaw: I would flare up on occasions. But I would cool down quite quickly too!

I have noted that there are many people who keep thinking about what they should do. They procrastinate so much that before they know it the time for doing anything is over and they can never do what they wanted to do. These people keep vacillating between 'Should I?' and 'Shouldn't I?' and never manage to accomplish anything. When I decide on doing something I go ahead and do it. If I find out that I was wrong, I try to correct myself. This is because I know that only doers are capable of making errors; people who never do anything make no mistakes!

~

During this period, I had the good fortune of going with Mr Suhrawardy to a number of places. He was working with Mahatma Gandhi to establish communal harmony among Hindus and Muslims. This was the time Muslims were being attacked every now and then. One Sunday I went to Mr Suhrawardy's house in the morning. He told me, 'Let's go to Barrackpore. Things are bad there. Mahatma Gandhi will also be going there.' I said, 'Let's.' I got into his car and we went to Narkeldanga. There the Mahatma, Manu Gandhi, Abha Gandhi and his secretary and a few Congress leaders joined him. We headed towards Barrackpore. Thousands of people had lined up and were chanting, 'Long live Gandhiji.' When we reached Barrackpore I found out that arrangements had been made there for a huge public meeting. But Gandhi would not speak to anyone or give speeches on Sundays. Manu Gandhi and Abha Gandhi recited 'Alhamdulillahu' and 'Kulhu Allahu', two suras from the Koran. They then sang two Hindu religious songs. The Mahatma wrote something for the occasion and his secretary read it out. The man was a magician. People cried out immediately, 'Muslims and Hindus are brothers.' The whole atmosphere changed instantly.

Two days later we were going to have the Eid prayer. Muslims were apprehensive and in a dilemma—should they hold the annual public prayer or not? The Mahatma declared that if there was another riot and if anyone inflicted violence on the Muslims he would start to fast. In neighbourhoods Hindi-speaking people brought out processions chanting slogans, 'Don't kill Muslims, Bapuji will start fasting then. Hindus and Muslims are brothers.' Eid day, in fact, passed peacefully. Yakub, a photographer friend of mine, and I decided that we would come up with a present for the Mahatma. Yakub said, 'Do you remember that when we were in Bihar you and I had taken photographs of the riots there?' I said, 'Yes, I remember.' Yakub said, ' I have been all over Calcutta taking pictures. You probably don't know that I have made copies of them. How about making a selection of those photographs and then presenting them to the Mahatma?' I said, 'That's an excellent idea. Let's go and make a packet immediately.' We sat down and did just that. We then made a packet consisting of photographs, wrapping it in such a manner that it would take anyone ten minutes to open it. Our plan was to give him the 'present' and then vanish. Among the photographs we had collected were some of Muslim women whose breasts had been cut off, little babies who had been beheaded, mosques burning, corpses lying in streets and many such gruesome scenes from the riots. We wanted the Mahatma to see how his people had been guilty of such crimes and how they had killed innocents.

We came to the Mahatma's place in Narkeldanga a little later. We let it be known that we had come there to exchange greetings on Eid day. We were taken inside. The Mahatma offered us some apples. We presented him the packet. He accepted it gladly. It didn't seem to bother him that we were strangers. But we realized that his granddaughter Manu Gandhi could recognize us since she had seen us sitting on the platform with Mr Suhrawardy in the Barrackpore meeting. We departed as soon as we could after handing over the package to him. Mr Suhrawardy was away at that time. There can be little doubt that the photographs we presented to the Mahatma left a deep impression on his mind. Later I informed Mr Suhrawardy of what we had done.

~

It was not possible for us to stay in Calcutta any longer since a lot of people were being arrested. Zahiruddin's house had been raided. If we were caught we wouldn't be spared. The best thing to do would be to flee Calcutta. There was one problem though: my brother-in-law Abdur Rab Serniabat and I were operating a restaurant in Park Circus. He had gone to his village home with my sister and my wife Renu. He was taking his time to return to the city. Since I wasn't looking after the restaurant at all the manager was pocketing all the profits. I decided that I would telegram him to come back quickly and then leave Calcutta.

I went to tell Mr Suhrawardy that I was leaving. I was feeling very sad at the idea of leaving him behind in the city. I kept asking myself: how long would the Mahatma be able to protect Mr Suhrawardy? He had been attacked a number of times already. The Hindus were trying very hard to get rid of him. His car had been bombed in front of Science College and had gone up in flames. He had managed to survive somehow. I told him, 'Sir, let's go to Pakistan; what is the point in staying here?' He said, 'I'll have to go in the end, but how can I abandon the hapless Muslims and leave without doing anything for them? Can't you see how horrible the situation is all over India? All you read about nowadays is accounts of riots breaking out everywhere. All the other leaders have left; if I leave they will have nobody to look after them. When you go back to your country try to ensure communal harmony. If there is trouble in East Bengal it will be catastrophic. Try to ensure that the Hindus don't flee Pakistan. If they are forced to come here they will stir up trouble and that will result in an exodus of Muslims to East Bengal. If all the Muslims of West Bengal, Bihar and Assam leave for East Bengal, it will be difficult to protect Pakistan, especially East Bengal. I know very well you won't be able to accommodate so many people. For the good of Pakistan make sure that there are no communal riots in Pakistan.' I said, 'I'll have to leave for Dhaka since Shamsul Haq wants me to be there. There will be a meeting of all political workers in the city. I will come back later and meet you one more time before leaving.' He said, 'Please do.'

Nuruddin didn't come with me because he had his MA examination. He intended to return as soon as his exams were over. He had all sorts of problems; his wife was studying in the medical college then. He would have to wait for her to finish before coming back.

I thought at the time we have attained Pakistan, what more could we want? I will now go to Dhaka and enrol in a law course there and concentrate on my studies for a while. I would try to involve all Muslim League workers in an attempt to ensure that there would be no rioting in our part of Bengal.

I stayed with my parents and my wife for a few days and then came to Dhaka in September. I had been to the city only on a couple of occasions and wasn't familiar with its landmarks. I had no idea where my relatives who were working in the city were living. I decided that I would first stay in the Muslim League office at 150 Mughaltuli. Shawkat Mia, an old League hand, and a good friend, used to look after the office building. Mr Shamsul Huq was also living there. Mr Huq summoned a meeting of the workers of our party and other parties in the office to discuss the political situation. He had informed me of the meeting beforehand. I therefore arrived in the office a few days before the meeting. I took a horse carriage to the office. I found out that the man who was driving the carriage was a wit. He knew where the office was. He said, 'I'll take you there.' It seemed to me that he didn't charge me much. I have heard many stories about these Dhaka cabbies and their behaviour. But this man wasn't representative of the type who would insist on an exorbitant fare. Mr Shamsul Huq and Mr Shawkat seemed to be very happy to see me. Indeed, Mr Shawkat appeared to be so overjoyed at my coming that he seemed at a loss to decide on what he could do for me. He had a spare room and he put me up in it. We used to address each other formally then.

The conference was to be held in a couple of days' time. Many delegates had started to come from different districts. Many of them were staying with us in the Mughaltuli office building. Mr Shamsul Huq told me, 'We are running out of space and I don't know where to hold the conference. The government too is unhappy about our plans to hold a conference. It is trying to prevent us from staging it and is planning to thwart it any which way it can.' I said, 'How is it that they are beginning to ignore us so soon?' Mr Huq smiled and said, 'That is the way of the world!'

In the evening Mr Huq held a meeting with us to discuss the agenda of the conference. We decided that we would organize a youth front to prevent our younger students from dispersing. I told Huq, 'We can have a youth front but we should consider whether it should be involved in political activity. We are still members of the Muslim League and are bound by its rules.' Mr Huq replied, 'But we aren't going to make it a political machine.'

Mr Huq soon got involved in finding a site for the meeting. In the end it was decided that the conference would be held in the house of the vice chairman of the municipality, Khan Saheb Abul Hasnat. His house had a huge lawn and hall. He was the only one with the courage to make us the offer of a conference site.

The conference began. Mr Ataur Rahman Khan and Mr Kamruddin were two individuals who tried to help us make it a success. I knew Mr Kamruddin well but this was my first meeting with Mr Ataur Rahman Khan. At the end of the first session we formed a subject committee. In the course of the discussions it became obvious to me that some communists had joined us. They began to air their views openly. The first decision that we took was to organize a youth front where anyone could join in. But the idea was to keep it as far away from active politics as was possible. It would be treated as a cultural organization. It would be called Democratic Youth League. I declared that its only objective would be to promote communal harmony so that there could be no riots that would lead to the exodus of Hindus from our country. Many of the delegates present supported me. However, the pro-communist delegates said that we needed to do more. For example, we should take up schemes for economic development. We pointed out that this would steer us towards politics.

After much discussion it was decided that we would form a subcommittee that would work out a detailed programme and present it to the executive council of the Democratic Youth League. That body would have the right to vet the programme and accept or reject it. The committee was constituted. It would have seventeen members but would have the power of co-opting more members if and when necessary. We could see that people who were on our side constituted the majority. A few members with Marxist leanings were also part of the council. A few days later a draft was submitted to the executive committee of the council that amounted to a party manifesto. I strongly opposed the adoption of the draft since I felt that the committee was not empowered to adopt any comprehensive programme. I declared that we had no other objective for the moment except to rush headlong into a movement to ensure communal harmony. Only two months of independence had passed. It wouldn't be proper to raise any other demand at this moment. That would divide us from the people. This was when the communist leaders began saying, 'We haven't achieved true freedom; we have to attain it through a revolutionary programme.' The communist colleagues would have liked us to incorporate this goal in our programme. But if we went to the people with their ideas people would lose their trust in us and we would lose sight of the most pressing need of our time—communal harmony. They failed to pass their resolution in the first meeting since we constituted the majority. But when Mr Huq began to take a middle position we found ourselves in a more precarious position.

At around this time I had to go away to Calcutta for a while. I had to find out whether the restaurant I co-owned had been sold or not. If it hadn't, I had to find a way of exchanging it with some shop in Dhaka. When I went to Calcutta I found out that Mr Rab had managed to sell it. What a relief! Mr Suhrawardy had just returned from a tour of East Punjab, Delhi, Jaipur and Alwar that had made him a worried man since these were all places that had witnessed violent riots. He was the only Muslim leader of either India or Pakistan who had the courage to go and witness at first hand what was happening there. He was very happy to see me again. He said, 'The Muslims of East Bengal are really a civilized lot; there have been no riots or outbreaks of violence there. But the Hindus have been coming away regardless and they will create trouble here. I will go to East Bengal soon and address some public meetings there so that more Hindus don't flee the country.' He decided that he would consult Mr Nazimuddin in Dhaka and then go to Barisal for a public meeting.

~

I came away to Dhaka. A huge meeting was organized in Barisal. Mr Suhrawardy stayed with Mr Nazimuddin whenever he was in Dhaka and he did so this time too. We headed for Barisal in a steamer. Calcutta's Prafulla Chandra Ghosh had accompanied him on this trip. The Barisal meeting started in the afternoon. When I was about to address the meeting around 8 p.m. someone handed me a slip of paper. I was sitting next to Mr Suhrawardy. Mr Rab, my brother-in-law, had scrawled on the slip the following message: 'Your father is very ill and close to death. They have been trying to reach you for a while now. If you want to meet him you will have to head home by night-time. Helen [author's younger sister] has already left.' I read out the message to Mr Suhrawardy. He ordered me to leave for home immediately. I took my leave from him.

When I got down from the dais I found out that Mr Rab was waiting to receive me. He said, 'When did you get my message?' I replied, 'Yesterday evening.' He told me, 'Helen has left already and I have been waiting to accompany you.' I headed directly from the station to the dock to take a steamer since it was leaving in half an hour. If I missed it I would have to wait for the next steamer which would leave the next evening.

I boarded the steamer. The whole night I kept thinking of all sorts of things. I was the eldest son of my father. I didn't know much about running the family. I kept thinking of my thoughtlessness and the many ways in which I had hurt my father. But he had never rebuked me. All fathers love their sons and all sons love and respect their fathers. But I am unable to express the extent of my father's love for me and the love I felt for him.

In the morning the steamer reached Patgati station which was only two and a half miles away from our home. I asked the stationmaster and a few other people in the station if they had heard anything about my father. They all said the same thing: 'He is very ill.' Because it would take a long time to reach home by boat I left my luggage with the stationmaster and decided to walk home. I had to cross the Modhumati river. I decided to head home through the fields not bothering to stick to the roadways. It didn't matter to me that I was walking through paddy fields. When I came home I found that my father was suffering from cholera. He was in a bad shape and the doctor had given up on him. As soon as I called out 'Abba' he opened his eyes and looked at me. A few teardrops trickled down his face. I broke down in tears. Suddenly he seemed to show more signs of life. The doctor now said he appeared to be breathing better. Soon his condition took a turn for the better. The doctor told us then that we had no more reason to worry. He had stopped urinating but now he was passing water after a long time. He was beginning to look better too. The worst seemed to be over. A little later, the doctor declared, 'You have no more reason for worry since he has started to pass urine again.' Two or three hours later the doctor said that he would leave since he had stayed back for the night. He reassured us that there was no danger and that he would visit us again in the evening. I stayed back in our village home for a few more days. My father's condition began to improve steadily. Children who are deprived of their parents' affection are the most wretched people of the earth. And who can be more fortunate than children who have the blessings of their parents?

~

I returned to Dhaka. I enrolled in the university, having decided to study law. I bought a few books. In Dhaka, I came to know of a meeting of the Democratic Youth League. The executive committee had co-opted some new members and its size had increased from seventeen to thirty-four now. However, the real reason for the expansion was to make a minority out of us. Many of us hadn't got any notice of the meeting where this expansion had taken place. Calcutta's daily *Ittehad* was one paper where such news was usually printed but this time it failed to print this information. I objected to what had been done by asking a simple question: how could seventeen members co-opt seventeen more? I asked for a meeting. A few days later I learned that a meeting had already been called and it was to be held in Mymensingh. But while everyone had been given notice of the meeting I had been kept in the dark about it. I came to know about it from Noakhali's Aziz Mohammad, secretary of the Dhaka City Muslim League at that time; he had got the notice and he informed me about the meeting. He pointed out that it was going to be held the next day at 9 a.m. We found out that three members of the committee were in Dhaka then—Mr Aziz, Mr Shamsul Huda (now in the Convention Muslim League) and I. We decided that we too would join the meeting and oppose their scheming. We didn't have the time to inform members from other districts who were on our side. We would have to leave Dhaka that very evening since there was only one train that left at night and reached Mymensingh at 3 a.m. We stayed in the station till it was dawn. But Mr Huq was nowhere to be found and did not show up for the meeting.

When we came to the meeting we challenged its validity. Why weren't so many of us informed about it? How had they drafted a manifesto without our input? We demanded that notices should be sent out for another meeting to be held in Dhaka where this manifesto could be discussed to decide whether it should be adopted or not. We stressed that it wasn't right to adopt it in a hurry in this meeting. Besides we couldn't join any political party since we were all members of the Muslim League's council. We argued with them for a long time over the issue. At last, when we found out that they weren't going to accept our arguments and that almost all of them were communists or left-leaning people we decided that we had no option but to walk out of the meeting. But as we left it we made it known to them that no Muslim League worker would be part of their conspiracy. The Youth League was dead from this day onward. We told them that we knew exactly how powerful they all were and how popular. We said that they had no right to use our names in anything they did.

We took down the signboard of the Youth League office from the

Mughaltuli Muslim League office building. By this time they had printed their manifesto and had even brought it to the office. But since Shawkat Mia was in charge of the office he ordered them to remove everything belonging to the Youth League from it. But who would take away their things? Nobody showed up to claim responsibility. The police raided the office. Our name, it seemed, was in their books. The house at 150 Mughaltuli from which the movement for Pakistan had been directed in this part of the country now became a building under surveillance. Officials of the special branch of the police were now secretly keeping an eye on the office. Our fault was that we were all admirers of Mr Suhrawardy. But we continued to do our best to maintain communal harmony.

Manik Mia was then the secretary of Calcutta's daily *Ittehad*. We desperately needed money for our activities. But who would finance us? I could ask for some money from home for my studies, but where would I get the money for political activities? I was better off than most of us because I was the East Pakistani representative of the *Ittehad*. I used to get three hundred rupees a month for my work. My job was to collect money from the distribution agencies and to see that the paper continued to be sold and new distributors appointed to increase circulation. I didn't work for the paper for a long time. But the work was easy since the paper had a good reputation. The money I got from it and from my home was sufficient for my needs.

The All Bengal Muslim Students' League had been renamed the All East Pakistan Muslim Students' League. Shah Azizur Rahman continued to work as its general secretary. But instead of holding the council meeting in the open in Dhaka they held it secretly [to avoid the democratic process] somewhere else. Most members of the executive committee were no longer students since they had graduated by then. The committee was elected in 1944 when the last election was held. We refused to accept this committee any more. Many students from Calcutta's Islamia College and from other districts had now taken readmission in Dhaka University. They were not involved with this organization. I initiated a series of meetings with Students' League workers. Among others Aziz Ahmed, Mohammad Toaha, Oli Ahad, Abdul Hamid Chowdhury, Dabirul Islam, Naimuddin, Mollah Jalaluddin, Abdur Rahman Chowdhury, Abdul Matin Khan Chowdhury and Syed Nazrul Islam agreed with me that we needed a new organization for ourselves.

On 4 January 1948 we called a meeting in the assembly hall of Fazlul Huq Muslim Hall. Here we decided that we would form a new students' front. We would call it East Pakistan Muslim Students' League. Naimuddin was made its convener. Oli Ahad, however, decided not to be part of it since he felt that he no longer wanted to be involved in any organization with a religious bias. He was interested in becoming part of it only if it was called East Pakistan Students' League. We tried to dissuade him and said, 'The time hasn't come for such a name yet. We have to take into consideration the political situation and the mood of the people. The name itself isn't important. If we hold on to our principles we could change the name at a later date. We have attained Pakistan only a few months back. It will take some time to change the mindset of the people and even the educated section of society, and turn them away from the mindset that had made them participate in the movement for Pakistan.'

The office of our organization was going to remain at 150 Mughaltuli. Muslim League leaders made several attempts to take over the office but failed to do so because of Shawkat Mia. We put up a signboard which said 'Muslim League Workers' Camp' to stake our claim. This is where the East Pakistan Muslim Students' League began functioning. Shawkat Mia made arrangements for the necessary tables, chairs and cabinets. It wouldn't have been possible to do anything without him then. He also looked after our food and accommodation needs. We used to give him whatever we could as our monthly expenses. He really used to look after us well.

The response to the formation of the Students' League was overwhelming. We were able to form committees in almost every district of the province within a month. Even though Naimuddin was the convener I ended up doing most of the work. I was fortunate in having a few truly selfless people with me. The East Pakistan government was overtly supporting the All East Pakistan Muslim Students' League by now. On the other hand, they had let loose the secret police on us.

Meanwhile, Khawaja Nazimuddin gave orders for the dissolution of the Muslim League National Guard. Mirza Golam Hafiz, Zahiruddin and a few others opposed this move since this institution had worked for the creation of Pakistan and had been striving to prop up the nascent state. It used to try to solve the problems created by the lack of trained workers in the railways and help tackle law and order problems and so on. There were thousands of people working for the National Guard. When it was dissolved instead of being employed in nation-building activities its members became very frustrated. The leaders of the National Guard organized a meeting in which they decided that they would continue to keep the organization functional. Zahiruddin was made its chief. But soon after he came to Dhaka he was arrested from the Mughaltuli office one day under the Public Security Act.

It should be mentioned here that the National Guard office was also in Mughaltuli and was housed in a spacious three-storeyed building. Although he was released from prison after six or eight weeks, many leaders now took fright. I am not sure what Mr Nazimuddin told Mr Mojaher, the man in charge of the National Guard in Bengal. Mojaher gave a statement in the papers saying that since the country had achieved independence it no longer needed a National Guard. By not utilizing such an effective organization for the purpose of national development, the government managed to harm the national interest. Many members of the organization had made huge sacrifices to create Pakistan. In some cases they had done much more than some of the leaders. Many people kept telling me, 'Where would we get the money to engage them in any kind of work?' But they didn't want money. They had been working month after month for very little. The government could have absorbed them gradually into the Ansar battalions.[14] Many of them had received extensive civil defence training. It was difficult for us to figure out the antics of our leaders in this case. The National Guard wasn't paid salaries. The government failed to use the enthusiasm that the National Guard and Muslim League workers had in them to build Pakistan.

Ordinary people as well as government officials were working day and night for the new nation. I know that in some instances one official would run an entire office. In one case only one jamadar and a guard worked with League workers to help maintain law and order in an entire thana. People travelling in trains often found no tickets available, yet paid in cash when boarding railcars. As if by magic, symptoms of corruption vanished.

But slowly everything once again took a turn for the worse because of government policies. The government seemed to have no clue as to how it could channelize the energy of a country which had just emerged from inertia into nation-building activities. Thousands of workers began to disperse aimlessly. There was plenty to do and plenty of people available to do the needful but no plan or direction to guide them. A major reason for this is that the men who had come to power had no confidence in the masses and were cut off from them. Indeed, the men who took over the reins of government in the province had been intimate with the British and had propped them up. They had received titles like 'Sir', 'Khan Bahadur' 'Khan Saheb', etc. from them in return. They now began to rely entirely on bureaucrats from the British era. They would do exactly what the men at the top would tell them to do. There is abundant proof of the way these bureaucrats oppressed and suppressed the selfless workers who had striven for independence to appease their English masters and to earn promotions for themselves.

Soon after independence these lackeys of the government got promoted in quick succession and became heady with success. The 'Sirs' and 'Khan Bahadurs' for their part became transformed into their puppets. These people didn't have the mindset required to build self-reliant people for an independent country and to earn the confidence of the masses. On the contrary, to consolidate their power they began to manoeuvre to control the Muslim League. Soon after independence the party itself had split into two. One part remained in India and called itself the All India Muslim League while the other became known as the Pakistan Muslim League.

Since Muhammad Ali Jinnah had become the Governor General of Pakistan he could no longer remain president of the Muslim League. Consequently, Chaudhury Khaliquzzaman was given charge of running the Pakistan Muslim League. The League decided to dissolve the East Pakistan Muslim League and form an ad hoc committee to run it. But although the Punjab, like Bengal, had been split, nobody thought it necessary to dissolve the Muslim League there. Neither the Sind nor the Frontier Provincial Muslim League was split. Only the East Pakistan Muslim League had to be broken into two since there were too many Suhrawardy supporters in it! They were, therefore, reconstituted with Nazimuddin supporters. Maulana Akram Khan was made the chief here.

We quickly managed to get 112 council members to sign a petition demanding a requisition meeting to discuss the situation. Among the people who signed the petition were Mohammad Ali, Tafazzal Ali, Dr Malek, Abdus Salam Khan, M.A. Sabur, Ataur Rahman Khan, Kamruddin, Shamsul Huq, Anwara Khatun and Khairat Hussein. I did a lot of work to collect these signatures. I had to travel to a couple of districts for this purpose.

After attaining the requisite number of signatures, we drafted a notice asking for a requisition meeting. Now we had to hand the notice over to Maulana Akram Khan. Since nobody wanted to take on this responsibility I ended up doing so. At this time, we used to have our meetings in Mr Tafazzal Ali's house. Somehow, I was feeling embarrassed about handing over the notice to the Maulana there. Ultimately, I found myself in his daily *Azad* office at Kaltabazar. When he came to know that I was waiting to meet him he summoned me. I greeted him respectfully and told him that I would be happy to have him acknowledge officially that he had received the notice. He did so. He treated me well and asked about my health. But all I wanted to do then was leave his presence as soon as possible! I thus took my leave from him as quickly as I could.

The next day he printed the notice in the daily *Azad* and also the list of signatories. Through a press release he let it be known that nobody had the power to call a requisition meeting since the old Muslim League had been dissolved. He was now president of the East Pakistan Muslim League Ad Hoc Committee. In other words, none of us were any longer members of the Muslim League Council. And so this is how we were thrown out of the Muslim League! Many accepted the situation without protesting but we decided not to do so. We would try till the end to do something about the situation.

~

It was probably on 8 February 1948 that the Pakistan Constituent Assembly met in Karachi. A topic that came up for discussion there was that of the national language of Pakistan. Muslim League leaders wanted to make Urdu the state language. Most League members from East Pakistan were of the same view. Babu Dhirendra Nath Dutt, the member from the Comilla Congress, demanded that Bengali should be chosen since the majority of the population spoke the language. The Muslim League leaders did not agree.[15] It soon became obvious that a great conspiracy was afoot to make Urdu and not Bengali the state language. The East Pakistan Muslim Students' League and the Tamuddun Majlish[16] protested against the move and demanded that both Bengali and Urdu should be considered state languages. We met to protest against the imposition of Urdu as the sole state language. This East Pakistan Muslim Students' League and the Tamuddun Majlish decided in a joint meeting that they would form a committee to establish Bengali as the state language. The East Pakistan Muslim Students' League had by this time formed a few branches in some districts and subdivisions of the province. The Tamuddun Majlish, it should be mentioned, was a cultural organization headed by Professor Abul Kashem.

Meanwhile, from among the old Muslim League workers, Mr Kamruddin, Mr Shamsul Huq and many others joined the central committee formed to direct the action. We decided that 11 March would be declared 'Bengali Language Demand Day'. We also decided to spring into action in all the districts on that day. I gave speeches at student meetings in Faridpur, Jessore, Daulatpur, Khulna and Barisal on the subject before arriving in Dhaka three days before. In Daulatpur students, incited by the Muslim League, tried to disrupt our meeting. This led to a violent clash in which some people were wounded. But they failed to prevent us from carrying on with the meeting and I managed to finish my speech successfully. At this time Mr Abdus Sabur Khan lent us his support.

Barisal's Mr Mohiuddin Ahmed was a member of the All East Pakistan Students' League and a strong supporter of both the Muslim League and the government. We were led by Kazi Bahauddin Ahmed. I spoke at a meeting in a college. Mr Mohiuddin Ahmed did not attempt to thwart our meeting.

I then came back to Dhaka. The night before 'Bengali Language Demand Day' we met to decide on our strategy so that we could man the picket lines adequately. Except for a few university students, it could be said that 90 per cent of the students of the province joined us in protesting against the move to make Urdu the state language. In particular, students of Jagannath College, Mitford Medical School and Engineering College were active participants. The Muslim League let loose their goons on us. They managed to rally most of the people against us. In some places of old Dhaka our students got beaten up. They wanted everyone to believe that we were out to destroy Pakistan.

On the morning of 11 March hundreds of student workers set up pickets in Eden Building, the General Post Office and other places. There was no need to organize any pickets at the university and in colleges. The whole of Dhaka city was covered with posters. Most shops were closed and only a few stayed open. Only a part of the old city did not observe the general strike.[17] At 8 a.m. police attacked students who had assembled in front of the General Post Office. But when one group of students was driven away another took its place. We had kept some workers in reserve in Fazlul Huq Hall who could act as reinforcements. The day passed in this fashion for some time. At nine o'clock the police attacked the students who had gathered in front of Eden Building. Khaleque Nawaz Khan, Bakhtiar and the City Students' League's general secretary M.A. Wadud were badly injured in the police action. In Topkhana Road Kazi Golam Mahbub, Shawkat Mia and many other students were hurt. The students standing in front of the gate at Abdul Ghani Road were unable to withstand the force of the police assaults after a while. Many of our workers were wounded and some of them had to flee. I rushed towards Eden Building with some fresh workers who had joined us at the General Post Office.

Meanwhile, the police had encircled Mr Shamsul Huq's group in front of Eden Building. The gate had by this time become deserted. I was on a cycle then. The city Superintendent of Police (SP) tried to chase me in his jeep but failed to catch hold of me. I realized that I was going to be cornered. I gave my cycle to a friend and then decided I would sit down in front of the Eden Building gate with four or five other students. I told the friend to whom I had given my cycle that he should send us some more students as soon as possible to help us in our resistance. There were only a few of us and by ourselves we wouldn't be able to hold out for long. Some students saw what we were doing and decided to join us in the sit-down strike. Some of us got beaten up and some were arrested and hauled into jeeps. Mr Huq had already been forcibly taken to one of the jeeps. Many students were hurt and arrested. A few students were driven to a jungle 30 to 40 miles away from the city and dumped there. A few girl students too were beaten up. Oli Ahad had also been arrested. Tajuddin, Toaha and a few others had managed to elude the police. Seventy to seventy-five of us were tied up and sent to jail in the evening. The movement, however, had picked up momentum by then. We had managed to get the support of the people of Dhaka in the end.

At this time the East Pakistan Legislative Assembly was in session. Processions too were a daily affair. Mr Nazimuddin realized that things were getting out of control and that the protest movement was gathering momentum. Wadud and Bakhtiar, both Students' League workers, had been badly hurt and were in the jail hospital. This was the moment when Mr A.K. Fazlul Huq, Mohammad Ali of Bogra, Tafazzal Ali, Dr Malek, Mr Sabur, Khairat Hussein, Anwara Khatun and many others began to protest vehemently against the Muslim League's stand. Also, Mr Suhrawardy's party had reunited under him. Mr Nazimuddin became worried and agreed to discuss the issue with the committee we had set up to organize the protest against the decision to make Urdu the state language.

We were in jail and so I was unaware of the discussions taking place. But Mr Kamruddin met us in jail on behalf of the committee and told us that Mr Nazimuddin had agreed to our demand that the official language of East Pakistan would be Bengali. The East Pakistan Legislative Assembly would send a recommendation to the centre so that the Bengali language would have the status of a state language. He would also withdraw all the cases filed against us, release all prisoners, and would himself undertake an investigation of the excesses committed by the police. There were other points which Kamruddin reported that I do not remember now. But it seemed farcical that he had agreed to investigate the actions that he himself had initiated as home minister.

We were put up in Ward 4. It was housed in a three-storeyed building. Outside the walls of the jail was Muslim Girls' School. All the five days that we were in jail, the schoolgirls began their morning raising slogans from the school's rooftop and ended their day doing the same at four in the afternoon. They seemed indefatigable as they cried out, 'The state language must be Bengali', 'Our brothers in prison must be freed', 'Police brutality must end', and so on. I remember telling Mr Huq then, 'See how even our sisters have come out in the open for our cause. Surely Bengali will be the state language after such an event.' Mr Huq said, 'I agree, Mujib.'

We were taken to jail on the 11th and released on the 15th [of March]. We were then taken in a procession from the jail gate to Salimullah Muslim Hall. On the 13th, however, we had an unpleasant encounter inside the jail. A non-Bengali jamadar had come to lock us up that day. We were sitting on our beds at that time. He was counting heads to see if everyone was there. He did this every day and if the numbers tallied he would lock us up from the outside. This was how all the wards were locked up in the evening. That day the jamadar did a headcount many times but the numbers did not add up. However, everything seemed fine in the next room where a number of students had been interned. The problem was that there were some really junior students who had been locked up with us and would not listen to us. They would often move to another room when the time for counting heads came. Mr Huq and I would often scold them and force them to sit still on such occasions. Mr Abdul Mannan—now the headmaster of Nabakumar High School—and the two of us were older than the rest who had been imprisoned. Mr Mannan was in charge of distributing the food among us. When he failed to tally our numbers the jamadar flew into a rage and used abusive language. This upset the students and they stood up and began to shout. Mr Huq and I forced everyone to sit down. The jamadar began to count again and the numbers finally tallied. But when he got outside the door he blew his whistle. The jail alarm bell began to sound. This was tantamount to a warning signal. No matter what they were doing, the moment they heard the bell go off, prison personnel rushed in with guns, sticks and any other weapons they had and beat up prisoners indiscriminately. On such occasions there was no restraining them. Even ordinary sepoys had the legal right to act as they thought fit as long as there were non-commissioned officers with them. The jailers and deputy jailers would join them as soon as they could.

We couldn't figure out what had led to this situation. The Bengali sepoy who was on duty had locked us all up. The jamadar wanted the key from him but he refused to hand it over. We saw them scuffle over this. The sepoy ran downstairs with the key. The jamadar, it seems, wanted to storm our rooms with the other sepoys so that they could all beat us up. As soon as we realized what would happen when the jailer, deputy jailer, and superintendent entered, Shamsul Huq and I told everyone to sit down in their assigned seats. The two of us then stood by the door, intending to take the brunt of any attacks made on all of us. We also told the others that they shouldn't make a move unless we were assaulted. But if they did beat us up the others were to resist with chairs, tables, dishes, pots and pans, and anything they could get their hands on. Both Mr Huq and I could be pretty tough customers. If necessary, we could go on the offensive and fight with our bare hands, something I was used to doing from childhood. There could be no doubt that if the sepoy had not fled with the keys we would have been beaten up by the lower-ranked jail personnel since we were being confined to a room. By this time many sepoys had taken up positions and were hurling abuse at us. The jailer and Mr Mokhlesur Rahman, the deputy jailer, turned up in front of our gate and ordered all the sepoys to go downstairs. Soon the jail superintendent, Mr Bill, showed up and, gauging what was going on, ordered all the sepoys to disperse.

Later, the superintendent told Mr Huq what had happened. In 1950 he himself had been responsible for firing on political prisoners under his care in Rajshahi jail's Khapra ward, which had led to the death of some patriots. That incident had led to the death of many. Later, we found out that there had been a conspiracy afoot to create a pretext for beating us up. The next day the deputy jailer, Mr Mokhlesur Rahman, informed us about the many laws governing prison conduct. Even though I had gone to jail once when I was quite young, I did not know till then the different laws relating to prisoners. All the knowledge I had gathered of jail was based on a book or two that I had read on the subject. But it is true that students who had been jailed did not care much about laws in any case. The burden was on Mr Huq, Mr Mannan and me to coax the others into complying with the rules and regulations of prison life.

Indeed, many of our fellow prisoners were school-going boys. One of them was only nine or ten years old. When his father came to the jail gate to meet him he said, 'I will take you out of jail today.' But the boy replied that he wouldn't leave until the other students were released. When he came back and told us about the exchange with his father all of us patted him on the back and raised slogans praising his stand. I can't remember his name now but I remember his exact words. He was a very determined fellow. In fact, the students who had been arrested were all determined to make Bengali the state language and ready to make any sacrifice for its sake.

We took part in the students' general meeting held at the university on 16 March 1948 at 10 a.m. Suddenly someone proposed that I should preside over the meeting. All the students present supported this proposal. This was the first time I had to preside over a meeting in the famous university hub called Amtala. Many people spoke on the occasion. The meeting approved all the resolutions adopted by the student committee that had negotiated with the government to end our protest. But no one agreed to have Khawaja Nazimuddin head an investigation into the police brutality since he was the home minister as well as the chief minister. I said in my speech, 'We must abide by the decisions taken by the action committee; all we can do is propose that this one change be made in the compromise we had worked out with them; we can't do much more than that.' The students insisted that they would go in a procession to the Legislative Assembly when it was in session to submit this demand to Mr Nazimuddin. I said we could do that but immediately on submitting our demand to him we would have to leave the premises of the Legislative Assembly. Nobody would be allowed to remain there since our action committee had decided to suspend any further action for the time being. Everyone agreed with me.

We went in a procession to confront Mr Nazimuddin. Once we reached his office, we sent him a note that contained our demands. I gave another speech asking everyone to leave and got ready to go back to Salimullah Muslim Hall myself. As I left the place I could see that many students had already left. But some students and members of the public were still around and raising slogans from time to time. I went back and gave another speech then. By now some more students had left. This time I left the hall for good. At 4 p.m. I learned that many people had once again congregated in front of Mr Nazimuddin's office. Most of them were government employees and members of the public, although there were some students amongst them too. Mr Huq kept trying to send some of the students back.

From time to time students were trying to get an MLA or two to come to Muslim Hall. They were making them sign a statement saying that if they failed to make Bengali the state language they would resign from their seats. The ministers were trapped inside. Mr Nazimuddin had managed to get out of his office through the back door with the help of the army. Many people had gathered at the spot once again. I rushed towards the Assembly. As I came close to it I could see the police firing tear gas shells and attacking the crowd with their batons. My eyes started to burn. They soon filled with tears and I was unable to see anything at all. Some students and members of the general public seemed to have been injured. A few of us went to the pond inside Palassey Barrack to wash our eyes. After some time we were able to get some relief from the effects of the gas.

We now discovered that Muslim Hall was astir. Bagerhat's Dr Muzammel Huq had been seized by the students and had been brought to the hall. He was an MLA. We knew each other well. I requested the students to release him. He was a good man and a follower of Mr Suhrawardy. I managed to persuade them to let him go after much effort. I put him on a rickshaw afterwards. All of a sudden we found out that Mr Shawkat Mia had been hurt and hospitalized. I rushed to see him and found out that he had been severely hurt. His hands and back had been bruised. When the police had attacked them with batons, a few other students had also been wounded slightly. I told everyone that they should leave the hospital as soon as they had recovered a little since the police could arrest them again.

Later in the evening we were informed that the action committee that had been formed to protest against making Urdu the state language would meet in Fazlul Haq Hall soon. I was a little late for this meeting. As I reached it I could hear someone abusing me loudly. I stopped to listen to what he had to say. I moved towards the dais as soon as this man stopped speaking. I then had my say. I said: didn't everyone know that I had declared at the Amtala meeting that we should deliver the note and come away and hadn't I announced as much in my speech? In any case, this was how the meeting ended and there wasn't much discussed afterwards. We all agreed that we would postpone our movement for the time being since Muhammad Ali Jinnah was scheduled to come to Dhaka for the first time after the creation of Pakistan. He would have to be given a public reception by us students as well as other people. We would have to make the necessary arrangements so that all students could go to the airport in a procession.

The movement to make Bengali a state language was not limited to Dhaka city. A few hundred students went to jail in Faridpur and Jessore for this cause. Movements supporting the cause also took place in Rajshahi, Khulna, Dinajpur, and a few other districts. The East Pakistan Muslim Students' League tried to thwart this movement but failed to do so in the end. There can be no doubt that students initiated this movement by themselves. But it soon became obvious that people as a whole were determined to make Bengali a state language. Particular mention should be made of government officials who supported the movement wholeheartedly. When the students of Engineering College were attacked by a group of goons some government officials from Palassey Barrack rallied to thwart them. As a result the goons were beaten up and had to disperse. It was obvious that the people of Dhaka changed their opinion about the issue in course of time. The government propaganda machine claimed that Hindu students from Calcutta had come to support the movement and had put on pyjamas to pass off as Bengali Muslim students. But of the seventy or so students who had been arrested not one was a Hindu. None of the wounded students were Hindus either. From this time on the government tried to label us as 'agents of India', 'communist' and 'traitor' to drive the masses against us. Government press notes also tried to blame us in this fashion.

Bengali was the mother tongue of 56 per cent of the people of Pakistan. Thus it should have been the only state language of the country. Nevertheless, we wanted both Bengali and Urdu to be state languages. The Punjab's people spoke Punjabi, Sind's Sindhi, those of the Frontier Province Pashto, and Baluchistan Baluchi. Urdu was not spoken in any of the provinces of Pakistan, but if this was the language that our brothers in West Pakistan wanted as a state language, why should we oppose their wishes? But those who wanted Urdu as the only state language had just one argument to back them: it was, they said, an 'Islamic language'. But we could not figure out how Urdu had ended up becoming an Islamic language.

Muslims in different parts of the world speak different languages. The people of Arabia speak Arabic, those of Iran Persian. The Turks speak Turkish, the Indonesians Indonesian, Malaysians Malay, while Chinese Muslims speak Chinese. Many other arguments could have been forwarded to defend their position but to hoodwink the religious-minded people of East Pakistan with the argument that Urdu should be the state language since it was an Islamic language was simply not possible. Every race loves its mother tongue. No nation has tolerated any attempt to insult its mother tongue.

The Muslim League leaders at one point seemed ready to sacrifice everything they had for the sake of Urdu but when they saw that people were not with them they began to get a little worried. At one point they even resorted to their ultimate weapon to block the movement. They believed that if they could make Jinnah speak in support of Urdu nobody would dare oppose their motion since everyone respected him irrespective of their party affiliation. Everyone would surely listen to him if he made a reasonable point. But nobody had the guts to tell Jinnah that that was not what the people of East Pakistan really wanted.

On 19 March when Jinnah landed in Dhaka's Tejgaon airport thousands of people went there to greet him. I remember that it was raining heavily that day. We had all got drenched in the rain and yet we waited to greet him in our wet clothes. Jinnah went to the Race Course ground and declared at a huge meeting, 'Urdu will be the only state language of Pakistan.' Some four or five hundred of us students were sitting in one corner of the field. Many of us raised our hands in protest and shouted, 'No, no.' Later when he went to Dhaka University's Convocation Centre and again announced Urdu would be the only state language of Pakistan the students sitting in front of him shouted out, 'No, no, no.' Jinnah paused for about five minutes and then resumed his speech. I believe that this was the first time that Bengali students had dared to oppose him. From this time on till he died Jinnah never again said that he wanted Urdu as the only state language of Pakistan.

In Dhaka Jinnah invited two representatives from the two leading student organizations of the time to talk with him. They belonged to the East Pakistan Muslim Students' League and the All East Pakistan Muslim Students' League. It is possible that he also invited the leaders of the All-Party State Language Action Committee but I am not sure about this now. He didn't like the idea of two different organizations existing at that moment. Mr Toaha and Mr Shamsul Huq represented us but I was not asked to go with them. Jinnah liked the name of our organization. When our representatives submitted a list of names of the All East Pakistan Muslim Students' League they tried to point out that most of them were now working full-time or had quit studying. Jinnah was upset when he found this out. Shamsul Huq got into an argument with Jinnah when he went to meet him about the question of the state language of Pakistan. Mr Huq told me this himself when he came back from the meeting. Mr Huq was the kind of man who would say what he believed in; he was never afraid of anyone when it came to stating the truth.

A few days after Jinnah left Dhaka a meeting of students was held in front of Fazlul Huq Hall. A student whose name I can't recall now gave a speech saying, 'We will have to accept whatever Jinnah tells us. Since he wants Urdu as our state language we must accept it as our state language.' What I remember now is that I protested against his statement in my speech. I said, 'If any leader does something which is wrong, people have the right to protest and persuade him to abandon his position. For example, ordinary people had once queried Caliph Omar himself about the long dress that he was wearing.[18] Bengali is the language spoken by 56 per cent of the people of Pakistan; it is a democratic country, and therefore the demand of the majority must be met. We will continue our movement till Bengali is made the state language. Certainly, we are ready to work for this cause.' The students assembled supported me. Subsequently, students and young people in Pakistan began to hold meetings and come out in processions to assert their demand to make Bengali a state language. Day by day public opinion continued to mount on this issue. In a few months it became obvious that the All East Pakistan Muslim Students' League had lost all support. All that was left of the party were some 'leaders' whose job was limited to courting ministers and supporting the government on every issue.

Before the language movement had started a group of MLAs had come together under the leadership of Mohammad Ali, Tafazzal Ali and

Dr Malek. This was because Khawaja Nazimuddin had not given any ministerial position to any Suhrawardy supporter. He had not even made anyone of them a parliamentary secretary. The number of people he had thus deprived of positions was not by any means negligible. These people would often meet in Tafazzal Ali's house. It soon became obvious that their numbers had grown to such an extent that if they cared to raise a no-confidence move against Mr Nazimuddin they would win the motion. A couple of them went to Calcutta to invite Mr Suhrawardy to Dhaka. It was widely assumed that as soon as Mr Suhrawardy came to Dhaka the group would raise a no-confidence motion against Mr Nazimuddin. But Mr Suhrawardy did not agree to this move. He told them, 'I don't want to cause trouble at this point. Let Mr Nazimuddin continue.' He added, 'Do you want me to align with those old MLAs? Why, only some days back they had voted against me. Today they are going to vote against Mr Nazimuddin and tomorrow they are going to go against me once again. We don't need to get involved in such situations. I have a lot of work to do here yet. If I don't attend to them Muslims will be forced to leave India and hundreds of thousands of them will die. My only goal is to bring permanent peace amongst the Hindus and Muslims of India and the Muslims and Hindus of Pakistan.'

Meanwhile, Mr Jinnah summoned Mr Mohammad Ali and chided him for fomenting factions. He also asked him to become ambassador to Burma. Mohammad Ali came to Mr Tafazzal Ali's house to tell us about his exchange with Mr Jinnah. He informed us that he had accepted the offer to go to Burma. A few days later it was announced that Dr Malek would become a minister. Only Mr Tafazzal Ali remained without a post. He told me one day, 'Mujib, have you noticed how Mohammad Ali has left and Dr Malek has become a minister? Now I have been offered a ministership too. What should I do? I can't do anything all by myself and remain outside the party. I need your advice.' I could see that there would be no point in trying to oppose his wish to accept the offer. Everyone had joined Mr Nazimuddin's party by now. But I told him, 'At least you wanted my advice and for this I must thank you. Nobody else bothered to do so. You won't be able to do anything on your own. Accept the offer and become a minister. We will continue our movement. Till I fulfil the goals we have set for ourselves in working for independence I will continue the struggle.' I respected him for the courtesy he had shown by consulting me on the issue and we continued to enjoy a good relationship. He always used to treat me like his younger brother even though we belonged to different political parties in later years.

After Maulana Akram Khan's statement we no longer remained members of the Muslim League. In other words, we had been driven out of the party! We had intended to make the Muslim League a progressive party. Two seats of the Legislative Assembly had fallen vacant in Tangail. We wondered if we could get someone to oppose Mr Nazimuddin. Maulana Bhasani had by this time returned from Assam and was staying in Kagmari, Tangail. We approached him. But he decided that he would contest from one seat and would allow the other one to be Mr Nazimuddin's. Later, however, his victory was invalidated because he had failed to file his election expenses.

Maulana Bhasani had supported us during the language movement. A meeting of Muslim League workers was organized in Tangail to find out what could be done at this point. After much discussion it was decided that we would organize another meeting in Narayanganj to decide on our future course of action. It was agreed that Maulana Bhasani, Abdus Salam Khan, Ataur Rahman Khan, Shamsul Huq and many other Muslim League leaders and workers would attend this meeting. Salman Ali, Abdul Awal, Shamsuzzoha and many others had organized the meeting. The local MLA, Khan Saheb Osman Ali, had lent his support to it. But before the meeting could begin Section 144 was imposed in Narayanganj. We therefore had to reschedule the meeting and hold it in Paikpara Club. Many leaders and workers from different districts had come to attend it. At this point goons hired by the Muslim League assaulted Shamsuzzoha. What was unfortunate was that he and his allies had formed the Narayanganj Muslim League and had played active roles in the creation of Pakistan. On the other hand, the people who were behind the attacks had once fought against the creation of Pakistan and had even opposed the Muslim League! Now the Muslim League committee was being reconstituted in every district and the committee that had once been active was being disbanded in favour of an ad hoc one. Because almost everywhere supporters of Mr Suhrawardy constituted the majority they had to be replaced, even if this involved recruiting people who had once opposed the League and Pakistan itself. But when ordinary people continued to talk about the Muslim League they had these old party workers in their mind.

Maulana Bhasani presided over the meeting. It was decided that we would select two from our midst to go to Karachi to discuss the situation with Mr Chaudhury Khaliquzzaman and to present him with a list of our demands. Our main demand was that the old Muslim League should be allowed to continue to do its work. If they were not willing to agree to this demand, we should at least be allowed to have the receipt books[19] and arrangements should be made to hold free and fair elections. Then it would become clear who the people would really like to retain as their leaders.

In those days it wasn't easy to go to Karachi. To reach the city one would have to go through Calcutta and Delhi. It was decided that two MLAs, Mr Ataur Rahman Khan and Mrs Anwara Khatun, would make the journey. And so they did, meeting Mr Khaliquzzaman and submitting our list of demands to him. But he told them, 'Forget what happened in the past. Only those who support Mr Nazimuddin can remain part of the Muslim League now.' About the receipt books he said, 'It is difficult to buy paper nowadays and so making of receipt books has become even more difficult. Go and talk to Mr Akram Khan and the ad hoc committee formed in East Pakistan; if they are willing you will get the receipt books.' The two of them came back and pointed out how a lot of money had been wasted on the trip with nothing to show for it. They told us that Mr Khaliquzzaman had not shown much interest in them.

Mr Suhrawardy came to Dhaka at this time and addressed meetings in Madaripur, Gopalganj and a few other places. This bore dividends immediately since it stopped many Hindus from leaving the country and also reduced the flow of Muslim refugees from West Bengal and Bihar. It will be difficult now to imagine how well attended these meetings were and the rush of people to welcome Mr Suhrawardy wherever he went. It certainly seemed to have scared Mr Nazimuddin's government. On this trip Mr Suhrawardy stayed in Nawabzada Nasrullah Khan's house since the latter respected and supported him. I said goodbye to Mr Suhrawardy in Gopalganj. Mr [Abdus] Sabur [Khan] received him in Khulna since he still felt obliged to him and used to support him and our stand then. During his visit to Khulna, Mr Suhrawardy talked informally with Hindu and Muslim leaders about ensuring communal harmony and urged everyone to work for this goal. In the huge meeting in Gopalganj both Mr Suhrawardy and I had to address the crowd without microphones since we hadn't been able to arrange for them. This was because he had arrived unexpectedly and we didn't even get the time to send for a public address system from Khulna.

It was obvious to us that the East Pakistan government was not happy about Mr Suhrawardy's trip. On previous occasions government employees had specific instructions to look after him when he was in our part of Bengal. But now they seemed to be deliberately staying away from him. A couple of them even confided to us, 'We have instructions from up above not to cooperate with him.' It also seemed that the detective branch had become very active.

It was clear to us though that it was essential to ensure communal harmony in Pakistan for the nation's future. If refugees started to flood in, the nation would be in dire straits, something that should have been obvious to anyone who had given thought to the situation. It would, of course, appear different to those who approached politics with a closed mind. There were hundreds of thousands of Muslims still living in West Bengal, Bihar, Assam and other states of India whose contribution was by no means less significant than those of us involved in the movement for Pakistan. We believed that we should ensure harmony keeping their lot in mind. The truth was that East Pakistani Muslims had accepted Mr Suhrawardy's advice on the matter. As a result there were no riots or violence here. Muslims even requested Hindus not to leave the country. I went to many places to work for communal harmony. I know of many incidents that testify to what I have just said. What was unfortunate was that our progressive-minded Hindu brothers in West Bengal failed to ensure communal harmony there. From time to time there were outbreaks of violence in the state and homes and properties of innocent Muslims were ransacked and destroyed in many places.

At this point of time, food scarcity was recorded in many places. In particular, people of Faridpur, Comilla and Dhaka districts were facing a calamity due to acute shortage of foodgrain. The government now introduced the 'cordon' system. This meant that there was to be no movement of food from one district to another. People of Dhaka and Faridpur used to work as day labourers to harvest rice in the fields of Khulna and Barisal. They would help reap the harvest and take it to homes there. In return they would get a share of the harvest. They were called 'dawals'. Thousands of them would come in boats. When they went back they would take their share of rice in their boats to their homes. This was how the dawals of Comilla would go to Sylhet, for instance. Almost all of them were very poor and day labourers. They would leave their homes for two months at a stretch. When leaving they would take a loan from moneylenders so that they could leave behind money for their families' daily expenses. On their return they would repay the loans. They would also have to pay a share to the people whose boats they had used. When dawals went to harvest paddy no one obstructed them since they were indispensable. This was because all the paddy strains ripen at about the same time and have to be harvested quickly. It is difficult to get so many hands to harvest the paddy locally then. This system had been in place for centuries.

Thousands and thousands of people in Faridpur, Dhaka and Comilla were dependent on this system. When the dawals left for harvesting that year the government did not obstruct them. But when they had finished their work within two months and had loaded their boats with their share of the harvest to feed their hungry families and to pay off their debts, ready to go back to those who were waiting eagerly for their husbands, brothers and fathers to return, their paths were obstructed. They were told, 'You can't take the rice back with you according to the government's directive.' They were informed that they would have to surrender the rice and failure to do so would mean that their boats and goods would be seized. Did they give up their share of the rice so easily? Of course in the end they were allowed to leave after their share had been offloaded. As soon as I came to know about this, I protested strongly against the directive since it was not possible to accept it silently. I organized protest meetings and talked to government officials but to no avail. Meanwhile, I came to know that Khondokar Mushtaq Ahmed had also organized protest meetings against the directive. But all the meetings we organized and resolutions we adopted failed to dissuade the government. And yet these people were day labourers who weren't going to receive wages for the two months of hard work they had put in. Nor would they be able to pay off their debts to the moneylenders, debts they had incurred to meet their expenses for these months! In many cases, as soon as they came back they had to sell their ancestral homes.

I know of hundreds of such instances. On the other hand, many people who had a fleet of boats in Faridpur, Dhaka and Comilla districts and who would transport rice from surplus districts to their own had to shut down their carrying business while those who did the actual work of sailing the boats became unemployed. Many of them ended up as rickshaw pullers or coolies subsequently to make ends meet. When we all got intensely involved in the movement to oppose the government ban on transporting food grain, the government announced that it no longer had any objection to labourers moving from one district to another to harvest rice. But they would not be able to move the paddy across district lines. They would have to deposit the rice they had received for their work in the nearest government godown. In exchange government officials employed there would issue them a receipt. The dawals would then return to their own districts and submit these receipts to the godown closest to their homes. They would then get an equivalent amount of rice from that godown. The government was well aware that if dawals were not allowed to move across district lines, in Khulna alone half the paddy would never get harvested. It issued its revised ruling on the subject either in late 1948 or in early 1949. Unfortunately, half the dawals who followed the government directive were not given their due share when they returned to their own districts. They had been issued no valid printed receipts and had to accept handwritten ones when they deposited the paddy they had helped harvest. When they showed this receipt to the godowns in their districts they were turned back by those in charge of the godown and were even shouted at! Only when they bribed local officials did they receive some rice as their share. The net result was that the dawals eventually lost everything they had.

An unfortunate incident occurred around this time in Khulna. One night, officials intercepted nearly 200 boats loaded with rice owned by dawals of Faridpur district. Under cover of darkness, the dawals ignored the government officials' orders. Shouting 'God is great' and 'Pakistan Zindabad' they sailed the boats loaded with rice. After they had travelled for ten to fifteen miles, a police team in a launch caught up with them and attempted to prevent them from going any further. The dawals tried to thwart the police but failed. Finally, the police resorted to firing. The dawals were forced to get down in a field by a river and offload their rice. Then they were chased away. However, the confiscated rice did not end up in government godowns because the next day it was swept away by heavy showers. As soon as I heard of this, I went to Khulna where many boats that had been seized along with their cargo of rice had not yet left the district. I led a procession of the dawals whose boats had been seized and taken to the district magistrate's house. The district magistrate happened to be Professor Munier Chowdhury's father, Mr Abdul Halim Chowdhury. He lent me his ear but said he was helpless as government orders had to be followed. But he promised to telegram the higher-ups to inform them about the situation. I returned to Faridpur with the dawals and sent a telegram to the government on my own. I asked the dawals not to venture out again to harvest paddy till they had settled the issue with the government. Mr Nazimuddin was then the highest-ranking government official, having stepped into Jinnah's shoes to become Governor General after the latter had died in September 1948.

This time another arbitrary measure was imposed, making everyone suffer as in a plague. The government opened what it called the 'Jinnah fund'. The government let it be known that everyone should contribute to it according to his or her capacity. I don't know of anyone who hesitated to contribute to the fund. Those who had money were happy to make donations to it. Many poor people also gave what they could. But some overzealous government officials tried to force others to donate money to make the government happy. Some SDOs acted on the assumption that the more money they could make people give to the fund the faster they would be promoted!

The situation in our subdivision was dismal. Mr Nazimuddin was scheduled to visit Gopalganj. The subdivisional magistrate organized a meeting to form a reception committee. It was decided there that since 600,000 people lived in Gopalganj, if all of them paid a rupee each, it should be possible to raise 600,000 rupees for the event. Those who had guns would have to pay an additional amount. Businessmen of course would have to pay much more. People owning big boats would also have to contribute a hefty sum. He gave a ruling binding on all union board presidents that those who failed to pay would be punished. Everywhere people were being coerced. Local watchmen were employed for the purpose. They seized cows, cooking utensils, indeed anything of any value. It all amounted to a reign of terror. Mr Wahiduzzaman had invited Mr Nazimuddin to our subdivision. He was still in the Muslim League then. Others who had worked for the Gopalganj Muslim League till 1947, however, had been bypassed and an ad hoc committee had been formed for the time being. This committee worked closely with the SDO.

~

I returned from Khulna to Gopalganj at this time. The steamer did not land at Gopalganj port in those days and one had to get down at a small station called Haridaspur that was two miles away from Gopalganj and then take a boat to reach town. When I got on a boat the boatman recognized me. As soon as the boat had started to move he told me, 'I have to tell you this: I am in dire straits. There are five of us in our family and we have thus been ordered to pay five rupees. After working the whole day we manage to earn only two rupees and sometimes even less; how then can we pay five rupees? Yesterday the local watchman seized a lead vessel I had inherited from my father since I couldn't pay him the money.' As he told me about his plight, tears formed in his eyes. He told me his story in detail. He was quite intelligent and lived close to the town. He said, 'You used to tell us to work for Pakistan. Is this the Pakistan you wanted?' All I could say was that it wasn't Pakistan's fault that such things were happening.

Soon after I reached my home in Gopalganj people from all walks of life came to me with their woes. They had the same story to tell. In the evening some businessmen showed up as well as some veteran Muslim League partymen. I sent out word to my former party colleagues that I would like to meet them the next morning. Almost all of them showed up. I said, 'We will have to prevent them from forcing everyone to pay. This is not a tax imposed by the government and we don't have to pay it. What law says that people have to contribute to the fund they have set up?' Before I had arrived in Gopalganj they had already raised 300,000 rupees. I don't know the exact figure. The SDO and the ad hoc committee had decided that the money would be spent mainly to organize the reception. Whatever was left would be given to Mr Nazimuddin for the Jinnah fund in a ceremony. If possible, some money would be set aside for the big mosque they were building in the town at that time.

We decided that this leftover money would not be allowed to leave Gopalganj. Whatever money remained after the expenses incurred on Mr Nazimuddin's reception would have to be spent on the Gopalganj mosque and on building a college for the town. We would oppose any attempt to send the fund elsewhere. The news spread that the reception ceremony would be a troubled one. This put a stop to the fund collection. My return to Gopalganj seemed to have strengthened the morale of the people protesting against the fund-raising. The people of Gopalganj remembered the part I had played in the creation of Pakistan. They were very fond of me. I had a group of young volunteers with me who would willingly leap into fire if I desired them to do so.

Two days before Nazimuddin's arrival the SDO conferred with the district magistrate to find out if I could be arrested. The district magistrate, Mr Golam Kabir, advised him not to be foolhardy and said he would come a day before the event to talk to me. Mr Kabir was very intelligent and sensible and knew me from my Calcutta days. He used to address me with the familiar 'tumi' in Bengali and I also used an honorific in Bengali, Bhai, to show my respect to him.

Mr Kabir sent for me as soon as he came to Gopalganj. When I went to meet him I found the district police superintendent was with him. I presented before him my views on the situation and a list of our demands. He said, 'The Governor General is not a politician but the head of the state; he does not belong to any political organization. He is also a guest; will it be right to offend him when he is here?' I told him, 'Whoever gave you the idea that we have any such intentions? Everyone is ready to receive him. All we would like you to do is tell him to order an investigation so that the people responsible for coercing everyone to contribute to the fund are punished. Second, we will give him all the money that has been collected and make no claims to it but he should donate this money so that we can build a college here.' Mr Kabir said, 'Promise me there won't be any trouble.' I said, 'Are you crazy? Don't I know that he is not the prime minister but the Governor General? There won't be any trouble; at least, we won't be creating any trouble. Please tell him about our demands and inform us about the outcome of your talks with him so that we know by ten in the morning what his responses are and can join the others in giving him a proper reception.'

The next day Mr Nazimuddin's official vessel reached Gopalganj at 11 a.m. I was summoned to the vessel. Mr Nazimuddin was in the room next to where I was asked to sit. Mr Kabir told me on his behalf that he found our demands just and that he would certainly consider them carefully. He was aware that Gopalganj didn't have a college and needed one.

In the meantime something else happened. The people of the town thought I had been arrested since a police official in uniform had escorted me to the meeting in the boat. Our workers broke through the police cordon and began moving towards the boat chanting slogans. The police responded by assaulting them with their batons. The whole area was in turmoil. The district magistrate asked me to go to that spot. I went there and appeased the people: 'I haven't been arrested. Mr Nazimuddin has said that he is going to examine the demands I have submitted carefully.' I had also told Mr Kabir to discuss the plight of the dawals with Mr Nazimuddin. This issue had been troubling Mr Kabir himself since he knew that a famine was imminent in Faridpur because of what had happened to them.

The meeting that took place was a huge one. Everyone showed up to welcome the Governor General. He inaugurated the mosque by ceremoniously opening its gate. I don't know whether Mr Nazimuddin had examined all the issues involved, but it was clear when he left that he had not taken away the money that had remained unused. In fact, he had donated the money for the construction of a college. Because the money had been raised for the Jinnah fund the college was named after Muhammad Ali Jinnah. The college still exists and is indeed doing very well to this day.

~

I can't remember the exact date now, but it must have been sometime in 1948 that Mr Suhrawardy came to Dhaka and addressed a gathering of students at Salimullah Muslim Hall. Mymensingh's Syed Nazrul Islam was vice-president of the Hall union at that time (he is now vice-president of the East Pakistan Awami League but because I am now in jail he is the acting president of the organization). Mr Suhrawardy spoke so eloquently that even those who used to oppose him became his supporters. On the other hand, ministers were unable to go near the halls or the university at this time.

When Mr Suhrawardy came to Dhaka next a number of meetings were arranged to enable him to speak on the subject of communal harmony. The first of these meetings was organized in Tangail. The steamer would touch Manikganj en route to the meeting and he was to address another meeting on his way. Mr Shamsul Huq had made all the arrangements for these meetings. Mr Suhrawardy would usually get down from the plane and go to Mrs Anwara Khatun's residence. She was an MLA then. He had his lunch there on this occasion. The steamer was to leave from Badamtali port in the evening. Maulana Bhasani and I were to accompany him. We left for the steamer with him. But though the steamer was supposed to leave at six o'clock it didn't. On inquiry, we learned that the government had ordered it not to depart. We stayed put in the port for nearly two hours. Kader Sardar and Mr Kamruddin were also present. At 8 p.m. the district magistrate and DIG [deputy inspector-general] of police handed over a piece of paper to him: it contained a government order forbidding him to leave Dhaka for the meetings. But it mentioned that the government had no objections to his returning to Calcutta or staying anywhere in Dhaka.

Mr Suhrawardy arrived at the port and I unloaded his luggage from the steamer. Where would he stay now? Who would put him up? There were no hotels available. Mrs Anwara Khatun had the courage to host him but her house was too small to accommodate him. This was also the case with Ataur Rahman and Kamruddin. Kamruddin met Captain Shahjahan and his wife Begum Noorjahan since they had a beautiful house and enough space. She (a professor now) said, 'It is my good fortune that I can have him as my guest. I respect him as I would my father. Please bring him to our house; he can stay with us.' If she had not done us this favour that day we would have ended up being very embarrassed. It had seemed for a while that the man who had been really responsible for the birth of Pakistan had no place to stay in the country! For the two days Mr Suhrawardy stayed in her house, Mrs Noorjahan saw to it that he was completely happy. Indeed, words cannot describe the kind of care she took of him. Possibly even a daughter wouldn't be able to show as much devotion for her father. Captain Shahjahan also worked very hard to keep him happy.

Two days later I took Mr Suhrawardy to Narayanganj where he boarded a ship. I wanted to accompany him part of the way but he wouldn't agree.

He said, 'There is no need for you to come along. There are other people with me and I will be fine.' I saw to it that his bed was properly made and that everything was just right for him. When I bade him goodbye, he said, 'You are going to be punished by them. These people have become crazy. If they continue to rule in this heavy-handed manner nobody knows what might happen.' I said, 'Sir, don't worry. God has given me the strength to stand up against injustice and oppression. And you have taught me to deal with such things too.'

We didn't have the strength to protest against such repressive measures. Nor were we ready to do so. The students did protest a bit. But there was no one capable of leading us. If we had plunged headlong into a protest movement we would surely have found support among the people since they loved Mr Suhrawardy. When a few of us wanted to launch a movement some of the senior leaders based in old Dhaka prohibited us from doing anything. Most of us had only just arrived in Dhaka and had not yet made a name for ourselves in the city. Maulana Bhasani left with Mr Suhrawardy but he had attended our meetings too. If Mr Shamsul Huq had been with us that day I have no doubt that we would have been able to launch our protest movement successfully.

~

On 11 September 1948 when Muhammad Ali Jinnah died, Khawaja Nazimuddin had replaced him as Governor General and Mr Nurul Amin had become the prime minister of East Bengal. At this point a few MLAs had requested Mr Suhrawardy to move to Dhaka to become the prime minister of East Bengal. He, however, did not agree to do so. In the Legislative Assembly a new law was passed expelling him from it.

I turned my attention now to the organizational matters of the East Pakistan Muslim Students' League. We began to build our units in every school and college. Soon we were able to create effective organizations at the district level. The government student organization, on the other hand, existed only on paper. The Students' League took up the protest against the government's unfair decisions and began to criticize it. Since Pakistan had no opposition parties the government had left the path of democracy and opted for dictatorship. The prime minister of the country, Mr Liaquat Ali Khan, became the most powerful person in the country. He could not stand any criticism at all.

There were a few left-leaning students who disliked the government. But the kind of ideas they tried to propagate offended the general students and the public. I used to tell them, 'While ordinary people still like to walk you all tend to have your heads in the clouds and fly. They do not understand your language and will not accompany you in your flights. You should only give the public as much food for thought as they can digest.' This made these communists speak out against me but they failed to attract the student world in any way.

At about this time Rajshahi Government College students were beaten up. Most of them were members of the Students' League. Twenty-one students were expelled from the college and the government asked them to leave Rajshahi district. In many other districts too students were being tortured and arrested. In January or February 1949 students were arrested in Dinajpur as well. Dabirul Islam was beaten up mercilessly inside the jail. In fact, so brutal was the punishment he received that it would affect his health for the rest of his life. Students now made me the convener of a committee that was to organize a 'Resistance Day Against Repression'. They even chose a date for this event. It was eventually observed in district after district throughout East Pakistan. On that day demands were made to free all students and political prisoners and to withdraw all punitive measures undertaken against students.

This was the first time that a movement had been launched asking for all political prisoners to be released and protesting against repression. Nobody had dared launch such a movement before. In those days whenever we wanted to hold a meeting or go out in a procession some goons would be hired to beat us up and break up the meeting. On the 'Resistance Day Against Repression' they were imported into the university campus. When I heard about this I decided to hold the meeting in the evening. I told everyone present that we would have to resist any attempt to use the goons to attack us.

We were supposed to hold the meeting in the Amtala *math* that had become famous as a site for political meetings. When the authorities prevented us from holding our meeting we held it in the field that faced the university. I placed a special group of loyal volunteers near the university gate to obstruct the goons from attacking us and thwarting our meeting. The idea was to teach them a lesson through a three-pronged attack so that they would refrain in the future from coming to Ramna to carry out such acts of disruption. What was surprising was that the government party would openly patronize such action and assist the thugs when they launched their attacks. Sometimes when the students of Jagannath College, Mitford Medical School brought out processions headed for the university they would be ambushed and beaten up by these goons. The Muslim League leaders were thereby creating an atmosphere of terror so that nobody would dare criticize the government. They seemed incapable of understanding that such tactics would one day boomerang on them. They were assuming that hired goons could stifle people's demands. That such measures have never succeeded and would not succeed in this case did not seem to have occurred to them.

Around this time Mr Rafiqul Hussein of Krishnanagar, in Brahmanbaria subdivision's Nabinagar thana, organized a meeting in his locality. The idea was to raise funds so that Krishnanagar High School could formally begin operations. Mr N.M. Khan, of the Pakistan Civil Service, was invited as the chief guest with a view to raising funds. He was then director general of the food department. He agreed to attend the event. The famous singers Abbasuddin Ahmed, Shohrab Hussein and Bedaruddin Ahmed were supposed to perform on this occasion. I was also invited. Mr N.M. Khan had become very popular in this part of the country for the good work he had done here before independence as the SDO. When I reached the place I saw that thousands of people had turned up hoping to listen to Mr Khan and Mr Abbasuddin. The latter was immensely popular in villages all over Bengal. People used to go crazy when they heard him singing. His songs were dear to their hearts. He was very much part of the land. It was unfortunate that a man of his stature had to work in the publicity department of the government.

When the meeting began I gave a speech at the invitation of Mr Rafiqul Hussein. Addressing Mr Khan in my speech I said, 'You know the situation that we are living in now. You have worked in this land for a long time and are director general of the food department at the moment. Consider the condition of the dawals at this time. How will they survive! The government won't be able to feed them. If it is unable to help them why is it depriving them of food?' I went on to highlight the difficulties the dawals were facing. I appealed to the public to help the school.

Mr Khan assured the meeting that he would do his utmost to help. After he left in the evening the musical show began. Mr Abbasuddin, Mr Shohrab Hussein and Mr Bedaruddin sang on the occasion. The singing continued till late at night. Mr Abbasuddin as well as the rest of us stayed the night at Mr Rafiqul Hussein's house. Mr Hussein's brothers were accomplished singers. Our companions Hasnat and Barkat were good singers too and I was as fond of them as I was of my younger brother. They had also spent time in jail with me. The next day we left by boat for Ashuganj rail station. On the way our companions kept up their singing. I would consider a part of my life incomplete if I hadn't had the occasion that day to hear

Mr Abbasuddin sing bhatiali songs as we crossed the river. When he was singing these songs as we crossed the river that day, it seemed to me that the gently lapping waves were entranced by his singing. His disciples Shohrab Hussein and Bedaruddin have managed to keep his style of singing alive to an extent. I had become Mr Abbasuddin's devotee by this time. He told me at one point, 'Mujib, there is a conspiracy afoot against the Bengali language. If Bengali isn't made a state language, Bengal's culture and civilization will be under threat. The songs that you have appreciated so much today will lose all their charm and melody. Whatever happens, Bengali must be made the state language.' I pledged to him that I would try to make it our state language and have done my best to achieve this goal.

We reached Dhaka by night. When we reached 150 Mughaltuli we heard that the lower-class employees of the university were on strike and that students had joined them to show solidarity with their cause. I was aware that staff who were at the bottom of the pay scale had been petitioning for some time for their demands to be considered by the authorities. They had met me to acquaint me with their demands. Before the creation of Pakistan the University of Dhaka was a residential university. Now it was the only university in the province. The number of students had increased substantially. But the numbers of employees hadn't increased correspondingly. They had to work throughout the day. Previously, they had been provided with accommodation but now their flats were being taken away from them since the new capital of the province was short of residential space for government employees. They used to get uniforms at one time but after Pakistan this benefit too was withdrawn. On the other hand, the price of rice and other essentials had risen. There was no job security. They would be hired and fired according to the whims of their employers.

I told them to first get organized and then submit their list of demands. Otherwise, I pointed out, the authorities would not bother to listen to them at all. They formed a union then and one of the students became its president. That was all that I knew about their situation. I was actually travelling from district to district then. Thus when I found out in Dhaka that they had gone on strike it was easy for me to see that they had taken the measure because the people in power had decided to ignore their demands. Nevertheless, they shouldn't have gone on strike so quickly since they didn't have the funds to sustain a prolonged strike. Their organization had been set up only a short while back. But there was no way out now since they had already gone on strike. When I went to the university in the morning I found out that the students were on strike too to show their support for the staff. The workers had started to demonstrate and the students had joined their procession. I took some student leaders along with me to the vice chancellor and communicated to him the demand of the employees. The university authorities had by this time made up their mind to dismiss the striking workers. In the evening I met him again but this time I brought along with me the vice-presidents of Fazlul Huq Hall and Salimullah Muslim Hall. I told him, 'Please assure us that you will do your best to meet their demands by representing their case to the people in power and also seeing to it that no one will be sacked and no punitive measures will be taken against the striking workers.' The negotiations went on for a long time. In the end he agreed to our request. He told us, 'If you withdraw the strike tomorrow and resume work nobody will be punished and I will talk to the people in charge and try to persuade them to accept your legitimate demands.'

We returned to the university, trusting him to keep his word. It was 3 p.m. We negotiated with their representatives and then announced that the students' strike would be withdrawn from the next day. This was because most of the workers had decided to end the strike after receiving the Vice Chancellor's assurance. Since many of the employees lived quite far away I told everyone to spread the news of our decision to withdraw the strike everywhere as effectively as was possible.

The next day students went back to their classes and many employees resumed work. Those who came to join by 12 noon were allowed to do so but those who came after this time were turned away. Many employees who commuted to work from Narayanganj fell in this latter category. In all about 50 per cent of the employees who commuted to work from far-off places failed to come by the deadline, for they had come to know about the withdrawal of the strike rather late. These people told my colleagues and me about their plight. They began to gather in one place. We were now in a difficult position since it was our assurance that had made them withdraw the strike and join work. We asked them to wait and went to meet the Vice Chancellor at his residence once again. We asked him, 'What happened?' He said, 'When I asked them to join today I had made it clear that they should join by 11 a.m. and this meant that they would have to come no later than that time.' We tried to convince him that he should be a little more flexible but he refused to relent, having been pressurized by the government not to budge an inch. We said, 'Are you going to take such drastic action just because of an hour or two?' But nothing we said had any effect. We then pointed out, 'You should have specified that you wanted everyone to join by 11 a.m. All you had said was that people would have to join by today.' At this point he said that he didn't want to talk to us any more. We told him then that we would continue our strike.

Students and employees held a joint meeting in the university. In it I told those present what had happened in our discussion with the Vice Chancellor. I also declared that we would go on strike again from the next day and that employees and students would continue their strike till their legitimate demands were met. We brought out a procession and decided to continue to demonstrate in this manner once more the next day at 11 a.m. I had to take an active part in the procession then. I was finding it difficult to believe that an educationist and top-ranking officer of the university would allow himself to be used by the government into making such a double-edged statement.

Shortly after we had finished our meeting that night the university administration announced that the university would be closed sine die. Everybody was asked to vacate the halls in twenty-four hours. It was also announced that the employees who had demonstrated would be fired. I was in Salimullah Hall then. We organized a meeting immediately. We decided that we wouldn't leave the halls and made an announcement to that effect. The same decision was taken for Fazlul Huq Hall and a similar announcement made. A committee was formed to raise funds for the employees who had gone on strike. We would go to the streets to raise money to help them. This was because most of the employees were paid only between 20 and 30 rupees. How would they look after their families now? We chose a few of them to raise funds for the affected families.

By the next day half the student population had left the halls of residence. The day after more students left for their homes. Three days later there were only 30 to 35 of us left in Salimullah Muslim Hall and 20 to 25 in Fazlul Haq Hall. The police had encircled the halls in the meantime. We decided to meet in a room in our hall. We realized that we wouldn't be able to keep the police away any more. We decided unanimously to leave the halls and to raise more money to help the affected employees since without funds they would not be able to continue their strike. Four days later we were forced to leave the halls. We now worked on collecting funds to help the striking employees. Ten to fifteen days later we found out that one by one employees were signing bonds and rejoining work. Within a month most of them had resumed work. The strike was effectively over.

Around this time some of my colleagues and I went to Dinajpur. This was because some students had been jailed and Dabirul Islam had been beaten up inside the Dinajpur jail. Section 144 had been imposed in the town and we weren't able to hold meetings outside. We decided to hold an indoor meeting. We had put up in a hostel. Abdur Rahman Chowdhury was the secretary of the Student League then. On the train from Dinajpur to Dhaka we read in a newspaper that 27 of us students had been expelled from the university. Among the students who had been expelled for four years were Dabirul Islam, Oli Ahad, Mollah Jalaluddin (now an advocate) and Abdul Hamid Chowdhury. Others were expelled for different time periods. But except for the four students listed above the others would be allowed to resume their studies if they signed a bond and if they paid a fine. Among the girl students only Lulu Bilkis Banu was expelled. She was the convener of the women's section of the Students' League.

At the end of the month then most employees had gone back to work. The university had been shut down. The students had left. The administration had taken advantage of the situation and had managed to break the resolve of the low-ranking employees.

Now older League workers and leaders began to discuss the future: what could be done? Would it be a good idea to form a new party? I let my views be known. As far as I was concerned, it wasn't possible to do politics by relying entirely on a student organization. In addition to the official Muslim League, the Congress had an organization active in our country at this time. But except for a handful of representatives in the Constituent Assembly and the East Bengal Legislative Assembly they didn't make their presence felt. They were all Hindus and if they said anything much they would be promptly labelled 'traitors'. Consequently, they had become demoralized. They were also afraid of being caught in communal riots. The Muslim community was always suspicious about anything to do with the Congress. It didn't even have one Muslim member. On the other hand, all the leading Muslim League leaders of the past had become government supporters. They had been rewarded with ministries or been made parliamentary secretaries or given other such posts. We didn't have anybody famous to turn to.

Maulana Abdul Hamid Khan Bhasani had just returned from Assam at this time. The people of East Bengal didn't know much about him. Only people in Mymensingh, Pabna and Rangpur were aware of his activities. This was because he had been in Assam till then. However, educated people were aware of what he had done. Even though he was a leader of the Muslim community he had successfully resisted the 'Expel Bengalis' movement in Assam and had even gone to jail for it. The people of Tangail were very fond of him. Mr Shamsul Huq was genuinely fond of him since he was from this area. It was decided that he would talk to the Maulana. He had attended meetings with senior Muslim League leaders in the past. He was in Assam for a visit at this time. It was decided that as soon as he came back workers would hold a meeting and form a new political organization. In the Frontier Province, Pir Manki Sharif had formed an organization called the Awami Muslim League. He became the president and Khan Ghulam Muhammad Khan Lundkhar the general secretary of the Awami Muslim League. The chief minister of the province, Khan Abdul Quayyum Khan, had distanced veteran Muslim League leaders from the party and was ruling with an iron hand. He hadn't hesitated to put some Muslim League workers behind bars. He had now become the 'Frontier Leopard'! The movement for Pakistan had not been able to attract 'Frontier Gandhi' Khan Abdul Ghaffar Khan and Doctor Khan Saheb. As a result a Congress government had been established in the province. Only Pir Manki Sharif had been able to rally the Muslim League to oppose the 'red shirts'. And yet the Muslim League had discarded him later!

~

It must have been either in late March 1949 or in early April that the election in Tangail was announced. We decided to request Mr Shamsul Huq to contest the election against the Muslim League candidate. He agreed to our request, but where was the money going to come from? He didn't have any money and neither did we. But nothing was going to deter us. He headed for Tangail and we did whatever we could to raise funds for him. However, we succeeded only in collecting a few hundred rupees. The students and the workers managed to raise this amount by selling their pens and watches.

Meanwhile, the student leaders who had led the movement had been expelled from the university. This needed to be opposed. The authorities announced that the university would reopen on 17 April. Students' League workers and other students and workers who were involved in the movement met at 150 Mughaltuli and decided that they would observe 17 April as 'Protest Day'. They would keep protesting till the authorities withdrew the punitive measures taken. A few of our workers headed for Tangail. Most of them were veteran Muslim League workers. The Muslim League ministers and MLAs too had started to assemble in Tangail, armed with their funds and resources such as motor cars. The Muslim League candidate was the famous zamindar of Tangail, Khurram Khan Panni. Most voters were his tenants and thus obligated to him. In addition he could make use of the government's funds and resources.

Mr Huq, our candidate, on the other hand, was a poor but selfless man and a worker who was ready to give his all for the people. Moreover, he was idealistic and efficient. At that time no political organization was backing us. Our workers would campaign on foot and often go without food. Students in Dhaka were still involved in the strike. It was decided that all of us would head for Tangail. I would reach there on 19 April.

On 16 April we found out that the Students' League convener Naimuddin Ahmed; the vice-president of the Salimullah Hall Student League, Abdur Rahman Chowdhury (now an advocate); Dewan Mahbub Ali (also an advocate now); and many others had secretly signed a bond with the university. Many who weren't Students' League members but self-proclaimed progressive students had also signed the bond. Indeed, out of twenty-seven students, almost half had put their signature to it. This was because they had been informed that if they had failed to sign it by the 17th they would be expelled from the university.

When the news spread that the convener of the Students' League as well as the Salimullah Hall vice-president had signed the bond students got disheartened. I gathered as many of them as I could and tried to catch hold of Naimuddin. But it was difficult to track him down and he managed to elude us. Finally, we managed to get hold of him one evening in the house where he used to lodge then. He confessed that he had signed the bond and said, 'What else could I do? I had no other option. I have all sorts of problems.' I lost my temper with him. When I got back I summoned those Students' League workers still with us to a meeting that night. Many of them turned up. We decided at the meeting to expel students who had signed the bonds. We decided that we would print pamphlets at night and then distribute them in the university. Kazi Golam Mahbub was made our joint convener. He had been working for us selflessly all along.

In those days law classes were held in the morning. The students of the law department went on strike and picketing began at 10 a.m. Student workers decided to lie down in front of the university gate. Only one girl student took an active part in the strike. Her name is Nadira Begum. She is Professor Munier Chowdhury's sister. She sat down in front of the gate with the male students. Only 10 to 15 students were supporters of the All East Pakistan Student League. They trampled all over the prostrate students. One of them began abusing Nadira in filthy language. The general students got upset at their actions. I saw what was going on and requested everyone to stay away from trouble. I told them, 'We have no objections if you want to attend classes or go in. But please don't trample over the protesting students. And please don't use obscene language.'

They ignored us and kept going in and coming out of the gate, walking over the striking students. I couldn't do anything about the situation. By now many students had gathered on the spot. They now attacked these disorderly students who fled upstairs and took refuge wherever they could. I stood in front of the gate and tried to prevent the enraged students from taking any further action. In any case, the strike was observed successfully. A meeting was held and the strike ended.

Dr Osman Ghani was the provost of Salimullah Hall then. At the meeting of the executive committee he requested that the expulsion order against us should be withdrawn. Principal Ibrahim Khan supported him. However, the other members of the committee didn't agree to his proposal.

The strike was held on the 18th as well. It was decided that there would be another strike the next day. It seemed to me that students on the whole were losing interest in the protest movement. On the afternoon of the 18th I concluded that there was no point in going ahead with the strike. We therefore went out in a procession that evening to the Vice Chancellor's house. We told him, 'We take our positions here and won't budge from this place till the expulsion orders are withdrawn.' We were going to have a hundred students sit down in front of the Vice Chancellor's residence through the day and night. We then took over the rooms in the ground floor of the Vice Chancellor's residence. We began to occupy these rooms turn by turn. This is how the 18th ended. However, I was the only one who stayed there all the time. This is because I came to know that the Vice Chancellor was planning to call the police at any moment.

At 3 p.m. on the 19th a big contingent of police force arrived led by a district magistrate and an SP. I immediately asked the others to organize a meeting where they could elect a committee to carry on the movement. I felt that I should be ready to go to jail like the rest.

The district magistrate gave us five minutes to leave the spot. I told eight of the students that they should stay put but asked the others to leave. The eight students and I did not budge from our positions. The student representatives felt that the movement had slackened and believed that my being arrested and sent to jail would give the movement a boost. I accepted their line of reasoning.

When the five-minute deadline elapsed, the district magistrate ordered the police to arrest us. Tajuddin Ahmed (now general secretary of the Awami League) was among those hauled up although he had been told not to court arrest. He now did a smart thing by pretending he was a press reporter. He took out a slip of paper and started noting down the names of the students who had been arrested. This ruse worked and he was let off. I winked at him. They took us in a van and brought us to the jail.

From the next day our protest movement gained momentum. A complete general strike was observed. Even those I had dissuaded from courting arrest got themselves arrested in the next three days. Among them were Khaleque Nawaz Khan, Kazi Golam Mahbub, Aziz Ahmed, Oli Ahad, Abul Hasnat, Abul Barkat, K.G. Mustafa and Bahauddin Chowdhury. They were all front-ranking workers of our party. It was obvious that we would be unable to continue the movement without them. Classes resumed and we remained in jail. Thirty to thirty-five of us had been arrested and were being held in Dhaka jail. We were in Ward 5, which was on the second floor. Some of us had been given the status of upper-class prisoners but others had been denied this privilege and had a more miserable time. For example, the food supplied to the latter group was not wholesome. Nevertheless, we decided that we would stick together and share whatever food was given to us.

Those of us in jail belonged to two groups. Three were radicals and were called 'communists' by the rest. None of the three belonged to the Students' League. The rest of us did. We spent our time playing games. Barkat shared a room with me. At night he used to sing. He was good at it. We had some books with us and the jail library gave us access to some more. Everyone would spend some time studying. Since all of us were still students we were also quite naughty. Aziz Ahmed and I were the oldest of the prisoners. The jail physicians were authorized to recommend special diets for prisoners and were thus besieged with requests by us. Barkat exceeded all of us in naughtiness. Every time a physician came to see us he would cry out, 'My leg hurts. Please prescribe some eggs and milk for me.' Everyone would laugh at his antics. We would also spend hour after hour discussing politics.

Only Bahauddin Chowdhury's parents lived in Dhaka. He was the youngest of us all and I was very fond of him. Bahauddin's mother would send him loads of food. He would share it with everyone. Still, when he went to sleep at night the others would gang up and raid his food or hide it. Bahauddin wouldn't rebuke them but would tell me about his plight. I would shout at the others. But no one would confess to having been party to the raids. The ones who stayed up at night playing cards were supporting them. Barkat was never able to hide anything from me and would tell me the truth.

Khaleque Nawaz had a tough time too. He was very hirsute. Some of the boys would capture bedbugs and release them over his body. He would shout obscenities at them. In the evening we would play volleyball. Mr Amiruddin Khan was the superintendent. He was very fond of us. He would provide us with whatever we needed. He had instructed everyone working in the jail to ensure that we were comfortable.

One day I hurt myself in the arm while playing. I was in great pain and was unable to bear it any more. They were about to send me to Medical College. However, a physician who had just started working in the jail somehow managed to fix my arm and the pain began to subside gradually. In the end I didn't have to go to hospital.

In my village home my parents had become quite upset when they heard about my condition. Renu and my daughter Hasina used to stay with them. Hasina had just learned to walk then. I received a letter from Renu in jail. My father also sent me some cash since Renu knew that I used to smoke and that I might have run out of money. She asked me to let her know if I needed more.

They began to release us in ones and twos from the first week of June. The university had quieted down by now. Mr Shamsul Huq had managed to defeat the Muslim League candidate Khurram Khan Panni and was now an MLA. This was the first time the Muslim League had tasted defeat in Pakistan. They had to pay this price for indulging in coterie politics. We had been very apprehensive about the outcome of the elections when we were in jail. Mr Huq, on the other hand, had been unhappy with us because we had courted arrest instead of going to Tangail to campaign for him. However, when he found out what had really happened he saw that we had had no other option.

How had the Muslim League, a party that had been so enthusiastically supported by people in 1947, tasted defeat so swiftly? It could be put down to coterie politics, rule of tyranny, inefficient administration and absence of sound economic planning. The country continued to be ruled according to British policies. But people had expected the administration to run according to different principles in a free land. They had hoped that after the English left they wouldn't be exploited and would truly get the opportunity to improve their lot. Now their hopes were belied. People were getting frustrated.

Unfortunately, our leaders weren't bothered by the discontent being expressed by the masses. Jinnah's death had seen the birth of cliques and the beginning of the politics of conspiracy. Liaquat Ali Khan had now monopolized power. He couldn't tolerate anyone else. He used to talk about democracy but he never practised it. The people of East Bengal had loved and respected Jinnah. People had his name on their lips everywhere. When Liaquat Ali Khan became the prime minister, educated people expected that at the very least he would rule efficiently and follow the ideals of Jinnah, his guru. One wonders if things would have turned out differently if Mr Jinnah had left behind a constitution. Whatever he did or had to say used to be accepted by the masses. Liaquat Ali Khan failed to wield that kind of power. When Jinnah was the Governor General he made very good use of the power vested in him. Khawaja Saheb was too amiable and weak to be effective. He didn't have much of a personality.

Liaquat Ali didn't approve of the movement that we had launched. The leaders of his party in East Bengal had managed to mislead him about us. The prime minister of East Bengal, Nurul Amin, was too dependent on government officials and their reports. He began to believe the reports they had filed and act brutally on the basis of what he read in them. Even the defeat they suffered in the Tangail by-election didn't open their eyes or that of his cronies. The government party declared, 'No matter what has happened, Shamsul Huq will not be allowed to sit in the Legislative Assembly.' They filed a lawsuit against the election result. When Shamsul Huq came to Dhaka after having triumphed in the election, the people of Dhaka and its student community gave him a grand reception. They brought out a huge procession headed by him and went round Dhaka celebrating his victory. We enjoyed the whole spectacle from jail. On his return to Dhaka, the old Muslim League workers called a meeting of party workers in the city to discuss their future course of action. This meeting was scheduled for 23 June 1949.

~

Most of us had been released from jail. Only Bahauddin Chowdhury and I were left in prison. Bahauddin, though quite young, wasn't being allowed to leave because he was suspected of being a communist. At this time they were imprisoning quite a few people under the Public Security Act on this ground. It is what we otherwise know as imprisonment without trial. Among the people thus imprisoned many had been in jail during British rule too.

Now I found out how painful imprisonment could be. When they locked us in the evening I used to feel horrible. As soon as the sun set every prisoner was confined to his room, the door was locked and the counting of inmates began. I used to like listening to the stories the other prisoners had to tell about their lives and the good times and bad times they had been through. In those days it was illegal for prisoners to smoke or chew tobacco. However, political prisoners were exempted from this law. They could buy cigarettes and tobacco with their own money. Ordinary prisoners would go crazy for a smoke. But the prison authorities would try anyone who was found smoking illegally. Prisoners would be delighted if the guards were generous enough to allow them to smoke a cigarette. I used to give the non-political prisoners a bidi or two to smoke, which they enjoyed furtively.

People were gearing up for a grand meeting of workers. From our jail cells we came to know of the elaborate preparations going on. An office had been set up at 150 Mughaltuli. Shawkat Mia was looking after all the logistical details. Who else in Dhaka was competent enough to take care of food and accommodation matters? Yar Mohammad Khan, a veteran League worker of Dhaka, was assisting him. Mr Khan was resourceful in that he had the finances and the manpower to help. Advocate Ataur Rahman Khan, Ali Amjad Khan, and Anwara Khatun MLA were also helping them. We were anxiously awaiting the outcome of the preparatory work being done in the run-up to the meeting. They had contacted me for my views on the matter. I told them, 'There is no point in pursuing the Muslim League any longer. This party has now become the establishment. We shouldn't become part of the Muslim League even if they invite us to join them. This is because they now operate through coteries. They can no longer be called a party of the people. They have no policy at all.' They also wanted to find out from me whether I would like to continue to work in the student front or join the political organization they were thinking of creating. This was because if we didn't form an organization that could take on the role of the opposition this country would turn into a dictatorship.

Some time back Mr Kamruddin had created an organization called Gana Azadi League but its activities never went beyond the paperwork he did. In the end, the meeting that the others were organizing was scheduled to be held in Mr Humayun's Rose Garden house since no halls or space was available. Prominent political leaders as well as workers attended this meeting. Sher-e-Bangla A.K. Fazlul Huq, Maulana Abdul Hamid Khan Bhasani and Allama Maulana Ragib Ahsan were among those present. MLAs who attended included Khairat Hussein, Mrs Anwara Khatun, Ali Ahmed Khan and Habibur Rahman Chowdhury alias Dhonu Mia. Veteran leaders from different districts also joined the meeting. Everyone agreed on creating a new political organization. It was named East Pakistan Awami Muslim League. Maulana Abdul Hamid Khan Bhasani was made its president, Mr Shamsul Huq its general secretary, and I the joint secretary. I read in the papers that I was identified in reports as a 'security prisoner'. However, it was my view that since Pakistan had been achieved there was no further reason to create a political organization tied to communal ideals. I was for a non-communal party based on a sound manifesto. In the end I decided that the time had not yet come for such an organization. Perhaps those who had devised the East Pakistan Awami Muslim League had created it after thinking over all the issues involved.

A few days after the Awami Muslim League was formed, it was announced that Bahauddin and I would be released. My fellow workers must have heard of this announcement. When we left the jail gate we saw a large crowd led by Maulana Bhasani waiting to receive us. Bahauddin whispered to me, 'Previously nobody would have bothered to greet me with a garland but because I am accompanying you I will get at least one garland as my share.' I laughed and told him, 'If no one has a garland to spare for you I myself will deck you with one.' When we went out I saw that my father was waiting for me too. He had come all the way from our village home to greet me. I bowed down and touched my father's feet and did the same with Maulana Bhasani. At this time shouts of 'Long live Awami Muslim League', 'Long live Students' League' and, for the first time, 'Long live Awami League' could be heard. I greeted Mr Shamsul Huq and said, 'Mr Huq, your victory is the victory of the people.' He embraced me and said, 'Let's start moving.' Later the Awami Muslim League came to be known as the Awami League.

A few people were made vice presidents of the Awami League. They were Mr Ataur Rahman Khan, Abdus Salam Khan, Ali Ahmed Khan and Ali Amjad Khan. There was someone else elected to this position but I can't remember his name now. The first meeting of the working committee of the Awami League was held at 150 Mughaltuli. Sher-e-Bangla A.K. Fazlul Huq joined this meeting. A subcommittee to work on a constitution and another one to work out our future course of action were formed. We began working for the party in earnest. Shawkat Mia put up a huge signboard. He arranged for chairs, tables and everything else that we needed. Before I had been released from jail the Awami League had already held a public meeting at Armanitola Maidan. This was the first time Maulana Bhasani gave a public speech in Dhaka. The people of Dhaka had heard Mr Shamsul Huq before. Huq too was a good orator.

The Muslim League had resorted to strong-arm tactics to prevent the Awami Muslim League from holding this meeting. Numerous people had gathered for the event but just as it was to start some hired goons damaged the microphone and smashed the stage that had been erected for the occasion. They beat up many of our workers too. Badshah Mia, who was notorious for his violent behaviour, used to live in Babu Bazar (Badamtali Ghat) at this time. He had a lot of followers who used to flex their muscles and lord it over everyone else in these parts of Dhaka. He had been told that those who were working for the Awami League and organizing its meetings were out to destroy Pakistan. They should therefore be prevented from organizing any meetings in the area. He was paid 500 rupees to deploy his thugs to prevent us from holding the meeting.

Badshah Mia came from a good family but he had got into bad company and had taken part in the Hindu–Muslim riots. Quite a few lawsuits had been filed against him for his role in them. After he had disrupted the proceedings and left, Mr Arifur Rahman Chowdhury, a long-time resident of the neighbourhood, went to him and said, 'Mr Mia, you've managed to break up our meeting. However, we're going to reorganize and start again. First listen to what we have to say before taking any further action. If you hear us saying anything contrary to Pakistan then go ahead and disrupt it once again'. Mr Chowdhury was very soft-spoken. He had been active in politics since the time of the Khilafat movement of the 1920s. He had sacrificed everything that he had for the nation and was a descendant of Barisal's Ulania family of zamindars.

Badshah Mia and his gang members began to listen to the speeches being delivered from a street corner. After the first few speakers had delivered their speeches Badshah Mia went to the dais and declared, 'I have something to say. You'll have to let me speak.' Who had the guts to oppose him? For all practical purposes the whole of Armanitola Maidan was his fiefdom. Badshah Mia took the microphone and said, 'Muslim League leaders have misled us about you all. They gave me 500 rupees to break up your meeting. I have that money in my pocket now. It will be a sin for me to accept their money. I'm going to tear up the money in front of your eyes.' As he spoke, he took out a bundle of five-rupee notes and threw it at the audience. The notes began to fly all over the meeting. Some of the people present picked up a few of the notes while others tore them up. Badshah Mia went on to say, 'From this day onward I've decided to join the Awami League. I challenge anyone to disrupt an Awami League meeting in Armanitola Maidan from now on.' Members of the audience now garlanded Badshah Mia.

Those present felt heartened by the incident. It was now obvious that the Muslim League had stooped to strong-arm tactics and had even paid thugs to disrupt Awami League proceedings. Indeed, they had no sense of shame and had been pursuing such tactics for a long time now. They continued to do so till we succeeded in forcing them to abandon such policies. They had made up their minds that they wouldn't allow any sort of opposition to their rule. Why didn't they realize that they had lost support among the masses and should now take steps to regain their confidence? Why had they attempted to use repressive measures against the opposition and resorted to force?

I had just been released from jail, and my father had travelled to Dhaka in order to take me to our village home. I told my father, 'Please go home alone for now. I'll join you all in a week's time.' However, I needed money and had to return home soon to get some. Moreover, I had a strong urge to see my ageing mother and my wife and daughter. I sent word to Faridpur's Mr Salam that I would like to address a public meeting in Gopalganj and that he should be present there. A branch of the Awami Muslim League had been formed in Gopalganj. The old Muslim League committee had now become transformed into the Awami Muslim League committee. This was because the Government of Pakistan had facilitated the formation of a subdivisional Muslim League organizing committee consisting of the people who were our opponents.

~

I left for home soon after I had sent the message to Mr Salam asking him to organize a meeting in Gopalganj. This meeting was actually held sometime in mid-July. Mr Salam agreed to take part in it and I came from my village home to speak on the occasion. Thousands of people were thronging to the venue. In the morning all of a sudden the government imposed Section 144. We decided that we would hold the meeting in the mosque compound. If this meant breaking the law, so be it! The mosque was huge and the field in front of it was big enough to hold thousands of people. Mr Salam endorsed our plan. When the meeting began, the SDO entered the mosque premises and imposed Section 144 inside it. We protested. The police entered the mosque and started to beat up people. They used their batons and a scuffle ensued in which people and the police got hurt. Mr Salam and I expressed our unwillingness to leave the meeting. We were arrested. The people decided to encircle the mosque to prevent the police from taking us away. The police officers realized that they wouldn't be able to remove us from the spot and take us to prison or court without resorting to shooting at us.

As far as we could tell, even the police personnel were reluctant to impose Section 144 inside the mosque and had to do so at the insistence of the SDO. When the subdivisional police officer saw that the public had blocked the roads, he realized that things had taken an ugly turn and that a violent outbreak was imminent. So he told Mr Salam and me, 'If there is violence a lot of people will die. You will get bail immediately. Tell the people to disperse and remove the roadblocks. We will take you to court now and arrange for your bail.'

It was evening by then. People had come to attend the meeting from far away. It was drizzling too. It was hard for us to predict how things would turn out in the dark. Many people who had come to the meeting had armed themselves with sticks and oars. The SDOs began to pressurize me in particular to speak to the crowd and placate them. Mr Salam and the Gopalganj subdivisional district leaders conferred with me and we decided that I would give a speech requesting the audience to disperse. I spoke to the crowd, had my say and requested everyone to remove the roadblocks and leave. The crowd had confined the police and us for a few hours already. Now the public decided to let us go. It took three minutes to travel from the mosque to the court. The public escorted us, chanting slogans supporting our movement. We were freed on bail at 8 p.m. The crowd then dispersed. This was the first public meeting organized by the Awami League outside Dhaka. What was notable was that the government had tried to prevent it by imposing Section 144.

The next day the local Awami League held a meeting. Kazi Altaf Hussein was made the convener of the Gopalganj Awami League. The local Muslim League president, Advocate Kazi Mozzaffar Hussein, was made the chair. Something that happened at this time is still etched in my memory. Kazi Altaf Hussein and I had decided that we would meet Maulana Shamsul Huq (now the principal of Lalbagh Madrasa). His house was in our union. People as a whole venerated him. The two of us took a boat to his house at 10 p.m. It was a small boat and it was operated by a single boatman. We were sailing on the river Modhumati and the boatman lived on its banks. On one bank of the river was Faridpur district and on the other Jessore and Khulna. At one point the river was very wide. We knew that river pirates were particularly active here. I had dozed off out of sheer fatigue and had no idea that our boat had reached this area. This was quite typical of those of us who grew up in this land of rivers. My companion, however, was still awake. Another boat soon came close to ours. The people aboard asked our boatman if we had some matches with us. This was a well-known gambit used by river pirates before raiding other boats. Coming still closer to our boat they said, 'Where is this boat going?' Our boatman said, 'To Tungipara,' which is the name of my village. They then asked him, 'Who is on the boat?' The boatman said that I was on it. One of the pirates immediately hit our man with an oar and saying, 'You swine, why didn't you tell us that this is the boat of our honoured Sheikh?' they left quickly.

Our boatman came inside the passenger area of the boat and started weeping. This woke me up. Mr Hussein had hidden his watch and ring by this time. He was a rich businessman and liked to wear expensive things. I said to him, 'What's happening?' He and the boatman told me what had happened. Mr Hussein joked with me, 'The river pirates respect you a lot and we've survived just because your name came up. It was a close shave!' I replied, 'I guess they think I am one of them!' We had a hearty laugh at this. However, the boatman was inconsolable. His back had been badly hurt. We were therefore forced to moor the boat in a nearby village. As a result, we reached our destination at 10 a.m. even though we should have been there by daybreak. We found Maulana Huq in the madrasa. We conferred with him and left for our homes.

I stayed back in our village home for a few days. My father was very upset when he heard that I didn't want to study law at Dhaka University any more. He said, 'If you don't want to continue your studies at the university go to England and get a bar at law degree from there. If necessary, I will sell my land to finance your studies.' I said, 'What is the point of my going to England now? I don't want to run after money by becoming a lawyer.'

I was still angry at the Muslim League leaders. What they were doing with Pakistan was contrary to the Pakistan I had dreamed of. Things needed to change. Ordinary people depended on us and would direct their questions at us. The country had become independent: why wasn't anything being done to alleviate their sufferings? Corruption had increased and there were reports of food scarcity. Political prisoners were being jailed without trial. Muslim League leaders seemed unwilling to accept Bengali as the state language. Already West Pakistan was seeing a lot of industrial activity. East Pakistan, on the other hand, was being ignored. The capital of the country was in Karachi and everything was concentrated in West Pakistan. East Bengal was getting nothing.

I shared my thoughts about the situation and my plans for the future with my father. He said, 'You don't have to do anything for us. But you are married and have a daughter. You need to do something for their sake.' I said, 'You have managed to keep aside some land for us. If I can't manage to do anything I'll come back and do something here. But injustice shouldn't be left unopposed.' My father said nothing more to me.

No sooner had I left my father than my wife, Renu, told me, 'How long do you plan to go on like this?' I realized that she had been listening to our conversation. Renu suffered a lot but she never complained. She used to do her best to save money for me so that I could be financially unencumbered.

I returned to Dhaka. When I left Renu wasn't well at all. I still had my job with the *Ittehad* newspaper. They still paid me but did so irregularly since they were facing financial difficulties. This was because the East Pakistan government would often ban the paper. Besides, newsagents would often not pay them for copies sold. The paper was more popular in East Bengal.

~

When I came back to Dhaka I got involved in organizing the annual meeting of the Students' League as soon as possible. We were going to stage a council meeting for the first time. We all wanted elections immediately and I wanted to be relieved from my position.

The conference was ultimately held in Dhaka's Tajmahal Cinema Hall and I presided over the session. In my speech I said, 'From this day I don't want to be a member of your organization. I don't have the right to be part of a student organization since I am no longer a student. I will therefore say goodbye to you all. But the people of East Bengal will never forget the part played by the Students' League in leading them forward. The sacrifices you have made to uphold the dignity of our mother tongue will always be in the minds of the people. You have also managed to play the role of the opposition. And without an opposition party democracy cannot flourish.' This was the sum of what I said on the occasion. I had written my speech down before speaking but I no longer have a copy of the speech.

The elections were held next. Dabirul Islam, then in jail, became the president and Khaleque Nawaz Khan the general secretary. Nobody had any reservations about Dabirul Islam but not everyone was for Khaleque since he tended to be garrulous and often let his tongue run away with him. In the end I managed to convince everyone that he should be elected. The people present honoured my last request to them by electing him. But I must confess with the benefit of hindsight that the man I had succeeded in getting elected to the position of general secretary ended up doing more harm than good for the organization. This was because Khaleque wasn't able to take firm decisions despite the best intentions. He wasn't able to judge the pros and cons of issues put forward by others perhaps because he lacked the ability to do so. It was only because of the efforts of the Dhaka City Students' League General Secretary Abdul Wadud that the party set-up wasn't irreparably affected during Khaleque's tenure. Later Wadud became General Secretary of the East Pakistan Students' League. Although I had ceased being a member, the leaders of the organization kept in touch with me. I never hesitated to offer them advice when they needed it. They continued to respect me as the founder of the Students' League.

After much hard work, Mr Shamsul Huq managed to produce a draft manifesto and the outline of a constitution for our party. He consulted us repeatedly during the process. We worked through consensus in our working committee meetings to help him formulate the manifesto and constitution. The meetings went on for a few days. Once in a while there were heated exchanges between Mr Huq and Maulana Bhasani on some points. One day Mr Huq became very upset and told the Maulana, 'You won't understand these things. This is because to understand them you need to be a highly educated person and that is precisely what you aren't.' The Maulana got so mad at this that he left the meeting in a huff. I went over to Mr Huq and told him that he shouldn't have said such a thing to the Maulana even if it was true. Mr Huq then went over to the Maulana, apologized to him, and persuaded him to return to our meetings. Mr Huq wasn't the type who nursed a grudge for too long.

Maulana Bhasani was given the responsibility of selecting the members of the working committee. We didn't like the people he had chosen at all. I said to him, 'Where did you get such people and why did you make them members of the working committee? They will leave us at the first opportunity.' The Maulana replied, 'What else could I do? I don't know too many people here. I chose from the names given to me by your students.' I said, 'Just you see what these people do in times of crisis.'

The working committee adopted the draft manifesto. We decided that we would approve it at our council meeting. We would print the draft manifesto and circulate it before the meeting so that people would be ready with their proposals for consideration. We decided to get the draft ready to elicit public opinion on it. In it we proposed that East Pakistan be given complete autonomy. Only defence, foreign affairs and monetary policy would be vested with the centre. We also emphasized that Bengali would have to be made one of the major state languages of Pakistan. We had come up with many other economic and political programmes.

We began to devote ourselves completely to organizational work. Maulana Bhasani, Mr Huq and I went to Jamalpur subdivision of Mymensingh for the first meeting. Mr Haider Ali Mollick, a lawyer of Jamalpur, had set up the Awami League there. Hatem Ali Talukdar, a student leader of the subdivision, had worked hard to make the meeting successful. When we reached the meeting site we saw that there was a huge turnout. Just when the meeting was to begin, ten to fifteen people started to shout. We decided to ignore them and went on with our programme. The leaders of our Jamalpur wing had decided that Shamsul Huq would preside over the meeting and Maulana Bhasani would be the chief speaker.

But no sooner had we begun the meeting than we found out that Section 144 had been imposed. The police came and handed a piece of paper to the Maulana informing him of this. I said, 'I refuse to obey this injunction; I am going to give my speech regardless.' The Maulana stood up and said, 'Section 144 has been imposed. They won't let us hold the meeting but let us pray to God.' He then led the prayer. For half an hour he led the prayer and in the process he managed to say everything that he wanted to say. The police officers and staff had no option except to join him. By the time he had finished the Maulana had managed to insert a full speech into his prayer. The police and Muslim League people present could only watch helplessly!

That night we had been invited to dinner and Maulana Bhasani accompanied us to the venue. But he was clearly upset and wouldn't eat. What had annoyed him was that Mr Huq had been asked to preside over the meeting and not he. This put us in a fix. I tried to point out to him how people would misconstrue his stance. But nothing I said could placate him. He felt that he had been insulted. Mr Huq also spoke out and expressed his dissatisfaction at the Maulana's outburst in public. This was the day I realized that the Maulana wasn't very broad-minded. Nevertheless, I used to respect him since he was ready to sacrifice everything for the cause of the people. To do anything great, one has to be ready to sacrifice and show one's devotion. I believe that those who are not ready to sacrifice are not capable of doing anything worthy. I was able to come to the conclusion that to engage in politics in our country one must be ready to make huge sacrifices to make our people happy. The Muslim League government, I was convinced, would continue to be repressive and would try to stay in power by adopting brutal means. But cowering from its oppression would only make us susceptible to more of the same treatment. The reputation of the Muslim League was being used to hoodwink people for the time being, but this wouldn't last forever. It was still able to cast a spell on people but if we could expose what was going on inside the League and if we could build an effective opposition to it the party would not dare adopt brutal tactics any more!

We returned to Dhaka and called a public meeting at Armanitola Maidan to address the food shortage crisis. People were living under miserable conditions. The Maulana presided over this meeting while Ataur Rahman Khan, Shamsul Huq and I spoke on the occasion. The Muslim League was planning to disrupt proceedings but since Badshah Mia had now joined us they didn't have the courage to do anything much. The result was a meeting that attracted an immense crowd. Nothing like this had happened before here. The people in general and the citizens of Dhaka in particular were now accepting us. Besides all of us speakers had been actively involved in the movement to attain independence for Pakistan. That is why the masses wouldn't be persuaded by any attempts to characterize us as 'enemies of the state'. After all, we had been in the forefront of that movement.

Maulana Bhasani declared, 'When Mr Liaquat Ali Khan comes to Dhaka in October we would like to discuss the food situation and the issue of political prisoners and their release. If he refuses to meet us we'll have another meeting and then go to meet him en masse.' A few days later the newspapers reported that Mr Khan was scheduled to arrive in Dhaka on 11 October. The Maulana asked me to send him a telegram so that he could set up a meeting with a delegation representing our party. The telegram was sent in the Maulana's name. Mr Shamsul Huq was quite busy at this time with his marriage preparations. I therefore had to look after all the activities of the party. However, I would confer with Mr Huq all the time. He had told me that I should direct all the organizational activities of our party. We were so close that there was no possibility of misunderstanding between us.

I could see that Maulana Bhasani was beginning to dislike Mr Huq. He would speak out against him at every opportunity. I would try my best to prevent a confrontation between the two of them. However, the Maulana didn't dare criticize him to his face.

It will be unfair if I fail to record the contributions of Mrs Anwara Khatun who was a member of the Legislative Assembly and who would pitch in with her own money when the need arose. Mr Ataur Rahman Khan was also always available when his services were needed. He had no previous political experience and he wasn't politically astute. Nevertheless, he was well educated, sincere and ready to work for the party. I managed to develop a good rapport with him.

In district after district Mr Suhrawardy's supporters had started to join the Awami League. At about this time Calcutta's daily *Ittehad* was on the verge of closing down. Mr Suhrawardy had left Calcutta for good for Karachi. Mr Manik Mia had also left Calcutta but when he reached Dhaka he had almost nothing with him. He too now lodged with us in Mughaltuli.

Mr Suhrawardy himself had managed to come away with nothing much except a few clothes. The Indian government had confiscated all his possessions. Many will be surprised to hear that he didn't own a house in Calcutta. The house he lived in at 40 Theatre Road was a rented one. He had put up with his brother in Karachi because he didn't even have the means to feed himself!

Of the older leaders of Dhaka, only Mr Kamruddin didn't join our party. Abdul Kader Sardar supported us financially. He had the financial resources as well as a loyal following and was therefore able to help. He had confronted the Khawaja family of Dhaka all his life. He used to help the poor and that is why the masses loved him.

We hadn't been able to form our district committees as yet but there were a few exceptions. In Chittagong Mr M.A. Aziz and Zahur Ahmad Chowdhury and in Jessore the Pir Saheb of Kharki and Habibur Rahman headed the district committees. Mr Mashiur Rahman and Khaleque supported us but not openly. In Faridpur an organizing committee had been formed with the help of Salam Khan. We had decided that we would form branches of our party in every district by the end of 1949. We would head for the districts whenever we managed to get a break. The response was inspiring.

The Nawab that he was, Liaquat Ali Khan did not feel that he had to condescend to reply to the Maulana's telegram. We of course knew that he was coming to Dhaka on 11 October. He had told journalists he had no idea what the Awami League was!

We called another public meeting in Armanitola Maidan on 11 October. We had one microphone and our workers went around on a horse carriage to announce the date and time of the meeting. They were in Nawabpur Road when some hired goons of the Muslim League attacked them, around three or perhaps four in the afternoon. The goons beat up our workers and snatched away the microphone from them. There were three of our workers in the horse carriage at that time. It was as if there was no law and order in the country at all!

Our workers came to our Mughaltuli Awami League office to report what had happened. I was in a meeting with eight or ten of our workers then. Some of them had managed to recognize a few of the assailants since they had worked together in the Muslim League not too long ago. I said, 'This is very unfair. Let's go to them and ask them why they have acted in this manner and demand our microphone back from them. It will be best if they return it. If not, what should we do? We can at least lodge a complaint with the police.' I took along with me the Students' League's Nurul Islam (he worked for the *Ittefaq* later) and Chawk Bazar's Nazir Mia and Abdul Halim (he is now joint secretary of the National Awami Party. At that time he was joint secretary of the City Awami League). We headed for their Victoria Park office since I had found out that they had reassembled there. They used to hang around the first floor of the Cooperative Bank building.

When we reached the building we found them deep in discussion. I knew two of them, Ibrahim and Alauddin, from my Muslim League days. I said, 'Why have you snatched our microphone away? That is very unfair. Give it back to us.' They said, 'We didn't take it and have no idea who is responsible for it.' But we knew for sure that they had been present when the microphone was taken away from Nurul Islam. He said as much to them, pointing out that they had argued with him before snatching away the microphone.

Right then two Awami League workers, Yar Mohammad Khan and Hafizuddin, were passing by in a rickshaw. I hailed Yar Mohammad and appraised him about what was happening. He was a long-time resident of the city. He came from a good family, was well-off, and had many people working for him. He told them, 'Why did you take away the microphone?' One of them replied, 'So what if we have?' At this Yar Mohammad raised his fist and hit the man. Halim landed a blow too. Their colleagues at the Muslim League now joined in and attacked us. Halim sprinted to his neighbourhood to assign people from there to defend us. The owner of Presidency Library, Mr Humayun, came out and took Yar Mohammad to his office. Meanwhile our opponents began to hail abuse on us from outside the office. I took a rickshaw and rushed to the Awami League office where I recruited some ten to twelve of our workers. Our opponents did not notice my exit; otherwise they would have targeted me. Hafizuddin took a rickshaw too and sped to Yar Mohammad's neighbourhood. Instantly, his brother, relatives, friends and neighbours thronged to the spot. Halim too came back with a group of men from his neighbourhood. Those who were abusing Yar Mohammad vanished immediately.

Many members of the Khawaja family had joined hands with our assailants. A government minister had also witnessed the scuffle from the upper floor of a building in the neighbourhood. When I came back to the scene, the police had arrived. Yar Mohammad's men accompanied him and they attacked the local Muslim League office, which was just round the corner in Roy Saheb Bazar. There were some criminal elements in this neighbourhood. They used to beat up people and were basically goons for hire who specialized in beating up students. Whenever they saw our workers or students cross Roy Saheb Bazar in a procession they would swoop upon them and beat them up. Many workers and students had suffered because of their brutal activities. These goons were brought to justice at the mosque by the neighbourhood. At the time in old Dhaka petty justice was served at the neighbourhood mosque, where the accused was brought forward and socially tried. If found guilty, he was beaten up.

From this day forward, no one had the courage to assault or harass us any more in this area.

From this time onward Yar Mohammad began to take an active part in politics too, consolidating our party's strength in Dhaka city. I was able to create a group of youth volunteers by going from neighbourhood to neighbourhood. This was when a group of youths from Shamsabad and Bangshal joined the Awami League. Shamsabad was next to Bangshal and Armanitola Maidan. These young men took over the organization of our meetings in Armanitola Maidan from then onward. The Muslim League was unable to disrupt them, although they did their utmost to prevent us from holding meetings.

On 11 October we held a mammoth meeting at Armanitola Maidan. The entire maidan and the roads around it filled up with people. I spoke after Mr Shamsul Huq had delivered his speech. Maulana Bhasani had already addressed the crowd. Because we knew that the meeting could be disrupted at any time, we had ensured that the Maulana would be the first speaker. The Maulana told me that I should deliver my speech keeping in mind that we would go out in a procession as soon as I had finished speaking. I stood up and delivered my speech and then put this question to the people: 'If a man is murdered, what should the punishment be?' The crowd said in unison, 'Hanging.' I asked the crowd again, 'And what punishment should await those who have killed thousands of people?' The crowd yelled once more, 'Hanging.' I said, 'No! They should be shot dead.' I still remember the exchanges that took place then. I concluded my speech by saying, 'Let's march in a procession so that Mr Liaquat Ali Khan is able to see what exactly it is that the people of East Bengal want.'

The procession then began. The Maulana, Mr Huq and I led it. When we reached Nawabpur rail crossing I noticed that the police had blocked the road and were waiting for us with raised rifles. But we had no intention of breaking the law. In any case we had no desire to battle the police. We took a turn towards the rail station and the crowd followed us. Our plan was to cross the Nazirabazar rail line and enter Nimtali and then turn around at Dhaka Museum and take the road that would bring us back to Armanitola Maidan. But when we reached Nazirabazar we discovered that the police was blocking our way and would not allow us to proceed any further. By now it was time for the evening prayer. The Maulana started to pray on the road. Mr Shamsul Huq joined him immediately. The police began to fire tear gas shells. The crowd retaliated by throwing stones and bricks at them. This went on for about five minutes. The police kept advancing towards us and then assaulted us. A group of our workers lifted the Maulana on their shoulders and took him inside a hotel. A few of our workers were hurt badly and some of them were arrested; Mr Shamsul Huq was among those arrested. Blows landed on me from many directions. I fell into a roadside ditch and almost fainted. Although Kazi Golam Mahbub was also hurt, he managed to remain fully conscious. Some people lifted me up and put me on a rickshaw which took me to Mughaltuli. My feet were bleeding profusely. Some said that I had been hit by a bullet while others declared that I must have been hit by a tear gas canister. Still others felt that I had hurt myself when I had slipped. A physician showed up and dressed my wounds. He gave me a sedative since I was in such intense pain. Chittagong's Fazlul Huq BSc, Abdur Rab and Rasul were among those who sustained head injuries. They had been arrested. My relative Saifuddin Chowdhury aka Surja Mia who belonged to the Faridpur Dattapara zamindar family was with me all this time and took good care of me. I stayed awake till 9 p.m. Around this time the police surrounded our Mughaltuli office where I was living then and asked us to open the doors. Because this was an iron door and could be locked from inside forcing it open was not going to be easy for them. Saifuddin Chowdhury woke Kazi Golam Mahbub, Mofiz and me and said, 'The police have come to arrest you all.'

While I was in the sedative-induced sleep, Maulana Bhasani had sent instructions directing me to evade arrest. My body was sore and I had fever. I could hardly move. Nevertheless, I got up and began to think of various ways of making my escape. Shawkat Mia had already fled. He was familiar with the roads of this part of town. We used to live on the third floor and there was a two-storeyed building next to ours. One way out was to jump down from the third floor of our building to the roof of the other one. However, there was a gap between the two buildings and if I failed to land properly I would surely die. But I took the risk and jumped. Kazi Ghulam Mahbub and Mofiz followed me. Because Saifuddin was not involved in politics there was no reason why anyone would arrest him. He thus stayed put. As we were going down the stairs from the rooftop one of us somehow managed to knock a bucket and it fell down with a bang. The owner of the house immediately began screaming. We froze in our tracks. The policemen were too busy trying to break the door open and so paid no heed to the racket. No sooner had we managed to cross the slums surrounding our building and hit the main road than we heard the police finally breaking the door and entering it.

We would have to cross Maulvibazar. Three policemen were patrolling the road, moving from one side of the road to the other. When we saw them far ahead of us we crossed the road. They were unable to detect our movement. After we had crossed Maulvibazar we decided to take refuge in a friend's house that was close by. We spent the night there. In the morning I bade farewell to my two companions since they had no arrest warrant against them. But if they were found with me they might be arrested. I stayed with Abdul Malek Sardar in his Mahutuli house. From here I moved to Captain Shahjahan's house. His wife Noorjahan Begum used to treat me like her brother. She had no interest in politics. I was injured and unwell—where else could I go in Dhaka then and who would give me refuge at this time? The lady looked after me well and brought some medicine for me from a physician.

I stayed in that house for a couple of days. However, the Intelligence Branch (IB) people were keeping a close eye on this house since I was a regular visitor here. At 8 p.m. two officers showed up. Just at this time one of the party workers began to approach Begum Noorjahan to inquire about my whereabouts. Seeing IB officers, the party worker's facial expression became such that it was quite apparent where I was. I was in the next room and could hear everything. However, she was quite shrewd and able to think on her feet. Excusing herself to go to the kitchen to serve them tea, she took me downstairs and told me about the interrogation. I asked her for a shawl since I only had a lungi and kurta with me. Luckily for me, she had washed these clothes and had them ironed for me. She brought me a shawl and showed me the safest way out. When I left the house the IB people were still talking to her. I was aware that they had posted two policemen outside the house but I managed to elude them.

Maulana Bhasani was putting up with Yar Mohammad. I had to meet him to find out why he had wanted me to evade arrest. Personally, I do not believe in the kind of politics where one takes refuge underground since I detested covert politics and did not approve of furtive actions. I took a rickshaw to a fellow party worker's house. The two of us then headed for Yar Mohammad's house. One could enter the house through a rear door. We took this route in. The policemen who were guarding the front door thus failed to spot us. The Maulana and Yar Mohammad seemed very glad to see me. By this time I had recovered somewhat from my injury. I asked the Maulana why he had wanted me to flee and avoid arrest.

In a Muslim League meeting, Nawabzada Liaquat Ali Khan had declared: 'I will smash the head of anyone who dares to take part in Awami League activities.' This, despite his assertions that he believed in democracy! The fact is he didn't like the idea of an opposition at all. He couldn't stand the idea that anyone would dare criticize his government's policies. If anyone within his party had the temerity to speak out, he would cause trouble for that man. An example is his treatment of Nawab Mamdot, the prime minister of West Punjab. He was absolutely dedicated to Mr Jinnah. At Jinnah's directive, he had given up his vast landholdings and his title of Nawab. That Liaquat Ali Khan was not ready to accept the existence of any other party except the Muslim League is also obvious in his speeches. Thus he declared in a speech at the Muslim League Council meeting in 1950:

> I have always said, rather it has always been my firm belief, that the existence of the League, not only the existence of the League, but its strength is equal to the existence and strength of Pakistan. So far as I am concerned, I had decided at the very beginning, and I reaffirm it today, that I have always considered myself the prime minister of the League. I never regarded myself as the prime minister chosen by the members of the Constituent Assembly.

He wanted to be the prime minister not of a people but of a party. He had forgotten that a country could not be equated with any one political party. A democratic state can have many political parties; this is only natural if one goes by the law. It is unfortunate that Liaquat Ali Khan was bent on preventing any political party other than his own from coming into existence in Pakistan. Only a dictator could say 'I will smash the head of anyone who takes part in Awami League activities', not anyone who believed in and upheld democracy. Having captured all political power after Jinnah's death, he had become intoxicated with a sense of unlimited power.

Maulana Bhasani said to me, 'Go to Lahore since Mr Suhrawardy is there at the moment. Try to meet him and Mia Iftekharuddin. Tell them about the state of affairs in East Bengal. We need a party that can be representative of the whole country. Talk with Pir Manki Sharif and see if we can transform the Awami League under Mr Suhrawardy's leadership into a party that is genuinely all-Pakistan. No one except Mr Suhrawardy has the ability to lead such a party.'

In Karachi, meanwhile, Liaquat Ali Khan had been denouncing Mr Suhrawardy in the filthiest language imaginable: 'India has let loose this dog on us,' he said publicly. And yet Mr Jinnah had never said anything derogatory about Mr Suhrawardy. Such are the ironies of fate! To elect Mr Liaquat Ali Khan all the students of Aligarh Muslim University had to take to the streets. If it were not for those students who had stayed behind in Aligarh, Rafi Ahmed Kidwai would have defeated him. I don't know what he had done for the birth of Pakistan except making statements in Delhi under Jinnah's shadow. Who knows how events would have turned out if Mr Suhrawardy had not succeeded in becoming the prime minister of Bengal and consolidated the Muslim League in India? Mr Jinnah was aware of Mr Suhrawardy's achievements and therefore accepted his deeds.

Mr Suhrawardy had taken up the case on behalf of Nawab Mamdot in Lahore.[20] No doubt Liaquat Ali Khan considered the charges he had brought against the Nawab as an achievement! He was out to harass him because the Nawab didn't care a fig about him.

I told Mr Bhasani, 'How will I go to Lahore? I will have to pass through the whole of India. I will have to prove that I am a Pakistani and only then will the Indians allow me to travel across their country to go to West Pakistan.' No passports and visas were being issued at that time. All my woollens were in my village home. I had no money. And in East Punjab anyone suspected of being a Muslim ran the risk of being murdered. I couldn't figure out how to reach Lahore in these circumstances. And over here there was a search warrant against me and the police were on the lookout for me. Mr Bhasani said, 'How can I tell you how you can go to Lahore? All I can say is you should go to Lahore any way you can. You should meet Mr Suhrawardy there and tell him everything.' Sometime early in 1949, Maulana Bhasani, Mia Iftekharuddin and many others had met Mr Suhrawardy and had decided that if the Muslim League continued to be controlled by a coterie they would form a new party. Mr Suhrawardy had approved of this. Now they needed Mr Shaheed Suhrawardy's and Mr Mia Iftekharuddin's help, both of whom were on the best of terms.

I took leave of the Maulana. The only warm clothing I had was an achkan. I borrowed some money from my uncle Zafar Sadek. I also drew upon part of the money being held for me in the *Ittehad* for the work I had done for them. I decided to leave for Lahore with this small amount of money. I knew if I could reach Lahore one way or the other and meet Mr Suhrawardy I would be fine.

Somehow I managed to do just that. I reached Lahore after an arduous journey. I slipped through the nets of the East Bengal police with great difficulty. They had been raiding house after house and had looked for me in many localities. They had gone to my village and discovered that I was not there.

~

Lahore was enduring a cold wave. I found it difficult to cope with the cold. Besides, I had never been to the city before. I knew nobody there except

Mia Iftekharuddin. I knew that Mr Suhrawardy was staying with Nawab Mamdot. I kept my baggage in front of a shop and called the Nawab's house. I was told that he was not in Lahore and would return to the city two days later. I had only two rupees with me. What was I supposed to do? Where was I to keep my baggage? It was 1 p.m. and I was feeling quite famished since I had not had anything since the morning. If I spent the two rupees what would I do afterwards? After pondering my predicament, I decided to phone Mr Iftekharuddin. He was not at home. I got on a tonga and gave directions to his house. I had his address with me. When I alighted in front of his house with my baggage, the security guard told me he wasn't home. He asked me to sit in the vestibule. I kept my suitcase in a corner. I wrote down my name and address on a slip of paper and asked the guard to give it to Mr Iftekharuddin when he came back.

As soon as he returned home and saw the slip, Mr Iftekharuddin came out to meet me. He recognized me instantly and treated me affectionately. Seeing how exhausted I was, he immediately had a room arranged for me. He advised me to shower and freshen up. He said we could discuss the situation in East Bengal over lunch. Barisal's S.A. Saleh had already written to Mia Saheb and Shaheed [Suhrawardy] Saheb and told them I would be in Lahore. Saleh was a boyhood friend and Mr Nuruddin's first cousin. We had worked together for the Pakistan movement for a while. Mia Iftekharuddin, his wife and I discussed the political situation of the country as we ate. I told him how things were in East Bengal. I informed him of Maulana Bhasani's views and narrated the way the government was using force to suppress dissent. Mr Iftekharuddin had already quit the ministry. He said, 'Look, it's been a while since I left politics. I won't be taking part in politics actively any more. I have work of my own for the time being.'

He asked, 'How is the Muslim League faring in East Bengal?' I said, 'If we have elections I believe we will be able to defeat them and they will lose by a huge margin.' He seemed reluctant to believe this. Begum Iftekharuddin, however, felt that this was possible since 'only recently East Bengal had witnessed a movement against the League'. The Begum seemed well informed about the political situation and about events at home and abroad; it seemed to me that she was very well read too.

That night I had fever. Mr Iftekharuddin got a physician to examine me. He bought the drugs prescribed for me and I recovered in a couple of days. He had only one guest room in the house. Mr Suhrawardy's brother Shahed Suhrawardy was due to visit Lahore and stay in the house. Therefore I had to leave in the next day or so. I sensed that they would prefer me to do so.

Mr Iftekharuddin said that he was willing to come up with a solution for me. Mr Suhrawardy had returned to Lahore by then. I was no longer ill but Lahore was very cold. I reached Nawab Mamdot's house at 11 a.m. one day. Mr Suhrawardy was in the lawn, discussing a lawsuit with some lawyers. As soon as he saw me approaching he rose from his chair and embraced me warmly. He said to me affectionately, 'How did you come? You look ill; where have you put up?' He introduced me to everyone present. When they had left he turned his attention to me. I told him all that had happened in East Bengal. He inquired about the leaders and workers he knew. He wanted detailed information about the situation in our country. Those who have not met him will not be able to imagine the extent of his love for East Bengal. Mr Suhrawardy told me that he would have been in a terrible spot financially if he hadn't started working on the case he had on his hands then. He refused to allow me to return to Mr Iftekharuddin's house. We had dinner together along with Nawab Mamdot who had joined us. Mr Suhrawardy told the Nawab about my situation. The Nawab too asked me all sorts of questions to find out how things were in our country.

In the evening Khan Ghulam Muhammad Khan Lundkhar and Pir Salahuddin (then a student) came to meet Mr Suhrawardy. Mr Lundkhar had been expelled from the Frontier Province recently and was banned from ever returning to the province. He had been the general secretary of the Frontier Muslim League. He was very happy to see me. Mr Shaheed Suhrawardy requested him to find a hotel for me, preferably a low-cost one. Pir Jalaluddin was then a student leader of the Punjab who had already earned a name for himself as a party worker.

I took leave from Mr Iftekharuddin later. He said if he had had enough space in his house he would never have let me leave. I assured him I would be fine. Mr Suhrawardy took me to a shop and said, 'I have to get some clothes since the two suits I have aren't sufficient.' In addition to ordering some clothes for himself he bought a good-quality blanket, a sweater, some socks and a muffler, and inquired if I needed any clothes. But I was aware that he was struggling himself, so I said I wouldn't need anything at all. When he was dropping me off at my hotel he said, 'I have bought these clothes for you but let me know when you need anything.' I was relieved to have a really warm sweater and a blanket since the cold was getting to me.

Every morning I would go to meet Mr Suhrawardy and I would come back in the evening after spending the day with him. I became a good friend of the Nawab's brothers. Three days later Mr Lundkhar told me, 'Let's go visit Campbellpur. The Frontier Awami League is going to hold its executive committee meeting there. You can have discussions with Pir Manki Sharif and other leaders of the party there. I agree with you that the party branches of the two provinces should get together and form an All Pakistan Awami League under the leadership of Mr Suhrawardy.' The two of us approached Mr Suhrawardy. He said, 'Go and talk things out with them. It will be a good thing if we can get all the Awami Leagues of the provinces together; I myself am discussing the issue with the Nawab in Punjab.'

Mr Suhrawardy gave me some money. The two of us got into Mr Lundkhar's car and headed for Campbellpur at ten that night. Mr Lundkhar was driving the car himself. By the time we reached Rawalpindi it was early morning. We rested there for a while, took our breakfast and headed for Campbellpur afterwards, arriving in the town around afternoon. This was the first time I was entering the Punjab or the Land of Five Rivers. I took an instant liking to it.

People still haven't forgotten the terrible riots that broke out in East and West Punjab at that period. Hundreds of thousands of refugees flooded the province of West Punjab but things eased up soon since hundreds of thousands of Sikhs and Hindus had also left at the same time. Muslims had taken over their property.

Just before leaving for Campbellpur I had issued a press statement on the state of affairs in East Bengal mentioning the imprisonment of Maulana Bhasani and Shamsul Huq, the harassment of political workers and the food crisis in the province. Both the *Pakistan Times* and *Imroze* featured the press release prominently since both were owned by Mia Iftekharuddin. It was at this time that I became acquainted with the editor, the famous poet Faiz Ahmed Faiz, and his associate Mr Mazhar. It won't be an exaggeration to say that these men were learned and brilliant. Both of them as well as Mr Iftekharuddin believed that Bengali should be a state language of Pakistan. They also agreed that our demands were just. Before writing down my statement I had showed it to Mr Suhrawardy. He had gone through it and approved it.

We reached Campbellpur eventually. The District Bungalow had been reserved for the Pir Saheb. In a short time executive committee members as well as general members of the Frontier Awami League reached the venue. The meeting was being held here because Mr Lundkhar was not allowed to travel from West Punjab to the Frontier Province. It was here that I first met Pir Manki Sharif, Sardar Abdul Ghafur, Sardar Sikander and Mr Shamim Jung, who had once been a minister, and other prominent leaders of the region. The meeting went on for a long time. At one stage, they allowed me to join the meeting. It was taking place in the District Bungalow. Two armed guards made sure that no one from the detective branch was allowed inside the bungalow. The meeting went on till late at night. I gave a speech in English there. One gentleman whose name I have now forgotten translated my speech into Pashto. When I finished speaking, the issue I had raised of creating a trans-Pakistani organization was taken up. I could see that in the end almost everyone agreed to my proposal. After Ghulam Muhammad Lundkhar had ended his speech they decided to send a delegation comprising three members to Mr Suhrawardy to invite him to head the organization. The meeting ended late that night. At that time special permission was needed to cross Attock Bridge. The Pir Saheb had the necessary papers and was thus able to leave that night. Some of us stayed back in the bungalow. Mr Lundkhar took me to a small hotel. I had my dinner there and spent the night in it. That night it struck me forcefully how cold Punjab could be in winter!

I am from East Bengal, a land where one can go through an entire winter with only a light blanket. Here you have to wear layer upon layer of warm clothes and wrap yourself in blanket after blanket. And yet it is so cold that sleep evades you despite the layers of clothes and the blankets!

The Pir was saddened by what he had heard about East Bengal and told us about the atrocities being perpetrated by Quayyum Khan in the Frontier Province. Khan was guilty of incarcerating many leaders and workers there. He would impose Section 144 as soon as he heard of a meeting being held. Apparently, he would never think twice about employing the police to assault a procession with batons and bullets. The situation had become unbearable. It could be said that the tyranny of the state in East Bengal was nothing compared to that in the Frontier Province. He had thrown Lundkhar in jail. Although Khan released him later, he saw to it that Lundkhar was expelled from the Frontier Province. Lundkhar was therefore in Lahore.

We left for Lahore the next morning. Before that I had one request to make: how could I go back without seeing Attock Bridge and Attock Fort? After all, it was only a few miles away. Mr Lundkhar agreed to take me to see the bridge. I crossed the bridge and entered the Frontier Province. He sent a guide with me. There were a few fruit shops along the way. I bought some fruits and returned. You needed a pass to enter Attock Fort since a few war prisoners were interned within. From a distance I could see a few Sikh prisoners working inside. After I had returned Mr Lundkhar took us all back to Lahore. We stopped at Rawalpindi on the way. We rested there for a while. I saw that Mr Lundkhar knew quite a few people there. He would stop the car every once in a while to smoke the hookah. Wherever he stopped at a wayside hotel or a restaurant someone or the other was sure to bring a hookah for him. All these people seemed to belong to the Frontier Province. We stopped for tea in Jhelum, Gujrat and Gujranwala. When we reached Lahore it was almost 10.30 p.m. Mr Lundkhar dropped me off at my hotel promising to take me back to Suhrawardy and give me a report on the decisions taken.

Followers of the Punjab's Nawab Mamdot increasingly found themselves sidelined in the Muslim League. He had not formed a party yet. But he was considering it and hoping to form one after the conclusion of the lawsuit. Many well-known workers and leaders, all veteran Muslim Leaguers, had been meeting Mr Suhrawardy. He had agreed to address a public meeting in Sargodha district. He asked me to accompany him. Since I had very little to do I agreed to accompany him. Sargodha was full of refugees from India and it was obvious that there was no end to their misery. Mr Suhrawardy gave his speech. I was also asked to speak by many people but I told them that I didn't understand Urdu or Punjabi and the people here could not understand English and so how could I speak to them? Mr Suhrawardy said that I could be excused from speaking. However, I was introduced to the assembly. I greeted everyone and then sat down. I could see that Mr Suhrawardy's popularity extended to a place even as remote as Sargodha.

In the Lahore hotel where I was staying, Mr Aziz Beg and Mr Khurshid (who would later become president of Azad Kashmir) had rented two rooms from which they were publishing the weekly *Guardian*. They had read the statement I had made in the *Pakistan Times* and had published extracts from it in their paper. I met them and discussed all the issues with them. A *Guardian* representative met me and brought out a feature about me. Slowly the politicians of Lahore became aware that I was staying in Lahore. The hotel manager had already informed me that the detective branch was shadowing me. He also told me that someone was always tailing me on a full-time basis. Whenever I went out on a walk or on a tonga my tail would follow me on a bicycle.

Courtesy of Pir Jalaluddin I met a representative of the Punjab Muslim Students' Federation. We talked about the importance of forming an all-Pakistani student organization. Others like Mr Fahmi and Mr Nur Mohammad (he had just come from Delhi) who were leaders of the student fronts also agreed with me on this issue. I went to the Law College hostel on a few occasions to talk over the issue with them. I said, 'Even if I am no longer involved in a student organization, if you are ready to form an all-Pakistani organization, I will be able to persuade the East Pakistan Students' League to join you.' They said yes to my proposal and we decided to form such an organization. They drafted a constitution for it and asked me to carry it to Dhaka. I agreed and volunteered to inform the leaders of the Students' League in East Pakistan about their view. They would then write to their West Pakistani counterparts and a joint declaration would be issued from the Punjab and Bengal.

An unfortunate incident took place at this time. I went to the *Pakistan Times* office to meet Mr Mia. It was around 11 a.m. Mr Mia was not in his office. I waited for him for a while but he didn't show up. I had work to do with Mr Suhrawardy and was supposed to meet him in the high court. Soon after I had set out three or four people confronted me and asked me where I was from. I said, 'From East Pakistan.' Suddenly, one of them grabbed me by my hand while another one held on to my shirt and yelled, 'You are Pakistan's enemy.' Another brought out a hunter and the fourth a knife. I managed to free my hand and told them, 'Do you know who I am?' They said, 'Yes, we do.' I said, 'Either listen to me or if you want to have a fight let's do so on a one-to-one basis.' One of them tried to box me but I managed to deflect his blow. By this time a crowd had gathered. Some of them asked me what was going on. I said, 'I have no idea. I am from East Bengal. I had gone to the *Pakistan Times* office to meet Mr Mia. I can't understand why these people want to beat me up.' Among the people who had assembled were some students and some gentlemen. They told my attackers something and one of them actually abused my assailants. In the end the thugs left the scene. I went to the Law College hostel to inform Kazmi about what had taken place but he was not there. I hired a tonga and went to the high court to meet Mr Suhrawardy. I was all worked up and hadn't eaten anything. When we went out in the evening to the Nawab's house I told him about the incident. Mr Suhrawardy informed the Nawab about my encounter. I returned to my hotel before dusk set in. When Kazmi met me in the evening and found out what had happened he took some students along with him to the site of the incident and tried to find out from the shopkeepers of the area the identity of my assailants. They told him that they were not from the neighbourhood and must have come there from another area. It was obvious that they had been let loose on me by the Muslim League. Here too they were using strong-arm tactics. Lundkhar said to me, 'You will have to be on your guard from now on.'

I decided that I wouldn't tell anyone else about this incident. Senior government officials of the Punjab treated the Nawab with great respect. They soon came to know of what had happened to me. My problem was that I had difficulty in communicating in Urdu. On the other hand, the ordinary Punjabi didn't speak Urdu fluently. What they used was a mixture of Urdu and Punjabi while I could only use a mixture of Bengali and Urdu.

At around this time a conference organized by progressive writers of the Punjab took place. Mr Mia requested me to take part in it. I did so but as a guest since I wasn't a writer myself. The conference went on for two days. Mr Lundkhar also took part. Unfortunately, when he went to attend a session, someone or the other or perhaps a band of men set his car aflame. In the 1942 movement his house had already been torched since he was president of the Frontier Congress at that time. He had joined the Muslim League as soon as he had left jail. Lundkhar told me, 'These incidents are not unusual in Lahore. However, I am a Pathan and they are scared of me. They don't have the guts to confront me and so will always try to attack me when my back is turned.'

A month had gone by; how much longer would I have to stay in Lahore? I pointed out to Mr Suhrawardy that Maulana Bhasani, Mr Shamsul Huq and our fellow workers were behind bars in Dhaka. But Mr Suhrawardy said, 'As soon as you reach Dhaka they are going to jail you but this may not happen here in Lahore.' I replied, 'But they can arrest me here and send me to Dhaka since Mr Liaquat Ali is angry with me. Moreover, the government in East Pakistan must also be out to get me wherever I am. They will tell the central government to force the Punjab government to hand me over to them. This may happen any time now. After all, I haven't been quiet here. If anything is going to happen to me, it's best that it happens in East Bengal since in prison in East Bengal they will serve me rice and I will not survive if I have to eat the roti they serve in West Pakistani prisons! Indeed, I am fed up with the roti and meat I have to eat here every day. And if I have to stay in jail anywhere, it's best to serve time with my fellow workers.' Mr Suhrawardy said, 'In that case, make arrangements to go back.' He asked me what route I would like to take. I said, 'There is only one land route and that is through East Punjab. I don't want to take this route. I would like to fly from Lahore to Delhi and take the train from there. I'll need a permit to travel through India. Such a permit can be issued only by the Indian deputy high commissioner in Lahore.' I added, 'I have already talked to Mr Mia and he has assured me that he will tell the deputy high commissioner to issue me a permit since he knows him well.' Mr Suhrawardy asked me to get ready to leave.

A few of my friends were then undergoing training in Lahore's Civil Service Academy. I went to meet them there. I ended up meeting a lot of my friends. One of them was a leader of the government party and had opposed the movement that had gone on to establish the claim of our mother tongue. He said, 'You must have tea with me. Having come to Lahore I realize that you all were right to launch the movement for Bengali and I was wrong to oppose it. Many of the people here hate Bengalis.' I didn't say anything in response since that would be inappropriate. After all, everyone present was in government service and someone or the other could take offence.

I got my permit and decided to leave immediately since Mr Mia had told me not to waste any time. The permit said that I would have to leave India within three days. Three days was all the time I had! I calculated that I would just about manage to pass through India in that time. Mr Suhrawardy paid my hotel bills and bought me an Orient Airlines plane ticket to Delhi (this was then a Pakistani carrier). He also gave me some money for my incidental expenses. At that time you were permitted to take only fifty Pakistani rupees to India and only fifty Indian rupees to Pakistan. But it was difficult to procure Indian currency in Pakistan. Mr Suhrawardy asked Nawabzada Zulfikar (Nawab Mamdot's younger brother) to put me on the plane since he had heard that there was a move to arrest me at the airport. In that event the Nawabzada was to inform Mr Suhrawardy about my predicament. The Nawabzada therefore accompanied me to the airport. I noticed that he kept my luggage at a distance. He then took me to an official's room. That man examined my permit. He went through my luggage and said, 'Sit down here for a while and don't go anywhere.' Nawabzada Zulfikar told me, 'They seem to be up to something because it is time for the flight to leave but nothing is happening.' The passengers were made to board the plane and then asked to deboard. They seemed to be waiting for directions from above. The Nawabzada eventually found out that the whole delay was on my account. An hour later the plane was given permission to leave and I was told I could board it. I took leave from him and got on the plane, requesting him as I did that he should inform Mr Suhrawardy of the incident. I could see that they had taken all this time to decide whether I should be allowed to leave or be detained here. In the end they must have come to the conclusion that they shouldn't make the Punjab suffer for what was really Bengal's headache!

I was acutely aware that I had only three days to cross all of India. If the East Pakistan government was alerted, they would arrest me either at Darshana or Benapole border crossing. The permit clearly said that I would not be allowed to stay in India. If the Calcutta government officials knew about me they would not hesitate to intern me in their prison since I was Shaheed Suhrawardy's follower!

I was feeling sad about leaving Mr Suhrawardy behind since I had spent a lot of time under his tutelage. I had been showered with his affection and had worked under his leadership. In Bengal people venerated him and the Muslims of the region had joined the movement for Pakistan at his call. Unfortunately, the man whose gesture had inspired thousands to sacrifice their lives without hesitation had nothing now. The colleagues he had once taken pride in now considered him an enemy. Who knows how long it would be before I could meet him again? Without his guidance and help, we would not be able to establish a political party in East Bengal and prevent the Muslim League from establishing itself in the province. I felt that the nation would once more be able to benefit from his organizational acumen and leadership skills.

I reached Delhi and immediately headed for the second-class railway waiting room, where I kept my luggage. I showered, ate, left my luggage with a guard and then went out. I had already bought my ticket. The train was scheduled to leave that night and I had a lot of time on my hands. I took a tonga to Jama Masjid since I wanted to see how the Muslims were doing. During Partition the city had witnessed fierce riots. I found that Muslims were still doing business in some of their shops. However, I didn't have the courage to talk to anyone. I walked to the Red Fort. I had been there before but now the Indian flag was flying on it. Inside, things had changed somewhat. Muslims now had only a few shops inside it. I didn't feel like staying there for long. I therefore left, took another tonga and headed for the Anglo-Arabian College, where I had participated in the Muslim League Convention in 1946.

I then decided to go around New Delhi. This part of the city was being transformed and looked very different. It was now the capital of India. Muslims had ruled India for hundreds of years here but they were of no consequence at present. Their presence was tangible only in the pages of history. Who knows if even this memory would be retained in the future? The Hindu bigots who were responsible for the assassination of Mahatma Gandhi would surely not tolerate people from another religious community. It was here in Delhi that conspiracies were hatched to kill Mahatma Gandhi, Pandit Nehru and Huseyn Shaheed Suhrawardy. God had saved Mr Suhrawardy from death. Those who had assisted Nathuram Godse, Gandhi's assassin, had confessed as much during Gandhi's murder trial.

I boarded my train that night. I had a reserved seat. There were three other gentlemen in the second-class car with me. I didn't have the courage to talk to anyone. I began to read a newspaper. This was a time when India was witnessing intermittent communal outbreaks. But after the death of the Mahatma the Congress government was compelled to take punitive measures against the communal RSS [Rashtriya Swayamsevak Sangh] and Hindu Mahasabha workers. In the wake of the Mahatma's martyrdom—brought on by his determination to safeguard the lives of Muslims—his followers had begun to react against the forces of communalism. They had also started to behave in a friendly manner with Muslims.

When I woke up the next morning I saw that two of the passengers had left and there was only one other person in the car with me. He was from West Bengal. He asked me where I was from and where I was heading. I told him the truth. I said I was on my way to East Bengal from Lahore and that my home was in Faridpur district. The man said, 'I am from Barisal myself. I am now working in Delhi.' We talked for a long time. He was feeling sad because he wouldn't be able to eat the fish and vegetables of East Bengal, or breathe its air, or ever return to his land of birth, since all his relatives had left Barisal. The gentleman asked me to get down at Howrah and spend the night with him in his house. He said, 'Please stay with me; you won't have any problems there at all.' I thanked him saying, 'I'll have to leave tomorrow morning and that's why I'll spend the night in a friend's house.'

But when I was all alone I thought: where should I go now? I didn't want to stay in a hotel. In the end I decided that I would go to my friend Khondokar Nurul Alam's house and stay with him. I went to his Park Circus house to find he was not in, but his brother received me warmly. Nurul Alam returned home after a while. He seemed delighted to see me again. We dined together and then went out for a stroll. Alam told me, 'I don't know what to do; I'm here all by myself; my friends have all left. But what will I do in Dhaka? I don't have any money to invest in a business. Mr Nurul Amin will never offer me a job since I was on Mr Suhrawardy's side and was working with Mr Hashim for him.' I couldn't say anything to Alam since I didn't have the ability to offer him anything in Dhaka. My own future was quite uncertain and for all I knew I might have to eat jail food tomorrow! However, Nurul Alam told me that he had applied for a job in the Pakistani deputy high commissioner's office.

I telephoned the railway people and found out that the train to Khulna would leave at 11 a.m., reach Benapole in the evening and Khulna at 10 p.m. I bought an inter-class ticket. I knew I would have to hoodwink the police at the Benapole border. The East Bengal government would surely have alerted their people that I would be attempting to cross the border in a day or two. Its detective branch was no doubt busy trying to trace me so that I could be put behind bars. I was also ready for jail but before I was interned I wanted to meet my parents, family members and my children. I had written to Renu from Lahore and she would be looking forward to my visit. Everyone at home would be eagerly awaiting me. I also needed to go to Dhaka to talk things over with my colleagues. The work we were doing would have to go on even if I was arrested. I also needed to raise some money. Our party really was short of funds. I believed that I could raise some money for it on my own. I knew some admirers of Mr Suhrawardy who would not be able to refuse me if I approached them.

Our train stopped at Ranaghat for a long time. To find out if anyone was carrying any contraband items, the Indian customs officers searched the car as well as the passengers' baggage. They rummaged through my luggage too. By evening we came to Benapole. I got off the train before it stopped at the station. I had become familiar with a passenger in my car and enlisted his help. I requested him to show my luggage to the Pakistan customs official if they wanted to inspect it since I had some work to do. I also told him that it might be a while before I returned. Since it was dark I felt that I could take shelter under a tree. Members of the detective branch and some police officers were going from car to car and examining everything in sight. When I saw them approaching I went to the other side of the train to hide myself. I was determined to elude them.

I was thinking of my loved ones all the time. A few months back my eldest son, Kamal, had been born but I had not been able to spend any time with him. Hasina saw so little of me that whenever I met her she would not let go of me. I was overwhelmed by the thought that I was a father as well as a son and wanted to be with my family members once again. I knew they were all looking forward to my visit home and were sure that I would go and meet them as soon as I returned from Lahore. Certainly, Renu would be staying awake for me. She always endured hardship and never protested. Because she kept quiet and never complained I felt even sadder!

Maulana Bhasani, Mr Shamsul Huq and my co-workers were languishing in jail. I felt depressed thinking about them too. Even if I was unable to do anything to change the situation, to be near them would be some consolation. As the train started to move again, and as it began to gather speed, I ran and caught up with it and boarded it. I doubt if I could have been able to do that if I was even a minute late. The train had now picked up speed but I kept thinking I would have to be on my guard when we arrived in Jessore. I was aware that the rail station was normally full of people from the detective branch. A few minutes before the train reached Jessore station I went into our car's toilet. I came out only after the train had started to move again. A student had now entered our car. As soon as I came out of the toilet he said to me, 'Aren't you Mujib?' I asked him to move closer to me and whispered, 'Don't call me by my name.' He was in the Students' League and immediately understood why I didn't want to be identified by my name. Because the train was full no one seemed to have noticed. And that was a time when I wasn't that well known. Also, the student got down at the next station.

I knew what the situation in Khulna would be like. Since my childhood I had travelled through this city. To go to Calcutta for my studies, I had to cross it. The train reached Khulna at around 11 p.m. When all the passengers had got down from the train I took out my kurta, folded it and wrapped it inside my bedding. I rolled my lungi to my knees. I carried my bedding on my head and my suitcase in my hand. I hurried towards the river landing station as if I were a coolie. The men from the detective branch failed to detect me. I crossed the railroad and entered the river landing station. I exited from another gate and took a rickshaw. I retrieved my kurta from my bedding and wore it once more. The rickshaw puller was from Gopalganj and recognized me immediately. He said, 'Sir, how come you are dressing up here?' I told him, 'There is a lot that I could tell you but I will have to explain everything to you later. First, let's leave the station right away.' I knew I would have to tell him at least a few things that had happened to me. Since he was from Gopalganj he would not betray me.

I had a cousin who worked in Khulna. I knew where he lived and so headed for his house. I sent the rickshaw puller to my uncle's house. My uncle was a very capable man. I sent him to the landing station to buy two first-class reserved tickets on the steamer for me so that I could travel in privacy. I also got in touch with a friend who worked for the river steamship company. He advised me to board the steamer just a couple of minutes before it started. He would see to it that the steamer left as soon as I boarded it. He was aware that the landing station too was teeming with men from the detective branch. Unfortunately, because of fog the steamer took a long time to dock in the station and had to delay its departure by an hour. In other words, it would now leave at 7 a.m. This was a problem since at 6 a.m. it is still quite dark at this time of the year but by seven the sun would be up and I would be quite conspicuous. My uncle had loaded our baggage on the steamer by then. He had helped me don a coat and trousers and even a hat. When the steamer finally started to leave I sprinted on to it. My friend was still standing on the landing station. As soon as he saw me he ordered that the walkway be withdrawn, and the steamer was on its way. I managed to exchange glances with him and thus convey my gratitude.

Now my hopes were up—I would be able to reach home! I stayed inside the cabin the whole day and had food brought to it. Quite a few people had seen me board the ship. The ship stopped in Gopalganj before moving on to Barisal and then Narayanganj. Many of the people were travelling to Gopalganj. The steamer itself wouldn't go all the way to Gopalganj town but would offload passengers three miles away at a place called Manikdaha where they had constructed a new landing station. This is because the river had silted up near the town. When the ship landed at Manikdaha I surveyed the scene outside. Two of our workers—Rahmat Jan and Yunus—recognized me instantly when they looked my way and called out my name excitedly. I signalled to them to shut up since the police would be raiding our village home in a bid to nab me if they got wind of my arrival. Rahmat Jan and Yunus were actually travelling to Barisal where they studied at the college. They came to me right away. The ship was leaving then. I said, 'How did you recognize me?' They said, 'We know your eyes so well!' I told them, 'If the police find out that I am around they will try to arrest me as I walk home.' They said, 'Mujib Bhai, this is Gopalganj; unless you want to be arrested, no one will dare arrest you from here.' The people of Gopalganj usually added the honorific 'Bhai' or brother to my name when addressing me. On occasions both the father and son of a family would end up calling me 'Bhai'!

It usually took me two hours from Gopalganj to the landing station closest to our house. We arrived at the Gopalganj landing station around evening. It took me another hour by boat to get home. When I reached it, everyone was surprised as well as delighted. Nobody had imagined that I would be able to return home. My daughter just wouldn't let go of me and refused to go to sleep. I told my father about everything that had happened to me. I asked someone to keep an eye on the road. We posted a guard so that he would stay awake in the outhouse throughout the night to ensure that no one entered undetected. Our house was big and always full of people.

I wouldn't be unhappy if I was arrested now. However, I would still have liked to go to Dhaka once more before they interned me. I explained to my father as well as Renu that I wouldn't be able to stay home for long. In the end, I stayed with my family for seven to eight days. I told them, 'I won't be able to go to Dhaka via Barisal; neither can I travel through Gopalganj. They will be on the lookout for me and will arrest me if they can trace me. What I can try to do is board a launch from a landing station that is two stops away from Gopalganj. Then I will get down at Kabirajpur and take a boat to Shibchar in Madaripur subdivision. From Shibchar I will board another launch. But before I do so I will spend a day or two with my sister [who lived five miles away from Shibchar] and her family.'

Renu said to me, 'Who knows how long we will have to stay apart! Let me come along with you to Shibchar and take the opportunity to spend two more days with you. I will take our children along. Your father can come later to bring us back home.' I gave in to her proposal since I knew that if they got hold of me this time they would keep me in jail forever. Although going all the way to Shibchar by boat was quite arduous we decided to leave. Two of our workers, Shahidul Islam and Siraj, accompanied us. They were still in school but were very fond of me. Now the two of them are businessmen. Shahid is still very loyal to me and backs me up in everything I do. Siraj has switched his allegiance to another party but still respects me. They went with us as far as Kabirajpur and stayed awake the whole night to make sure that we were safe. They had left their homes without warm clothes on a wintry night. In fact, Renu gave them her own shawl so that they could stay warm that night.

We eventually arrived at my sister's house and ended up staying there for seven days. I was getting more and more attached to my children. I didn't feel like leaving them but knew I would have to. I had consecrated myself to the cause of my country—so what was the point of becoming sentimental about my family? If one loves one's country and its people one must be ready to sacrifice something and in the end might have to give up everything.

My father had given me some money when I left our home. Renu had also brought along some money for me. I told Renu, 'You were by yourself for a long time but now there are two of our children to keep you company. I know you can't expect any sort of financial assistance from me. You will have to manage on your own somehow. I am aware that you won't be asking for help from my father again and again. And in any case, where will my father get the money to meet all our needs? I don't need a lot of money. They are certain to detain me soon. I won't be able to elude them forever. There is no knowing when I'll be meeting you again. Don't come to Dhaka. The children will have a hard time there. Moreover, there isn't much space in my sister's house. I don't want any of my near ones to have a hard time on my account. Keep writing to me and I'll write back!'

I left them at night since Hasina would not stop crying if she saw me leave. Kamal of course was too young to understand anything at this time. Shibchar couldn't be accessed by steamer and so I would have to go to Chanderchar, which was ten miles away. My eldest sister's brother-in-law, Saifuddin Chowdhury, who happened to be a good friend as well as a relative, was to accompany me all the way to Dhaka. As I took leave of her, Renu started to shed tears silently. I didn't try to console her and left quietly. What could I say to her? I had explained everything to her already!

We left on a boat that night and reached Chanderchar Ghat in the morning. The steamer was supposed to leave later in the day. One of my co-workers, Samad Morol, had a house nearby. I sent word to him that I was in the landing station. He immediately came around to see me. He kept insisting that I should go to his house for refreshments but I told him that I wouldn't have the time to do so. The ferry steamer would take me as far as Tarpasha and from there I would have to board the mail steamer that sailed on the Goalando–Narayanganj route. By the time I reached Tarpasha the mail steamer had left. So I had to stay back for a whole day. The next ship was supposed to leave late at night and I had no option other than to spend the night on the landing station platform.

I reached Munshiganj next morning. I had met a Students' League worker in the steamer who knew my predicament. I gave our luggage to him and said, 'Make sure that you deposit our baggage with Shawkat Mia at 150 Mughaltuli. If I get down at Narayanganj in broad daylight I will be going to jail straight away instead of Dhaka! The ever-helpful Shawkat Mia should see to it that I have a place to sleep in. And if he can do so, he should meet me this evening in Narayanganj at Khan Saheb Osman Ali's residence. Please tell Khan Saheb's eldest son Shamsuzzoha to be there in the evening too.'

We got down at Munshiganj and started walking towards Mirkadim. After having food at a relative's house, we started moving towards Narayanganj in a boat just before dusk. Once it was dark we took a rickshaw to Khan Saheb's house. Mr Zoha had not been informed about our coming and wasn't in. His younger brother Mustafa Sarwar was a schoolboy then. He knew me well and went out to get his brother to come home immediately. We went inside to have tea and snacks. Khan Saheb's house was one of our favourite haunts. If any worker of our party was fatigued and happened to pass by the house they would inevitably be offered refreshments. Khan Saheb had suffered reverses in business but he had a huge heart. Mr Zoha got a taxi for us and saw us off. I had delayed our departure as much as I could, hoping that Shawkat Mia would show up. Unfortunately, he reached Narayanganj after we had left. So he set out for Dhaka immediately in our pursuit. We left our taxi at one point and took a rickshaw to Mughaltuli. We saw that our luggage had already found a place inside the house. Shawkat Mia was there too! He embraced me and said, 'Mujib Bhai, tell me how you managed to leave for Lahore and come back from there.' I replied, 'But before I do so tell me: how are Maulana Bhasani and Mr Shamsul Huq doing? Who all are in jail now? How is the Awami League doing?' What Shawkat Mia told me saddened me a little but didn't leave me completely unhappy.

Almost a dozen men who had been made members of the Awami League central committee had resigned from their positions out of fear. Among them were people who had been leading the party for a long time but had now not only resigned from it but also given statements against it to escape punitive measures. Sher-e-Bangla Fazlul Huq had talked to Maulana Bhasani and me soon after he had become a member of our party and had told us, 'I am in financial difficulty. I am going to accept the job of Advocate General that has been offered me. It isn't possible for me to take an active part in politics any more. For the time being I am withdrawing from the party. But you all have my blessings and support.' We appreciated his problem. Later he even took the trouble to come to one of our meetings. Among those who remained in the Awami League at this time were Maulana Bhasani, Mr Shamsul Huq, Ataur Rahman Khan, Abdus Salam Khan, Anwara Khatun, MLA, Khairat Hussein, MLA, Ali Ahmed Khan, MLA, Khondokar Mushtaq Ahmed, Yar Mohammad Khan, Narayanganj's Abdul Awal, Almas Ali, Shamsuzzoha and a few others besides me whose names I can't remember at this point.

Shawkat Mia arranged interim lodging for me. During the day I stayed put and went out to meet people only at night. I tried to seek advice on what my future course of action should be. Mr Manik Mia was in Mughaltuli too and could not decide on what he should do next. Abdul Halim kept me in his house for some time. A few people pledged to have some money allotted for my use. One night when I went to meet a friend who was an important government official, he was quite surprised to see me. He wasn't the kind to take fright easily. He was, in fact, very fond of me. He knew our plight and was sympathetic towards us. But I noted his discomfort and left his house as soon as I could.

I was getting tired of living like a fugitive. I told Abdul Hamid Chowdhury and Mollah Jalaluddin that I would stay with them. They were staying on the ground floor of Ali Amjad Khan's old house in the Khawaja Dewan area. I moved into their house. Throughout the day I would read books and at night I would go from place to place.

We decided to hold a meeting at Armanitola Maidan. I would give a speech there and court arrest. When arrangements were almost done, just a day or two before the meeting, I came back to the flat to find the police had encircled it. Two plainclothesmen of the detective branch had taken their positions inside the house. They knocked gently on my door. I told them to come in. I said to them, 'I have been waiting for you to show up for some time now but you will have to sit here for a while. I'll have to eat something for I haven't had anything to eat yet though it is 2 p.m. already. Someone has gone out to bring me lunch and will be back soon.'

It was Hamid who had gone to fetch my lunch but when he found out that the police was with me he decided to stay away. How long would they keep waiting for my food to arrive? Since there was no sign of Hamid and since Jalal too was away and there was no telling when he would be back I decided to send word to Ali Amjad Khan's eldest son, Henry, to come. He did so immediately. When he heard that I had had nothing to eat he went home and came back with some food for me. His brother Shahjahan who was studying in grade seven accompanied him. He began to berate his uncle loudly. That man used to live upstairs then. Shahjahan kept saying, 'It must be Uncle who informed the police about you for it couldn't be anyone else. Let my father come back and he will teach my uncle a lesson.' Shahjahan was very fond of me and used to come and talk to me whenever he had the time. When the police made me board their van he started to cry. I was feeling awful. I have never been able to forget Shahjahan's distress at my arrest. I later came to know that it was indeed his uncle who had betrayed me to the police for money. Mr Ali Amjad and Anwara Khatun kicked him out of the house for this misdeed.

I was taken to Lalbagh police station. Two Intelligence Branch officers began interrogating me. This lasted for two hours. I told them, 'I'll go on working for the Awami League.' They had innumerable questions for me: Why did I go to Lahore? Where did I stay there? What did I do then? When did I come back to Dhaka? How long did I stay in my village home? What were my plans? What did Mr Suhrawardy say to me? And so on. I said as much as I wanted to and kept mum about what I didn't want to disclose. They booked me under the Public Security Act and took me to the Kotwali police station after dusk.

~

I was made to spend the night in the police station. Jalal took my suitcase and bedding to the police station.

That night Anwara Khatun, MLA, Mr Ataur Rahman Khan and my relation through marriage Mr Shamsuddin Ahmed Chowdhury, who was also the zamindar of Dattapara, came to visit me. Later that night Mr Siddique Dewan, probably an inspector of police then, brought a bed and a mosquito net for me from his own house. My bed had been brought too and so I had no problem on that account. Mr Dewan and the other police officials treated me well and did their best to ensure that I was comfortable.

I was sent to Dhaka jail the next day. When I entered the jail I was told that I hadn't been given division status as yet.[21] I would have to stay there just like any other prisoner. At that time political prisoners had no status. The government would give division status to whoever it pleased and the rest would have to languish as ordinary prisoners. This meant hard labour and having the food that convicts were served. I ate nothing that afternoon. I was being confined with ordinary prisoners. There were two or three other political prisoners who were in my situation. They took me to their corner. At night I had some food with them since I was quite hungry by then. Maulana Bhasani and Mr Shamsul Huq were in Ward 5. They were given division status. Since this was withheld from me I couldn't be with them.

Very early in the morning a policeman came to me and said, 'Let me take you to another place.' I told him, 'First tell me where you plan to take me and only then will I move.' He said, 'You were granted division status at night. I have been instructed to take you to where Maulana Bhasani is. That's all I know.'

I took leave from everyone in my cell. The two or three political prisoners there had not been arrested under the Public Security Act. Separate cases had been filed against them. It was believed that they would be granted bail in a couple of days. I was taken to the ward where Maulana Bhasani and Mr Shamsul Huq were. I would stay in the same room with them. I decided to sleep next to Mr Huq since I used to smoke cigarettes then but would not smoke in front of the Maulana out of deference to him.

I was taken to jail in December 1949. Pakistan had been created in 1947. This was my third visit to jail in these two years. I told the Maulana everything that had happened to me. He also had questions to ask me: What had Mr Suhrawardy said? What were Pir Manki Sharif's views? Was Mr Mia going to take active part in politics now? Would an All Pakistan Awami League party be floated? If so, how long would that process take? Where did I stay in Lahore? What was the situation in Dhaka now? The Maulana told me that a case had already been filed against our party. In it I was indicted along with him, Mr Huq, Abdur Rab and Fazlul Huq BSc. Later Abdur Rab and Fazlul Huq BSc had been released on bail. Since they hadn't been charged with violating the Public Security Act, they were allowed to remain outside. But legal proceedings hadn't started because I had eluded them till now. The case was filed on the basis of the confrontation we had with the Nazirabazar police on 11 October.

In the cell, there were a few other division prisoners besides the three of us, who were here for political reasons. Some of them were sentenced for as many as twenty years while some others were there for shorter periods. They were here because they were financially sound and they were entitled to beds, mosquito nets, a bedcover and white clothes like us. One of them was a manager who used to supervise the food arrangements and see that we were well fed. I was fine here for a while. However, Mr Shamsul Huq was quite upset with me since he felt that I was responsible for our situation; I had proposed the procession that had led to all the trouble. Without it we would not have ended up in jail.

Mr Huq had been married only a month and a half back. He and his wife, Afia Khatun, were both studying in Dhaka University when they fell in love and wed. Whenever Mr Huq berated me for our situation I would tease him and call him 'wife crazy'. He would get even more enraged and shower abuses on me. Maulana Bhasani would smile at our exchanges and this made Mr Huq angry with the Maulana too.

The three of us used to say our prayers together. After we had finished our evening prayers the Maulana would teach us about religion from the Koran. This became a routine. But Mr Huq was a bit of a problem since he seemed unable to finish any prayer in under an hour. Each part of the prayer would take him ten minutes! At times he would just shut his eyes and lose sense of time as he went into meditation.

Out trial started. We had to go to court once every fifteen days. We were given chairs to sit in the cell for prisoners in the court building. We were summoned from there and sent back to it immediately after the hearings.

Many of our colleagues would come to visit us. Students' League workers would meet us on most visiting days. Mr Ataur Rahman Khan was pleading our case in the court. On days when Mr Huq's wife came to visit it would be impossible to talk to him afterwards! I would really feel bad about his situation then. It was unfortunate that he had to stay away from his wife so soon after their marriage. It was obvious that they were very much in love. I would call her 'Bhabhi', and she would always bring along a book or two for me when she came to visit him. She would always tell him that I should let him know if I ever needed anything. I used to tend the garden in the jail yard. The days Mr Huq would meet his wife I would pass on a bouquet of flowers or make a garland for him to present to her. Certainly, Mr Huq was finding confinement more and more impossible.

He now began to bother us in another way. Every night after 12 he would loudly chant 'Allah' over and over again. This would last anywhere from one to two hours. Sometimes he would start his chants at midnight. The ten or fifteen of us in the cell wouldn't be able to sleep because of his chanting. The first few days we kept quiet. Prisoners have to work throughout the day and therefore need sleep badly. We complained to the

Maulana and he advised Mr Huq to pray silently since we were unable to sleep because of his chanting. However, Mr Huq chose to ignore the Maulana's advice. My bed was next to Mr Huq's. He would spread his prayer mat next to mine and begin chanting. Sometimes I would wake up after half an hour or so and hear him chanting loudly next to my ear. What could I do? I had to somehow endure him. When he got into this mood, he would continue for ten to fifteen days. One afternoon I told him, 'How long can I go on like this? If I can't sleep properly I will have a breakdown.' He got mad and said, 'I'll have to chant and you'll have to bear it. If not, do what you can. Go somewhere else.' For the moment I said nothing. A little later, however, I told him, 'If you start your chants again tonight, I'll pour a bucket of water on your head and I don't care what happens afterwards.' He, however, didn't take offence and merely told me, 'You don't seem to understand that I am into meditation. You will see the result of my efforts one of these days.' What could I do except continue to endure him! But it was clear that his health was deteriorating.

While we were in jail bloody communal riots broke out in both Calcutta and Dhaka. Many innocent Muslims in Calcutta and equally innocent Hindus in Dhaka and Barisal died in the riots. Apparently, someone had spread a rumour about Sher-e-Bangla Fazlul Huq's death. That was enough stimulus for the riots to start and for some Muslims to spring into action. Many people were arrested and brought to Dhaka jail. They were put in Ward 5 with us during daytime. It seemed to me that some 700–800 people were arrested. I would chat with them. Not all of them were guilty of rioting; in fact, only a few of them were directly involved. The culpable ones managed to get off scot-free and people who merely happened to be at the scene ended up in jail. I tried to tell the jailed ones that it wasn't right to get involved in rioting and the killing of people; it was, in fact, a sin to kill innocent people. A true Muslim couldn't kill anyone who was blameless; God and his Prophet had forbidden such action. God had created Hindus as well as us. They deserved to be treated as human beings too. Just because some Hindus in India were involved in heinous actions did not mean we should be perpetrating violence here. I exchanged views with many people of our city who were known for their violent tendencies; many of them told me that they would stay away from rioting from now on. Who knows if they were influenced by me afterwards? But it was obvious that many of them had become devoted to me, for when I was released from jail they would literally flock to me. When I got into difficulties they would do their best to protect me and help me out.

The jail authorities weren't happy about my exchanges with them. One day they took me away from this cell to Cell 20, which was one of many recently constructed cells. These were well-built cells. In all, there were ten of them upstairs and ten on the ground floor. The Maulana decided to opt for an upstairs cell and asked me to take the one next to his. Mr Huq decided that he would be my neighbour and told me, 'Good! Now I will be able to chant all night long without being interrupted!' I said to myself, 'Good grief!' However, I told him, 'Either you stay upstairs or I will. If you choose to be my neighbour I will have to say goodbye to sleep.' He was mad at my comment and decided to take a downstairs cell. I pleaded with him to cool down, as did the Maulana. Now he began to chant even more loudly than before. The result was that even though we were upstairs and he on the ground floor we had trouble sleeping.

A few days later Haji Danesh was brought to Dhaka jail. He now became our companion. Two days later he was removed to some other place since the government had decided that we would have to be isolated from everyone else. In particular, anyone the government considered a communist had to be kept away from us. It appeared to be fearful of the idea that we could turn communist. Political prisoners had been interned in two or three parts of this jail. This was the first time I had been given an entire cell to myself and I now began to realize the truth of the expression 'a jail within a jail, that's what a solitary cell is'. Two months later, when most of the people charged with rioting had been released on bail and the few that remained had been removed from Ward 5 to Ward 4, we were taken back to Ward 5.

We were staying in a three-storeyed building. Young boys were kept on the top floor; we were confined on one side of the second floor while the others were accommodated in the jail office. The ground floor was used as a warehouse. Things produced by the inmates were stocked in it. The jail housed the only blanket factory of East Bengal. The inmates designed beautiful blankets. A team of tailors was responsible for making them. They worked in shifts of a hundred people. Uniforms were made here for the police, guards and other government department employees. Carpenters of Dhaka were well known for their craftsmanship in making good-quality beds, tables and chairs. Cane furniture was also made in this building. A deputy superintendent was in charge of these activities. The prisoners would refer to this department as ASD.[22] I would go round the different sections of this department to see the people at work. The warehouse was next to the stairway and on the other side was an office.

I had started work on a garden since the place had no such thing. I would send the prison guards to the different ward grounds to get me flowering plants. My garden soon started to look beautiful. Adjacent to my garden was a press owned by the government. This too was part of the prison. There was a door built into the wall that separated these two parts of the prison. We could hear the press machines but were never able to see that section. When I looked out of my window in the mornings and evenings I could see its employees come and go. Looking at them made me feel that they were working in another prison; only it was larger than ours. What could be a greater cause for regret than the fact that we were in an independent country and yet didn't have the most basic rights?

In Pakistan people were being confined in jail year after year without trial. Every six months the government issued a directive extending the term of imprisonment. In the English phase of our history political prisoners were given certain rights but now that we had become an independent country these rights had been taken away from us. In the British period, political prisoners were entitled to quality food, clothes, medicines, newspapers, sports equipment and even a family allowance. Mr Nurul Amin's Muslim League government deprived political prisoners of all these facilities. Many political prisoners were treated as ordinary convicts. The government seemed reluctant to acknowledge the fact that many of these political prisoners had made a lot of sacrifices for the sake of the nation. Muslim League leaders had even started to claim that only if someone had gone to jail in a movement against an alien ruler could they be termed patriotic. Now people who were ending up in jail were being labelled as traitors. They were to be stripped of their rights. People who had been given titles such as Sir and Khan Bahadur for their loyalty to the British crown were making these statements, denouncing us and taking advantage of the fact that they were in the government now.

Mr Liaquat Ali Khan was the prime minister of Pakistan and Mr Nurul Amin the prime minister of East Pakistan. The kind of torture and harassment of political prisoners that was going on during their rule had no precedence in any civilized country at any stage of history. Political prisoners appealed time and again for the rights and privileges people in their position enjoyed during the British period. Unfortunately, their petitions were ignored. They were therefore forced to resort to hunger strikes. In 1949 political prisoners went on hunger strike for 200 days. As a consequence Shiben Roy died in jail that year. Of the ones that survived many ruined their health permanently. Many were later struck by tuberculosis because of the action they had taken to protest their treatment. Many went mad. No one except those directly involved will be able to imagine how desperate our plight was in prison because of lack of proper food and medicine.

In 1950, seven political prisoners were shot dead in Rajshahi's Khapra ward. The doors of the ward had been locked up from the outside when this happened. The prisoners inside who had survived were beaten up so badly that they were maimed for life. Such incidents of torture were commonplace in different jails of the country even as political prisoners continued to go on hunger strikes to demand their rights all over the region. In some cases family members of political prisoners had to resort to begging to survive. Such is the irony of fate that people who had been sentenced to life imprisonment in the Andaman Island penitentiaries and had survived them in the British period were now languishing in jails after their country had become independent.

Liaquat Ali was doing his best to stick to his word. He had said, after all, that he would wring the neck of anyone who dared oppose him or who got involved with the Awami League. Even though he had failed to wring our necks he had succeeded in breaking the party's back by interning many of us and by adopting torture as policy. All three of us had protested vehemently against the measures his government had adopted.

But despite the Muslim League government's efforts we didn't have to starve in jail. This was because we had sympathizers even within the government. The jail authorities were doing their best to look after us. Mr Amir Hossain was the superintendent of Dhaka jail at that time. He tried to see to it that we were comfortable. Both the Maulana and I would tell him on his weekly visit that he should also try to ensure that other political prisoners were not suffering either. But our sympathizers within the government were also forced to be subdued. This was because the government had informers inside the jail. Many of the people who wanted to help us were so wary of them that they would often hesitate to help us out of fear. When Liaquat Ali Khan became the leader of the nation after Muhammad Ali Jinnah's death he unleashed a reign of terror in the country. It was under his directives that the provincial leaders pounced on opposition leaders and workers. Both the Frontier Province and East Pakistan jails of the period were now overflowing with political prisoners.

The draft manifesto we had produced at the time the Awami League was formed had stressed the need for autonomy. This aspect of the manifesto had infuriated Liaquat Ali Khan. Considering that they constituted the majority, the generosity of the East Bengalis had no parallel anywhere else in the world. In the first Constituent Assembly there were forty-four members from East Pakistan. The Punjab, Sind, the Frontier Province and Baluchistan together had twenty-eight members. From its quota of forty-four seats the people of East Pakistan had set aside six for West Pakistanis living in the province. Nobody in East Pakistan had objected to this arrangement. Even though we constituted the majority, none of us objected to having Karachi as the capital of the country. But when we saw that all the industrial development was taking place in the west, and that except for a few ministers all important positions, especially those in the higher echelons of administration, were being filled up by West Pakistanis, we began to take note.

Liaquat Ali Khan tried to operate by creating a rift between Bengali and Punjabi MPs since he himself was a migrant from India. He was particularly dependent on bureaucrats, who were all from West Pakistan. All these people were Muslims. The people of East Bengal had not trusted Hindus and high officials of their own region with governance and had empowered these people from the west to rule over them. The consequence was that, though West Pakistanis kept calling the people of the east their brothers, in practice they kept on building their own part of the country at the expense of East Bengal.

In 1950 a Grand National Convention was organized in Dhaka [by all parties]. Educated people of Bengal in general and those involved in the Awami League in particular got involved in this event. People like Ataur Rahman Khan and Kamruddin Ahmed took an active part in the proceedings. Mr Hamidul Huq Chowdhury was forced to resign from his position as a minister at this time. He too had played an active role in the convention. He was publishing the daily *Pakistan Observer* by this time. This was a big help to our cause. The Grand National Convention resolved to demand full autonomy for our entire region. When Liaquat Ali Khan came to Dhaka, representatives elected by the convention met him and informed him of the demands of the people of East Pakistan. Mr Khan of course disapproved of the movement for autonomy.

Mr Suhrawardy was not the type of leader who would stay mum at such a moment. He had been involved in political movements all his life. He had even succeeded in forming a party in the west. Some Muslim emigrants from India who had settled down in Karachi met him there and requested him to form a branch of the Awami League in this wing of Pakistan. Politicians from the Punjab and Sind also came forward to show their support for him. Nawab Mamdot's party had decided by this time that it would try to defeat Liaquat Ali Khan in the polls.

Mr Ghulam Muhammad [from West Pakistan] used to be a government official before Partition. When he was made finance minister after Jinnah died, bureaucracy in Pakistan got a boost. Chaudhury Muhammad Ali became the secretary general of the central government, and he was able to create a powerful political lobby [of West Pakistani civil servants] from within the civil servants. In East Pakistan Aziz Ahmed was the chief secretary and used to wield power decisively in the province. Mr Nurul Amin never dared to take a step without his approval.

I was having to spend all my time in jail. It seemed to us that there was no one to speak up for us. We learned from a newspaper that Mr Suhrawardy had issued a statement on our behalf in Lahore. A case had been filed against us in the court. Meanwhile, the Maulana and I were having a tough time putting up with Mr Shamsul Huq. His health was also deteriorating fast. He had lost almost 10 kilos. Moreover, he would spend the whole time chanting. Sometimes on hot summer days he would lie in bed the whole afternoon with only a blanket covering him. The Maulana and I had long discussions about his condition. It appeared to us that if he stayed in jail much longer he would go completely mad. On a couple of occasions he became angry with me and said, 'If they don't let me go I'll do so by signing a bond. Should I spend all my time in jail because of you and Bhasani's antics?' One day when the civil surgeon came for a visit we talked to him about Mr Huq's health. We pointed out that the way he was losing weight indicated he could have a breakdown at any moment. He said that he couldn't submit a report on him till the government asked for one although he could comment on Mr Huq's health in any petition submitted by him. Mr Shamsul Huq had already written a petition that he intended to submit to the authorities but I persuaded him not to do so. Instead, he wrote another one applying for release from confinement on health grounds. Although its argument was weak in places, there was no other alternative to submitting it. The civil surgeon wrote on it that he believed Mr Huq's health was in bad shape. Five or seven days later he was released from jail and he left immediately. Maulana Bhasani and I continued to be in confinement. We would meet Mr Shamsul Huq when we were taken to the court. Apparently, the government believed that if someone as strong as Shamsul Huq could be won over, people like the Maulana and myself would have to bend. One of my sisters who lived in Dhaka (Sheikh Fazlul Huq Moni's mother) would visit me in jail. I had asked everyone in my own village not to bother about visiting me in Dhaka; nevertheless, my father came to see me once.

One day when we were in court we came across Mr Manik Mia. He was waiting there to talk to us. After we had talked for a while, he said, 'I'm going through a hard time but no one seems to be giving me any attention. There is little that I can do here now. I've been offered a big position in Karachi and would like to take it. What do you think?' I said, 'Manik Bhai, are you going to desert us too? I guess we'll have no one to help us through this ordeal.' I was aware that he and his family consisting of four children were going through a lot of hardship. He had left his children behind in Pirojpur and was staying on his own in Dhaka. He kept quiet for a while and then responded to my plea by saying, 'No, I'll not desert you all.'

The Maulana had published the weekly *Ittefaq* for some time. But after the paper had come out for a few weeks he had had to suspend publication. After all, where would he have got the money to sustain it for any length of time? He told Manik Bhai, 'If you can, try to publish it once again.' The latter said, 'Where will I get the money to publish it? Nevertheless, I'll give it a try.' I told Manik Bhai about a friend who loved me like he did his own brother. He used to work in Calcutta and was totally devoted to Mr Suhrawardy. Even though he didn't live in Bangladesh he was very fond of the country and its people. He might offer some help if he was told that I had recommended him. The next time we saw him in the court when we went there for a hearing, Manik Bhai told me that he would try to publish the paper regularly. And so the paper was revived. To keep it going he had to raise money from various sources. He had to spend whatever money he had to keep it afloat. Within a few days the paper became very popular. Awami League supporters would help him run the paper and distribute it everywhere. This paper wasn't supplied to us in jail. I would get hold of a copy and read it when we were taken to court. Workers of the Awami League began to distribute the paper in every district of the country. It soon became identified with the Awami League. Initially, Manik Bhai preferred to write in English and was reluctant to write in Bengali. And yet he soon came to be seen as East Pakistan's finest columnist in Bengali. He was writing brilliantly. He edited the paper himself. Two or three Students' League workers assisted him. He got most of the money he needed from my friend. It was difficult to get ads for the paper then for there was little commercial activity going on at that time. And of course an Awami League paper could not expect any government ads. Nevertheless, Manik Bhai managed to get the paper going on his own.

The hearing of our case ended in late 1950. The magistrate's verdict led to the Maulana's and Shamsul Huq's acquittal. Abdur Rauf, Fazlul Huq BSc and I were sentenced to three months of hard labour in prison. But what did it matter in my case whether I was given a sentence by the court or not? I was going to be held for much longer for security reasons, regardless of the outcome. Mr Ataur Rahman Khan, Mr Kamruddin and many others argued our case in court. I was also given division status. But I had to serve my sentence despite the appeal that they filed on my behalf. After a few days I was sent to Gopalganj since a case had been filed against me there too.

I had been staying close to the Maulana for a long time and felt bad about having to stay without him now. But I had no option except to leave him. I now began to serve my sentence as well as continue to serve time as a prisoner held under the Public Security Act. In Dhaka jail I was made to weave thread. I did what I could. I actually liked making thread. I had been feeling quite depressed and my body was suffering too from continued inactivity.

I was taken to Gopalganj via Narayanganj on a ship called the *Khulna Mail*. This ship stopped in Barisal on its journey. I had a sister living in Barisal as well as many other relatives. Because the ship touched Barisal only for a short while I ended up meeting none of them. I had requested a rickshaw puller to try and inform my cousin Jahangir to come and meet me. Everybody knew Jahangir in that town. Just when the ship was leaving I saw him cycling towards the ship. By this time they had withdrawn the planks. I talked to him for a minute or two from where I was. He said, 'I found out that you are here only a moment ago.'

The ship left for Gopalganj. On its way it would have to stop at two river ports. I would have to get down at Gopalganj and enter the town after crossing the station. We used to touch Patgati station every time we travelled this route. Everybody knew me in this region. I asked the stationmaster if he knew how my family was doing. He told me exactly what I was apprehending: the previous night my parents, wife and children had left for Dhaka to meet me. I had boarded the ship that was coming to Gopalganj while they had boarded the one leaving for Dhaka! In fact, the two ships must have crossed each other. Unfortunately, we had failed to meet. I felt depressed. I didn't inform anyone in our village home that I was in Gopalganj. Renu had written to me a few days back saying that she wanted to come to Dhaka to meet me. But I had no idea that she would be going there soon after.

I reached Manikdaha station late at night. In order to reach Gopalganj town you needed to get on a boat and travel for at least a few miles. I was being escorted by some armed guards, a constable, two men from the detective branch, a sub-inspector, and either an orderly or a bodyguard. We reached Gopalganj in the early hours of the next day. I was taken to the police line. My Gopalganj house was a short distance away from the police line. Some students were staying in our house. The Awami League and Students' League offices were located in it.

I was feeling very depressed and was exhausted by this time. The people in charge tried their best to make me comfortable. They arranged a bed for me as quickly as they could. I went to sleep immediately.

I began to get ready for the day as soon as I got up the next morning. The news had spread in Gopalganj town that I had been brought here for my trial. Next to the police line was the house of Shamsul Huq Muktar, popularly known by his nickname, Basu Mia. His wife was very fond of me and I used to call her mother-in-law since she was distantly related to my wife's mother. She was very pleasant as well as bright. She had food sent for me as soon as she knew that I was being confined in the police line. I was summoned by the court at ten o'clock. A crowd had congregated outside. The magistrate ruled that I would have to be kept within the area under the police station's jurisdiction. The case would be heard in court the next day.

Gopalganj jail had no provisions for keeping prisoners who had been granted division status or who were being tried for breach of public security. The court was one mile away from the police station and I would have to walk this distance. This was because Gopalganj had no rickshaws at that time. A lot of people accompanied me as I began my walk to the court. I knew every bit of Gopalganj intimately. I had studied in its school, played in its fields, swum in its river, and I knew everyone in the town just as everyone here knew me well. I had grown up breathing the air of this place. This is where I was initiated into politics. Next to the river were the court and the Mission School. There was a college in the vicinity too. The students of the college abandoned their studies and flocked to see me. A little farther away were rows of shops, whose owners I knew by name. As I walked to the court I exchanged greetings with all of them.

As soon as I reached the police station, the police sub-inspector in charge put me in a room where in the pre-Partition days political prisoners were confined. We used to live in this neighbourhood when I was a child. I used to chat with the political prisoners confined in that room then. Since I was a small boy at that time everyone would ignore me and allow me to mix freely with the prisoners. But today I was being kept in this little room so soon after we had become independent!

Next to the police station was the house of an uncle of mine. He was a well-known lawyer. He is no longer with us now. His name was Abdur Razzaque Khan and he was the brother of Abdus Salam Khan. He used to spend a lot of time reading and was quite knowledgeable about politics. He was also well liked by everyone. I have rarely seen such a selfless and patriotic man. He never wanted anything from anyone. On many an occasion I had made unfair demands on him but he never took offence.

Mr Salam Khan was his stepbrother even though no one ever got to know that fact. When Mr Salam Khan deserted the Awami League he did not follow his brother. He was exemplary in every way. It could be said that his death left Gopalganj poorer. People of our area were devoted to him and had a lot of faith in him. Government officials too would respect him. People called him 'Raja Mia'. To me, he was Uncle Raja. The court informed him about my being there. My food was supposed to be sent from his house. Before I had reached the police station I was informed that Raja Mia's mother and wife, my maternal grandmother and aunt respectively, had sent me food and that I should take a bath and then eat. When I stepped out of my room in the police station I saw that my maternal grandmother and aunt had come to see me. I greeted them respectfully. On both sides of the police station people had gathered to meet me. I greeted all of them. I then wished them all well and went back to my room in the police station. Someone had come from my own home to meet me.

It had been a while since I had been allowed to stay outdoors after sunset. I had spent a year in jail by this time and every day the door was locked from outside as the sun set. All I could do then was peep out to catch a glimpse of a moonlit night or the stars in the sky. Today I didn't feel like going indoors again. I stayed outside as the police kept watch over me. The policeman in charge of guarding me sat down next to me. We talked for a long time. A couple of friends who lived in the area joined us. By the time I went to bed it was late night but sleep evaded me. The problem was that in the next room a telegraph machine sounded away. I decided to sit outdoors again. I wanted to go to sleep under the sky but that was impossible what with Gopalganj's notorious mosquitoes all around me. Exposing myself to them was not a good idea. I eventually went to sleep when it was early morning and woke up quite late.

I reported to the court later that day and the time was set for my hearing since the court inspector had come from Faridpur for that purpose. He informed me that the case would be prosecuted on behalf of the government by its public prosecutor, Rai Bahadur Binod Bhadra. But he did not show up and the date of my hearing was set back by a month. I was to stay in Faridpur district jail till my hearing was over. I would stay there and would be brought to Gopalganj every month close to the date of my hearing. Although Gopalganj was a subdivision of Faridpur district, travelling back and forth between these two places was arduous because of the state of the roads. Twice a day steamers would sail from Khulna to Gopalganj. You could also go to Barisal directly by ship from Gopalganj. I was taken to Madaripur from Gopalganj. I would have to spend the night in a place called Sindhia Ghat en route. The next morning I would have to go to Bhanga by launch and from there board a taxi for Faridpur. All in all it would take me a day and a half to travel from Gopalganj to Faridpur!

We reached Sindhia Ghat in the evening and stayed in a bungalow owned by the irrigation department. This bungalow stood at the confluence of three rivers. I had decided to spend the night there and the policemen guarding me had agreed to let me do so, for where else could they keep me at night? This was a river port and the guard of the bungalow knew me well. An official of the irrigation department used to stay in one of the two rooms of the bungalow and I was given the other room.

Some people of the neighbouring village were devoted to me. As soon as they heard that I had been brought there, they rushed to see me. I requested the guard to arrange for our dinner and the other guards helped him with the arrangements. Two employees of the establishment named Korban Ali and Azhar had homes nearby. They kept insisting that I should have dinner in their houses. I said I didn't mind myself but that it probably wasn't a good thing for them since they would lose their jobs if the government came to know. In the end they sent me curry from their homes. I stayed up late, looking at the river flow by. I could see boats criss-crossing it. I told the police not to worry about me and asked them to go to sleep. I said, 'Even if you try to remove me by force I won't budge from here.' They laughed at this and said, 'We know that you won't flee and aren't worried about you.'

I couldn't sit down for a long time for there seemed to be an overwhelming silence everywhere. It seemed as if the whole country was asleep. All I could hear was the splash made by a boat or two.

I woke up in the morning. The launch would come from Madaripur in the morning. I would have to take it to Bhanga. When it arrived we got on it. We met a lot of people. Bhanga had a subdivision court. Here I had a distant cousin who was a lawyer. Next to Bhanga was Nurpur village, where one of my uncles used to live. The launch stopped at a landing yard that was next to this court. When one of my cousins came to know that I was here he came to see me. We went to the taxi stand. However, my uncle's family had not been informed about my arrival. We hired a taxi to take us to Faridpur. It was evening by this time and we were told that prison laws prevented their managers from taking anyone in at night. I therefore had to go to the police line. It was arranged that I would stay in a room there in what was probably the clubhouse. The reserve inspector arrived and instructed his people to ensure I was happy with the arrangements.

I didn't inform anyone here of my arrival though I had many relatives in Faridpur. Nevertheless, a lot of people turned up to see me. But I never wanted anyone to get into trouble on my account. The next morning the police people arranged for my breakfast and I had to oblige them. I kept thinking, 'How you people are showing your love for me!' The people with whom I had worked very closely before Pakistan's independence, people with whom I had been intimate once upon a time and who used to praise me saying 'there is no one as efficient as you are in party work' were now conniving to keep me in jail without trial and were doing their best to punish me.

I took leave of the police officials and came to Faridpur jail. The jail administration had already been informed by the DIG about my arrival. I reached the jail gate in the morning. Both the jailer and the deputy jailer were in their offices. I was made to sit in the deputy jailer's office room. He looked through my papers and pointed out that I still had to serve three months of my sentence. However, I was also being confined under the Public Security Act. I said that I could not have more than a month of my sentence left to serve. He tried to figure out where I should be staying within the jail. He probably had to be on the phone for this reason. A few political prisoners were being kept in a ward. Should I be kept with them or separately? In the end I heard him say that a room in the hospital wing of the jail should be cleared so that I could be put up there. My box and clothes were inspected by his people. I kept quiet while all these activities were going on. A jamadar eventually came to me and said, 'Come to this room.' When I went inside the room he put a hand in my pocket. I told him, 'Please don't touch me. You can't search me physically since this is not permitted by the law. Only the jailer and his deputy can examine me physically if they so desire.' I was quite angry when I said these words and the poor fellow became flustered. I told him, 'Who ordered you to subject me to a physical examination?' I then addressed the deputy jailer: 'What is going on? Have you ordered him to examine me physically?' The deputy jailer asked the man to leave and apologized to me: 'Forgive him. He was ignorant of the rules.' I told the deputy jailer, 'Go ahead and see what I have with me: cigarettes, a matchbox and a handkerchief.' He was embarrassed by my outburst. He sent me away as soon as he could.

This was the first time I had been in Faridpur jail. Its hospital had two floors. I stayed all by myself in a ground-floor room. The other rooms of the floor were for patients. The floor had a veranda, something that pleased me. Since I hailed from Faridpur, I was bound to know some of the other inmates. I was given a boy to look after my needs. My food would be brought from the dining room of the political prisoners' ward. I had come to know that there were five or six of them in the ward. All I had as companions were the books I had brought along. I also asked for newspapers. There were some open spaces in front of the hospital and a flower garden. I decided that I would be responsible for looking after them. I would have to find means of spending my time and I thought this was as good a way as any as I wouldn't get the opportunity to meet the political prisoners. Even though the prison was small, they lived in a part of it that was still some distance away from where I was staying.

I would pray regularly and also recite verses from the Koran every day. I had the Bengali translation of the Koran in several volumes. While I was in Dhaka jail I had taken Maulana Muhammed Ali's English translation of the Koran and had read it.

The jailer himself came up to me on one occasion to tell me that I should let him know if I faced any problems. I didn't like the idea of taking naps inside my jail room during the day. Nevertheless, I went to sleep in it the first day of my stay here. I woke up in the evening, had a cup of tea and walked about a bit. As the sun set, they locked me in. There would be five prisoners-cum-guards guarding my room and there was the boy to look after my needs. The prisoners-cum-guards had two-hour shifts and they stayed with me inside the room. The jail watchman standing outside would ask them periodically if everything was all right inside the room and they would answer, 'Yes, fine.' They also had to verify the number of prisoners inside the room. I had instructed them not to shout out their answers and to respond to the jail watchmen softly so that my sleep wouldn't be disturbed. But if the guards in my room responded softly to the queries directed at them from outside, this wasn't the case in the other rooms. Fortunately, all the wards were some distance away from the hospital; otherwise I would have really suffered.

I was being kept in solitary confinement as part of the punishment. Only those who have endured this form of punishment can imagine how difficult it is to stay all by oneself in a dark room. The jail code specifies that no prisoner should be allowed to stay in solitary confinement for more than three consecutive months. When any prisoner violated prison regulations he would often be punished by the jail wardens with solitary confinement. But even the wardens didn't have the right to keep anyone in isolation for more than three months at a time!

The next morning when I was having tea after a walk a middle-aged prisoner who was a patient in the hospital came towards me and sat down on the floor. I asked him where he was from. He replied, 'I am from

Gopalganj and the name of my village is Vhennabari and I am called Rahim.' I said, 'And so you are Rahim!' Everyone in our region knew him well. Never in the whole of Gopalganj subdivision was such a notorious dacoit born. People used to be scared of the very name. He was always trying to steal things but whenever this proved impossible he would turn into a dacoit. I asked him if he was responsible for the theft of almost all the valuables in our house a while ago. He kept quiet for a long time and didn't respond to my query. Sometime either in 1938 or in 1939 thousands of takas worth of jewellery belonging to my mother and my sisters was stolen. My father used to be in Gopalganj then. In the almost 400-year history of our house this was the only time that a theft of this nature had occurred. Rahim eventually said, 'Yes, I stole the jewellery.' I told him, 'How did you work up the courage to break into our house? We have a gun, as do many other people in the cluster of houses that make up our homestead. We live in such a huge house and there are so many people living in it.' He said, 'I was helped by some villagers and people from your own house.' Indeed, we had found out later that a man who used to work for us but had a boat of his own had used it to bring Rahim to our house. Three days after the theft he had confessed to his role in the crime. Since most of the stolen goods had not been traced the case didn't appear before the courts. Moreover, the police sub-inspector in charge of filing the case had done his best to prevent it from happening. If Rahim had been arrested we would have got more jewellery. But he was not to be found anywhere for a long time. My father had done his best to expose the sub-inspector's complicity and had managed to put him in a tight spot. In fact, the then police superintendent had taken punitive measures against the sub-inspector.

Rahim began narrating his life story. He had been in jail for a long spell. He said, 'When I failed to become rich even after burgling your house I made it known that I would build a house even though people assume that a mere thief manages to build nothing. The people of my village could see what I was up to. A few days later I went to Bagerhat intending to commit a robbery there but was captured. I had to spend a lot of money to free myself on bail and return home. I then made another attempt to burgle the home of Roy Chowdhury of Gopalganj's Ulpur village. When I was on my way back after committing the crime the police captured me once again since they had been tipped off about the route I would be taking to return home. I managed to get bail once more but made yet another attempt to commit robbery. This time too I was arrested but now I was refused bail. I will have to be in jail for fifteen to sixteen years in all now for all the offences I have committed. Before Pakistan achieved independence I had already served a term in Dum Dum jail in Calcutta. From there I was sent to Rajshahi and finally to Faridpur jail. Do you know that I had never been caught for theft till I attempted to steal from your house? Afterwards every attempt I made has landed me in jail! In jail it occurred to me that there must be something sacred about your house because I scorched myself the moment I tried to put my hand into it. I guess I will be forgiven if I plead to your mother to forgive me.' I told him, 'Rahim Mia, my parents were saddened by your actions. We wouldn't have been upset if we had lost everything else, but you managed to steal my elder sister's jewellery. Since she was nineteen she has lived the life of a widow with a son and a daughter and that is all the wealth she had.' He replied, 'I will never steal again in my life. I still have to serve a few more years in jail. My health is deteriorating.' He requested me to let him know if I needed anything since he had a gold coin tucked away in his throat somewhere. I said I didn't need anything. But I said to myself, 'Of course you would have a gold coin stowed away somewhere!' After all, he had stolen a lot of jewellery from our house.

It was obvious that this man had managed to buy off a lot of the guards in Faridpur jail for they would leave him alone. It was easy to see why he had such a free hand compared to other convicts. He would stay in the jail hospital for prolonged periods of time. Health-wise, he was in bad shape. He would come and talk to me whenever he got the opportunity. He would tell me all sorts of things then. It seemed to me that perhaps he was turning over a new leaf.

Mr Syed Ahmed was the jailer at that time. He would always inquire about my health. He would tell me that I should contact him the moment I needed something or was uncomfortable. Even though prisoners were not supposed to press oil manually, Faridpur jail employed prisoners for the purpose regularly. I asked him, 'Why are you still persisting with such a practice?' He replied, 'We will stop doing so as soon as we can purchase cows.' In a few days' time he stopped this inhuman practice.

I had conversations with many notorious thieves and robbers staying in Dhaka and Faridpur jails when I was interned in them. Many of them would somehow stow away gold coins in their body. They managed to keep money, gold rings or gold guineas in their body parts. They would sell them from time to time to buy themselves necessities. They would spend money to live rather comfortably. Many would beg for cigarette paper from me. One day while I was in Dhaka jail I told one of them, 'Show me how you manage to stow away gold in your body and I will give you cigarette paper.' He said, 'I'll do so but you'll have to wait.' When the guard moved away he seemed to throw up and in the process managed to emit a taka coin. I said, 'Enough! I can see what your method is.'

~

A month went by. It was time for me to go to Gopalganj again. Just before dusk, a detective branch official and a gun-toting guard escorted me from the jail gate. I had to stay in the police line that night because I would have to leave for Bhanga at five the next morning. Prisoners were not allowed to leave the jail that early in the morning. Next to the police line was a friend's house. When I sent word to him that I was staying in the police line he came to see me. We talked for a long time. He wasn't involved in politics of any kind and so no one had any objections to our meeting. That night I slept in the clubhouse of the police line.

We left for Bhanga very early in the morning. In those days it took a few hours to travel to Bhanga. One had to cross two ferries to do so. The road was in a bad shape. Two or three of my relatives were present. They had arranged for my food. The launch didn't delay. We boarded a launch, which arrived in Sindhia Ghat in the afternoon. We would have to spend the night here. I said, 'Why bother spending the night here? Let's go to Madaripur. A ship will be leaving at 11 p.m. from there. Boarding the ship from Sindhia Ghat so early in the morning is quite tough!' My guards found my suggestion acceptable. But we would have to travel a much longer distance to take this route. However, we reached Madaripur late in the afternoon. The ship was still in the landing station.

I ordered supper for all of us on the ship. The guards said, 'Why do you want to spend so much money?' There was a hotel in the landing station and departure was still some hours away. We could easily have our food before that. We would have to wait for five or six hours in Madaripur Ghat. By then my relatives and friends had come to know of my arrival in Madaripur. Many of them came to meet me. I talked to them for a while and found out how everyone was doing. They brought refreshments for me. I asked the ship's butler to ensure that everyone got something to eat. The ship eventually left at 11 p.m. I felt free even though I was in police captivity. After all, I could feel the breeze still caressing me.

We got down at Haridaspur station at 8 a.m. and reached Gopalganj by boat afterwards. I told the police who were escorting me to take me to the police station so that they could be relieved of their charge immediately. As soon as we landed in Gopalganj I saw our boat. My father had come to meet me along with my mother, my wife, Renu, and my children, Hasina and Kamal. They had arrived at the same time and so we managed to talk to each other. Our home was 14 miles away from Gopalganj. I was meeting them after a year. Hasina embraced me and wouldn't let go of me. Kamal kept looking at me but didn't seem to recognize me. He wasn't old enough to figure out our relationship. My mother kept crying. My father rebuked my mother and told her to stop shedding tears. I came to the police station and those who had come to see me went back to our house in Gopalganj. I reached the police station to find that a flat here had recently fallen vacant when a sub-inspector had been transferred. I was allowed to stay in it.

I would have to go to the court without delay. I got ready to do so. By this time the road was full of people eager to meet me. Many of my co-workers and supporters had come to see me. When I came to the court, the magistrate began proceedings immediately. The hearing continued till the next day. I asked my lawyer to request the court to allow my parents and wife and children to meet me in the flat I was staying in. The magistrate agreed to our request. The man who had accompanied me from Faridpur and the Gopalganj detective branch official were not in favour of me meeting outsiders but they did not object to me meeting my family members. So I asked my co-workers and friends not to come to the police station since what good would it do me to put these people under a cloud of suspicion? After all, I could meet them all in the court. I returned to the police station. My baggage was in the care of the station-in-charge. My parents and wife came to see me there as soon as they were informed of my arrival. The police contingent, which had escorted me from Faridpur, continued to keep watch on me and would take me back to Faridpur as soon as the hearing was over. My family stayed with me for a few hours. Nothing would induce Kamal to approach me. He kept staring at me from a distance. No doubt he was thinking, 'Who could this man be?'

We met again next morning. However, I had to leave soon after I returned from the court. By evening I had taken leave of everyone and boarded the launch to reach Sindhia Ghat. I would have to spend the night there. I stayed in the government inspection bungalow. The night went quite smoothly even though the food they served me wasn't good at all. Luckily, I had some food that had been sent from our house.

Very early in the morning I boarded the launch again. Some of our party workers had come to Sindhia Ghat to see me off. Since the launch had left Sindhia Ghat on time I was able to reach Faridpur by evening and I could be sent to the jail that very night. The jail was full of locks—the gates, the ward doors and my rooms, all were locked up. I would have to spend the night in a room that had been locked up from outside.

And so this was how I had to spend three to four months of my life—going back and forth from Faridpur to Gopalganj for my hearings. But every time I went to Gopalganj I was at least able to see my family. Nevertheless, travelling between Faridpur and Gopalganj was quite tiresome. So I petitioned the government to allow me to stay either in Barisal or Khulna jail since it would be easier for me to travel to Gopalganj from these places because of direct steamer services between them and because I would not have to get off and get on steamers repeatedly. The government consented to my request and I was sent to Khulna. I had to depart for Khulna via Rajbari and Jessore.

When I arrived in Khulna I was shocked: it had no space to accommodate me. There was only one building in this jail and all the prisoners were being kept in one place. Where would I be staying? There was only one cell exclusively confining all sorts of violent criminals. The jail warden showed me the cell and said, 'Where else can I accommodate you? We have such a small prison house!' I now had the status of a political prisoner. I had served my previous sentence as well. It included only three months of imprisonment. There were no other political prisoners in this place. I was shocked: how could the people in charge send me to a place like this? There were probably six cells in all and each of them had a fourteen-foot wall in front of them. Next to the cells was the hang room and on the other side were the lavatories. The inmates had to use these lavatories to relieve themselves. The odour was so unbearable that one couldn't stand in front of them. They couldn't make any arrangements for me to dine separately because there wasn't any space for that. And nothing could be done about that. I was kept in one of these cells and was to have food brought from the hospital. I would have to eat the rice and vegetables the hospital served its patients. I had been sent some dry food from our home. I would have to survive on that if I wanted to avoid hospital food. My life was turning out to be hell. I told the jail warden, 'Please write to the higher-ups that there isn't any space here for me. I won't be able to stay here on my own. And if they want me to stay here they'll have to provide me with adequate facilities.'

It was time for another hearing. I went to sleep on the steamer soon after I had boarded it. We were supposed to reach Gopalganj in the morning. My health had deteriorated considerably by this time. One day I was called to the jail office. At that time civil surgeons also used to serve as ex-officio superintendents of prisons. Now Mr Mohammad Hossain was acting as the civil surgeon of Khulna. When he came on an inspection of the jail and heard about my condition he sent for me. He was waiting for me when I reached the prison office. He asked me to sit next to him. As soon as I sat down he asked me, 'Why are you spending time in prison?' I said, 'Because I want to grab power!' He stared at me for a long time and then said, 'And what will you do once you have grabbed power?' I said, 'If I can I will try to do something for the people of the country. Can you do that by not assuming office?' He said to me, 'I have been associated with prison administration for a long time. I have met many political prisoners in the course of my work. Nobody has answered my question like you have. All of them say the same thing: they are in prison because they were working for the good of the people. They say they were serving the country and had protested because they couldn't bear the oppression of the government and that's why they were in prison. But I must thank you for answering my question so frankly.' He then discussed the facilities that I had been given. He told me that he had written to the higher-ups in the administration about the difficulties being faced by political prisoners. He was hoping to hear from them soon. He also told me that he was aware of the hardships that I had to endure.

In the evening I used to walk in the tiny space in front of the prison office. The jailer had given me this privilege. My room had no window and only one door and even that was facing a wall. A prison guard from Rajshahi often did duty as my guard. He was a terrific singer. I used to listen to his songs whenever he came to do guard duty.

I came to Gopalganj this time in the midst of the hearings. A government official was giving testimony against me. Most of the officials had been transferred by then. They had to come from places far away and every time I saw a new face giving testimony. I would come for the hearings from Khulna jail and the government lawyer and court inspector would come from Faridpur. As usual, when I was there, I would have food sent from our home. I had told my folks to have some eggs sent for me since lack of good food had weakened me considerably. In a month's time I had lost a lot of weight. My eyes were in bad shape too. My stomach was playing up. I was beginning to have chest pains. Renu warned me not to forget that I had once suffered from a heart problem and that my eyes had once been operated on. I tried to tell her that I would be fine. What else could I do? Hasina just wouldn't let go of me this time too. Nowadays whenever it was time for her to leave she would burst into tears. Kamal had started to come close to me recently. He had started to call me 'Abba' since he could hear Hasina calling me that. Because I was within the jurisdiction of Gopalganj police station on these occasions I could at least enjoy such moments with them for the time being.

Soon I had two new companions. A political prisoner called Nurunnabi had been brought here from Rajshahi because he had to appear before the court to defend himself in a case filed in the Khulna court. He had been in Rajshahi when political prisoners had been fired upon. A bullet had wounded him in the leg and the physicians had had to amputate it. He moved around on one leg now. He was a good-looking young man. His life was in ruins and yet they wouldn't release him. He was originally from Burdwan in West Bengal.

A few days later the peasant leader Bishnu Chatterjee was transferred here from Dhaka jail, his feet in chains. He had been sentenced after a trial and was now serving time as an ordinary prisoner. One case against him still awaited a court hearing. He always looked cheerful; it was as if he had no worries at all. One day he told me, 'I have only one cause for sorrow; they have made me an accused in a robbery case!' He was denied division status. He had to wear prison clothes and eat the food served to all ordinary prisoners.

Nurunnabi, on the other hand, always looked grim. He was depressed because he had become a cripple for life. From him I came to know the sad stories of the torture being inflicted on prisoners in Rajshahi jail. Even after the country had become independent an English prison official had ordered the prison guards to fire on prisoners mercilessly. This had led to the untimely death of seven political prisoners who had been serving sentences for fighting for the freedom of our country. The people who had survived were in a sad state too since they had been beaten up so badly that they would never be able to resume normal life again.

Three months had passed since I had been brought to Khulna jail. Prisoners detained under the Public Security Act would be issued directives from the government every six months. I think I must have been in jail for around eighteen months by now. The six-month detention period allotted for me was over and yet no new directive for me had reached Khulna jail. On what basis could the jail authorities keep me in prison now? I said, 'Since you have no orders to detain me, release me. If you continue to detain me, I will file a case against you for imprisoning me illegally.' The jail authorities now talked to the Khulna magistrate and the superintendent of police, who informed them that they had received no orders to extend my imprisonment. However, there was a production warrant issued against me for the case filed in Gopalganj even though there was no custody warrant that would justify my detention. They talked at length about my situation and decided in the end that they would send me to Gopalganj court as well as send a radiogram to Dhaka. In the meantime an order came from Dhaka to send me to Gopalganj. I was sent on a ship to Gopalganj accompanied by a police escort.

The Gopalganj court released me on bail the very next day. The people of Gopalganj brought out a huge procession, which I headed, to celebrate my release. I had sent word to my village home about my release and intended to head that way by nightfall. Meanwhile, I rested in our Gopalganj house while people were getting a boat ready for my journey. When the boat had arrived and I was about to take my leave a police inspector and a man from the detective branch approached me saying, 'We want to talk to you.' However, they had no police escort with them. On the other hand, at least a hundred people were with me at that time. I left my people and went to one side to hear what the two had to say. They handed me a piece of paper. It was a radiogram order to arrest me again under the Public Security Act. I said, 'All right, let's go.' One of the two said to me out of politeness, 'We won't escort you; it's okay if you go to the police station on your own.' I told my people, 'Please don't create a commotion but I have to tell you that I haven't been given freedom since they have issued an order to detain me once more. I have to go to the police station once again. But please don't harass these two. I have read the order myself.'

I sent word to the people who had got the boats ready to leave without me. I also arranged for a boxful of my clothes and books to be sent to the police station. Some of our party workers began to cry. Some of them shouted, 'No way! We won't let him go; let them snatch him away from us if they dare!' I tried to dissuade them but they just wouldn't listen to me. The detective branch official was a perfect gentleman. I told him, 'Come with me; otherwise it won't look correct. And don't worry—nothing untoward will happen.' I sent word to my family once again that very night to apprise them of what had happened. It was likely that I would be sent to some other jail the next day. I also forbade anyone from coming to see me in Gopalganj since it was likely that I would be taken elsewhere.

That night I stayed in the police station. The staff expressed regret at the turn of events. What reason could there be to arrest me after I had been incarcerated for seventeen–eighteen months? The next day I learned that my family had stayed awake the whole night in our village home thinking that I might show up at any time. My mother had cried inconsolably. I felt depressed. They shouldn't have hurt my parents, brothers and sisters and children in such a manner. I had signed no bond with the government. Why did they free me in the first place? Why hadn't the order to rearrest me come earlier? Surely I had committed no crime? Couldn't they behave more decently with me? The people with me decided to stay in the police station till it was quite late that night. I sat with them too. I kept thinking, 'I'll have to be in jail for a long term once more.'

I had to stay in Gopalganj police station for two more days. There was no directive from Dhaka regarding which jail I would be sent to. My health had deteriorated considerably while I served time in Khulna jail. After this turn of events it got worse.

Two days later word came that I was to be taken to Faridpur jail. And so I came back to that jail once more. This time I was kept in the ward set aside for political prisoners. There were two rooms in the ward. There were five political prisoners in one room. The prisoners in the other room included Gopalganj's Babu Chandra Ghosh, Madaripur's Phani Majumdar and myself. I had known the two of them for some time now. Phani Majumdar used to be a leader of the Forward Bloc party. He had been in prison for some eight or nine years during British rule and even after independence there was to be no respite for him! He hadn't married. His father was in India and used to receive a pension but Phani Majumdar himself wouldn't leave his country and so he stayed back. He was loved by Muslims as well as Hindus; people were fond of him irrespective of religion, nationality or caste. He would be there to lend a helping hand to anyone in distress. If any family had a sick person he would be there to look after that person. He was very fond of me. The government's policy, it seemed, was to keep people it deemed to be communists in one room. Since the three of us were not considered communists we were kept in the other room.

As for Chandra Ghosh, he was a social worker. He had never been involved in politics. Like Mahatma Gandhi, he used to wear a single piece of cloth whether it was summer or winter. On his feet he wore wooden clogs and he never put on leather shoes or sandals. He had established quite a few schools in Gopalganj subdivision. He had founded a degree college in Ramdia village, which is part of the Kashiani police zone. He had built many roads and had had many canals excavated for the public good. He was given to working for the people. After Pakistan was created an overzealous government official, thinking he would be rewarded for his effort, submitted a malicious report on him, which had led to his incarceration. When Mr Suhrawardy came to Gopalganj in 1948 he had told this man that by falsely accusing a person like Chandra Ghosh and then imprisoning him the Pakistani government had cast disrepute on itself. Chandra Ghosh, however, had served his sentence and yet he was being held under the Public Security Act. Since I was from Gopalganj I knew the truth about Mr Ghosh. I had been actively involved in the

Muslim League and the movement for Pakistan in this region. The Muslims as well as the Hindus of the region were very fond of Chandra Ghosh. In fact, there were many Muslims among his admirers. But his most devoted fans were scheduled caste Hindus. Some Hindus of Gopalganj who belonged to this caste had voted for Pakistan; in fact, I know that some 'untouchable' Hindus had worked with us in the Sylhet referendum. Chandra Ghosh had also built a school for girls. I had requested many government officials not to punish such a man since he had never been involved in politics. Society as a whole would benefit from such a selfless person. These people could be utilized to build the country now that it had become independent. But who was willing to listen to reason? Someone or the other had informed the government that Hindus were not paying heed to the law and had raised the Indian flag and one of their leaders was Chandra Ghosh. Among other things, these people asked for more armed police to be sent. But I know for sure that such talk was nonsensical. Muslims were quite strong in Gopalganj. If the Hindus had such intentions surely the region's Muslims would have opposed them. And if they were guilty of such a malicious act communal riots would certainly have broken out. In fact, nothing of that sort had taken place. But when Chandra Ghosh was arrested the Hindus of Gopalganj became scared. Upper-caste Hindus started to migrate to West Bengal. The few that had stayed back now tried to get ready to leave. The only reason the government had for detaining him was to give people the impression that they were very active in dealing with treason and had succeeded in saving Pakistan from dissolution by their alertness.

When I came to Faridpur jail I was already in poor health. Now I began to suffer from high fever, severe headaches and chest pains. Though the prison officials did their best for me I was very unwell for a while. Night after night Chandra Babu would sit beside me and try to bring down my fever by pouring water on my forehead. Whenever I regained my senses, I would see him sitting next to me. Phani Babu too stayed awake by me till late in the night. In fact I remember that at one point I didn't see Chandra Babu lie down at all for three whole days. He would rub my forehead all the time then to give me relief. At times he would pour water on my head and he also tried to persuade me to swallow my pills. If I refused to do so he would scold me. I would tell him not to work so hard on my behalf. His reply would be, 'I have done this sort of thing for people all my life and at this age I am accustomed to such acts and I never tire of doing them.' The prison physician wanted to remove me to the hospital but Mr Chandra and Mr Phani would not allow me to go there worrying no one would take care of me in that place like they were doing here. The other political prisoners also did their best for me.

I recovered after a few days. But because I had become very weak I couldn't go to Gopalganj for my hearing on the scheduled date. My folks therefore had to return home that day without meeting me. They had to come to Gopalganj by boat and had to stay there for a day and yet the trouble they took came to nothing. My father got so worried at not seeing me that he sent a telegram to me later.

Although I had recovered from the effects of high fever my heart had become weak. My eye condition worsened. I also suffered from stomach aches. In this condition another month passed by. And then once again I had to undergo the journey to Gopalganj on the date fixed for my hearing. This time the government inspection bungalow in Sindhia Ghat appealed to me more than it had before. I savoured the opportunity to breathe one more time the night air outside. Many thoughts went through my mind. In 1945 I had spent a night together with Mr Suhrawardy in this spot. My friend and co-worker Mollah Jalaluddin was with me then. It was from here that I accompanied the two of them to Gopalganj. In Faridpur Jalal and Hamid had worked with me for the movement to establish Pakistan.

Many people came to meet me late in the evening. Sindhia Ghat is nothing more than a small river port. A few low-ranking government officials are stationed there. Some of them came to see me when they heard that I was unwell. They took their leave one by one after spending a few minutes with me. After all, they could not stay for long since the detective branch people could file reports on them for seeing me.

Something else that had happened around this time is relevant in this context. A fellow working for the Madaripur detective branch had filed a report saying that people had once come to meet me when I was on a steamer in Madaripur. In the wake of that report the guards who used to escort me back and forth to these hearings became wary. They requested me not to talk to outsiders for long. But while I could refrain from initiating conversation with other people, how could I prevent people from meeting me if they wanted to do so? All these people usually did was greet me and ask me how I was and I would make the same inquiry as a matter of courtesy. My captors seemed to have forgotten that Faridpur was my district and that I had many relatives in the region. I had organized meetings in every part of the district and the people here knew me well. They should have had some twenty–thirty armed police escort me if they wanted to prevent anyone from exchanging greetings with me. They should have arranged for me to commute from Faridpur to Gopalganj and back on a government launch. Why blame the people who wanted to meet me? I did what I could to ensure that these unfortunate people did not have to suffer more on my account.

It wouldn't do for me, however, to stay outdoors for long because I couldn't afford to fall ill again. I would have to leave the bungalow early in the morning even though the landing station was nearby. I arrived in Gopalganj. This time too my folks had come from Tungipara to meet me in two or three big boats. All my relatives were alarmed at the state of my health. My mother began to wail loudly on seeing me. I returned from the court in the evening. I would have to go back the next day for another round of hearings. I told the court inspector, 'Why are you delaying proceedings? All the witnesses are here!' But the subdivisional police officer was absent, probably because he was in Chittagong then. But it was a good thing that he had decided to stay away since things had heated up to a boiling point and there could be trouble because people were in an explosive mood.

I now witnessed an amazing event. The former police inspector of Gopalganj had come to testify. In all probability he had been transferred to Dhaka. He was well known in Gopalganj for his honesty and for not accepting bribes. When he gave his testimony he didn't utter one falsehood; he truthfully narrated what he had witnessed. He testified that I had asked the crowd to disperse silently. I could see that this perturbed the government attorney. But the testimony had been recorded and the court official had got it down on paper. What could be done now? I realized that the case against me wouldn't stick but I also knew I would have to suffer a little longer. Pakistan, it was clear, still had police officials who didn't want to utter falsehoods. Because of the laws of our land no one could be prosecuted if someone failed to give false testimony when a person was in the right. Only in cases where you began with falsehood and ended with it could you hope to be successful. It is doubtful, however, if one can expect justice in a land where the law is based only on lies.

A date had been set for our hearing again for next month. I went back to the police station like on previous occasions. For two days I had got the opportunity to meet all the members of my family twice a day—in the morning and in the evening. Uncle Raja and his wife wouldn't allow me to have food supplied from anywhere except their home. His wife was especially fond of me. My maternal grandmother, Uncle Raja's mother, was staying with them at that time. My food would be sent from their house. Of the people who had come to see me from our village home the women were staying with my uncle and his wife and the men in the boats. When Renu got me to herself she said, 'I have no problem with your staying in jail but make sure that you have enough to eat. The sight of you has depressed me immensely. You should know that I have no one else in the world except you. My parents died when I was a child and I have no one else to look after me. How will I survive if something happens to you?' She broke into tears while saying this and when I tried to console her she began to cry even more. When they saw their mother sobbing, Hasina and Kamal started kissing her. I said, 'What God wills will happen, so why worry about it?' The next day I took leave from them. But consoling my mother proved to be a much more difficult task.

And so I came back to Faridpur jail once again. I found that Chandra Babu had been hospitalized and that he was in a critical condition. He had a hernia problem. He had somehow exerted pressure on his stomach and an artery had been displaced. As a result he had excreta coming out of his mouth and could die at any moment. The civil surgeon, however, was a very good physician. He wanted to risk an operation since the alternative was Chandra Babu's death. The man had no relatives around who would give the doctor the right to operate. Chandra Babu himself offered to give written permission for the surgery. He said, 'Since I have no kin what else is to be done?'

The civil surgeon ordered his removal to the General Hospital outside the prison. Chandra Babu said to him, 'I have nobody else but I would like to see Sheikh Mujibur Rahman once before I leave, for he is like a brother to me. I don't think I will meet him again in this life!' So under the directive of the civil surgeon and the jail superintendent I was taken out to the jail gate to meet him. He was lying on a stretcher. It seemed like he wouldn't survive. On seeing me he burst out crying and said, 'My brother, my only regret as I approach death is that they tried to smear me with the charge of communalism. I have never made any distinction between a Hindu and a Muslim throughout my life. Do tell everyone to forgive me. And it is my last request to you to always treat people as people. God made no distinctions between human beings. Since I have no kin of my own, I wanted to meet you before death since I consider you my relation. May God bless you.' He spoke in such a manner that the superintendent, the jailer, the physician and even the official of the detective branch had tears in their eyes. I too was crying. I told him, 'Don't worry; I always treat people as people. In politics I make no distinction between Muslims, Hindus and Christians; all are part of the same human race.' I didn't have the strength to say anything more. All I could tell him at the end is, 'If God wills it you may still get well again.' And so they took him away. The civil surgeon told us, 'There is little hope of success. But I am going to give it a final try by operating on him.'

We were all very apprehensive; who knew what the outcome of the operation would be? Two hours later the jail authorities informed us that the operation was over and he was doing fine. In the evening we were told that he was likely to survive though he was still not out of danger. We spent the night worrying about him but the morning news was that he was definitely improving. He was no longer throwing up excreta through his mouth. We had reason to hope that he had escaped death on this occasion. The next day the government made him a free man. But even though he was free he would have to stay in hospital a few more days because he still had to be certified out of danger. I think he had to remain in hospital for fifteen more days. He was clearly out of danger then even though his wounds hadn't healed completely. As soon as he was discharged from the hospital the district magistrate issued some fresh conditions for his release. He would have to live in his village, Ramdia. When Chandra Ghosh went to meet the magistrate he told him, 'If you want to remain in Pakistan you will have to confine yourself to your own village. And if you want to go to Calcutta for medical reasons we won't object. But when you come back you'll have to inform the police of your return.'

Chandra Babu agreed to these conditions and came to the prison gate to claim the few possessions he had. He had sent word to me of his departure. I was greatly saddened because he was leaving us. A few days later Phani Babu too had to be taken somewhere or the other. Now I had to stay in the room all by myself even though during the daytime I got to meet the other prisoners. But at night I was all by myself. However, Sunday we would all sit together and chat and tell each other stories. We wouldn't talk about politics much since the subject would inevitably lead to debates. Four of the other inmates had the same ideology while I had my own views and Babu Nepal Naha had his own ideas about politics. In other words, politically we didn't see eye to eye.

Dr Maruf Hassan was in charge of the food served in the jail. We used to call him 'manager'. We had a tough time surviving on the food that was served us. However, Faridpur is well known for its vegetables and we would be occasionally served some.

In any case, I would have to go to Gopalganj again though my heart had weakened even more and my eyesight had become worse, so much so that I couldn't read any more. I was also suffering from rheumatic pain in my left foot. The civil surgeon and the physician treated me as well as they could but I wasn't showing any improvement. They said they would like to send me to Dhaka jail since the Faridpur one didn't have facilities to treat inmates with heart and eye conditions and I could be best treated at Dhaka Medical College Hospital. I said, 'Do whatever you think is best—who am I to decide!'

It took a few more days for the jail authorities to exchange notes on my condition. Eventually the government sent orders to remove me to Dhaka jail. To go there I would have to be taken from Faridpur to Goalando by train and from Goalando by steamer to Narayanganj. From Narayanganj I would be taken in a taxi to Dhaka jail. From the prison gate I would be removed to the prison hospital. Goalando then had a very comfortable steamer service to Dhaka. The government had issued an inter-class ticket for me. I said I would go only on a first-class ticket. Since the steamer would be awfully crowded I wouldn't be able to get any sleep. Why couldn't they use my money which they had in deposit to buy me a first-class ticket? They realized that they had to give in since I wouldn't budge from my stance. Moreover, the poorer government employees never wanted me to be in any distress.

When I came to Dhaka this time it was the end of 1951. I stayed in the jail here for almost a month. My baggage was taken to the place I had been put up before. Maulana Bhasani had been released by this time. A few days later I came to know that Barisal's Mr Mohiuddin had been brought to Dhaka jail under the Public Security Act. Till recently he had been general secretary of the Muslim League. Apparently the government had arrested him for his involvement in communal riots. A violent communal riot had taken place in Barisal in 1951. Mohiuddin was a very able worker for the movement that had resulted in the creation of Pakistan. In the student movement he had belonged to my opposite camp. Even though we left the Muslim League he hadn't. In Barisal my good friend Kazi Bahauddin, once his co-worker, had opposed him as a member of the Students' League. My co-workers and I were always wary of him since he had been blind in his support of the government. But now when we met and exchanged views it was obvious that he had changed a lot. I could see that if released from jail he would no longer be part of Muslim League politics. He confessed to me that he could now see that communal politics was harmful for Pakistan.

Since I couldn't be treated properly in the Dhaka jail hospital I was sent to Medical College Hospital. I declared that they would have to give me a cabin, a private room, if they wanted me to go there. The government agreed. Due arrangements were being made. There had been a gulf of misunderstanding separating Mohiuddin and me but now the two of us became more intimate in prison and we soon became good friends. Mohiuddin said, 'Your party and the Students' League will launch a movement for your freedom. No one will do anything for me since I was in the Muslim League and it is a Muslim League government that has arrested me. You know very well that I am a political worker. It isn't possible for me to start riots on my own but they are making all kinds of false allegations against me. This is because of the two factions within the League. Since I am in the faction that opposes Mr Nurul Amin he had me arrested under the Public Security Act.' He went on to say, 'You have Mr Suhrawardy and Maulana Bhasani to launch a movement for you.' I replied, 'Let bygones be bygones; if I ask for my freedom now I will also ask for your freedom. Just wait and see.'

A few days later I was brought to Dhaka Medical College Hospital. My eyes were bothering me a lot now. The first thing they did was have my eyes examined. Captain Lashkar, the famous eye specialist, was looking after me. In a few days my eyes got better but I was told that it would take some time for them to be completely cured. Dr Shamsuddin began the treatment of my heart.

In the evenings a lot of people came to meet me since visiting hours were from 4 p.m. to 6 p.m. In those days the hospital had only a few cabins. My cabin was located right next to the stairway leading to the first floor. Medical College students would come in groups to see me and there was no stopping them. There were some policemen posted outside my cabin. When night fell and the crowd thinned I would walk in the veranda though I was still quite weak.

Maulana Bhasani had kept himself busy ever since his release from jail. Mr Shamsul Huq was quiet for a while. Mr Suhrawardy had come back to East Bengal by this time. Together with the Maulana, he addressed public meetings in Mymensingh, Comilla and other places. On every one of these occasions the Muslim League tried to create trouble. In the meeting held in Dhaka the government imposed Section 144. However, Mr Suhrawardy decided to go to Armanitola since many people had gathered in the meeting place. Mr Suhrawardy had requested everyone there to disperse since he didn't want anyone to violate Section 144. He and Maulana Bhasani had been vociferous in demanding my release from jail. They emphasized in their speeches that I was unwell and in hospital. Mr Suhrawardy and Mr Ataur Rahman Khan took special permission from the government to meet me. We talked about a lot of things and Mr Suhrawardy showed his affection for me in every way. He called for the attending physicians and told them that they must take good care of me.

I brought up the subject of Mohiuddin with Mr Suhrawardy. He reacted to this with dismay and said, 'I guess you don't know that this Mohiuddin is the person who sent a letter against me to Liaquat Ali Khan full of fabricated information when I had gone to Barisal as part of the peace mission in 1948. He also took active part in the communal riots that took place there in 1951.' I said, 'Sir, people can change. I think you know that he is a good worker. Now he is in jail and with me. Believe me, he has changed a lot. If we can bring him back to the right path, our country will benefit. It won't do us any harm if we decide to adopt a liberal policy. When you talk about securing my release in public, do mention his name too and please tell others to do the same.' Mr Suhrawardy was as broad-minded as the sea is vast. Whenever a man went to meet him no matter how great an offender he was, he would forgive him!

Mr Shawkat Mia and Students' League workers had printed a petition demanding my release. Many well-known political workers of Dhaka city had signed the petition. I requested Shawkat Mia to be kind enough to also include Mohiuddin's name with mine. The Student League activists became upset at my suggestion. They would often steal into my hospital room late at night to meet me. Now I tried to persuade them but the student leaders from Barisal misunderstood my intentions. However, I was able to clear their misunderstanding later after I was released from jail.

When Maulana Bhasani and I were in jail in October 1951, Mr Liaquat Ali Khan had been shot to death in Rawalpindi. Khawaja Nazimuddin then gave up his position as Governor General to become prime minister and chose Ghulam Muhammad, then finance minister, as his successor. Liaquat Ali Khan had become a victim of the kind of machinations that he himself had introduced into politics. Till now no one has nabbed his assassins or discovered whether it was the work of a single man. And you can be sure that the truth will never be uncovered. But it is pretty obvious that the people behind the assassination were very influential since they left behind no clues at all. The prime minister of Pakistan was shot dead in broad daylight. How did the assassin manage to find a spot so close to his victim? How could he fire a shot without being detected by anyone? Why was the assassin himself shot dead immediately afterwards? All these questions troubled many of us at that time. Even though it was at his instigation and Mr Nurul Amin's concern about us that had sent us to jail, I was saddened by the news of Liaquat Ali Khan's death. This is because I have never believed in the politics of conspiracy. Indeed, I was very fearful about a Pakistan where intrigue was becoming a constant leitmotif in politics. It is difficult to articulate the horror I feel at the thought of the kind of tactics adopted where you disposed of your opponent with a bullet. Those of us who believe in democracy abhor such a reprehensible mode of action.

Khawaja Nazimuddin now inducted, Chaudhury Muhammad Ali, a bureaucrat, into his administration. He was secretary general of the Pakistan government. He was now made the finance minister. From his appointment onward bureaucrats became active players in Pakistani politics. A government official had now become the Governor General and another one the finance minister. Mr Nazimuddin himself was a very weak-kneed sort. He had many positive aspects but he lacked initiative and was inefficient. As a consequence, bureaucrats now began to rule the roost. In particular, when one of them became the finance minister, other bureaucrats began to harbour ambitions of attaining great positions themselves. Politicians now began to yield to the bureaucracy. The Muslim League lacked a strong leader who could firmly deal with the machinations of these bureaucrats. Mr Nazimuddin himself had struck blows at the foundation of democracy. How else can one explain his decision to ask a government employee to resign from his position so that he could be appointed a minister? It seemed to me that Mr Nazimuddin had been coerced into this decision because of pressure from one particular province. Even though he was the prime minister two groups were really determining his cabinet's policies. One group was from the Punjab and the other from Bengal. Members of the cabinet who were from the other provinces were secretly supporting the Bengali group. However, Mr Nazimuddin was making a huge mistake by favouring the Punjab group.

Mr Nazimuddin had come to East Bengal soon after he became prime minister. He had said nothing much during his first trip there. But later, probably towards the end of 1951 or perhaps January 1952, he gave a speech in Paltan Maidan where he declared, 'Urdu will be the only state language of Pakistan.' He thereby broke the pledge he had made in 1948 when he was the chief minister of East Pakistan. In a written agreement with the committee set up to make Bengali the state language, he had pledged that it would be the official language of the province. He had later tabled a motion in the Provincial Assembly that year to this effect. He had also agreed to officially request the central government in the National Assembly to make Bengali the state language of Pakistan. Such a resolution had been adopted unanimously in the East Bengal Provincial Assembly. It was in Dhaka that he had made these pledges and it was in Dhaka that he would break them! His action caused a huge uproar throughout the country. The only party in opposition at that time, the East Pakistan Awami League, its student wing, the Student League, and its youth wing, the Youth League, protested against his decision as loudly as they could.

I remained in the hospital while all this was happening. One night Mohammad Toaha and Oli Ahad came to meet me, sneaking in through a window of my cabin that opened into a ward. I had told them to meet me after 1 a.m. I had also told them that I would like to talk to Khaleque Nawaz, Kazi Golam Mahbub and a few other Student League leaders. My door was being guarded by IB people but at this hour of the night most of them would be asleep. This was when five to seven of them came to meet me. I used to walk by myself till late at night. Since no one used to visit me then they allowed me to walk on my own. The police would lie down quietly knowing that I wasn't going to run away. The detective branch people tended to nod off to sleep. We could therefore talk in the veranda. I told them that we should form an all-party united front. The Awami League leaders had already been informed. The Student League was the only student organization with a following at this time. The Student League leaders agreed to my proposal. Oli Ahad and Toaha declared that the Youth League would also agree to it. There was a conspiracy afoot to thwart the demand for establishing Bengali as the state language. Now if there was no protest the National Assembly would introduce legislation to make Urdu the only state language. Mr Nazimuddin had not only talked about making Urdu the only state language, he had also come up with many new arguments to buttress its claim.

Although Oli Ahad wasn't a member either of the Awami League or the Students' League he was very fond of me and respected my views. I told him, 'I've come to know that they are going to send me back to jail soon since they believe that I've been busy politically in the hospital. Come again to meet me tomorrow night.' I also asked for a couple of other Students' League leaders to meet me then. I wanted Shawkat Mia and a few other Awami League workers to be there too.

The next night all these people came to see me one after the other. We decided in the meetings in my room to observe 21 February as State Language Day and to form a committee that day to conduct the movement to establish Bengali as the state language. The convener for that movement would be a member of the Students' League. A campaign would be launched from the beginning of February to mobilize public opinion. I told them, 'I myself will go on a hunger strike from the 16th of February demanding my release from prison. I have been in jail for twenty-six months already!' I added, 'Mohiuddin is in jail too and we live in cells close to each other. I will let you know if I can persuade him to join the hunger strike with me. In that case add his name to mine in your campaign to secure my release. When I give you notice that I am going on hunger strike Shawkat Mia will be responsible for printing pamphlets and posters, so see to it that they are distributed and posted.'

Two days later I found out that a medical board had been instituted to examine me. They declared that I was much better now and that my treatment could be continued in jail. The government sent me to Dhaka jail even though I hadn't recovered completely. As soon as I came back to jail I talked to Mohiuddin. He agreed to go on a hunger strike till death with me. The two of us sent a petition to the government on 1 February. When the jail administration requested me not to go on hunger strike I pointed out to them that I had languished in jail for twenty-six or twenty-seven months without a trial. I had been guilty of no crime. I had made up my mind now that I would force myself out of jail either alive or dead. In other words, 'either I will go out of the jail or my dead body will go out'. They informed the government of our resolution. We had already informed people outside that we would petition the government about our decision to go on a hunger strike. All Awami League offices outside the city and Student League workers of all branches were alerted. The Awami League had its offices only in a few districts at that time. But I had my friends and associates in all the districts of the country.

Meanwhile, the All-Party State Language Action Committee had been formed. February 21 had already been chosen as the State Language Day since the East Pakistan Provincial Assembly was scheduled to sit in session on that day. Kazi Golam Mahbub had been made the convener of the council. In 1948 students had launched the movement for establishing Bengali as the state language entirely on their own. I was sure that this time our people would come forward to support the movement since they could understand by now that if Bengali was not made the state language they would have to wear the chains of servitude once again. No nation can bear any insult directed at its mother tongue. Although 56 per cent of the people of Pakistan were Bengalis, the West Pakistanis didn't want Bengali to become the state language. On the other hand, Bengalis wanted to make their language the state language along with Urdu and had no objections against that language. But they mistook the generosity of Bengalis in this regard as a sign of weakness. By this time, however, Bengalis were beginning to perceive that they were being discriminated against in business, government service and all spheres of trade and commerce. Because Karachi was the capital of Pakistan, Bengalis were being deprived of all sorts of advantages. The East Pakistani Awami League's demand for regional autonomy and the 'Grand National Convention', where the call for autonomy had been voiced by all parties, had articulated the position of Bengalis effectively. The more the leaders of the East Pakistani Muslim League were getting alienated from their people the more dependent they were becoming on a West Pakistani coterie and the West

Pakistani bureaucracy. Khawaja Nazimuddin and Mr Nurul Amin were beginning to be afraid of the people. That is why after their party was defeated in the Tangail election they did not have the courage to go to the polls again even though many seats of the Provincial Assembly had fallen vacant since then.

Because they had started to lose the confidence of the people, Muslim Leaguers were becoming more and more dependent on the bureaucracy. The then chief secretary was Mr Aziz Ahmed (originally of the Indian Civil Service). He was a very intelligent and sagacious man and was also efficient and well-versed in administration. He used to work as the representative of the central government. As a witness in the Public Offices Disqualification Order (PODO)[23] trial of Mr Hamidul Huq Chowdhury, he had testified that he had files on all the ministers and kept the central government informed about their activities. Hamidul Huq Chowdhury had been forced to quit the ministry but his colleagues were still in power. They didn't have the guts to do anything though since most of them could not stand up to someone of Mr Aziz Ahmed's calibre. To enforce public opinion in their favour they resorted to assaulting the Awami League and the leaders and workers of all the parties opposed to them. They were beginning to invoke the Public Security Act at the slightest provocation.

Meanwhile, the two of us were getting ready to fast unto death in jail. We talked over our strategy and decided that we would not break our fast for any reason at all. If the consequence was death so be it. The people in charge of the jail—in particular, the superintendent, Mr Amir Hossain, and the deputy jailer in charge of political prisoners, Mr Mokhlesur Rahman—tried to dissuade us. I told them that we had nothing against them and that our hunger strike was not directed at them. If we were on a hunger strike it was only because the government had detained us for months without trial. We had been in jail for a long time now but had never had any differences with them. I assured them we were fully aware that they had to follow orders. Mr Rahman was a very amiable, gentle and well-read man.

On the morning of 15 February I was taken to the jail gate on the excuse that there would be talks with us about our decision to fast unto death. Immediately after, Mohiuddin too was brought to the gate under the same pretext. A few minutes later our baggage, clothes and linen were also brought there by the janitor. I said, 'What's going on?' The people in charge replied, 'We have orders to take you to another jail.' I asked, 'Which one?' No one had a reply to this query. Meanwhile, the armed police and IB officers were getting ready to escort us. But they couldn't hide our destination from us for long and I found out that I was being taken to Faridpur jail again. In fact, both of us were being sent there. It was 9 a.m. by then. We were supposed to board the steamer that left Narayanganj at eleven. I started to delay them as much as I could since I knew that if we left immediately no one would know where we were being sent to. I took out my books one by one and then all my clothes. I began to go over my accounts to find out how much money I had spent and how much I had left. I managed to procrastinate till it was ten o'clock. It took us another half hour to leave. The armed subedar and the officers of the detective branch were trying to rush us as much as they could. The sergeant was a man from Baluchistan and he had been posted in Gopalganj at the time of the Partition of India. He respected me and was also very fond of me. He had seen me work selflessly for the cause of Pakistan. As soon as he saw me, he said, 'How come you are in jail?' All I said in reply was, 'Fate!'

They had arranged a horse carriage which could be locked up from outside. As soon as we were put into it they rolled down the windows and shut the door. Two guards sat inside with us. A carriage followed ours along the road that runs parallel to Victoria Park. When we reached the park entrance we saw that a taxi reserved by the police was waiting for us; at this time of the day it was normally difficult to find a taxi for hire here. We got down from the carriage and got into the taxi slowly. However, we did not meet any of our acquaintances though we kept looking for them. Our escorts kept asking the taxi driver to speed up. I, on the other hand, kept urging the taxi driver not to rush lest we ended up losing our lives in a road accident.

When we reached the landing station we found that the steamer had left. What was to be done now? Where could they take us? The next ship was scheduled to leave at 1 a.m. We were taken to Narayanganj police station. They phoned their superiors and sought permission to keep us here. We were taken to a room in the police barracks. I met an acquaintance in the police station and requested him to get in touch with Shamsuzzoha. Everyone in this city knew where Khan Saheb Osman Ali's house was. Within an hour Mr Zoha, Bazlur Rahman and many others came to see us. They brought along food for us. Later, Mr Almas Ali too came to meet us. I told them, 'We are supposed to eat in a hotel tonight. Let me decide which hotel it will be. Make sure that you are there when we arrive. We need to talk over a few things.' I managed to tell them in the little time we had why we were being transferred from Dhaka to Faridpur jail. But the people handling us did not let them stay in the police station for long. So we said our goodbyes after giving them the name of the hotel where we would be meeting at night. I told them that they could expect us to be there between eight and nine. It was a new, two-storeyed hotel that had just been built on the Dhaka–Narayanganj highway.

I told the sergeant in charge of us, 'We need to eat, so let's go to a hotel; we can go to the landing station afterwards.' He agreed readily. I was confident that he would heed our request. Besides they would have to feed us somehow! He had our baggage sent to the station with a guard and we reached the hotel as scheduled. We sat down to eat. Mr Zoha was waiting for us along with eight to ten of our party workers. We had our food at a leisurely pace, discussing issues all the while. I found out how Maulana Bhasani, Mr Huq and the other leaders were doing. They told me that they would try to have newspapers sent to us so that we could keep abreast of current events. I pointed out that the weekly *Ittefaq* would do. I also let them know that we were going on a fast unto death from the next day but they seemed to already know of our resolution. No political activist can forget the sacrifices made by the party workers of Narayanganj and their patience and forbearance. They told us, 'On 21st February we are going to enforce a hartal in Narayanganj. We are going to strike to demand that Bengali be made the state language, but we are also going to demand your freedom that day.' Here too our leaders kept asking me if they could trust Mohiuddin and if he would change colour again and prove himself a Muslim Leaguer once he came out of prison. I told them, 'Let's do our duty and let him do what he is supposed to be doing. I am sure he won't return to the Muslim League. I have no doubts on that account. He is a prisoner, so why should we have any reservations about campaigning for his freedom? People can be won over by good manners, love and sympathy and not by force, hatred or oppressive means.'

We reached the landing station at eleven that night. The steamer was waiting in the station. Our fellow party workers stayed with us till the steamer left the river port. We took leave of everyone at 1 a.m. I told them, 'It is possible that we will never meet again in this life. I hope all of you will forgive me. I have no regrets. I will have to die sooner or later and if I do so while taking a stand against oppression and injustice such a death would be worth it.'

When the ship left we made our beds and went to sleep. In the morning we deliberated over the wisdom of going on a hunger strike on board the steamer. We decided we should be in jail before we started our fast. The steamer sailed throughout the day and we reached Goalando Ghat in the evening. From there we got on a train, which reached Faridpur at 4 a.m. The people in charge of the jail refused to accept us at that time of the night. The two of us spent the rest of the night in the veranda of the guards' quarters. In the morning the sergeant in charge of us said, 'You won't be taken inside the jail till the time the officers arrive, so let's go and have some breakfast.' We had no intention of having breakfast but we hoped to meet someone or the other when they took us out for breakfast. Then our party workers in Faridpur would come to know that we were in town and that we had begun to fast unto death. We prolonged our stay in the restaurant by half an hour and yet didn't manage to meet anyone. The owner of the restaurant arrived and I told him my name and asked him to inform my party people. Just when I had started for the jail we came across an Awami League worker called Mohiuddin, popularly known as Mohi. He had worked with us when I was in charge of the party workers of Faridpur in the run-up to the elections of 1946. Mohi was on a bicycle. As soon as I saw him I called out his name. He stopped his bike and came towards me. The IB people tried to block his way. I ignored them and even scolded them for coming in our way. I told Mohi why I was going to Faridpur and asked him to tell everyone that I was going on a fast unto death from that day. We headed for the prison with Mohi in tow.

When we reached the jail gate we saw that the jailer and his deputy had arrived. They instructed that we should be taken inside immediately. They had been informed of our arrival and were ready to take us in. They had prepared a place for us but we were not going to be kept with the political prisoners and were to stay separately. We decided to take our medicine immediately so that we could clear our stomachs. We then began our fast. Two days later our condition began to deteriorate and we were taken to hospital. Both of us were in poor health by this time. Mohiuddin was suffering from pleurisy and I from a number of ailments. Four days later they began to force-feed us by inserting tubes in our noses. This was a problem! They inserted a pipe through our noses that reached our stomachs. Then they tied a cap to the mouth of the pipe, which had a hole in it. They poured some milk-like liquid on the cup so that it could reach our stomachs. They seemed determined not to let us starve to death. However, my nose protested against this technique. After they had fed me through the pipe a number of times my nose became sore. It began to bleed and I was in pain. We began to object to this procedure but they ignored all our protests.

We were finding the situation too painful. I had sores inside both my nostrils. When we objected to such force-feeding they brought along people to handcuff us and tried to insert food into our stomachs. The two of us had become really weak by this time. After five or six days we were unable to even get up from bed. We did have a drink of lemon juice and salt since this had no food value. We began to lose weight rapidly. But if we moved around while they were trying to force-feed us we always ran great risks. The civil surgeon, the attending physician and the people in charge of the prison were doing their best to see that we were not uncomfortable. The civil surgeon kept prohibiting us from carrying on with the fast.

My heart began to act up. I began to have severe palpitation. I was having trouble breathing. I began to think that my time was up and that I would not last much longer. I persuaded another prisoner to get me a few scraps of paper. Although my hand shook while I was writing, I composed four short letters: one for my father, one for Renu, and one each to Mr Suhrawardy and Maulana Bhasani. I knew that in a day or two I would lose the little strength I had now and would not be able to write anything at all.

We spent all of 21st full of anxiety, worrying about what was happening. At night the guards on duty told us that there had been trouble in Dhaka. According to the radio, a few people had been shot to death. A general strike had been called in Faridpur and students had come up to the jail gate in a procession raising slogans such as 'We want Bengali as the state language', 'Exploitation of Bengalis shall not be tolerated any further', 'We want Sheikh Mujib's release' and 'All political prisoners should be released.' However, I was feeling a bit upset wondering why they weren't raising slogans in my own district Faridpur about Mohiuddin too. It would have sufficed if they had only said, 'We want all political prisoners to be freed.'

Later that night I became really worried when I heard what had happened in Dhaka. It was difficult to tell how many people had actually died in the city. However, we knew that many people had been shot to death. The two of us were lying in adjacent beds. The physician had asked us not to move at all. But such was our excitement that we were up soon. Two prisoners had been assigned to watch over us and to attend to our needs. They put us back to bed immediately. I was feeling very upset and seemed to have lost all capacity for thought. Why had they resorted to shooting the demonstrators? They were observing a strike and were in a procession, intending to hold a meeting but not to disrupt the law and order situation. Surely no one had any intention of becoming violent. The imposition of Section 144 always leads to violence and an administration is much better off without imposing it.

Very late that night a guard told me that many students had died and many more had been detained. That was all that we found out about the day's happening that night. As it is we were having a tough time going to sleep and now that we knew what had happened sleep proved impossible.

The next day around nine or ten a big procession came out on the wide road next to the jail. Had we been on the first floor we could have heard the slogans clearly and even seen the people in the procession but because they had kept us in a ground-floor room all we could hear was someone using a bullhorn to give a speech. Surely they were addressing us. We could understand a bit of what had happened in Dhaka from it. The jail administration wanted to keep us in the dark. They seemed determined to keep us away from people and to prevent others from talking to us. It would take another day for us to read in the newspaper about what had happened.

On the 22nd, people brought out processions in Faridpur throughout the day. Students raised slogans whenever they came together. Even little children began to chant slogans in the streets. On the 22nd when we got the newspaper we read some stories in it about what had transpired. We found out how rashly the Muslim League government had acted that day. For the first time in the history of the world a race had shed blood for its mother tongue. Nowhere in the world had people been shot to death for demonstrating on behalf of their language. Mr Nurul Amin had not been able to figure out where his dependency on the bureaucracy would ultimately take him. The bullets had been fired inside the Medical College Students' Hostel and not on the road. Even if Section 144 had been violated, it would have been enough to arrest the demonstrators; there was no need to shoot at them. I thought since our boys had shed blood they would end up making Bengali the state language even though I myself would never be able to see that day. When people are destined to self-destruct they tend to make one mistake after another. The leaders of the Muslim League in Bangladesh had failed to understand who were the people making Khawaja Nazimuddin talk in Urdu and why he preferred to speak only in that language. They knew that even a leader of Mr Jinnah's stature had not left our country unopposed after declaring that Urdu should be the only state language of Pakistan. And if that was the case with Jinnah what would Mr Khawaja Nazimuddin's and his followers' fate be? A coterie, adept at intrigue-based politics, was ensuring he was more and more alienated from the masses. They were also cutting off his disciple Nurul Amin from the people of the land. There could be little doubt that this coterie was hatching a deep conspiracy. But then Mr Nazimuddin had never had much of a following in Bangladesh.

I read in the newspaper that Maulana Abdur Rashid Tarkabagish, MLA, Khairat Hussein, MLA, Khan Saheb Osman Ali, MLA, Mohammed Abul Hossain, Khondokar Mushtaq Ahmed and hundreds of other students and party workers had been arrested. Two days later I read that a few professors, Maulana Bhasani, Mr Shamsul Huq and many Awami League leaders and workers had been arrested as well. Narayanganj's Khan Saheb Osman Ali's house had been ransacked and the people inside roughed up. The old man and his children had been roundly abused. People across Dhaka and Narayanganj had been brutalized. In all probability no Awami League workers were outside bars. Our own condition had deteriorated to a point that we could die at any moment. The civil surgeon was now coming to examine us five to seven times a day.

When he was examining me on 25th morning, I noticed his face suddenly turn grim. He left without a word, his face ashen. I realized my time was up. He came back a little later and said, 'What's the point of dying in such a manner? Bangladesh has great expectations of you.' I was having trouble talking but I said, 'There are many others still active. The work will go on. I am being punished because I love my country and its people but I am ready to give my life for it.' The deputy jailer said, 'Do you want us to inform anyone about your condition? Where are your wife and children now? Do you want to telegram your father?' I said, 'There is no need for all that. I don't want to cause them any more grief.' I had given up hope by this time and could feel my body stiffening. I wouldn't have been in such a sorry shape if my heart hadn't been so weak. A prisoner delegated to look after me now began to massage my body with mustard oil. Every now and then I felt that I was in a deep freeze.

Mohiuddin was in a sad shape too. He was suffering from pleurisy once again. I called a jail employee and gave him the four letters I had written and asked him to deliver them to one of my relatives who lived in Faridpur after my death. I had made him swear an oath to that effect. Again and again images of my father, mother, brothers and sisters kept coming to me. What would happen to Renu? She had no one else in this world to look after her. What would happen to my two little children? However, I was confident that my father and younger brother would never abandon them. I was slowly losing the ability to think things through. I kept thinking I would never see Hasina and Kamal again. No one in our home knew about the state I was in; surely they would have come to see me if they had an inkling about my condition!

Mohiuddin of course had no relatives in Faridpur. He is from Barisal. His brothers had good jobs. However, except for one of them the others didn't inquire much about him. That brother was a superintending engineer. I knew him well. In any case, Mohiuddin and I were lying in adjacent beds. We held hands now but kept quiet all the time. My heart was aching again.

The civil surgeon kept me under constant observation. My condition deteriorated further on 27th morning. It seemed I would be able to survive for a day or two more at the most.

At about 8 p.m. that day we were lying quietly in our beds. We didn't feel like talking to each other; nor did we have the strength to do so. Soon after the two of us had done our ablutions with the help of the prison guards assigned to us and had finished praying to God to forgive us, the deputy jailer unlocked the door and entered the room. He said, 'Will you eat if we free you?' I said, 'We will eat only if we are free and if we aren't freed we won't have anything. However, then our bodies will be free!' The attending physician and a few other people had come too. The deputy jailer said, 'Let me read out the release order which has been sent by radiogram; the district magistrate has a copy too.' He finished reading it out but I still could not believe it was genuine. Mohiuddin took it in his hands and read it and confirmed it was indeed for my release. He began to rub my forehead to make me feel better. The deputy jailer said, 'There is no reason for you to disbelieve me. I have no reason to deceive you; you really are free!' The physician had brought along some coconut water for me. Two people lifted Mohiuddin up. He said, 'I am going to help you drink the coconut water.' He made me drink two teaspoonfuls of coconut water to break my fast. But there was no release order for him. This began to bother me. How could I get him free? Besides, although I had been freed I didn't have the strength to go anywhere. The civil surgeon wouldn't let me go out because of my pathetic state. He was administering coconut water to me from time to time. The night passed in this manner. In the morning they gave me some food to eat and more coconut water. I began to feel better but how could I leave Mohiuddin behind? We had spent the whole time in jail together. What would happen to him if I left? Who would look after him? What if they failed to release him? But he was in the same situation that I was in so why shouldn't they release him? I had become the 'enemy' to the Muslim League politicians who had assumed power after the creation of Pakistan but Mohiuddin had been an important member of that party till the day he was jailed. It is often the case in politics that in case of strife party members can turn on each other's throats even more fiercely than they would on sworn enemies.

At 10 a.m. I realized that my father had come for me. But it was not possible for me to go up to the jail gate on my own. The people in charge therefore allowed him in. My father started to shed tears as soon as he saw my state. He was the kind of man who had great self-control. But even he could barely manage to keep himself from crying. He sat next to me and began to console me saying, 'You have been freed and I have come to take you away. I had gone to Dhaka to meet you along with your mother, Renu, Hasina and Kamal but for two days nobody bothered to inform me about your whereabouts. They told me that you weren't in Dhaka only at the jail gate. Only later did I find out that you had been taken to Faridpur jail. But by that time I couldn't travel to meet you. There was no way I could come to Narayanganj to take the steamer to Faridpur. In the end, I left your mother and Renu and the children in Dhaka and decided to come away on my own. This is because I had my doubts about whether you really had been taken to Faridpur. I am going to telegram them today asking them to head for our village immediately. I plan to take you home either tomorrow or the day after. The rest is up to God. The civil surgeon has told me that I will have to sign a statement saying that I am taking you on my own responsibility.' However, my father kept consoling me and told me that he had come to know that Mohiuddin too would be released a day or two later.

The next day my father took me out of the prison. A lot of people had come to the jail gate to see me. I was taken in a stretcher to the gate and kept outside. It was as if they were hoping that if anything was to happen to me it was best for them that it happened outside the jail. A few people carried my stretcher on their backs to Mr Alauddin Khan's house. I was kept here for a while. In the evening I was taken to my sister's house. I spent the night there. Many of my relatives as well as a lot of other people came to meet me there. My father remained with me all the while. The next morning one of my friends drove me all the way to Bhanga in a car. My father hired a big boat there. My aunt's house was close to the road. She came to the road to see me. She asked my father to stay with them in Nurpur village for the time being. However, my father said that he would take me in the boat to his older sister's house in Dattapara. We would stay there for a day till I recovered a little and then all of us would go home. By this time I was feeling much better, though I was still quite weak.

Dattapara is in Madaripur and from there it takes a day and a night to go to Gopalganj by boat. Our party workers were waiting for us in Sindhia Ghat and when they saw that I was on my way they headed for Gopalganj to receive me there. We reached Gopalganj a few hours later only to see that a huge crowd had gathered there to receive me. Indeed, the entire riverbank seemed to be full of people waiting for me. They wanted me to get down there. My father objected to this but they were in no mood to listen to him. They held me up and carried me in a procession and then brought me back to the boat again. My father decided to take me home without any further delay since my mother, Renu and everyone else in our house was waiting eagerly for me. My brother too was there, having come from Khulna to meet me.

I reached home after five days. It was difficult to explain to my mother what had happened. My daughter Hasina embraced me and said, 'Abba, we want Bengali to be the national language; we want all political prisoners to be freed.' She had picked up these slogans when she was in Dhaka on 21 February. Kamal wouldn't come to me although he kept staring at me. I was still very weak and had to lie down every now and then. When everyone had left my room one by one and we were finally all by ourselves Renu began to cry. She said, 'I knew as soon as I received your letter you had decided to do something drastic. I had become impatient to meet you. I didn't know whom to approach to take me to you; it was too embarrassing for me to request your father to do so. Your brother Nasser was elsewhere. When I read the news in the paper I decided that I would have to risk the embarrassment and asked your father to take me to you. He immediately made arrangements for our trip. And we were soon on our way to Dhaka in our big boat with the help of three oarsmen. Why did you go on a hunger strike? Do these people have any compassion? Didn't you think for a moment about us? Can you imagine what would happen to us without you? How would I survive with two little children? What would happen to Hasina and Kamal? You might say that even without you, we wouldn't starve. But is that all one wants? And even if you had died would it have helped the country in any way?' I kept quiet. I let her go on knowing that if we can give vent to pent-up emotions we would feel better. Renu was usually very composed but that day a dam seemed to have burst and words came out of her in torrents. All I said by way of reply was, 'I had no options.' The children had gone to sleep by then. In our house, in my own room, in my own bed after twenty-seven to twenty-eight months I kept thinking of the lonely days I had spent in prison and the agony I had gone through there. I had found out what was going on in Dhaka by this time. Mohiuddin had already been released. But just when I had been freed they put my fellow workers behind bars.

Next morning father called a physician over to our house to have me examined. I had brought along the civil surgeon's prescription. The physician told everyone that I should not be allowed to leave my bed. I would be permitted to walk only after ten days, but that too only in the evening. Some of my colleagues from Gopalganj, Khulna and Barisal had come to meet me in our house.

One morning Renu and I were chatting in bed while Hasina and Kamal were playing on the floor. Every now and then Hasina would come up to me leaving behind all her playthings. At one point she called out to me, 'Abba, Abba.' Kamal kept staring at me. Then Kamal told Hasina, 'Sister dear, can I call your abba my abba too?' Both Renu and I heard him say this. I got down from the bed slowly and took him in my lap and said to him, 'But I am your dad.' Kamal would normally stay away from me but today he hugged me. I realized that he couldn't keep away from me any longer. But how strange it is that one's own son can forget his father if he is away for a long time. When I went to jail he had been only a few months old. How inhuman can people be to keep a man away from his dear ones and his children because of political reasons? People become blinded by greed. Our nation had been freed just the other day after being in chains for 200 years. Even if I hadn't done a lot, I had contributed at least a little to our independence. And now my fellow workers and I had to endure life in prison for months despite all that we had done. Who knows how much longer we would have to be in prison? Was this what freedom amounted to? However, I wasn't frightened of imprisonment. I had sworn to do all I could to achieve the kind of Pakistan I had dreamt about.

Some of the people of Gopalganj who came to see me echoed my thoughts: 'Why did they imprison you? You were someone who had made us conscious of Pakistan.' Others said, 'You said so many things about how Pakistan would transform our lives. You said that people would be happy then and that we won't be oppressed any more. Now that a few years have gone by in Pakistan all we can feel is that there is more sorrow than before and there is no relief in sight. The price of rice is so high nowadays.' What could I tell them by way of a response! They were ordinary folks. How could I explain to them what had happened? A number of villagers, who were among its leaders, were quite intelligent and clear-eyed as well as articulate. How could one explain to them in a few words what had happened? There was nothing wrong with the concept of Pakistan; it was our country. But those who had been left in charge of the nation were more interested in their own fortunes than those of the people. They weren't bothered about how they could best build Pakistan and improve the lot of the people. After the bullets had been fired in Pakistan it was easy for people to see that the people in charge were not their friends. I found out that when the news of the police firing on 21 February reached the countryside people everywhere had observed a general strike. They had come to understand that a particular group of people was trying to snatch away their language from them.

~

The author.

The author (standing) with Mahatma Gandhi and Huseyn Shaheed Suhrawardy, 1947.

The author on his way to a workers' meeting accompanied by the Awami League leaders Shamsul Huq, Yar Mohammad Khan, his father, Sheikh Lutfar Rahman, and others, June 1949.

With Huseyn Shaheed Suhrawardy, 1949.

In a consultation with party co-workers.

Amongst party leaders and workers, 1952.

With Maulana Bhasani at the Provatferi (bare-footed procession in the early morning) to show respect for the 'Language Martyrs', 21 February 1953.

At a public meeting at Armanitola Maidan, May 1953.

Meeting of the Jukta (United) Front for selecting candidates prior to provincial elections of 1954, December 1953.

The author, 1954.

With Huseyn Shaheed Suhrawardy in Rajshahi, 1954.

Addressing a public meeting, 1954.

The author sporting a football jersey, 1940.

The author with his wife, Begum Fazilatunnesa, at Tungipara, 1947.

The author, 1949.

The author's ancestral home at Tungipara.

The author with Sheikh Russel on his lap. Begum Fazilatunnesa, Sheikh Jamal and Sheikh Hasina on his left. On his right, Sheikh Rehana and Sheikh Kamal, 1972.

The author with his parents: father, Sheikh Lutfar Rahman, and mother, Sayera Khatun.

The author in his personal library.

I began to believe that no one could shut us up any more. There was no way out for them except to make Bengali our state language. People had responded enthusiastically to the movement for Bengali and had come forward to join it. Some religious leaders had issued religious decrees against Bengali. But they had become frightened. They could no longer say anything against Bengali in the open. Public opinion had been mobilized, and oppressors are always afraid of public opinion. When rulers become oppressors or assist them the country and its people are bound to suffer.

The whole of March I had to stay home. My health had improved somewhat but my heart was still weak. My father just wouldn't let go of me. The physician who was attending to me also objected to my leaving home. Renu was apprehensive that once I went to Dhaka I would start airing my views publicly and could therefore be arrested again. Many Students' League leaders and workers were still in jail. The Awami League had stopped functioning. Nobody had the guts to say anything any more. The League government had flattened all opposition with its steamroller of tyranny. But it wouldn't do to keep silent, no matter how difficult the situation had become.

At about this time I received a letter from Manik Bhai asking me to come to Dhaka. He felt that my treatment could continue in Dhaka and I could keep working while in the city. I showed the letter to my father. He kept quiet for a while. He then told me that if I really wanted to leave I could. Renu had no objections. I needed some money, however. I had been told by now that I no longer had a bed or clothes in Dhaka. I would have to buy a new set of clothes and furniture again. I told my father that I would need some money to buy a bed, a table and chair and linen. I would also need some money to see me through the first few months. Mollah Jalaluddin and Abdul Hamid Chowdhury contacted me to say that they had managed to rent a house in Tantibazar and I would be welcome to stay with them. I didn't want to go back to 150 Mughaltuli because it was so crowded with people all the time that I had no privacy there at all. Nevertheless, there was still a lot there to attract me. If you had someone who took care of you as well as Mr Shawkat did, you could relax! I was still in poor health and needed to be on a drug regime for some time. I took some money from father and left for Dhaka in the second week of April. Renu, Hasina and Kamal didn't want to let go of me; they had become really attached to me by now. When I was leaving brother and sister were inconsolable. I went to Dhaka via Barisal. Since I had informed him of my schedule Jalal was waiting to receive me in Narayanganj and took me to his house immediately. He had a room ready for me.

Mr Shamsul Huq had shifted the Awami League office to Nawabpur by this time. Manik Bhai and his family had been residing in two rooms of this building for some time now. I met him, Ataur Rahman Khan and many others here. I went to Dr Nandi and got a thorough check-up. He prescribed some medicines for me. I also went to the Awami League office. I saw that the furniture there consisted of one table, two or three chairs and a bench. A boy worked as a peon here. Professor Qamruzzaman looked after the office since Mr Huq was in jail again. As joint secretary of the party I convened a meeting of its working committee. The twelve or thirteen members who turned up for the meeting made me acting general secretary and gave me the responsibility of running the organization for the time being. Mr Ataur Rahman Khan was the senior vice-president and he presided over the meeting.

Dhaka was under a very tyrannical and ruthless regime in those days. People were too scared to open their mouths since they risked imprisonment if they did so. The universities and colleges were under siege too. People were too scared to come to the Awami League office. Mr Qamruzzaman and I spent our evenings sitting in the office and doing nothing much. People we knew averted their eyes as they passed our Nawabpur office. One or two of them were actually members of our party! But if anyone wanted to meet me I would tell them that I would do so only in the office.

After Mr Shaheed Suhrawardy had come to our office he had managed to send us a typewriter that he had got from one of his admirers. A student from Dhaka called Siraj would type on it with one finger. I requested him to do the office correspondence with it and he did so readily. He soon began to type quite well. The peon we employed for the office would also work in Professor Qamruzzaman's house later in the day.

One day a lawyer came to our office. He said, 'I would like to become a member of your party. You won't get me to do a lot of work but I'll try to do what I can in the evenings.' I was elated. This gentleman used to talk very slowly. He was about my age. I liked him a lot. I soon requested him to take the responsibility of running the office. He said that he would come and do what he could every day on his way back home after the courts closed. He was as good as his word and began to come regularly. He worked steadily. The man who had been our secretary had vanished without a trace. In a working committee meeting later I proposed that the lawyer be made the office secretary. Everyone agreed. Sixteen years later he is still our office secretary. He has never wanted any reward from anyone for the work he has been doing. He has become my good friend too. However, he never speaks on public occasions. Nor has he been asked to do anything besides office work. For his part, he too has not wanted to do anything else. I had entrusted him with all office expenditures. He would also keep all accounts. Our income was meagre and so was our expenditure. No government had ever looked at what he was doing suspiciously or put him behind bars until recently when he had to spend a few days in jail. But he was now in poor health. Because we had been fortunate in getting a secretary of his ability the East Pakistan Awami League office has managed to function efficiently. I haven't mentioned his name yet but he is Mr Mohammadullah. Mr Suhrawardy and Maulana Bhasani were fond of him and trusted him too. He would never neglect work that came his way.

In any case, with two or three exceptions, district committees had not yet been formed. If we worked steadfastly we would be able to build our organization since the people were now against the Muslim League. The Awami League, on the other hand, was the only opposition party and was guided by ideals and was principled in its actions. But the main obstacle in its way was a shortage of finances.

Meanwhile, Muslim League leaders had published a statement it attributed to Mr Suhrawardy distorting it in such a manner that it would appear to anyone reading it that he would have liked Urdu to be the only state language of Pakistan. As the general secretary I held a press conference on this issue. In it I demanded that Bengali be made a state language and all political prisoners should be freed. I also demanded compensations for the families of those who had died on 21 February and insisted that the brutal oppressors of that day be punished. I also asked the government to provide proof that a foreign country was responsible for instigating the language movement. The Muslim League had not hesitated to come up with the story that Hindu students from Calcutta had put on pyjamas and taken the guise of Muslims and were behind what had happened. I asked the Muslim League whether they agreed that the five or six people who had died were Muslims and whether 99 per cent of the people arrested were Muslims or not. If it was true that Dhaka was overflowing with Hindu students from Calcutta and if the government was unable to capture even one of them, did it have any right to stay in power?

Mr Ataur Rahman Khan was assisting me in every manner possible in running the party. Mr Yar Mohammad Khan was also helping me in many ways. We organized a meeting in which it was decided that I would have to go to Karachi where I would meet the prime minister of Pakistan, Khawaja Nazimuddin, and demand that all political prisoners be freed. I also needed to talk to Mr Suhrawardy. We needed his guidance badly.

By this time the Awami League party had been formed in the Punjab, the Frontier Province, Sind and Karachi. But because Nawab Mamdot's Awami League party had joined the Jinnah Muslim League, the party in Punjab had now become the Jinnah Awami Muslim League. We had agreed in a meeting of the East Pakistan Awami League Working Committee that we would not change the name of our party. It was not right to have any political party named after Mr Jinnah since no political organization should be called by the name of a person. We also decided not to alter our manifesto. We had not taken any affiliation at this time. Mr Suhrawardy was unhappy at this decision. It was necessary to discuss these issues with him. He had written a letter to me from Hyderabad, Sind. He was then involved in defending the people who had been arrested under what was known as the Rawalpindi Conspiracy case.[24]

~

I reached Karachi in May. Mr Mahmudul Huq Osmani, president of the Karachi Awami League, and its general secretary, Sheikh Manzurul Huq, were there to receive me on my arrival. I was to stay in Mr Osmani's house. A meeting of the Awami League was called where I spoke in English since the people there did not understand Bengali while I would not speak in Urdu.

As soon as I reached Karachi, I sent a letter to Khawaja Nazimuddin asking for an audience with him. He complied and scheduled a meeting with me and sent me a pass so that I could get to see him.

At that time there was a young Bengali man called Amanullah who was staying in Karachi. He acted as my secretary and assisted me in every way and stayed with me all the time. He was a member of the Karachi Awami League. He was a tireless worker and was adept at doing all sorts of things. He was in the centre of things here too and would carry on the battle to establish Bengali as a state language single-handedly. The Karachi Coffee House was then the centre of all political activities in the city. Osmani and Manzur decided that I should hold a press conference there to give everyone a detailed picture of the ground realities in East Pakistan since West Pakistanis had only heard one side of the story about the movement for establishing Bengali as a state language.

I went to see Prime Minister Khawaja Nazimuddin at the appointed time in his office. His assistant secretary, Sajed Ali, greeted me on arrival. I knew him from my Calcutta days. He had previously been the personal assistant of the prime minister of East Bengal. He took me to his office room. The prime minister had allotted me twenty minutes of his time. As soon as I entered his office Mr Nazimuddin rose from his chair to receive me. He was quite polite. He asked about my health and wanted to find out how long I would be staying. He knew that personally I held him in high esteem. I knew that he thought highly of my abilities as a party worker and was fond of me. I requested him to release Maulana Bhasani, Shamsul Huq, Maulana Tarkabagish, Khairat Hussein, Khan Saheb Osman Ali, Abul Hashim and our other workers who had been imprisoned. I asked him to order a judicial inquiry into the firing and killing of students on 21 February. He said, 'This matter is under the jurisdiction of the provincial government; what can I do here?' I replied, 'You are the prime minister of a Muslim League government and East Bengal has a Muslim League government. So you certainly have the right to tell them what to do. Surely you don't want unrest in the country; nor do we. I have come all the way to Karachi to meet you since I know that the provincial government will not heed my demands. They continue to commit one brutal act after another to protect themselves from the consequences of that first brutal action.' In the end we talked for an hour instead of the allotted twenty minutes.

I said to him, 'The Awami League is in the opposition. It should be given the opportunity to act unhindered. After all, a democracy cannot function without an opposition. I know very well that you believe in democracy.' He conceded that the Awami League was the opposing political party. I asked him, 'Can I tell the newspapers that you are willing to accept the Awami League as the opposition party?' He replied, 'Certainly.' He said though he did not normally interfere in any provincial activity he would try to resolve matters in this case. I took my leave. I was grateful to him for patiently listening to me. Two days later I held a press conference. After I had read a statement I had composed myself, I fielded questions posed by many journalists. I was able to answer them satisfactorily and give them a clear picture of the situation in East Bengal. In answer to a question I said, 'Elections to nearly thirty seats are not being held. Let there be elections in any one of them and watch us defeat the Muslim League candidate by a wide margin.'

At that time, the West Pakistani people, including the educated elite, believed that the Awami League was hardly popular. They believed that the Muslim League would win hands down in any election. This was because of the election results in the Punjab. They did not know anything about the people of Bengal; they had no idea of their thoughts on such an issue. This was also the result of the concerted campaign carried out by the government-supported media. The West Pakistanis had never got the opportunity to learn the truth. They asked me about self-rule; I responded by asking them to think about Pakistan's geographic situation.

The press conference lasted for over two hours. When it ended, I believed that they were able to gather something of the truth. Both the *Pakistan Times* and *Imroze* gave prominence to the coverage of the press conference. I met many people who had once worked with me in the Muslim League. Sheikh Manzurul Huq, for example, was a leader of the national guard of the Muslim League in Delhi when I had met him there. Now he had become secretary of the Awami League

This was my first visit to Karachi. I thought: so this is our capital! How many Bengalis would ever get the opportunity to see their capital? We were born in a country that was green everywhere; wherever one looked in Bengal one saw a sea of green. How could we ever get to like the pitiless sandscape? People have an intimate relationship with their environment. Desert denizens have minds that wavered like the sand blowing in a desert. On the other hand, people of an alluvial region like Bengal have minds that were soft and verdant like the land. We were born into a world that abounded in beauty; we loved whatever was beautiful.

Manzur took us in his jeep to Hyderabad. We came across the desert after we left Karachi. There were no signs of habitation within minutes of leaving the city; only once in a while did we pass small bazars. And even these had only a few people in them. I said to Manzur, 'How do you manage to survive in such a barren land?' Manzur replied, 'Because we have no other option! We are migrants, this is where we have built our homes, and this is where we'll have to die. You have seen Delhi; you saw that it was nowhere as barren as this land; when we first came here we felt miserable but now we are used to this environment. We have decided to migrate to Karachi in great numbers; when you come to Karachi next you will see how we have managed to fill the city with flowers and fruit-bearing trees.'

We reached Hyderabad in the evening. Manzur was driving the jeep and he was doing it expertly. We were getting to be good friends. We had both been through much turmoil but our friendship had survived all vicissitudes. Whenever I went back to Karachi later, he was always by my side.

In any case, we went straight to the local government bungalow. Mr Suhrawardy was not in and was expected to return at night. The two of us went to a hotel and freshened up. When we went to the bungalow to meet Mr Suhrawardy at about nine that night he still hadn't come back. We kept waiting for him. Finally, he showed up at ten. As soon as he saw me he said, 'Quite a press conference you held in West Pakistan.' I replied,

'What else could I have done!' He had known I was coming to Hyderabad. We talked for long. He asked a lot of questions about the situation in East Bengal; he wanted to know if all our leaders had been jailed and expressed his doubts on whether they would be looked after well. I gave him details of my meeting with Mr Nazimuddin. I also told him about the events of 21 February. I informed him that the newspapers had published his views on the question of the state language of Pakistan. He said, 'What have they been publishing about my thoughts on the issue?' I said, 'Apparently, you had told some reporter that Urdu should be the only state language.' Visibly angry at this, he said, 'I made no such comment. What would be wrong if both Bengali and Urdu were made state languages of the country? That is exactly what I had said.' He added that he had issued statements protesting against the use of force that day. I told him that no newspaper had reported this. I said, 'The people of Bengal were very hurt when they found out that you had said nothing in their support.'

He asked me to meet him again the next evening since he would be attending the court in the morning. Proceedings of the Pindi Conspiracy trial were being held inside Hyderabad jail then. He would return from Hyderabad to Karachi later in the evening. He said I could go back with him to Karachi since Manzur was planning to return that very morning. The two of us returned to the hotel. Manzur set out in the morning in search of Mr Masud, hoping to bring him to our hotel. This gentleman was once secretary of the All India State Muslim League and had settled down in Hyderabad after Partition. He was devoted to Mr Suhrawardy and had joined the Awami League. Manzur left me with Mr Masud and went his own way. Mr Masud took me out and we were together till 1 p.m. We had lunch together and he introduced me to a lot of people in this city.

At two I went to Mr Suhrawardy's place with my baggage. He had a few biscuits and drank some Horlicks. This was what he usually had for lunch. With him was an advocate who had come from Peshawar to consult him on a case involving another prisoner. That night Mr Suhrawardy treated the two of us to dinner. I told him, 'How can you go on living in this manner?' He said, 'All I need for lunch is some biscuits, butter and bread.' He had no one to look after him and managed things all by himself.

We resumed our conversation on the political situation. He said, 'The East Pakistan Awami League is not affiliated to me in any way. I am nobody as far as your organization is concerned.' I said we would have to build up our organization before we started to seek affiliations. 'You continue to be our leader. The East Pakistan Awami League considers you its leader and the people of East Pakistan support you.' He said, 'Summon a conference; but before that the East Pakistan Awami League must seek affiliation.' I told him, 'You are involved in the Jinnah Awami League but we can't change our party's name. We don't want to link a political organization to any person's name. Second, we have our own manifesto, our own constitution; it won't be possible to alter them. Maulana Bhasani had sent me to meet you in 1949. Even then he had requested you to form an All Pakistan Awami League. He won't have any objections if you agree to accept our manifesto and constitution.'

After extensive discussions he agreed to my proposals and gave us his written consent. I needed to present this at the next meeting of our party's working committee and get them to apply for an affiliation. I said, 'If they see your signature no one will have any objections. I discussed your situation with Maulana Bhasani when I met him in jail. If our manifesto, name and constitution are all acceptable to you there should be no problem about seeking affiliation.' I made another request to him: he would have to assure us in writing that he supported the idea of having both Bengali and Urdu as state languages of Pakistan. After all, there had been a lot of misunderstanding about his stand on the issue. The Muslim League as well as the so-called progressives had been trying to discredit him through their propaganda. He readily agreed to put his signature to such a statement, as it was something he believed in. And he did exactly that.

He promised to come to East Pakistan as soon as the trial had run its course. He would stay in our part of the country for a month and asked me to make arrangements for him to address at least one public meeting in every district of the country. There was no time to lose. But the real problem was that he had no idea how long the trial would drag on. When I asked him, 'Is what is being said about the Pindi Conspiracy case true? Will you be able to acquit the accused? And if those accused are really guilty should they not be punished?' He said, 'Don't ask those questions; I won't tell you anything since as an advocate I am under oath not to divulge any information about cases under trial.' Seeing him visibly upset at my questions, I decided to keep quiet.

We left for Karachi late in the afternoon. Mr Suhrawardy drove the car himself and I sat beside him. A few lawyers were sitting in the backseat. On the way they asked me about the situation in East Pakistan. Why did we want Bengali to be a state language? Were the Hindus behind the movement? I tried to explain to them what was really going on. Mr Suhrawardy also tried to give them a clear picture and pointed out that the role of the Hindus in the movement had been distorted in the portrayals they knew of. They wanted me to recite Kazi Nazrul Islam's poems. I recited some lines from 'Who calls you a bandit, my friend?', 'Women', 'Equality' and other poems. I also recited a few lines from Tagore's poems. Mr Suhrawardy translated those lines into English for them. A couple of them said that they had read a few of Tagore's poems in their English versions. Time passed quite quickly in this manner. We reached Karachi in the evening. Mr Suhrawardy dropped me off at Mr Osmani's home and asked me to come to 13 Kachari Road the next morning.

When I went to meet him the next day he asked me to go to Dhaka via Lahore. He told me that he would telegram Khawaja Abdur Rahim, Bar at Law, and Raja Hassan Akhter about my trip to Lahore. He also asked me to hold a press conference in Lahore and to address party workers of the city. Since I had already spent many days in Karachi I decided to head for Lahore by train immediately. Khawaja Abdur Rahim, formerly an officer of the Indian Civil Service, was a perfect gentleman. He invited me to stay with him in 'Javed Manzil' where he was staying. This house was once owned by the poet Allama Iqbal, where he had had his vision of Pakistan. He was not only a poet but also a philosopher. I went to his mausoleum and prayed for his soul and felt myself honoured to be doing so. How fortunate I was to have been able to stay in the same house where Allama Iqbal once spent his time in meditation!

The admirers of Khawaja Abdur Rahim and Mr Suhrawardy's followers in the city worked together for the press conference I would be holding. I met a lot of people on this trip to Lahore. For instance, I met Mr Hamid Nizami, an acquaintance from a previous visit to the city, who had entertained me lavishly then. He assured me he would be present at the press conference and would ask everyone he knew to attend it.

The press conference was attended by reporters of all the major dailies of the city. The representative of APP [Associated Press of Pakistan] himself was present. After my opening statement they asked me many questions, which I was able to answer satisfactorily. They seemed unaware of the fact that we wanted both Bengali and Urdu to be state languages. They had been given the impression we wanted Bengali to be the only state language. I was able to prove to them that the members of the Awami League were all the same people who had worked for the movement for Pakistan. They were convinced when I began to name the members of our party one by one.

The members of Lahore's Awami League thanked me profusely for my performance at the press conference. I told them that I say exactly what I believe in. There is no discrepancy between what I feel and what I say. I don't mince words and will give voice to whatever I have in my mind. This attitude often landed me in trouble; you could even say that this was a defect of my personality or you could interpret this as one of my strengths! The one thing that I could drive home in Lahore was that any election would completely expose the vulnerability of the Muslim League. I told them that they could not imagine how badly the Muslim League would be mauled.

A problem cropped up now: there was only one flight a week from Lahore to Dhaka and there was no ticket available on the next flight, which was three days later. Also, I still had some unfinished business. Moreover, the next flight had been cancelled and I would have to stay in Lahore for seventeen to eighteen days. Khawaja Abdur Rahim and Raja Hassan were going to holiday in Rawalpindi and Murree and wanted me to accompany them. I agreed. In Rawalpindi I saw our military headquarters and the park where Liaquat Ali Khan was shot dead by an assassin. The next day we arrived in Murree. It was very cold. One needed woollens and at night a blanket. In contrast, Rawalpindi had been so hot that I had broken into a rash. And yet Murree was only thirty to thirty-five miles from Pindi and it had such lovely weather! I truly relaxed there. The town was on a mountain. Many Punjabi zamindars and businessmen had built summer houses here, where they spent their summers with their families. I really liked the place. The mountains were all green now and the city too was full of greenery. I was there for a day but felt like staying on. However, I left the town the next day. Lahore's Pir Salahuddin was my companion during my stay. I went round everywhere with him.

Newspapers like *Nawa-i-Waqt* and *Pakistan Times* had given my press conference ample space. The government newspapers, on the other hand, had been very critical of my statement. I had stressed that Bengali should be one of the state languages and emphasized the need to free political prisoners. I had protested against the way people had been shot to death. I had also emphasized our economic problems and the importance of giving us autonomy.

From Lahore I took the plane to Dhaka. In those days there were no direct flights between the two cities and one had to travel via Delhi or Calcutta. As soon as I reached Dhaka I summoned a meeting of our working committee. I contacted Maulana Bhasani too. I informed everyone about Mr Suhrawardy's views. We arrived at a consensus to seek affiliation. By this time the weekly *Ittefaq* had become very popular. Manik Bhai had mortgaged everything that he had to run it successfully. I helped him whenever I could. Mr Ataur Rahman Khan also made every attempt to be of assistance.

~

At about this time the Maulana became ill and had to be admitted to Dhaka Medical College Hospital. The government refused to meet his expenses. They were willing to let him stay in a cabin but we would have to bear all costs. Maulana Bhasani, on the other hand, was a prisoner and how would he be able to generate the money needed for his treatment? The government should have underwritten his treatment costs but was not prepared to do anything for him. Maulana Bhasani contacted me to ask what he could do. I was in a spot: where could I raise the money and who would be willing to help us? After every ten days of stay he would have to pay 150 rupees a day for his treatment. He would also have to pay for his medicines as well as for any other expense incurred while staying in the cabin. However, I told the Maulana to get himself admitted and started to raise a fund for his treatment. Mr Ataur Rahman Khan promised to try to help as much as possible. One of my friends who was in government service and Mrs Anwara Khatun also helped from time to time. But there was one person whose contribution must be acknowledged: a friend called Haji Giasuddin who was in business and who had never become a member of the Awami League but who was very fond of me. He was from Comilla. Whenever I ran out of means to raise money, I would go to him and never returned empty-handed. I had to raise the money in ten days' time. If the payment was delayed the Maulana would get a reminder from the hospital. He, in turn, would write to me from his hospital bed informing me about the reminder.

Once or twice I went to the hospital to see the Maulana. However, I couldn't get to have much of a conversation with him since the police or IB official guarding him would plead to me that his job would be at stake if anyone found out that we had been talking. At around this time many political workers from Dhaka's Bangshal area joined the Awami League under the leadership of Abdul Malek and Habibur Rahman. They tried to help us by raising funds on their own. In those days Awami League workers helped keep the party afloat financially by raising funds themselves.

While the Maulana was in the hospital I drew up a programme to go to every district to hold public meetings. This was when Mr Ataur Rahman Khan and Mr Abdus Salam Khan were at loggerheads. Mr Salam felt that though he was the deputy vice-president he was being bypassed and Mr Khan was getting all the attention. He kept pointing out that while he was an advocate of the high court Ataur Rahman Khan practised in the judges' court. He also stressed that he was older and had more experience in politics and yet was being ignored. I tried to convince him not to mind. I said, 'Ataur Rahman Khan has been living in Dhaka from before you and the people of the city know him well. On the other hand, you are a newcomer in Dhaka. Also, why bother over such issues?' I pointed out that they could alternate in presiding over our working committee meetings. Maulana Bhasani was of course still in jail.

However, the tension between the two men increased and I found myself in a tough spot. Mr Salam was not always available and could not mix easily with our party workers. On the other hand, Ataur Rahman Khan was always around. When Kazi Golam Mahbub went into hiding and was subsequently imprisoned Ataur Rahman Khan had become acting convener of the All-Party State Language Action Committee. In this capacity he had been in contact with our workers and students involved in the movement. I could depend on him whenever I needed his help. For all these reasons I myself was inclined to support him. He would never protest if he was given a responsibility. True, he lacked initiative, but at least he was ever ready to respond to our call. I tried not to let my bias for him show. I told Mr Salam that I would be touring North Bengal with Mr Ataur Rahman Khan and would take him along when we held meetings in Faridpur, Kushtia, Jessore and Khulna.

Mr Ataur Rahman Khan and I set out to address meetings in Pabna, Bogra, Rangpur and Dinajpur. We had succeeded in forming committees in Natore and Naogaon but had failed to set up one in Rajshahi. On the day we addressed the meeting in Dinajpur, it had rained a lot and attendance was poor. At night we held a meeting and our party workers managed to form a district committee under the leadership of Mr Rahimuddin. We were thus able to set up committees in different districts. However, Rajshahi proved resistant to our efforts and in Pabna too no one came forward to assume responsibility on the party's behalf. We had a tough time finding a place to stay in this district. Later we managed to form a committee that included Captain Mansur Ali and Abdur Rab, aka Boga. Since we could not get others to join we nominated some students. The Pabna Students' League called a meeting at two hours' notice in the Town Hall. We couldn't get a microphone for the meeting. Nevertheless, Mr Ataur Rahman Khan and I managed to address the meeting.

Similarly, we continued to organize meetings in the south of Bengal after we had finished with the north. We managed to form strong committees in Kushtia and Jessore. However, we couldn't find mature people to work for us in Khulna. I had to make a younger colleague, Sheikh Abdul Aziz, president and we made Momenuddin general secretary. Mr Salam kept objecting to our decision to appoint younger people. I pointed out, 'What makes you think we will not be able to build up our party if we fail to attract the attention of older people? Just wait and see—the younger people we have recruited will one day develop into able leaders of our district committees.' Where our two advocates were not available for travel I would go alone and organize and address meetings. I would form committees everywhere. All through June, July and August I kept working non-stop, touring all the districts and subdivisions, and managed to form branches of the Awami League everywhere I went.

Mr Shamsul Huq had already formed a committee in Mymensingh. Mr Abul Mansur Ahmed had returned from Calcutta by this time. He became president of the Awami League while Mr Hashimuddin Ahmed became secretary. Mr Hashimuddin Ahmed, Mr Rafiqueuddin Bhuiyan and Mr Hatem Ali Talukdar had been arrested during the state language movement and had spent time in jail. In Noakhali Mr Abdul Jabbar Khaddar formed the district committee. In Chittagong Mr Abdul Aziz, Mozaffar Ahmed and Zahur Ahmad Chowdhury and in Comilla Abdur Rahman Khan, Lal Mia and Khondokar Mushtaq Ahmed formed Awami League branches. I toured these districts and tried to make the party organization more effective there.

At the end of August I went to Barisal and then to my village home since I was running short of money. After staying in our village for a while I returned to Dhaka. I had quit my law studies by then. My father was very unhappy with my decision and reluctant to give me any more money. I had to make my living somehow. I had my children to look after and how long could I go on at this rate? Renu would say nothing and endured all hardship silently. Whenever I went to our village home she knew I would be needing money and she tried to raise whatever amount she could. In the end my father gave me some money though he was not able to give me much. However, he never really declined to give me enough to meet my expenses. I spent very little and the one luxury I permitted myself was cigarettes. My younger brother Nasser was doing business by this time in Khulna. He used to meet the expenses of my children. He had quit studies but did not have to rely on my father for any funds. On the contrary, he was able to send money home from time to time.

~

Soon after I returned to Dhaka I attended a meeting of the East Pakistan Peace Committee. Mr Ataur Rahman Khan presided over the meeting. Our slogan was 'We want peace and not war'. On 15 or perhaps 16 September [1952] we were informed that delegates from South-East Asia and Pacific Rim countries would be attending the 'Peace Conference'. We would be going to Peking by invitation. Thirty people from Pakistan had been invited, of whom only five were from East Pakistan, namely, Ataur Rahman Khan, Tofazzal Hossain, editor of *Ittefaq*, Khondokar Mohammad Ilias, the Urdu writer Ibne Hassan and myself. There was little time to make preparations. Also, where was the money for the trip to come from? When would we get our passports? All we knew was that the Peace Conference committee would send us our tickets to travel to Peking.

We applied for our passports even though we had little hopes of getting them. This was because the government and its partymen were very upset with us. Could anyone be invited to go to communist China if he wasn't a communist? They did their best to convey the impression that we had been invited not to a peace conference but to a Communist Party meeting. However, in Karachi Mia Iftekharuddin was sparing no effort to get us our passports. A passport officer we knew told us, 'I have everything ready and will issue you your passports as soon I get the order to do so.' He personally contacted Karachi to know the status of our case. We tried to find out the fate of our application from the home ministry. Mr Ataur Rahman met the joint secretary and the secretary. Nobody could give us much information. We kept trying our best and contacted the BOAC [British Overseas Airways Corporation] office. They told us that our tickets had arrived. However, they wouldn't be able to reserve our seats and issue our tickets without our passports. The BOAC flight landed in Dhaka once a week. We found out that the plane would leave Dhaka either on the 23rd or the 24th and fly via Rangoon and Hong Kong.

We learned that Peking would be very cold at this time of the year and we would need warm clothes. I didn't have any woollens but knew I could buy them cheap in Hong Kong. By the 23rd we had given up any hope of going. But then we found out that a flight would be landing in Dhaka on the 24th. We then came to know that the government had given the go-ahead to the passport office to issue our passports. We realized that it was not being generous but merely acting to save its face. We received our passport at 1 p.m. Did we have enough time to go home, get our clothes and then board the plane? Mr Ataur Rahman phoned the BOAC office to find out when the plane would land. They had no information about its arrival. All they could say was that it would be a few hours late. This made us hopeful that we would be able to board the plane after all. We kept waiting at Mr Khan's house. We would be informed in an hour's time when exactly the plane would take off. Manik Bhai kept telling us he wouldn't be able to accompany us for there was no one to look after *Ittefaq*.

We soon got news that the plane would be twenty-four hours late. It would be landing in Dhaka the next day at 12 noon and it would leave an hour later. We felt relieved at getting some time. We could take some measures to ensure that the Awami League's activities would continue in our absence. When I came back home, Mollah Jalal and Hamid Chowdhury ensured that everything had been arranged for me. I went to the Awami League office and then to Manik Bhai's *Ittefaq* office. I kept insisting that he should come along with us and he began to give in gradually but couldn't yet make up his mind fully. We had agreed to meet in Mr Ataur Rahman Khan's house at ten and leave from there for the airport. Khondokar Ilias was a good friend and editor of the weekly *Juger Dabi*. We were about the same age. We decided that we would stay together. But we were still having problems with Manik Bhai. What would he finally decide?

In the morning I got ready and left for Manik Bhai's house. In those days rickshaws were the only mode of transport available in Dhaka. It was eight o'clock when I reached his house—only to find him fast asleep! I woke him up with a lot of effort. He said, 'What am I to do? I can't see myself going. You guys go ahead with the tour.' This made me angry. I told his wife, 'Why don't you ask him to go? What will it matter if he goes away for ten–fifteen days? Manik Bhai is a writer and will be able to write about his trip and this will give the people of our country a chance to learn about the new China. Where are his clothes? Please pack his suitcase. And as for you, Manik Bhai, please get ready. We are not going anywhere without you.' Manik Bhai knew how stubborn I could be and so got ready quickly.

Next, we came to Mr Ataur Rahman Khan's house. We found there that the plane would be landing on time. We would have to be in the airport by eleven since there were lots of formalities to go through. We had collected our tickets a long time back. Our seats had already been reserved.

By the time we came to the airport the plane had already landed. A few of our friends had turned up to see us off. Mr Ali Aksad, secretary of the Peace Committee, had even arranged some bouquets for our farewell. Our luggage and our passports were duly examined. On board the plane were Mian Mahmud Ali Kasuri and two or three other West Pakistani leaders also travelling to China. We found out that the other Pakistani delegates had left Karachi for Hong Kong and we would be meeting them there. We would then leave for China together. Our plane would first land in Rangoon and we would spend the night there. We would therefore have a lot of time to spend there. Indeed, we would be there for one full evening and night. Mr Ataur Rahman Khan told us that Barrister Shaukat Ali Khan's older brother lived in Rangoon. He had a thriving business there and he would be able to provide us with his address.

When we reached Rangoon arrangements were made for us to spend the night at BOAC's rest house. We saw that Burma and Bangladesh had the same kind of flowers. Burma was then in turmoil for though the country had become independent the situation there bordered on anarchy. Some citizens had managed to get a lot of arms from Japan and China after the Second World War. They were now using those weapons indiscriminately. The communists and Karens had rebelled against the administration. The country, in fact, was disintegrating because of a situation bordering on civil war. Law and order was non-existent. In Rangoon city there were daylight robberies and hijackings. People were generally too scared to leave their homes at night. Those who had businesses and were well-off had the most to fear and were worried stiff. Their children could be kidnapped for ransom at any moment. If the kidnappers did not get the money they demanded they would threaten to kill the children. Such incidents were quite common. We had been warned about the situation. We had been instructed to inform the authorities if we wanted to go out. Indeed, our hotel was surrounded by armed guards. But we were foreigners and in any case what valuables did we have that the miscreants would want to rob from us?

When we reached the rest house Mr Ataur Rahman Khan phoned Amjad Ali, the proprietor of Royal Stationery shop. He was not in but returned the call later and met us in the rest house. He was delighted to see us in Rangoon. After all, who isn't happy to come across a countryman in a foreign land? He had a car of his own and drove us around the city. However, he first took us to his shop, Royal Stationery, which was among the best shops in Rangoon.

It seemed to us that the city was dozing off by then. He filled us in about the way things were in the city. But he was determined not to leave it. The Burmese government had control over the city and around twenty miles of the surrounding countryside. Nevertheless, it couldn't do anything to suppress the rebels. Mr Ali took us to his house and introduced us to his wife. She was a very amiable and polite lady. They insisted that we should have dinner with them and would not take no for an answer.

Mr Ali took us out once more to make us see the city's sights. We saw some huge pagodas. We went inside one of them. However, the largest pagoda was a few miles away from the city and it would be late by the time we returned. Moreover, the roads were unsafe. So we ended up going to the house of an East Bengali acquaintance of Mr Ataur Rahman Khan who also lived in the city and had once been a minister. He wasn't home though and after we had knocked on the door for a long time a Burmese woman peeped out to tell us nobody was in. She wouldn't open the door since we were all strangers to her. We asked for a piece of paper. She said, 'I am not going to open the door for anything. There is some paper outside; please write what you want on it and then slip it in through the window.' When we asked her why she was so wary of us she said, 'But this is exactly how the bandits enter. They come in a car and ask for the owner of the house. Previously, the people of the houses here would respond to their call and ask them in. The bandits would immediately tie them up at gunpoint and then loot everything that they could get hold of.' Such incidents were commonplace in Rangoon and people were naturally wary of strangers and would not allow them entry into their houses.

Rangoon must have been beautiful once. There were some beautiful places still to see but it had lost its charm somewhat. Mr Amjad took us around the city for hours. Later, he took us to the Burma Club. Before the country was independent, membership was open to Europeans only. Natives were not permitted to enter it. The club was on a lake and was very beautiful. Mr Amjad was well respected there and everyone inside seemed to know him. He was with us throughout the day and took us back to our rest house at night. He invited us to spend a day or two with him on our way back.

Ilias and I shared a room that night. A few members of the Rangoon Peace Committee came to meet us the next morning. We had extensive discussions. Their leader informed us that a few members of their committee had already left for China. A few more of them were scheduled to leave for the country as soon as their passports were ready. A few of their members had even fled to China!

We had to leave Rangoon very early that morning. We arrived in Bangkok later that day. The capital city of Thailand, it had a big airport. Here we had tea and snacks. We left for Hong Kong an hour later on a direct flight. I have no problems sleeping on planes. We traversed Thai and Vietnamese airspace and then flew over the South China Sea. We landed in Hong Kong's Kaitak airport at 1 p.m. We were greeted at the airport by representatives of the Xinhua news agency, also known as New China News Agency in English. Arrangements had been made for us to stay in Kowloon Hotel. Ten to twelve delegates from West Pakistan had already arrived. More delegates from that part of the country were expected later that evening. The next day all of us met and decided to make Pir Manki Sharif the leader of our delegation.

That night and the next morning we toured Hong Kong. The English used to call this city Victoria. On one side of the river was Hong Kong and on the other Kowloon. All of us bought some warm clothes. I had very little money but things were very cheap. However, you had to be careful since they would ask twenty-five takas for something that really cost one taka and if you didn't quote this price you were going to be fleeced! It wasn't a good idea to buy anything here without the assistance of someone who had lived in the city for a while and knew its customs and prices. Indeed, another name of the city could have been 'Con Town'. When you were walking the streets you had to keep your hands in your pockets for if you didn't you ran the risk of it being picked. Such a beautiful city and yet such risks! It was still an English colony. Many wealthy Chinese had fled from the mainland to Hong Kong and the many homeless people here had to resort to illicit ways to make ends meet.

I talked about the situation of the city with a West Pakistani friend. He had a home in Sind but was now living in the city. He told me quite a few stories of what was happening in Hong Kong. I would have many more occasions to travel to the city and stay there but I always wondered how it managed to hold its head up high despite what was happening in it.

It must have been on the 27th that we took the train from Hong Kong to Canton. The first Chinese station on our way was Shenzhen. The British railroad ended when we reached the limit of British territory. We had to walk over a bridge to reach the Chinese station. Volunteers of the Peace Committee greeted us warmly on our arrival. We had no reason to worry about our journey from here on. They accepted all responsibility for our luggage. They had made decent arrangements and we were comfortable in the train. They had assigned an interpreter for every two to three delegates. Almost all of them were school and college students.

I decided to explore the train. You could travel from one end of the train to the other. The people of the new China that was emerging were quite eager to show us their achievements. A race that had once been notorious for its opium addiction suddenly seemed to have woken up from sleep. Now no one took opium and you couldn't see anyone dozing off under its influence. It appeared to me that this was a new country and its people a new race. They were now full of hope, and they had left behind despair. They had become free. I wondered: how could they have made such an impact on the world in three years' time?

We reached Canton late in the evening. Hundreds of children had assembled at the station, bouquets in their hands. The members of the Peace Committee were at the station to greet us. Arrangements had been made to accommodate us in a huge hotel located on the banks of the Pearl river. We had been invited to a dinner that night by the Peace Committee.

The people of China were like us Bengalis in that they seemed to give long speeches and enjoyed listening to them!

The speeches began before dinner was served. Pir Manki Sharif spoke on our behalf. Every line that he uttered was greeted with applause and we had to join in all the time. We were to leave for Peking early next morning. We had reached China quite late. In fact, the conference had already been postponed so that we could be present. Delegates from quite a few countries had not yet managed to reach China. From Canton the distance to Peking by plane was 1500 miles. We began our journey after breakfast. I saw the Chinese countryside from my seat and was overwhelmed by its beauty.

The province of Canton was verdant like Bengal. Even though foreigners had exploited this country for hundreds of years they had not been able to exhaust its resources. The people of new China had resolved to build their country anew with all their hearts. At night we reached Peking airport. Little children, some Indian delegates and members of the Peking Peace Committee were among those who had turned up to welcome us. As soon as the welcoming rituals were over we were taken to Peking Hotel. And so we were finally in Peking, the capital of China! Many nations had conquered Peking at one time or the other. The English and the Japanese had destroyed many landmarks of the city. They had taken away much of the city's treasures when they had captured it. Now the entire city had taken on a festive look. It was as if it had decided to smile at us to show its happiness at throwing off the foreign yoke.

We were to stay in Peking Hotel. This was the largest and most beautiful hotel in the city. I was to share a room with Mr Ataur Rahman Khan and Manik Bhai. We had become exhausted by now and had decided not to go out that night. The leader of our delegation, Pir Manki Sharif, had asked our hosts to ensure that we would be eating in a restaurant run by Muslims. We would have to take a bus to this place at night. It was freezing outside and we didn't feel like going out at all but we really had no other option.

The restaurant was nearly two miles away. As soon as we entered, food was served. The owner of the restaurant appeared delighted to host us. However, the people in the hotel could only speak in Chinese. Fortunately, we had interpreters with us. We started to eat but soon found that the food was too spicy for us. We managed to somehow eat a few pieces of bread before making our exit. But whatever we had eaten disagreed with us and soon we were suffering from stomach pain. When we went to our room we had tea and ate the grapes and other fruit that had been served us and somehow got through the night. Manik Bhai now decided to play the rebel and refused to eat in that restaurant. Everything, after all, could be got in Peking Hotel. They were ready to serve us anything we wanted. Manik Bhai and a few others decided the next afternoon to have lunch in the Peking Hotel restaurant and then take a nap. Mr Ataur Rahman and I felt obliged to go to the Muslim-run restaurant for our meals. That night Pir Manki Sharif and four or five of his companions were going to eat in the restaurant once again. But the next day Mr Sharif and his secretary Hanif Khan (now the Central Parliamentary Secretary) were the only ones willing to go to the Muslim hotel for food. In fact, Peking Hotel served rice, vegetables, prawns, chicken, beef, egg and everything else we were used to eating. If we gave them some time they were even willing to cook these dishes in a manner acceptable to us. We thus felt satisfied as far as food was concerned. A few days before we checked in, the famous West Bengali man of letters Manoj Bose and the celebrated singer Khitesh Bose had been guests in the hotel. They had ensured that the food served was acceptable to our palates. Food-wise, things became even better for us when we came to know them.

We had two or three days still in hand. October 1 was New China's Independence Day. This nation had declared its independence on 1 October 1949. That was when Chiang Kai-shek and his followers had fled the mainland and taken refuge in Formosa.

The Peace Conference was to begin on 2 October. I thought it would be good to catch the sights and sounds of the city before the conference began. Inside Peking city was another city called Forbidden City, where the emperors of old had stayed with their retinue. Ordinary people had no access to this part of the city. The Forbidden City had everything you could think of: parks, a palace, lakes, everything! I had already seen India's Red Fort, Agra Fort and Fatehpur Sikri but this place appeared larger. Now its doors were open to everyone, especially workers. The city's museums, libraries, parks and lake were all open to visitors. Thousands of people were thronging them. Taking in these sights, I said to myself: monarchs behave the same everywhere in the world, spending the wealth created by ordinary people for their own gratification and doing so without having to encounter any objections.

The next day we saw the Summer Palace. It was full of sculptures of all sorts of animals, a huge Buddhist temple and a very big lake, which had an island in it. One could call it the biggest tourist city of the world.

Major General Reza, the Pakistani ambassador, came to meet us in Peking Hotel. He said we should contact him if we had any problems or needed anything. He invited us for dinner. He shared many stories with us.

Apparently the black market had been rendered inoperative and people were getting employment easily. Robberies, thefts and abductions were now things of the past. The new government was bent on curbing any unlawful act with an iron hand. Whatever you wanted to buy could be found at a fixed price. I bought a few things by myself in a market. The price was listed on every product and there was no scope for bargaining. I even rode on a rickshaw even though I didn't know Chinese. I would hold out some yuan, the Chinese currency, to the rickshaw puller. And they took only the exact fare and not a bit more.

This year 1 October was the third anniversary of China's independence. Special arrangements had been made for the delegates of the Peace Conference attending the inaugural ceremony. Positioned right behind us, Mao Zedong, Chu Teh, Madam Sun Yat-Sen (Soong Ching-Ling), Zhou Enlai, Liu Shao-Chi and many others would take the salute. People began to come in processions. There was a sea of people everywhere. Contingents from the infantry, navy and air force marched past us, displaying their skills. They were followed by processions featuring workers, farmers, young pioneers, all with red flags in their hands. I noticed one thing everywhere: although there were a huge number of people involved, everyone showed utmost discipline. There must have been five to seven lakh people in all. The revolutionary government had succeeded in instilling a sense of discipline in the people through its ideology.

I had no idea that Mahbub was posted here as third secretary at the Pakistan embassy. We had studied law together once upon a time. I also knew his father, Mr Abul Kashem, a sub-judge in our country. They were from Chittagong. Fiercely independent, he was never afraid to speak out for what he believed in. Mahbub had brought his wife along to witness the Independence Day festivities. I greeted Mahbub as soon as I spotted him in the crowd. He was surprised to be called by name in Peking. He was delighted to see me. He had read in the papers that I was coming. In the evening he came to the hotel with his wife to meet me. He took me around the city and showed me many of its interesting spots. Because we had a dinner party scheduled for that night I could not stay with him long. However, he promised to come again the next day. In fact, I had dinner with him and his family for the rest of my stay in Peking. I am one who is never happy until I have Bengali food. Mahbub's wife presented me a camera. Because I had run short of money he also gave me some. He asked me to buy some things from Hong Kong with the money because you could get stuff very cheap there. He expressed regret at not being able to buy my wife a gift but said I should spend some of the money he had given me to buy something for her.

Mahbub's wife narrated the following story to me. One day while coming home in a rickshaw she had accidentally dropped her pen. She came home and searched for it everywhere but just couldn't find it. She concluded that she must have dropped it in the rickshaw and lost all hope of getting it back. But the next day the rickshaw puller himself came back to return the pen to her. Such incidents were apparently everyday occurrences in China these days. One could see many such ways in which the Chinese people were changing. I will never forget Mahbub and his wife's hospitality. He was the only Bengali working in the Pakistani embassy in China.

The Peace Conference had 338 delegates attending it from thirty-seven countries. Flags of these countries fluttered in the Peking sky. The conference venue had been decorated with images of the dove of peace and the hall looked very beautiful indeed. Every table had a headphone on it. The Pakistani delegates were bunched together in one place. Leaders of different countries gave speeches. Every country would take turns in providing the president for the different sessions. Many people spoke on the occasion. From East Pakistan Ataur Rahman Khan and I delivered speeches. I spoke in Bengali while Mr Khan gave his speech in English. Chinese, Russian and Spanish were being used in addition to English, so why should I not speak in Bengali? Representing India, Manoj Bose also spoke in Bengali. The students of East Pakistan had sacrificed their lives for their mother tongue. Bengali was the language spoken by the majority of Pakistan's population. I have hardly come across any educated people in China or anywhere else in the world who did not know our great poet Rabindranath Tagore. I could speak English fluently but I felt it was my duty to speak in my mother tongue. After I had finished speaking Manoj Bose rushed to me and, embracing me warmly, said, 'My brother Mujib, now we belong to two separate nations but no one has been able to divide our language. And no one will be able to do so. All Bengali-speaking Indians are very proud of the sacrifices you all have made for our mother tongue.'

After I had finished speaking, Khondokar Ilias refused to let go of me! He was that overwhelmed, even though we had discussed my speech before I delivered it. Mr Khitesh was from Pirojpur and was keeping us all entertained with Bengali songs. He told everyone how all of us are proud of the Bengali language (I have copies of the speech I gave with me; I'll insert it later).[25]

The conference now split into different commissions and we sat in separate rooms to discuss the issues assigned to us. I was a member of one such commission and took part in its deliberations. Once we were through, the resolutions we had adopted were provided to the draft committee. The drafts based on the recommendations were then submitted to the general assembly and adopted unanimously.

It could be said that Manik Bhai took no part at all in the commission proceedings. He said that the resolutions had been formulated already and there was no point in being present in the proceedings. After the conference, a public meeting was organized. This was a huge affair in which representatives from all the countries spoke. All of them emphasized the same point: 'We want peace and not war.' People from different religions also came in processions and joined the meeting. Chinese Confucians constituted the majority here. Then there were Buddhists and a not inconsiderable number of Muslims and a few Christians. We visited a mosque where we were told by the people in charge that nobody interfered with them but that no help was forthcoming either. It seemed to me that Tahera Mazhar gave a very good speech in the meeting. She was the only woman in the Pakistani delegation who spoke. Her speech managed to raise Pakistan's image quite a bit.

After deliberating long on the question of Kashmir, the Pakistani and the Indian delegates came up with a joint statement on the issue. In it the Indian delegates acknowledged that the Kashmir problem should be resolved through peaceful means and a plebiscite. We had succeeded in presenting the Kashmir issue to all the delegates clearly and fully.

We invited the Indian delegates to dinner and they reciprocated the gesture. However, the Muslim League delegates amidst us were not happy with these exchanges. But participating in conferences such as this one can only have positive repercussions for a country. Pakistan was a new country and many people outside it had no clear notions about it. When the Pakistani flag flew next to the flag of other nations, when the Pakistani delegates spoke along with the delegates of other nations and when the name of the country came up in their speeches, others became interested in it and wanted to learn more about Pakistan.

We invited the Russian delegates to dinner too. Here I was fortunate to make the acquaintance of the Russian writer Asimov. It was at this conference that I became acquainted with the famous Turkish poet Nazim Hikmet. He had been imprisoned in his own country for a long time. He had left his country and was now staying in exile in Russia. His only fault was that he was a communist. His country did not want him although he was world famous. I also became acquainted with Dr Saifuddin Kitchlu, Dr Faridi and many other leaders. Ilias and I looked for an opportunity to talk to Madam Sun Yat-Sen and when it came we grabbed it and talked to her for a while.

The one thing I came to understand was that the Chinese government and people were really interested in getting to know the people of the Indian subcontinent. They were interested in becoming friendly with Pakistan but they saw India as a friendly country and liked everything about it. In our talks with the Chinese we tried to impress on them that the people of Pakistan were interested in friendship with them. I got the opportunity to talk to the mayor of Peking, Che Peng, for a while.

We visited Pe Yong Park and the Temple of Heaven. The Chinese used to pray in these temples for a good harvest. But the people of China no longer believed that merely praying for a good harvest would lead to one. The communist government had confiscated the land owned by landlords and had distributed it among all farmers. Thus landless peasants had become landowners. They were trying to increase the harvest and help the government. They no longer gave a part of the harvest to landlords who had done no work. The farmers were working indefatigably. All of them believed that China now belonged to peasants and workers and that the class that used to dominate and exploit them had had their day.

After eleven days spent at the conference it was time for us to return to our country. The organizers of the Peace Conference asked us if we wanted to visit other places in China and expressed their willingness to accommodate us if we wanted to extend our stay. They would bear all the expense incurred. Mr Ataur Rahman Khan and Manik Bhai were eager to return home and so they left. Ilias and I decided to visit a few other places. Since it made better sense to travel in a group we joined Pir Manki Sharif and a few other Pakistani leaders. It occurred to the two of us that with the kind of attitude being displayed by our government we would never get the opportunity to visit China again. But we also knew that we could not stay in China for too long. If we spent too much time there it was very likely that when we landed in our own country our government would take us straight from the airport to its hotel for its special guests! In any case, Yusuf Hassan joined another group. The rest of us decided to travel by train. We left Peking and our first halt was Tien Shin port. But we were having problems with Pir Manki Sharif. He was more interested in visiting places of worship such as pagodas, temples and mosques. We, on the other hand, wanted to spend all our time visiting industries, agricultural facilities, cultural centres and museums. However, since he was the head of our delegation, we were bound to follow him. Nevertheless, the two of us took every opportunity we could to go to the places we fancied although the people there did not understand us and we were unable to understand them. The only way we could communicate, in fact, was through an interpreter.

Tien Shin was a deep-sea port. We saw many Russians there. Ilias and I went to the park in the evening. We tried to talk to a Russian family we met there. But communication proved to be impossible in the absence of an interpreter. In the end we had to depart from them without fulfilling our wish to communicate with them. All we could do was wave our hands to say goodbye. Although we had the desire, we didn't have the means to satisfy it since we didn't know each other's language.

In the evening arrangements had been made for us to dine with the imam of a mosque and a few other Muslims. The Muslims attending the dinner as well as the imam told us that they were happy with the way things were in their country. The communist government did not interfere in their practice of religion. However, they were not allowed to proselytize.

After staying in Tien Shin for a couple of days we headed for Nanking. There wasn't much by way of motorized traffic and all one could see on the roads were cycles, cycle rickshaws and a few buses. There were very few cars to be seen. This was because the new government was more interested in building the country than spending its resources on buying cars.

I faced one problem there. I was in the habit of shaving myself. I have never gone to the barber for a shave. But I had run out of shaving blades. When I went to buy some I was told that the local shops did not stock them since they could not be imported. I had tried to get some blades in Peking but had been unable to find them there too. I had then thought that I would surely find some in a port city like Tien Shin, which was also a big industrial centre. I did manage to locate a shop where they had some blades but they had become so rusty that it was impossible to use them. The Chinese were not going to use anything that they themselves had not manufactured. They shaved with old-fashioned razors. In the end I had to go to the hotel barbershop for a shave. The Chinese spent their foreign exchange only on importing machinery for their factories and industries. At the same time the foreign exchange our country had amassed during the Korean War was largely being spent on purchasing Japanese dolls and luxuries. How different the policy adopted by the Chinese government was! In this country you could not buy an imported cigarette anywhere. The cigarettes that the Chinese produced were of poor quality but they smoked them regardless of their purchasing power. We too were forced to smoke Chinese cigarettes. We struggled with them initially since they were very strong but we gradually got used to them.

Nanking is an ancient city. It had been China's capital for a long time. Now it housed Sun Yat-Sen's mausoleum. The first thing we did on reaching the city was pay our respects to him. Pir Manki Sharif placed some flowers on his grave while we stood silently before the mausoleum to pay homage to this revolutionary leader. He had fought the imperialist forces and the Manchu dynasty all his life and had sacrificed endlessly for the sake of his country. He had succeeded in eliminating monarchy and earning new respect for China in the eyes of the world. The imperialist countries had been forced to acknowledge China as a force to reckon with, which could not be dominated or exploited any more.

From Nanking we went to Shanghai. This was one of the leading cities of the world and a major centre of trade and commerce. Foreign forces had captured it again and again. Before the new China came into being foreigners used to frequent it for a good time. It was like Hong Kong in this respect. The new Chinese government had dealt firmly with places that used to offer luxuries and entertainment to foreigners. Shanghai has many industrial establishments. The government had confiscated a few of those owned by admirers of Chiang Kai-shek. Many had fled the city fearing action against them. Many other establishments, which had not been confiscated, now jointly functioned under workers as well as management. We were taken to the world's largest textile mill. It had just been nationalized. Many new buildings had been erected to accommodate the workers of the mill. Schools had been built for their children and hospitals too. A huge colony had been set up. I spent some time in these places along with Pir Manki Sharif. Later, I told Ilias, 'Of course they will showcase these achievements; however, I want to visit the workers' houses and see how they actually live. They certainly will not want us to see the problem areas.' Ilias said, 'We must ask them to take us inside their homes.' I told him, 'Don't say anything now; let's take them by surprise by requesting them to show us these houses without warning and then we will get a better idea of the actual state of the people living in them.'

Pir Manki Sharif had gone to visit many places that he had wanted to see. On the other hand, we told the interpreter as soon as we got the opportunity, 'We would like you to take us inside any of the homes in this colony. We would like to see how these people actually live.' The interpreter told us to wait outside one of the houses while he went in. He came back five minutes later to tell us we could now go inside. When we went inside the house we saw a woman waiting for us. After greeting us, she invited us in and asked us to sit down. There were two or three chairs in the room, a bed and a comfortable-looking mattress. This woman had been married a month ago and her husband worked in a mill. She was all by herself then but she too would go out to work when her husband returned. She said, 'I am so sorry that my husband is not at home, and because you came without informing us, I am incapable of entertaining you all properly, but do have a cup of tea with me.' She brought tea for us as quickly as she could. We had Chinese tea—without milk and sugar. Our interpreter said, 'Come in and take a look at both the rooms they live in,' and we did exactly that. It was spacious enough for a comfortable middle-class lifestyle. The furnishings were also what one would see in a middle-class home. The house had a kitchen, a lavatory and a bathroom.

At one point I told Ilias, 'We are in a bit of a fix. This woman got married only a short while ago and yet we don't have any gift to give her. What will they think of us? Our country's reputation is at stake!' Ilias replied, 'Let me think for a moment and see what I can come up with.' I suddenly thought of the ring in my hand. I took out the ring and told the interpreter, 'We would like to present this little gift to this lady since it is the custom in our country to take something along as a gift for the bride and the groom whenever one goes to the house of a newly-wed couple.' But the lady did not want to accept the gift. We said, 'If you don't accept our gift we will be hurt and surely you don't want to hurt a foreign guest. We've known that the people of China are very hospitable and we have seen proof of this throughout our tour!' In the end we persuaded her to accept the ring and we took our leave. When we met Pir Manki Sharif we told him the entire incident. He was very happy to hear that we had gifted her a ring.

For the next few days we toured Shanghai extensively even though the city had lost its sheen after the expats had left. Nevertheless, what the city still had to offer the tourist was not all artificial. What is beautified by the mere application of an extra layer of paint will in fact destroy its innate beauty. It only serves to hide its unique quality. Whatever remained in Shanghai now was authentically Chinese and the people of China had a stake in it. We also saw a few seafaring ships in the port.

The next day the woman whose house we had visited came to visit us in King Kong Hotel along with her husband. They had brought two Chinese Liberation pens as gifts for us. I didn't want to accept their gift but in the end had to since this apparently was the custom of their country. The members of the Shanghai Peace Committee were present at that time.

Everywhere we could see new schools and colleges coming up. The government had taken charge of education. The Chinese were imparting education to their children according to their own system.

From Shanghai we went to Hangzhou, a city on the banks of a lake in the west of the country. The city is known as China's Kashmir. The countryside abounds with picturesque spots and flora and fauna. The city had spread along all sides of the lake. We were to stay in a newly constructed hotel on the lakeside. The Chinese here moved from one part of the city to the other in small boats. They came to this city to relax. The lake itself was dotted with small islands. Hangzhou and Canton remind one of East Bengal, for everything is lush green. Pir Manki Sharif had spent the first day visiting pagodas and was planning to spend the second day visiting more historical sites. Ilias and I decided to give him the slip. We resolved instead to take a boat tour of the entire lake. The islands had very nice resting places. Even the girls here rowed boats. Whether rich or poor, the people of this city had their own boats. In the rainy season the only way they could commute was by boat. I come from a land where I had to learn how to row a boat since Faridpur is full of rivers and canals. So I rowed a boat here too.

We got down on an island, which had a tea shop on it. We celebrated the end of our tour of the lake with tea. We then left Hangzhou and headed for Canton. From Canton we would return home via Hong Kong. Now we got the opportunity to tour Canton at leisure. I saw that the people of the new China had a wholly new way of thinking. Their eyes lighted up with ideas and hopes of a New World. They took pride in being citizens of an independent country. This was the same Canton that was invaded by Sun Yat-Sen's band in 1911. The people of Canton province are fiercely independent. Greeting the people of China and the government of Mao Zedong, we took leave of this fabled land. We were once again back in Hong Kong, an English colony, a place of synthetic beauty and artificial people and a haven for smugglers. We stayed there for a couple of days and then boarded a plane for our country. I returned to Dhaka inspired by what I had seen and with renewed enthusiasm. It is difficult to really know your own country well until you go overseas.

We had become independent in 1947 while China had attained freedom in 1949. The enthusiasm of the Pakistani people at the time of our independence had dimmed a lot by now. Instead of making good use of its people's energy, the government had been trying to suppress it. In contrast, the Chinese government was using its people to build the country. The big difference between us and them was that the people of China knew, and were made to feel, that the country and its resources were their own. On the other hand, our people had begun to comprehend that the resources of the nation were being enjoyed by a coterie while they themselves were getting no share of it. As a consequence the people of Pakistan were becoming increasingly disillusioned. The only difference, they were now beginning to see, was that the white-skinned rulers had been replaced by dark-skinned ones.

It was quite apparent that the Chinese were assisting the government enthusiastically. I saw that public opinion favoured the government. The Chinese government had not identified itself as a 'communist' one; it called itself 'the coalition government of a new democratic order'. The government had in it communists but it also had people with other beliefs. Nevertheless, I was convinced that the communists were controlling everything. I myself am no communist; I believe in socialism and not in capitalism. I believe that capital is a tool of the oppressor. As long as capitalism is the mainspring of the economic order, people all over the world will continue to be oppressed. The capitalists were quite bent on waging a world war to achieve their goals. People from newly liberated countries had an obligation to come together to work for world peace. Those who had been bound in chains for ages and those whose wealth had been looted by imperialist forces now needed to concentrate on building their countries and would have to devote all their energies into ensuring the economic and political freedom of the masses. It was vital to build public opinion in favour of world peace.

~

When I returned to Dhaka I devoted myself to building our party. Maulana Bhasani and many other colleagues were still in prison. It had become imperative to accelerate the movement to free political prisoners. I decided to hold a meeting in Paltan Maidan. This meeting turned out to be a big one. It was presided over by Mr Ataur Rahman Khan. I protested against the oppressive nature of the government. This was the first public meeting I had addressed after the state language movement of 1952, although after we had been freed the Students' League had organized a meeting at the Dhaka Bar Library to greet the party workers who had just been released from prison. It was also true that I had attended a number of meetings in different houses organized by the All-Party State Language Action Committee.

I dedicated myself completely to building the Awami League as an organization. I invited Mr Suhrawardy to visit us in East Bengal. He had given me his word that he would visit us for a month and address public meetings. I worked out a schedule and sent it to him. He would be addressing a meeting in each district and also in some of the prominent subdivisional headquarters. He was soon in Dhaka, where he addressed a meeting, which was bigger than any held in Dhaka after independence. Without mincing words he spoke in favour of making Bengali one of the state languages and demanded that all political prisoners be freed. He also asked for autonomy for the province. Awami League workers had organized meetings for him all over the country, beginning with Sylhet, Dinajpur and Bogra. He went as far south as Barisal, in fact to all districts. The only district where no meeting was held was Rajshahi, although he did address a meeting in Natore. This was because I had not yet succeeded in forming a district committee in Rajshahi. However, many leaders of Rajshahi met him in Natore and took him to the town where an Awami League chapter was finally formed. By now, therefore, Awami League organizations had been formed in almost every district and subdivision. At the end of Mr Suhrawardy's visit the people of the entire province seemed to have become influenced. People started to desert the Muslim League and join the Awami League. Ordinary people as well as the educated section of the population had confidence in Mr Suhrawardy's leadership. People as a whole believed that Mr Suhrawardy was the only leader who could offer the country a real alternative and the one man whom the country and its citizens would benefit from.

Meanwhile, the country was reeling under corruption, oppression and tyranny. Instead of concentrating on rational schemes for development the government was devoting its energies to the politics of conspiracy. The people in power were now indulging in bureaucratic rule and intrigue-based politics. They nurtured high hopes because of Mr Khawaja Nazimuddin's feeble grip over the administration. Retired government servants like Chaudhury Muhammad Ali, Ghulam Muhammad and Nawab Gurmani began to take an active part in politics. By trying to appease the Punjabi bureaucrats through his appointment of Chaudhury Muhammad Ali as finance minister, Khawaja Nazimuddin had entangled himself in the politics of conspiracy. As a consequence, the people of the country had become frustrated and were beginning to express their confidence in Mr Suhrawardy's leadership. Democracy cannot be established without political parties. And now the Awami League emerged as the only opposition party that could tackle the Muslim League. In West Pakistan too a group of selfless leaders and workers came forward to build the Awami League there under the leadership of Pir Manki Sharif.

Mr Suhrawardy assisted us in building our organization, by touring West Pakistan and East Bengal.[26] After every meeting, I held meetings with district and subdivisional leaders and workers and tried to assist them in forming a powerful organization. Many people who had admired

Mr Suhrawardy in the past began to join the Awami League. In particular, young workers came forward now to tackle head on the oppressive tactics employed by the Muslim League government. Hundreds of our workers were in jail serving sentences under the Public Security Act. Initially, the government tried its best to thwart our meetings but later it had to give up. Public opinion was in favour of Mr Suhrawardy and Maulana Bhasani. By now both had succeeded in arousing public opinion in favour of releasing all political prisoners. Maulana Bhasani was becoming immensely popular throughout East Pakistan.

Even though the Awami League had been formed in 1949, no council meeting of the party had been held till now since most of its proponents were spending time in jail. I directed all district and subdivisional Awami League offices to hold elections in three months' time. After this we were going to elect office bearers of the East Pakistan Awami League Council and adopt a constitution and manifesto. I began to work night and day towards attaining these goals. I went to the subdivisions that Mr Suhrawardy had been unable to visit to help strengthen the party. I could not initially anticipate the response I would get from the people and from our workers. The East Pakistan Students' League also helped the Awami League become a strong organization because without a really powerful organization it would have been difficult to oppose the tyrannical regime. Till the Awami League found its feet, only the Students' League had been able to stand up to the government's oppressive measures and combat the injustice it was perpetrating. The people of the country too were supporting the students. The leaders and workers of this student organization had to face great hardship. The Muslim League government for its part had tried its best to destroy this organization. In addition to the Awami League and the Students' League, under the leadership of Oli Ahad, the Democratic Youth League was also playing a part in arousing public opinion.

From the start of 1953, political and student workers began to be released from jail. Mr Shamsul Huq was also released but he had become sick by then. That he was mentally unhinged was obvious to anyone who was with him in prison. He was never violent but every time he started to say anything he would end up saying something completely different. We were very worried about him. A selfless patriot who had devoted himself to his country, he had been imprisoned for his work. This man was now coming out of the darkness of the jail an insane man. Who would listen to this sad story? His contribution to the movement that led to Pakistan's creation was greater than that of many who were now in power in the country. It won't be an exaggeration to say that of the workers in East

Bengal who had given their all to attain Pakistan he was the most outstanding. Certainly, Mr Shamsul Huq had been foremost among those who had emerged in 1943 to take the Muslim League away from the palaces and estates of Nawabs and zamindars to the homes of ordinary people. But such is fate that it was in a prison in the Pakistan that he had helped create that Mr Shamsul Huq would go mad.

I talked to many people about his condition and tried to have him treated but he wouldn't agree to any kind of treatment. Instead, he would rant at me for mentioning treatment. At the working committee meeting I formally requested him to take up his responsibilities as general secretary of our organization since I had been filling this position, as the acting general secretary in his absence. I believed that if we could get him absorbed in work he would get well. He came to the meeting but declared, 'I won't take the responsibility of running the organization as its general secretary; let Mujib carry on.' He also said several weird things which made it obvious to everyone present that he had become quite unstable mentally. I carried on with my work. I then tried to make Mr Huq preside over a council meeting of the Dhaka Awami League. But he ended up declaring himself the caliph of the whole world, and everyone felt sorry for him. We all despaired; how were we to cure him and prevent him from going completely crazy? Things got even worse for him when his wife, Professor Afia Khatun, went abroad for higher studies. Perhaps something could have been done for him if she had been around.

Yar Mohammad Khan began to assist me in party work and I found him indispensable. Manik Bhai had succeeded in making *Ittefaq* a really popular newspaper. Even though it was a weekly it had become very well liked in villages and towns through the country. The *Pakistan Observer* also published some stories about us from time to time. The Muslim League government as well as the party was fast losing popularity. I realized that all we needed now was able leadership and a disciplined organization. My colleagues and I made good use of this opportunity and succeeded in setting up Awami League organizations in almost 70 per cent of the unions. The younger workers were inclined towards me since I was fairly young too. Maulana Bhasani and other Awami League leaders were released from prison. I talked to the Maulana and Mr Ataur Rahman Khan about organizing a council meeting. They gave their assent. The first council meeting was summoned in Dhaka. However, getting a hall for the purpose proved difficult. In the end Yar Mohammad Khan managed to get Mukul Cinema Hall for the event. Since I couldn't get any accommodation for the council members who were coming to Dhaka from the other districts I rented big boats for them to stay for the duration of the meeting. These boats were anchored in Dhaka's Sadar Ghat. We decided that Mr Suhrawardy would be the chief guest.

As the day of the meeting drew nearer some senior leaders of the Awami League began to conspire to ensure that I would not be made the general secretary for the next term. I wasn't aware of their machinations since I was occupied all the time working for the organization, raising money and arranging accommodation and food for everyone. Those who were involved in the conspiracy to displace me were Abdus Salam Khan, Mymensingh's Hashimuddin Ahmed, Rangpur's Khairat Hussein, Narayanganj's Almas Ali and a few others. None of them had helped our organization by raising funds for it or donating anything. They wouldn't even work for it wholeheartedly. But now they were spending money to ensure I wouldn't become the general secretary. Mr Salam Khan was allegedly piqued because I had slighted him and had preferred Ataur Rahman Khan to him. Displeased with the goings-on, I requested Mr Ataur Rahman Khan a fortnight before the council meeting, 'Please agree to be the general secretary; I don't need any position. I have been working for the organization and will continue to do so and will ensure you have no problems running it.' Mr Khan replied, 'Where will I get the time to do all that? There is no way I can leave everything else I do to work only in this position. Anyone who becomes general secretary now will have to work full-time. No one but you can do this and you will have to accept this position.' I said to him, 'Some of our leaders are conspiring against me. They are claiming that only someone experienced should be made the general secretary. This is really unfortunate; these people have no sense of gratitude. After all, I have been working day and night ever since I was released from jail to give shape to our organization.' Mr Khan told me, 'Forget them; they aren't ready to work; what they do best is talk and they do a lot of that during our meetings.' I said to him, 'Think about what you have just told me, for once I declare publicly that I am going to stand for the position I won't be dissuaded by anyone from attaining it.' He said, 'You will have to become the general secretary.' Mr Khan knew it was because I favoured him that Mr Salam was angry with me. Maulana Bhasani was all for my being elected to this position. I had told him too that they should think of making someone else the general secretary. But he didn't agree and insisted, 'You will have to be the general secretary.' As for Mr Suhrawardy, he was in Karachi and oblivious of what was going on in Dhaka.

Following the communal riots of 1950, Mr Abul Hashim had left West Bengal and settled down in East Pakistan. Many of his co-workers had joined the Awami League by then. He too was jailed during the state language movement of 1952. While in jail he was able to talk to many Awami League leaders and workers who were fellow prisoners.

Those who were opposed to me failed to get anyone to stand against me despite their efforts. Nobody was bold enough to compete with me. Most councillors were inclined to vote for me. These people therefore altered their strategy. They met Mr Hashim repeatedly and asked him to join the party and become its general secretary. He agreed to do so but on one condition: he would have to be elected unanimously. He invited Maulana Bhasani to dinner. He informed the Maulana that some Awami League leaders wanted him to become the general secretary. He asked the Maulana for his thoughts on the proposal. The Maulana said, 'It is doubtful that you will be elected to the position unanimously since Mujib has reservations about you. But if you want to be the president of the party I am quite willing to give up this position for you.' Maulana Bhasani himself told me about his exchange with Mr Hashim.

After the first session of the council Maulana Bhasani announced the name of four of us who were to be given a special responsibility. Ataur Rahman Khan, Abdus Salam Khan, Abul Mansur Ahmed and I were entrusted to come up with a list of names of party executives by consensus and present them to the council. On the eve of the council meeting my opponents proposed to Mr Ataur Rahman Khan that he should be their candidate for the post of general secretary. Mr Khan softened a little but told them he would first talk to me about it. He called to inform me of the exchange he had had with those people. I said I was no longer inclined to listen to any such request, although I would have done so some time back. I asked him to suggest that one of them should stand for the position. Mr Khan conveyed my message to them. They now approached Maulana Bhasani but he said to them that they should entrust the four-member panel to come up with the name of the general secretary on the condition that the choice was unanimous. However, the meeting did not last long because they could not come up with any names. I told Maulana Bhasani at the council session that elections would be held for the position. There was no unanimity on the issue although Mr [Ataur Rahman] Khan supported my stance. We discussed the manifesto and the constitution through the night in the subject committee. The council meeting approved both and then elections were held even though there was complete unanimity about the candidates to be elected. Maulana Bhasani was made president, Mr Ataur Rahman Khan vice-president and I general secretary. (I don't have the manifesto with me at the moment but I will give extracts from it later.)[27] And so finally the Awami League emerged before the people as a truly complete political party. One thing is for sure—no political party can run without a manifesto or a declaration of its principles.

Before these developments took place we had attended the All Pakistan Awami League conference in Lahore. But because we couldn't see eye to eye with Nawab Mamdot about dissolving the zamindar system and other issues, he had quit the party. There is a major difference between politics in East Pakistan and politics in West Pakistan. There politics was something big businessmen, zamindars and Nawabs indulged in to while away their time. In contrast, politics in the eastern wing of the country was the domain of the middle class. Because West Pakistan did not have a powerful middle class the people of that wing paid little heed to the country or the country itself. Ordinary people tended to believe whatever they were told by the landlords and their religious gurus. On the other hand, since a peasant movement had taken root in Bengal a long time back, the people of the province were much better informed about political issues than the West Pakistanis. Moreover, Bengalis had taken an active part in the independence movement. For a long time now the people of Bangladesh had had a village-level government and had experience of Union Boards, Local Boards and District Boards. All this had made them much more politically informed. Even though the literacy rate in East Bengal was low, Bengalis were not indifferent or unaware of political issues. They could very well decide between right and wrong and they ably proved this in the general elections held in 1946 to decide on the question of Pakistan.

The Awami League had the support of the masses as well as the educated section of society. By this time the Muslim League had been bedevilled by the politics of conspiracy. They had become stuck in the web spun by these conspirators. These politicians had basically been bureaucrats in the British Raj. The organization was driven by factionalism. These people were splitting into increasingly small groups, and their sole aim was to hold on to power somehow or the other. The leaders at the helm of affairs at the subdivision and district levels had not participated in any movements; nor were they aware that the world was moving forward all the time. All they cared for was power!

Meanwhile, a group of West Pakistani leaders who saw themselves as representing the country at the centre and some senior bureaucrats were conniving to snatch away the resources of East Bengal and transfer them to the other wing of the country. They seemed to have convinced themselves that East Pakistan would not stay with them for long. Therefore, they were trying to build up their part of the country as fast as they could! When the

Awami League began to demonstrate with facts and figures how East Pakistan was being exploited, they became desperate and began to torture Awami League leaders and tried to suppress it by using force. Meanwhile, the people were getting increasingly angry with the Muslim League set-up and the oppressive nature of the government. In East Pakistan the Muslim League was beginning to show signs of exhaustion.

During Khawaja Nazimuddin's administration violent communal riots broke out in the Punjab too. Thousands of people died in them. Martial law had to be enforced in Lahore. The riots erupted from movements launched against the Ahmedias and the Kadiyani sects. Some famous Muslim scholars had instigated them. These spiritual leaders seemed bent on proving only one thing: Kadiyanis were not Muslims. I myself didn't know much about this issue. But I know at least this much: no one should be murdered because he holds views different from mine. That certainly was not what Islam taught and such an action was tantamount to a crime in the religion. Kadiyanis believed in God and the Prophet. Let alone the Kadiyanis, Islam forbids punishing even non-believers. In Lahore and other places husbands, wives and even children had been thrown into flames and roasted alive by these bigots. The people behind these gruesome deeds are even now very much part of Pakistani politics.

Pakistan was supposed to be a democracy. Here people of all faiths, irrespective of race and religion, were supposed to have equal rights. It is unfortunate that the people who had played a contrary role in the movement to create Pakistan were now trying to present Pakistan as an Islamic state and poisoning the nation's politics to achieve their own ends by using religion. Instead of adopting programmes of economic and social reform, the Muslim League leaders chanted one slogan in unison: 'Islam'. They seemed to feel that they had no reason to be concerned about the economic well-being of the people, which, after all, was the goal for which the working class, the peasants and the labourers had made sacrifices during the movement for independence. The Muslim League and its cohorts appeared more interested in helping the oppressors and the feudal class since these people had now taken over the reins of government.

On the other hand, the foreign exchange earned from East Pakistan's economy was now being used to build factories and industries in West Pakistan. A group of capitalists had sprung up, bent on making as much profit as they could by exploiting the people. Overnight, they had become millionaires. Many of them became wealthy and came to be known as industrialists merely by sitting in Karachi and by selling import–export licences. This too can be ascribed to the Muslim League government.

Khawaja Nazimuddin's weak hold over the administration was largely responsible for these people managing to make profits and aggrandizing themselves since he was perhaps never inclined to turn down even the unreasonable proposals submitted by these ex-bureaucrats-turned businessmen. Meanwhile, I believe he had come to rely on as predatory a person as Chaudhury Muhammad Ali, whom he had appointed finance minister. I am not sure about this point but no doubt some of the things being said about him were true. The late Fazlur Rahman was then a minister in the central government. I believe that he had tried to obstruct Chaudhury Muhammad Ali's machinations.

Khawaja Nazimuddin's government was split into two factions. Mr Fazlur Rahman headed the faction known as the 'Bengali' group. The other, led by Chaudhury Muhammad Ali, was known as the 'Punjabi' group. The so-called Bengali leaders of the central government could not make Chaudhury Muhammad Ali happy even after they had conceded to their Punjabi brothers the capital, military headquarters, all the major government positions and the bulk of the country's trade and commerce. In the Constituent Assembly the Bengalis constituted a majority even after they had handed over six seats to their West Pakistani 'brothers'. They could have upheld the interests of East Pakistanis if they had wanted to. But instead of standing up for their people they gave up everything they could to the Punjabis so that they themselves could hold on to power. Ironically, they failed to preserve their own positions in the end. The West Pakistani leaders realized they had managed to take as much from these people as they were capable of giving. Now they needed to take things from a new group of people since the older group would be reluctant to cede anything more. Perhaps they had managed to recognize their intentions and true nature after all! They had made the East Pakistani leadership act in a manner that would make them untrustworthy in the eyes of the people of East Pakistan. They would collapse like a pack of cards if one gave but a mere push. They had made Mr Khawaja Nazimuddin speak against the Bengali language so that whatever faith the Bengali people had in him would evaporate forever. They now tried some other moves. How would these people ever be able to stand up to the wily bureaucrats of the British Raj? They had lost the trust of the masses completely and were by now totally dependent on the bureaucracy, made up almost entirely of people from West Pakistan, particularly from the Punjab.

In April 1953, Governor General Ghulam Muhammad sacked Mr Khawaja Nazimuddin, who was president of the Muslim League, the party that had a majority in the Constituent Assembly and Parliament. In his place, he appointed as prime minister Pakistan's ambassador to America, Bogra's Mohammad Ali. This, even though Mr Ali was not a member of the Constituent Assembly. Indeed, he was not even a member of the Muslim League. He had been staying outside Pakistan since 1948 and did not bother to keep himself informed about the events in the country.

I remember a meeting that the Awami League had organized in Dhaka's Paltan Maidan. Mr Suhrawardy was addressing a huge crowd when someone informed us he had just heard on the radio that Mr Nazimuddin had been dismissed from the position of prime minister. Mr Suhrawardy told the people in the audience, 'Something important has happened in Pakistan today.' When the meeting ended and I was accompanying Mr Suhrawardy, he told me, 'True, Mr Nazimuddin has been dismissed but this isn't a piece of news that delights me.' I said to Mr Suhrawardy, 'This is exactly what he deserves!' Mr Suhrawardy agreed with me and said, 'Yes, instead of giving us a constitution and holding general elections they have mired Pakistan in the politics of conspiracy.'

We discussed many other issues that day. In any case, the other leaders of the Muslim League did not protest the very undemocratic manner in which Mr Nazimuddin had been dismissed. One by one they abandoned the man who had been their leader and lined up behind Mr Mohammad Ali propelled by their greed for power. Mr Nazimuddin even had to give up his position as president of the Muslim League. The leaders of the party now made Mr Ali president of the All Pakistan Muslim League. Not one voice was raised in protest. Only the East Pakistan Awami League protested against the very undemocratic manner in which Khawaja Nazimuddin had been sacked from his position.

The chief minister of East Bengal, Mr Nurul Amin, was an intimate disciple of Mr Khawaja Nazimuddin. He and the chief ministers of the other provinces declared that they too would back Mr Mohammad Ali as the prime minister of Pakistan. He was the leader they would all support. After such a display no one who was educated or had a conscience could have any faith in the Muslim League leadership. It was now obvious that this party was made up of opportunists and self-centred people. Where did Mr Ghulam Muhammad get the confidence to make such an audacious move? He must have been egged on by the top bureaucrats of the country and some invisible powers who must have assured him of their support if he ran into trouble. They seemed fully aware of the nature of Muslim League leaders and workers. Mr Khawaja Nazimuddin's followers joined Mr Mohammad Ali's cabinet one after the other. Mr Nazimuddin himself seemed afraid to do anything to stop this mass exodus. Just as he had retreated silently from everything in 1946, he decided to take rest this time too. No doubt his strategy was to show himself again if the smallest opportunity came his way. Bogra's Mohammad Ali had no real political ability. He had a very superficial approach to things. All he had done in America was pick up American manners and customs and their way of dressing. He seemed eager to do whatever Ghulam Muhammad wanted him to do. He also seemed quite happy to follow whatever the Americans told him. The American administration smelled communists everywhere and he appeared to have caught the same disease. Initially he addressed Mr Suhrawardy as his political 'father', but soon he began to speak against him.

Maulana Bhasani and I and our colleagues decided there was no time to waste. We concentrated all our energies on building up the Awami League. We toured the districts, subdivisions, police stations, thanas and villages and managed to raise an army of devoted and selfless workers. Under the leadership of the Students' League the students managed to stand up against the mighty Muslim League. The country was reeling under corruption and nepotism in the administration, which had taken an extreme form. The constitution had been watered down. Government officials were bent on doing whatever they fancied. The food situation had assumed critical proportions. Unemployment was a huge problem. The people in power seemed to be operating without any plans or programmes to address the situation. It was as if they were happy as long as they managed to hold on to power. Wherever the ministers of the East Pakistan government went to speak people stayed away. No one in the province had forgotten the events of 21 February [1952]. We tried to build public opinion in favour of drafting a new constitution. We were bent on making Bengali a state language and getting autonomy for East Bengal and would not compromise on these issues. Around this time Mr Fazlur Rahman tried to introduce a way of writing Bengali using the Arabic script. We were able to create public opinion against this move. Some Muslim League leaders were attempting to impose a centrally based government on the entire country through covert propaganda. The Awami League, on the other hand, was working to implement a government based on confederation and regional autonomy, and was trying to convince the people of its advantages.

It is wrong to keep anyone in prison without a trial. As a result of government policies, the movement to free political prisoners who had been imprisoned without trial had gathered momentum. Progressive youths and workers began to join the Awami League. In mid-1953 it was decided to hold elections for the Provincial Assembly in East Bengal. There was little doubt that the contest would be between the Awami League and the

Muslim League. True, an organization called the Ganatantrik Dal had been launched but its activities seemed confined to giving statements in newspapers. Mr A.K. Fazlul Huq was the Advocate General in the Dhaka High Court. After Pakistan had been established he had taken no part in politics. In 1953 he resigned from his position as Advocate General and joined the Muslim League. By then the Muslim League was in the throes of infighting. Mr Mohan Mia had formed a faction opposing Mr Nurul Amin and attempts to make Mr Huq president of the Muslim League had failed. The two factions confronted each other in a bloody fight in front of Curzon Hall. Mr Amin's faction won the 'battle' and Mr Mohan Mia and his people were driven out of the Muslim League.

I now met Mr Fazlul Huq and requested him to join the Awami League. He took part in our meeting held in Chandpur. Addressing the meeting, he declared: 'Those who are fond of thievery should join the Muslim League and those who are for the good of the masses should join the Awami League.' Holding up my hand in public, he told the crowd, 'Do what Mujib wants you to do. I can't talk for long since I am an old man now.' This speech was reported in the newspapers. At this time the older faction[28] of the Awami League revived its scheme of forming the United Front against the government. Abdus Salam Khan, Mymensingh's Hashimuddin and a few others began to campaign for this cause. Meanwhile, a group of so-called progressive people in the party began to clamour for unity among the opposition groups. The reactionaries and the radicals seemed to have united on this platform. In those days people had heard of no opposition party other than the Awami League. Maulana Bhasani and I discussed the situation to decide what course we should take. He told me unambiguously that if Mr Huq decided to join the Awami League we would accept him and give him a position worthy of his stature. But if he joined any other party we wouldn't form an alliance with it under any circumstances. The people who had been expelled from the Muslim League were now attempting to lean on his shoulders to stand up again. We should not align with them in any way. They had been involved with all the infamous deeds associated with the Muslim League till September 1953. These people had opposed making Bengali the state language. Maulana Bhasani consulted many of us on these issues. He had instructed me to ensure that the supporters of the United Front found no place within the Awami League.

The working committee discussed all these issues at great length in its meetings. Most of our members were against the United Front since forming an alliance despite ideological differences might give dividends for the time being but would not contribute to stability in the long run. In fact, this would do more harm than good to the country. Those people within the Awami League who were pressing for the United Front were really interested in ousting the Muslim League and grabbing power any which way they could. How could they stay out of power forever and remain in the opposition wing permanently!

The radicals, on the other hand, had a different motive for forming an alliance. They wanted the United Front so that they could cut down national-level leaders to size in front of the people and make people lose confidence in political institutions. In that event they could tell people in the future that no good could be expected of these leaders and their parties! These people were trying to muddy the waters that were clear.

The Muslim League had lost the confidence of the masses. It was a party sans principles. There was no heinous act that it had not done while in power. It had betrayed the people in general and East Bengal in particular. The people who had been expelled from this party had not been able to find a place for themselves amidst the devilish machinations going on in it. It is difficult to even imagine how anti-people the members of the party could be. But the people who were quitting it now were doing so not to uphold their principles but because they had been compelled to leave after losing out in the power struggle. These expelled people had not protested even once against the government's anti-people policies in independent Pakistan. On the contrary, they had tried to extract as many advantages as they could from the government. They now changed tack and tried to take advantage of Mr Huq's popularity with the people to enter into negotiations with the Awami League.

Mr Huq had by now made up his mind to join the Awami League. He had even talked about his decision with some people. These people now began to whisper to him that it would be better to form a separate party and then participate in the United Front. They said he would not be given a position worthy of his stature within the Awami League. They suggested that the chances of Mr Suhrawardy making him the prime minister of East Bengal were slim, and so on. If they had a party of their own they could overcome any obstacles put up by the Awami League by forming an alliance with the Muslim League. The Muslim League would definitely capture some seats in the elections, they argued. But their first option was to form an alliance with the Awami League and they would wait and see before making their next move. If they kept their options open they could take the path most profitable for them at every step. For our part, we had informed Mr Huq that he would become the leader of the Awami League in the East Bengal Provincial Assembly while Mr Suhrawardy would be our leader in the National Assembly.

At around this time, Maulana Bhasani wrote to me formally asking me to organize a meeting of the Awami League Council in Mymensingh. He did not consult me before sending me the letter. Mr Hashimuddin of the Mymensingh Awami League was all for the United Front. Maulana Bhasani knew that I wasn't fond of this man. He had formed an alliance with Mr Salam and was always conspiring to do something or the other with him. My supporters in the district, Mr Rafiqueuddin Bhuiyan and Mr Hatem Ali Talukder, were still in prison. It was difficult to figure out Maulana Bhasani's political tactics. I foresaw things coming to a head in the Mymensingh conference. Nevertheless, I convened the conference, letting everyone know that I had been instructed to organize it by Maulana Bhasani in his capacity as president of the Awami League. Mr Suhrawardy was also invited to the conference. I sent letters to all the districts about the conference. I requested Mr Hashimuddin to make arrangements to accommodate the delegates in hotels where they could pay for their own food, although it was really the district committee's responsibility to look after such expenses. Mr Abul Mansur Ahmed was the president of the District Awami League but he let Mr Hashimuddin look after all organizational matters. They did not make any arrangements for me to set up a temporary office of the East Pakistan Awami League there. Party people all over the province had been instructed to attend the conference. I was confident that no matter where the conference was organized no more than 10 per cent of the votes cast would go against me. However, delegates from many districts had not been provided with accommodation. Under such circumstances, I was lucky to get the help of Mr Abdur Rahman Siddiqui, a party worker. We managed to put up party workers from different districts in rooms in the small hotels of the town.

Three or four days before the conference, Maulana Bhasani let it be known that he would not attend it. However, he gave no reason for staying away. I was aware of his tendency to stay away from meetings whenever a major decision had to be taken. Khondokar Mohammad Ilias and I were therefore forced to go to Bogra's Panchbibi village to bring Maulana Bhasani to Mymensingh although we had little time on our hands and there was much pending work that we had to deal with. In fact, we were to have contacted party workers of different districts. The faction in our party which was all for a United Front had sent its people to the different districts. Khondokar Mushtaq Ahmed was one such who supported the United Front. Just as Ilias and I had crossed Bahadurabad Ghat and had boarded a train in Fulchari Ghat, we saw a train arriving from Bogra. I saw someone very much like Maulana Bhasani inside a second-class compartment. I said to Ilias, 'Can you find out if it is him inside that train?' Ilias took a good look and said, 'It is the Maulana!' We quickly collected our luggage and got down from the train and rushed to the Maulana's compartment. Without saying a word he began to walk away from us. We walked faster to keep pace with him. I said to him, 'So what's happening? You asked us to summon a conference and why are you not attending it?' He replied, 'I guess you don't know how crazy your leaders have become about forming a United Front. I don't want to work with such unprincipled people. The number of people in the Awami League who want a United Front are in the majority. You won't be able to defeat them when the issue comes to a vote. I don't want to be involved in such politics any more. In any case, I have nothing to gain at all. I don't intend to stand for a position in the elections. I don't even want to join the meeting of the council.' I got mad at him and said, 'It was you who asked me to summon the council meeting in Mymensingh without consulting any of us. The council meeting was scheduled to be held in Dhaka a few days later. But you don't really know what the council will decide. I doubt very much if they will be able to form a United Front even if they want to. Awami League members have suffered many humiliations at the hands of the expelled Muslim League leaders and they know that these people haven't joined us to stay in the opposition bench. They want to take advantage of us to get elected and once they get elected they will go their own way. If you don't show up at the conference I will telegram everyone to cancel the council meeting and head home from here!'

By this time we had reached Sarderer Char village and had landed up in the house of Musa Mia, who was the Maulana's disciple. He was really poor and all he had in his thatched house were two small rooms. We kept our luggage and bedding under a tree near his house and sat down on a mat. The man was at a loss as to how he could best look after us. He was a poor man but he sure had a big heart. There was no train to take us to Dhaka for a while then. Meanwhile, the Maulana was keeping quiet. We would have to spend the night here. Mr Musa must have spent all he had to ensure that we had a decent meal that night. He sent someone to Fulchari Ghat which was almost one and a half miles away so that we could have tea. We spent the night in a neighbouring house owned by another of the Maulana's admirers. This man had a room to spare. After we had some exchanges with the Maulana—some heated, some quite mild—he finally agreed to attend the council meeting. Ilias had extended discussions with him.

The next morning the two of us headed for Mymensingh to find Mr Mohammadullah. Korban Ali, Hamid Chowdhury and Mollah

Jalaluddin had already reached the place. However, we had to go to Dhaka again to receive Mr Suhrawardy. We then went back to Mymensingh with him. After failing to secure any space for the Awami League office, Hamid, Jalal and Mohammadullah managed to get a room in Mr Azizur Rahman's house for that purpose. Arrangements had been made for me to stay in Hashimuddin's house. But how could I leave the others and stay in his house? In my previous trips to Mymensingh I had stayed with Hashimuddin. Khaleque Nawaz, Shamsul Huq and Rashid were prominent party workers of Mymensingh and even though they were not particularly fond of Hashimuddin they were my great fans. They helped me find accommodation for all of our council members. The council meeting itself would be held in Aloka Cinema Hall. That night I came to know that Hashimuddin was planning to have outsiders sit inside the hall during the meeting or was going to position them inside masquerading as Awami League members so that his faction could claim that they constituted the majority in any voting.

I told Mr Abul Mansur Ahmed at 5 a.m. about the possibility of Mr Hashimuddin trying to upstage us. I said, 'Please tell Hashimuddin not to try anything fishy because if people get to know of any row within the party it will hurt our reputation.' Mr Ahmed replied, 'I don't know anything about this but I will investigate and see what I can do.' In the morning I directed Awami League party officials to position themselves, along with eight workers, at every door of the hall and to ensure that no one could enter without an invitation card bearing my signature. I entrusted this job to dedicated party workers from different districts. As a result, no outsider was able to make his way in. Some people tried to force their way in but to no avail and had to retreat in the face of the stiff resistance put up by our workers.

I submitted my report as the secretary of the party. Mr Suhrawardy and Mr Bhasani gave speeches. As far as I can remember Mia Iftekharuddin, who had been invited as special guest, spoke last. Two topics were discussed extensively: foreign policy and the formation of the United Front. A subject committee deliberated for a while but could not make much headway. I put forward a proposal on foreign policy. I suggested that the Awami League should have an independent and neutral foreign policy. Abdus Salam Khan opposed this suggestion and accused me of being too radical in my approach. I responded by labelling him as too reactionary and so he got exactly what he deserved. My proposal was approved and, realizing that the mood of the meeting was against him, he did not dare bring the issue to a vote.

We next discussed whether the Awami League would be forming a United Front with the other parties to combat the Muslim League—that old issue! Those who supported the idea spoke on its behalf but I spoke against the motion and raised the following questions in my speech: Was there any other opposition party worth the name then except the Awami League? To form an alliance with people who had no principles or ideals was tantamount to trying to breathe life into people who had already become fossils. These people had caused immense harm to the country already. They were in politics for personal gain and they did not really care about their country.

My speech was based on emotions brought on by my thoughts on the subject. The proponents of the United Front included many who were guilty of helping suppress the language movement in 1948 and 1952. The Muslim League government had imprisoned us without a trial for months. Maulana Bhasani too was staunchly opposed to the idea of a United Front while Mr Suhrawardy had shown no enthusiasm for it in his speech. The faction for the front seemed to have been taken back by the opposition to it. Mr Ataur Rahman Khan and I were united on the issue: 'We don't want a United Front.' This was a motion that had to be voted out. People, however, might end up thinking the Awami League was against unity. I asked my friends if they had received any proposals from people they knew who were overenthusiastic about the idea. For sure the issue of a United Front would have been rejected had it come to a vote. In the end it was decided to give Mr Suhrawardy and Mr Bhasani the responsibility of coming up with a solution. But they would have to agree to a solution and would have to discuss their thoughts with the members of the working committee before settling the issue. My friends knew that both Mr Suhrawardy and Maulana Bhasani were not fond of many of those in favour of a United Front.

Both the Maulana and Mr Suhrawardy declared unambiguously that if Mr Fazlul Huq wanted to be part of the Awami League he would be welcomed to the party and we would work to have him elected prime minister of East Bengal. He would be made the leader of the East Bengal parliamentary party. Mr Suhrawardy had said to me, 'He is a veteran politician; he has done a great deal for people throughout his life; he should be given one last chance to serve his country.'

Maulana Bhasani told me he wouldn't be part of any move to form a United Front. There could be no question of getting into politics with the likes of Hamidul Huq Chowdhury and Mohan Mia. They were guilty of the same crime committed by Nurul Amin. He directed me to make preparations for setting up an election office and to decide who would be nominated for high positions. I reassured the Maulana, 'The Awami League will win the election and there is no reason to worry on that account. And even if the Awami League fails to become the majority party in the Provincial Assembly it can work as the opposition party. Politics then will be transparent and not such a mishmash of opinions. The nation will not benefit from having unscrupulous people in power. That can only help men who are interested in their own advancement.' The Maulana agreed with me and asked me to make arrangements for meetings in different districts to discuss this issue. He and I would tour all the districts and we would decide who would be nominated where. Mr Suhrawardy too would join us after a few days when he returned from Karachi and would take overall charge of the election campaign. The Awami League had one deficiency: lack of funds. However, it had a big group of volunteer workers who were worth more than their weight in gold. We wouldn't need that much money, and candidates could go ahead and spend whatever they could raise. Public opinion, after all, favoured the Awami League.

Mr Salam, however, did not give up. He had to some extent taken on the role of Mr Huq's conscience keeper. Mr Huq managed to form a party of his own almost overnight. He named it Krisak Shramik Party. Although it didn't have any organizational strength anywhere in the country he managed to attract some leaders who had been expelled from the Muslim League and were led by Hamidul Huq Chowdhury and Mohan Mia as well as some of Mr Huq's old admirers. This latter group had quit politics by this time and had devoted themselves fully to their families. Most of them had been opposed to the establishment of Pakistan. Mr Abul Hashim had also advised Mr Huq not to join the Awami League and had told him to form his own party. Mr Salam did precious little to persuade Mr Huq to join the Awami League. This was because Mr Salam was aware that his own position within the Awami League was precarious. He told me one day, 'For how long can one stay in opposition? Unless we wield power the public will lose all faith in us. We will have to grab power any which way we can. We will surely be able to form the government if we constitute a United Front.' In response I had told him, 'We might attain a position of power one way or the other, but we won't be able to do anything for the people that way and in any case power got by expedient means will soon evaporate. Where we are not united on the basis of ideals no alliance will endure.' But he didn't agree with me. He was posing to be a problem because he was bent on achieving a position of power regardless of the means employed. He seemed to have figured out that if the Awami League was the sole party with a majority he would not get a powerful position; he would have a much better chance of attaining such a position if he sided with Mr Huq. Nobody was opposed to having Mr Fazlul Huq in the Awami League. But there could be little doubt that the kind of people who had gathered around him would bring about the ruin of his reputation as well as that of the Awami League and the country itself. I therefore continued to oppose Mr Salam's moves. It was true that there was a section of people who favoured the idea of a United Front but these people were driven solely by their emotions. They were eager to emerge from the clutches of the Muslim League. The people as a whole did not know much about any party other than the Awami League and the Muslim League.

Mr Suhrawardy began holding public meetings all over the country. He knew fully the implications of forming a United Front. One day when he and Maulana Bhasani were discussing the issue I happened to be present. I said, 'We can form an election alliance if we want to. In that event the Awami League will not nominate candidates in areas where Mr Huq's party can field sure winners as candidates. Similarly, they will have to withdraw their people from areas where the Awami League has men with solid reputation as candidates. And all candidates will contest the elections on the basis of their party manifestos.' But the Maulana was not ready to agree to even this concession. He said, 'The Awami League will contest the elections all by itself.' He instructed me to organize the party for the elections. It must have been towards the end of 1953 that Mr Suhrawardy told me he would have to go to Karachi for a few days to collect some funds and after that he would not be returning to West Pakistan again until the elections were over.

The Maulana and I went from district to district to hold meetings. We planned to be back in Dhaka two days before Mr Suhrawardy was scheduled to return to the city. We decided to first tour North Bengal. We would conclude this part of our tour with three meetings in Kushtia and then come to Dhaka. The response we got was tremendous. We informed the district officials of our party to send recommendations to help us decide on the candidates who would contest the elections on our behalf. They sent us the names of the people they had selected. We would nominate only those who had been chosen unanimously at the district level. If the district officials failed to agree on any one name in a particular constituency, it would fall on the East Pakistan Awami League to nominate someone from that place. However, if both Maulana Bhasani and Mr Suhrawardy agreed on a particular candidate for a particular constituency their choice would override other considerations.

As soon as Maulana Bhasani and I reached Kushtia I received a telegram that Mr Ataur Rahman Khan and Manik Mia wanted us to go back to Dhaka immediately. I called Mr Khan that night from Kushtia. He said we should abandon the idea of holding a meeting and head for Dhaka as soon as possible. I tried to tell him that the meeting was scheduled for the next day and if we cancelled it this late our workers would risk being beaten up by the locals for misleading them. This would also be bad for the reputation of the party. Mr Khan kept insisting that we should heed him. I agreed to send Maulana Bhasani back the next day but said I myself would return only three days later after addressing the public meetings that had been announced. He agreed to this proposal. Mr Khan was at first one with us in believing that a United Front wasn't a good idea. Unfortunately, he could never hold on to any opinion for any length of time. Whatever one said to him would be greeted with 'yes, yes'. In other words, all one had to do was hold his hand and he would melt and be incapable of saying 'no'. The Maulana returned to Dhaka as agreed. I was to follow as soon as I had addressed the meetings. But before I could do so, I was informed that Mr Fazlul Huq and Maulana Bhasani had signed an agreement to form a United Front.

I couldn't reconcile myself to what I had heard: why would Maulana Bhasani put his signature on such a document? Could they carry out a programme in Mr Shaheed Suhrawardy's absence? What would happen to our organization now? How would the nominations be made? Why had the Maulana showed such alacrity in signing the document? I just couldn't figure out how such a thing could have taken place. When I came back to Dhaka I went to Mr Yar Mohammad's house to meet Maulana Bhasani. The Awami League office was on the ground floor of the building in which Mr Mohammad lived. As soon as I entered our office and took a seat our workers explained to me the events behind the signing of the document. There could be no doubt that Mr Abul Mansur Ahmed was a shrewd man. He could sense what the times demanded and so with the assistance of Mr Kafiluddin Chowdhury he managed to have Mr Fazlul Huq sign the twenty-one-point manifesto. This document included the Awami League's demand for autonomy as well as the necessity of having Bengali as the state language and freeing all political prisoners. It also agreed to some other demands that we had made. However, those of us who are intimately involved with the politics of this country know full well that many do not believe in this document sincerely.

When I met Maulana Bhasani he told me, 'Look Mujib, I had objected to signing a document agreeing to form a United Front in your absence; I told

Ataur Rahman Khan and Manik Mia that since you are the general secretary of the Awami League I could not sign any document of this kind without consulting you. Both of them assured me that the responsibility of getting your assent was theirs. That is why when Mr Fazlul Huq turned up and requested me to sign the document I agreed to do so.' I replied, 'Never mind me; why didn't you wait for a couple of days till Mr Suhrawardy returned to Dhaka? He is due to be here in two or three days. You had said one thing to me a few days ago and now you come up with something quite different! You left me behind so that you could come here and sign the document. What method will we choose to decide on the nominations? How will we go ahead with our work? Who will take the responsibility for conducting the election campaign? How come you have decided to proclaim "Mr Huq and I have decided to form a United Front" without deciding on any of these issues?' However, I assured him, 'No doubt you have taken what you think is the best option—so what can I say now? And since Mr Khan and Manik Mia have taken upon themselves the responsibility of securing my assent how can I let them down? If this is good for the country, so be it. And if it turns out to be a bad move for the country I won't be responsible for it since I am merely the general secretary of the party and so had no role to play in it! You all are the leaders of the party and since you have decided to form the United Front it is up to you to ensure that the campaign runs smoothly.' The Maulana replied, 'I have let it be known that Mr Suhrawardy will decide all issues. Whatever needs to be done regarding nominations and framing policy will be done by him.'

Even though I had not agreed with the decision our leaders had taken I now consented to work for it considering our leaders must have arrived at it with the good of our country in their minds. I toiled towards making the United Front effective and well managed. But it took only a couple of days for me to realize the game being played behind the scenes. Parties that I didn't know existed surfaced. Mr Huq told us he had already signed an agreement with an organization calling itself the Nizam-E-Islami Party. I asked Maulana Bhasani if he knew anything about the party. He replied, 'I know nothing about it.' I asked, 'Where is this party based? Who are its officials? Do they have any base which necessitates us taking them on board? If we take them on board shouldn't we also take the party called the Ganatantrik Dal which has announced itself in the papers through one or two statements? At least that party has a handful of progressive-minded people. But we have a lot of democratic parties with us that are not acceptable to them.'

Mr Shaheed Suhrawardy returned and took charge of the office. Nobody had any objections to having him as the chair of the United Front. Mr Ataur Rahman Khan from the Awami League and Kafiluddin Chowdhury from the Krisak Shramik Party were made joint secretaries and Kamruddin Ahmed was made the office secretary. A steering committee was formed next. A board was created, consisting of an equal number of members from the three parties, whose task it would be to come up with the nominations. Mr Suhrawardy was made the chair of this body. It was decided that nominations would have to be made on the basis of consensus. There would be no scope for voting on such an issue. Mr Suhrawardy worked out a strategy for us after working night and day for it. He made arrangements so that he could stay in a room within the office building. He would be there all the time and would start working as soon as he could every morning. Applications were invited for nominations. Forms were printed. Applicants would have to mention the party they were representing and they would have to give a copy of their applications to their parties. Mr Suhrawardy soon began to feel the need for funds to run the campaign effectively.

The application form was to be submitted along with a fee. The fee was non-refundable and would not be returned even if the applicant failed to secure a nomination. Almost a lakh taka was thus collected. Mr Suhrawardy managed to acquire a number of microphones. However, we had almost no vehicles for campaigning. The only vehicle we had was an old jeep Mr Suhrawardy had bought.

There was no dearth of candidates to represent the Awami League. We were in a position to nominate an Awami League candidate for each constituency and these were people who had worked there steadily from 1949 to 1954. Because Mr Huq's Krisak Shramik Party was unable to field candidates in all constituencies, they were sometimes forced to induct whoever wanted to contest the elections on their behalf. Though they had agreed to refuse nominations to people who had never been active in politics or had quit politics by this time or were members of the Muslim League, we found such people becoming members of the Krisak Shramik Party after failing to get nominations from the Muslim League.

On the other hand, quite a few applicants were refused nominations even though they had gone to jail protesting against the Muslim League government's policies. For instance, the secretary of the Chittagong Awami League, Mr M.A. Aziz, had not been nominated. Instead, a businessman had been chosen. Someone like Khondokar Mushtaq, who had even gone to jail for the party, had been refused nomination. Noakhali's Abdul Jabbar Khaddar had been a member of the Awami League from the time of its inception and yet he was denied nomination. The Nizam-E-Islami Party submitted the names of a few religious leaders who had not even applied for nominations. And yet the same party submitted a list of people who were to be denied nominations because they were supposedly communists. Some people on the list were Awami League members who had been imprisoned for their political convictions while some were members of the Ganatantrik Dal. I protested against their submissions and declared, 'I too have a list of people who won't be nominated because they had opposed the formation of Pakistan.'

Nevertheless, these people went to such extremes that soon instead of nominating people of merit they merrily listed the names of men who had been with the Muslim League until only four or five months ago or those who had no political experience. From time to time Mr Huq would send us brief notes that we could not afford to ignore. Moreover, members of the steering committee belonging to the Krisak Shramik Party and the Nizam-E-Islami Party would often abandon our meetings saying that they had to consult Mr Huq on these issues. And so it went. After great effort, I was able to persuade Maulana Bhasani to come to Dhaka. But he wanted to leave as soon as he arrived. We told him about the seriousness of the situation. He said, 'How can we work with these people? I couldn't care a fig about them. I don't recognize your United Front. I am leaving.' I exchanged heated words with him. I said, 'When we are finalizing nominations these people suddenly leave to talk to Mr Huq, but who can we turn to? Since Mr Suhrawardy is the chairman he can't take sides. Please stay back in Dhaka since you are needed and talk to Mr Suhrawardy tomorrow about these issues.' He kept quiet. I had to leave for a meeting soon. Mr Ataur Rahman Khan also kept quiet. I was the one who had to argue all the time. I also had to keep track of every candidate's background. Although Mr Kafiluddin Chowdhury was a member of the Krisak Shramik Party he had become fed up with its leaders' behaviour. He took to supporting any candidate nominated by the Awami League if he considered him a good man. This enraged the members of his party. Mr Ataur Rahman Khan too would be upset at times and say, 'I hate talking to such people.'

Maulana Bhasani left Dhaka, once again without consulting anyone. As soon as I heard about his departure I rushed to the railway station and managed to talk to him. I pleaded with him to stay on but he just wouldn't listen. Things were so bad at that time that the United Front was on the point of disintegration; only Mr Suhrawardy's patience, restraint and judiciousness saved it.

Nominations had not yet been submitted in three or four districts. I had to deposit my own nomination paper with our Gopalganj election office. I left Dhaka a day before the deadline. Because I could not be physically present everywhere, some of our people who had made huge sacrifices for the party had been denied nominations. Those in charge were not willing to listen to even someone of Mr Suhrawardy's stature. Maulana Bhasani's tendency to disappear in times of crises was a constant in his political career. Many later incidents only confirmed this.

At Gopalganj I found the Muslim League candidate, Mr Wahiduzzaman, campaigning vigorously with his entourage. He had amassed a lot of wealth by then. He was able to employ everything that was needed for campaigning—be it a launch, a speedboat, bikes or microphones. All I could afford was a microphone and two bicycles. My constituency comprised two areas: Gopalganj and Kotalipara police stations. Both had no roads. Therefore communication was very difficult. My workers would ride their own bikes. I had limited funds. I could not afford to spend too much on anything. Since my family owned some country boats I was able to put them to good use. Students and youth volunteers of our party began to campaign for me using their own funds. After addressing a few meetings it became obvious to me that Mr Wahiduzzaman would be trounced. His resources wouldn't be enough to get him elected since public opinion was heavily in my favour. People in the villages that I visited would not only offer me refreshments, they would also offer me money and would be offended if I refused to take it. They insisted that I should utilize the money for my campaign.

I remember once how a very poor old woman had waited for a few hours by her hut because she had been told that I would be crossing it. When she finally met me she held my hand and said, 'Please come inside my hut because I would like you to sit inside it for a while.' Holding on to her hand, I went in. There were a lot of people with me and yet she spread out a mat for all of us and gave me a bowl of milk, a paan leaf and some coins. Handing me these things she said, 'My dear son, please drink the milk and have the paan leaf and take the money, little though it is, because that is all I have.' Tears came to my eyes. I drank the milk but returned the coins, along with some more money, saying, 'Your blessings are more than sufficient for me; they cannot be equated with money and I don't have enough to repay you.' But she refused to take the coins and the money I gave her. Instead, she told me affectionately, 'The prayers of the poor will be with you.' When I left her hut my eyes were moist with tears. On that day, I promised myself that I would do nothing to betray my people.

I had many such encounters during my campaign. I went from one union to another on foot. I stopped in village after village to take a break every now and then. Even the women of the villages were eager to have a glimpse of me. Even before the elections I was aware of how much the people of the villages loved me. A big change took place in my consciousness at this time.

When Mr Zaman and the Muslim League saw that the situation was not favourable to them, they decided to play their trump card. They enrolled in their service many famous religious divines. The union where I was born in Gopalganj was also the birthplace of Maulana Shamsul Huq, one of the most famous divines of East Bengal. I respected him a lot. He was quite knowledgeable about religious matters. I was sure that Maulana Huq would not campaign against me. But he soon joined the Muslim League and began to campaign against me. The Muslims of our community used to revere him. He visited union after union in a speedboat to oppose me. On one occasion he went so far as to issue a fatwa against me, proclaiming that voting for someone like me would be tantamount to eradicating Islam from the region and causing the death of the religion. In addition to him, other religious leaders such as the Pirs of Sarshina, Barguna and Shibpur, and Rahmatpur's Shah Saheb joined the fray to defeat me, sparing no fatwa in their arsenal. Except for a couple of maulanas almost all the divines of the region deployed their considerable wealth and influence and worked night and day to destroy me. A few government officials also joined them. The country's police chief came to Gopalganj from Dhaka and gave clear directions to his forces to support the Muslim League. Because Mr Altaf Gauhar, the district magistrate of Faridpur, refused to follow government orders, he was transferred and another officer was brought in. This man even went to my home village to give speeches against me. Three days before the election he moved the voting centres in a bid to help Mr Zaman.

On the other hand, people as a whole, and students and the youth of our area in particular, worked selflessly on my behalf. Four days before the election, Mr Shaheed Suhrawardy, having been informed of the devious methods being employed against me, came to my constituency and addressed two meetings. The day before the election Maulana Bhasani also turned up and spoke in my support. A few days before the election Mr Khondokar Shamsul Huq Muktar, Rahmat Jan, Shahidul Islam and Imdad were arrested under the Public Security Act and kept in Faridpur jail. Forty prominent people of one union were put behind bars. Three days before the election, arrest warrants were issued against fifty others (all from the United Front parties). Mr Shamsul Huq Muktar was hugely popular in our region. The people who worked for him were also famous people. When I heard that many more were going to be arrested, I told them not to show up in town. I also had to visit two other neighbouring constituencies. I thus went to Jessore to campaign for Abdul Hakim, who went on to become the Speaker, and to speak in support of Abdul Khaleque, who became a minister of the central government cabinet later.

In the elections Mr Wahiduzzaman lost by almost 10,000 votes. The people of my constituency had not only voted for me in large numbers but had also raised 5000 takas for my campaign. I clearly saw that if you loved the people they would reciprocate. If you are willing to sacrifice a little for them they will sacrifice even their lives for you. Maulana Shamsul Huq realized now that he had made a mistake and withdrew from active politics. The Muslim League was defeated by an overwhelming margin in the elections. A few days before the elections Mr Suhrawardy had issued a statement saying he would be very surprised if the Muslim League managed to win more than nine seats. Out of the 300 seats in the Assembly the Muslim League managed to win only nine![29]

Rarely had the ruling party of a country been humiliated in this manner anywhere in the world. That ordinary Bengalis are knowledgeable about politics and are very conscious of the political situation was once again proven in this election. They had demonstrated their sensitivity to politics earlier in the elections held in 1946 to decide the Pakistan issue. In this election many prominent leaders of the Muslim League, including some members of the National Assembly, not only lost their seats but also had to forfeit their deposits. The prime minister of East Bengal, Mr Nurul Amin, was defeated. The results bewildered the ruling coterie and high-ranking bureaucrats.

Nevertheless, they did not abandon hope of holding on to power. They now tried to adopt new strategies and began to hatch all sorts of conspiracies. In particular, West Pakistani industrialists and businessmen who had invested in East Bengal by building factories and setting up business houses and had openly aided the Muslim League with financial grants now found themselves in a tricky situation. They tried to find consolation in the fact that the central government was still run by the Muslim League and hoped it would shore up their investments. Those vanquished had never believed in democracy and therefore would not accept the verdict of the people. They now embarked on the politics of conspiracy. Almost all of them left East Bengal and took refuge in Karachi. The West Pakistani leaders, industrialists and bureaucrats were sorely hurt by the losses they had suffered in the elections: where would they get such a naive group of people to be their errand boys again? These people were only too willing to hand over East Bengal's wealth to West Pakistan without a murmur. In return for their labours they wanted to be ministers and wield a bit of power. The central rulers of the country realized that the Awami League had succeeded in creating opinion in favour of provincial autonomy among the people of East Bengal. The Awami League had produced, and distributed throughout the province, pamphlets packed with figures showing the financial gulf that was being created between the two wings of Pakistan day by day and the way Bengalis were being excluded from jobs, trade and commerce and the army. Throughout East Bengal folk musicians had composed and performed songs, which spread the word about the growing disparity between the two wings of Pakistan.

It had become obvious that you could not fool the people of the country by cooking up slogans in the name of 'Islam and Muslims'. Bengali Muslims loved their religion but they would not allow themselves to be made fools of by people who were interested in using Islam for political gains. What the masses wanted was an exploitation-free society and economic and social progress. Muslim League leaders had never presented any rational programmes to achieve these ends. All they said was 'Pakistan will be destroyed', 'The Muslim League has given birth to Pakistan and is thus the country's mother', 'Pakistan is synonymous with the Muslim League', and so on. They proclaimed that the people in the Awami League and other leaders of the opposition were traitors and agents of the Hindus of India. All they wanted, the Muslim League alleged, was to reunite West and East Bengal. Such were the slogans that they manufactured. But the masses knew that Shaheed Suhrawardy was one of the men instrumental in the birth of Pakistan. They were keenly aware of the achievements of Sher-e-Bangla Fazlul Huq and of his love for the people of our country. They recognized the work done by Maulana Bhasani for the sake of Pakistan. In addition, the people also knew of those of us who had had minor roles to play in the making of Pakistan and had made at least small sacrifices for that cause. Thus, it was not possible to hoodwink them.

The Awami League had submitted a list of twenty-one points framed for the overall welfare of the people. The masses were aware of this. A few days before the election, communal riots had erupted in Chandraghona's Karnaphuli factory where most workers were Bengalis, and most executives non-Bengali. The latter ill-treated the Bengalis. The Muslim League propaganda had it that if the Awami League came to power they would not allow non-Bengalis to live in East Bengal.

The Awami League and its workers loathe any form of communalism and prejudice. Most workers and leaders of the Awami League believed in socialist principles and were convinced that the path to the liberation of our people was through socialism. Capitalism was a way of holding the masses in bondage to exploit them. Those who believed in socialism could never subscribe to any form of communalism. For them Muslims, Hindus, Bengalis and non-Bengalis were all the same. On the whole, they disapproved of the exploiting class. In West Pakistan too attempts had been made to discredit the Awami League by accusing it of being communal and anti-non-Bengali.

After the election results were announced, I returned to Dhaka. I was given a rousing welcome at the Dhaka railway station and taken to the Awami League office in a procession. Mr Suhrawardy had had his doubts about whether I would be elected, even though when he met me in my village home he had reassured me: 'You have no reason to worry, for what I have seen tells me that you will surely win.'

A meeting of the United Front MLAs was called at the Dhaka Bar Library hall. Awami League MLAs were to meet in the Awami League office that very morning. We began to hear rumours that Bogra's Mohammad Ali was trying to contact Mr Fazlul Huq through the veteran Muslim Leaguers who had joined Mr Huq's party recently and had managed to get themselves elected under the banner of the Krisak Shramik Party. They may have changed parties but at heart they always remained Muslim Leaguers.

And so we had a meeting of all the Awami League MLAs in the morning and an all-party meeting in the evening at the Bar Library hall. Mr Suhrawardy and Maulana Bhasani were present at the Awami League meeting. Mr Khairat Hussein, a leader of the Rangpur Awami League, moved a resolution stating: 'Before Mr Fazlul Huq is elected a leader, Mr Suhrawardy and Mr Bhasani should work out with him the list of ministers. Once he is made the leader of the United Front in the Assembly it is likely that the very adept players in his party will hatch up conspiracies of all sorts. Moreover, the deputy leader should be elected from our party since the Awami League has the majority of seats within the United Front.' Mr Suhrawardy said, 'He will surely consult the two of us before deciding on the names of the ministers. He is an old man and therefore it would not be a good idea to bother him too much at this stage.' Maulana Bhasani agreed with Mr Suhrawardy. Although I was one with Mr Khairat Hussein I did not say anything. When I had returned from my village home in Tungipara after the elections Mr Suhrawardy had a meeting with me where he had asked me, 'Do you want to be a minister?' I had replied, 'I don't want to be a minister. There is a lot of work to be done for the party and we have many people within it that you can consider for ministerial positions. Mull over them and then elect them ministers.' Mr Suhrawardy said nothing more to me about this issue.

The United Front MLAs met in the Dhaka Bar Library as scheduled. Mr Shaheed Suhrawardy and Maulana Bhasani were present. Mr Fazlul Huq was elected the leader of the United Front unanimously. The second resolution adopted called for the resignation of the Muslim League leaders who had been nominated to the National Assembly by members of the previous Provincial Assembly who had not been able to hold on to their seats in this provincial election. Soon after Mr Huq was elected the leader of the United Front he was invited by the Governor of East Pakistan to form the ministry. He told the Governor that he would soon submit the list of ministers. That evening Mr Suhrawardy and Maulana Bhasani went to meet him. I accompanied the two to Mr Huq's house. However, I was not made privy to their discussions, which took place in another room.

While I waited outside, I was getting quite depressed by the behaviour of the leaders of the Krisak Shramik Party. The air seemed thick with conspiracy. After a while, Mr Suhrawardy and Maulana Bhasani came out and we headed straight for Mr Yar Mohammad's residence. Mr Ataur Rahman Khan was already there. They told us that Mr Huq wanted to form a cabinet consisting of four or five people for now, but would choose some more people as ministers later. His choice of ministers was Abu Hussein Sarkar, Syed Azizul Huq (Nanna Mia), Ashrafuddin Chowdhury, Ataur Rahman Khan and Abdus Salam Khan. Our leaders, however, tried to convey to Mr Huq the idea that it was best to start out with a full team of ministers: the people of the country were looking forward to the United Front working for them without wasting any time. They had one other reservation about Mr Huq's decision: they said it would be best if Mr Syed Azizul Huq were left out of the ministry for the moment and inducted later. But if a full ministry were being formed, they had no objection to having Mr Syed Azizul Huq in it. What they really wanted to see was such a ministry. Because Mr Huq would not concede to their demands, they told him no one from the Awami League would want to be part of the kind of ministry he had in mind. If he wanted to he could form his cabinet with only his [Krisak Shramik] party members. The Awami League would support it externally and would join it only when he expanded it into a full cabinet. Our leaders were able to see through the conspiracy to create factions within the Awami League in a bid to split it.

Mr Huq had declared to Mr Suhrawardy and Maulana Bhasani, 'I won't make Sheikh Mujib a minister in my cabinet.' Mr Suhrawardy had responded, 'It is up to me and the Maulana to decide who the Awami League will nominate; just as you have said that you won't be able to function without Nanna Mia we too can say that we can't do without Sheikh Mujib. He is the secretary of our party. Only the party can decide on these matters.'

I told Mr Suhrawardy and Maulana Bhasani, 'Please don't make me a bone of contention. I don't want to be a minister. If they are willing to form a full-fledged ministry without me, please go ahead.' Even as we were discussing these issues, Mr Huq sent word that he was willing to form a ministry comprising six members and would take me on board. Maulana Bhasani declared, 'If the Awami League is to join the ministry, all Awami League members will have to join at the same time. We don't want to do things in bits and pieces.' The next day Mr Huq took oath as did Abu Hussein Sarkar, Syed Azizul Huq Nanna Mia (all, Krisak Shramik Party) and Ashrafuddin Chowdhury (Nizam-E-Islami). A procession was taken out in front of the Governor's House, with people chanting 'We don't want nepotism' and 'No formation of coterie government'. If a full-fledged ministry had been announced, surely thousands and thousands of people would have gathered in the streets to greet the cabinet, but it was not to be. Within a day, it seemed, the momentum gathered through the mass movement had dissipated. The people seemed to have become indifferent to the whole democratic process. Mr Huq and his followers began to whisper that these negative reactions could be attributed to my manoeuvrings. But the truth is I had no hand to play in these developments. As I read in all the papers, people on the whole were upset at what was happening and the same group of men who had gone to greet the cabinet had raised slogans protesting against the selection of Nanna Mia as a minister. This was because he was not well known. His main claim to fame was that he was Fazlul Huq's nephew. As a man he was very amiable and polite. Besides, the two of us got along very well. I knew him from my Calcutta days. I have never seen him get perturbed about anything. In any case, Mr Fazlul Huq himself wasn't responsible for what was going on. He was an old man by this time. He would be persuaded by others, especially the group around him, whose members had been expelled from the Muslim League. This group was led by Yusuf Ali Chowdhury (Mohan Mia), who wanted to become a minister and who all his life had been adept at breaking up ministries and becoming part of them. One major handicap that he had was that he was not well educated and so was overlooked by everyone. But as a worker he has no parallel in this country. He has the ability to work night and day with the same energy; many people believe that he is an evil genius. If he had applied his skills and intelligence in achieving good things he would have been able to do a lot of good for the country.

I concentrated on building up our party instead of joining the ministry. Mr Suhrawardy returned to Karachi. His health had taken a beating due to overwork. When Mr Huq went to Karachi the East Bengali members of the National Assembly had asked him if they should resign. His response was to tell them, 'I myself have not resigned and so why should you do so?' This, despite the second resolution adopted at the United Front meeting demanding that these members resign. When in Karachi the Muslim League leaders who had assembled under the leadership of Mohammad Ali contacted him and let it be known that they were actually against the Awami League and supported him and would try to make him the chief minister of East Bengal. All he should do is keep the Awami League away from power. Secretly, attempts were being made to woo away our members but our enemies weren't making any headway. Nobody wanted to leave the Awami League. Even those who harboured dreams of being ministers were afraid to say so since they were wary of the public outcry it would elicit. Mr Huq's party continued to deceive him. There was no doubt that the central government formed by the Muslim League would pounce on the provincial government at any sign of weakness. They were well aware that the provincial government could not function without the support of the Awami League. Among the Muslim members of the Assembly, the Awami Leaguers constituted the majority. Even if all the other parties united they would not be able to outnumber the Awami League when it came to voting.

On his way back from Karachi, Mr Fazlul Huq stayed in Calcutta for a couple of days. Some newspapers published reports on speeches allegedly made by him around the time.[30] Mr Mohammad Ali and his gang tried to make use of the opportunity these reports provided them and started to conspire against Mr Huq. He now found himself in big trouble. However, the Awami League and its members refrained from attacking Mr Huq and his party on this count. They let it be known instead that they were fully behind Mr Huq's cabinet. Mr Huq now expressed his wish to discuss the issue of a cabinet expansion with the Awami League. Another one of Mr Huq's nephews, Mahbub Murshed (a barrister and subsequently the Chief Justice of the East Bengal High Court), had a consultation with Mr Huq and requested Ataur Rahman Khan and Manik Mia if the Awami League would join the ministry. He was assisted in these negotiations by

Dhaka's Kafiluddin Chowdhury and Mirza Abdul Kader Sardar. Meanwhile, Mr Suhrawardy's health had deteriorated in Karachi and he was unable to come to Dhaka.

Maulana Bhasani and I were touring the districts around this time and addressing public meetings. Our central office had our programme schedule. Mr Huq informed Ataur Rahman Khan and Manik Mia that he wanted me to become a minister too. While Maulana Bhasani and I were at a party workers' meeting in Tangail, giving speeches, the SDO of Tangail interrupted the meeting, a radiogram in his hand. The radiogram, he said, was from the chief minister asking me to go to Dhaka. I asked Maulana Bhasani for his advice. He said to me, 'If needed, you will have to join the cabinet. However, you must first consult Mr Suhrawardy to find out if it will be a good thing to join the cabinet in this manner at this time. Without a doubt Mr Huq's party must be in a spot and so they want you to help them out.'

I returned to Dhaka in the evening. When I reached home I found out that Renu had come to Dhaka the previous day with the children. She wanted to stay in Dhaka from now on since she believed that the children needed to study in the city. I was happy because I had been leading a very unsettled life. She would now put things in order in my house. Since she knew how hard up I was, she had also brought along some money with her. When I went to visit Mr Huq he told me, 'You will have to become a minister. I want you to be one and please don't say no. You all should get together and decide who else we should induct into the cabinet.' I said to him, 'I have no objections to that. However, Mr Suhrawardy is unwell and we will have to consult him. Also, Maulana Bhasani is not in Dhaka and I will have to talk to him.' I sat down in the *Ittefaq* office with Manik Mia and Ataur Rahman Khan to discuss the situation. A little later, Mr Murshed, Kader Sardar and Kafiluddin Chowdhury joined us. After we had finished, I tried to call Mr Suhrawardy on the phone but he was not in a position to talk. However, his son-in-law Ahmed Suleiman was able to convey our message to him. He eventually informed us that Mr Suhrawardy had no objections to our joining the cabinet.

Nevertheless, I felt strongly that we should not make a move without consulting Maulana Bhasani since the situation had become fairly complicated. Even though Mr Suhrawardy and Maulana Bhasani had decided on the people who would become ministers we still needed to go over the names with them. Meanwhile, the Krisak Shramik Party was not willing to nominate Mr Kafiluddin Chowdhury from their organization for a ministerial position. I let it be known to him that if necessary we could nominate him for a ministerial position from our party. We did not want him to be humiliated because he had dared to speak out. At 11 p.m. after our discussions with Mr Huq we (Mr Ataur Rahman Khan, Mr Murshed, Mr Kafiluddin Chowdhury, Abdul Kader Sardar and myself) headed for Tangail in a jeep. The road to Tangail was in bad shape and in those days it would take six hours for anyone to reach the town in a car. One had to cross four ferries en route. When we reached Tangail it was early morning. The Maulana was in a room on the second floor of the Awami League office building. We went in to talk to him but he became very agitated when he saw us. However, he eventually gave in to Mr Murshed's pleading. Mr Ataur Rahman showed him the list of names we had come up with: himself, Abul Mansur Ahmed, Abdus Salam Khan, Hashimuddin Ahmed and me. Since the Krisak Shramik Party had objections to Mr Kafiluddin Chowdhury the Awami League had decided to nominate him to the ministry. In addition to Mr Huq there would be twelve other ministers. Later, we would see the list expand overnight with the inclusion of a few more names.

One day in May 1954 all of us assembled at 9 a.m. at the Governor's House to take oath. No sooner had we finished taking our oaths than we learned that Bengali and non-Bengali workers had clashed in Adamjee Jute Mill, leading to widespread violence in the area. Syed Azizul Huq had gone there early in the morning. An EPR [East Pakistan Rifles] contingent and a police force had been stationed there overnight. A couple of high-ranking officials from Dhaka and police officials were also present on the scene. Why did the violence break out right at the moment when we were taking oath? There could be little doubt that this was a bad omen. Along with Mr Huq, we headed straight for Adamjee Jute Mill. In those days you could go to the mill on a launch via Narayanganj. A road to the mill had been built by then but it was not ready for car traffic although a truck or a jeep could make the trip with some difficulty. The rest of our company had departed but the crowd that had gathered outside the Governor's House now got hold of me. They wanted me to head a procession right then. It took me half an hour to convince them that this was not the time for me to parade with them.

When I reached Narayanganj I heard that Mr Huq had headed back to Dhaka after waiting there for me for some time. However, he had kept a launch waiting for me. As soon as I reached the spot I boarded the launch and directed it to the mill. There I was put in a jeep. There was still some rioting going on then. In whichever direction I travelled I found the roads strewn with dead bodies. Many wounded people were crying out for help but there seemed to be no one around to give them relief. The EPR forces were on patrol and had managed to separate the Bengalis and the non-Bengalis. Thousands of Bengalis living in neighbouring villages had been informed about the riots and had decided to intervene. Non-Bengalis living outside the mills were being herded into trucks and taken inside the mill premises. I felt quite helpless. All I had with me were two armed policemen. A little later I came across a few other policemen. I ordered them to stay with me. I set up a temporary office under a tree. The mill had four trucks but not one of them was to be seen anywhere near us. I managed to gather some men and entrusted them the task of providing the wounded with water, ignoring the dead bodies for the time being. When some officials noticed that I was taking part in the work they lent a helping hand. Then Mohan Mia appeared before me. Looking at him, I took heart. Three trucks also soon showed up. Their drivers tried to flee but I warned them that they risked being sent to jail for desertion. My wrath seemed to cow them down. Dhaka had been contacted over the phone and asked to send ambulances to this spot. Mohan Mia and I managed to send at least 300 wounded people to hospitals by working from 11 a.m. to nightfall. I went to the Bengalis who had come from everywhere and assembled there to assault the mill and managed to placate them through my speeches. They cooled down after they heard me. However, I doubt whether they would have been swayed by my words if they had discovered the truth. Just before evening set in I went all around the area and counted over 500 corpses myself. I have no doubt that there must have been at least a hundred bodies more in the pond.

The rioting had started over a trivial matter. Three days ago a Bengali worker had got into a fight with a non-Bengali guard. At one point the Bengali worker hit the guard who died on the spot. This led to tension and intrigue. The guards here were all non-Bengalis as were some of the workers. The incident led to a lot of resentment. The mill authorities kept on inciting the non-Bengalis to attack. They permitted them to hoist a black flag over the mill. Work was stopped in the mill and the Bengalis were asked to come inside to collect their wages one day. When they came to collect their wages armed guards and non-Bengalis pounced on them from all sides and began to assault them. The Bengalis were taken by surprise. Many were murdered. Next, the Bengalis who were outside the mill attacked the non-Bengalis and ended up killing many of them. What was the intention behind summoning all the Bengali workers to collect their wages at the time the new United Front cabinet members were taking oath? Although the EPR forces were present they had not fired a single bullet to stop the killing. As a consequence, over 500 people died in the riots. The police officials had been informed beforehand of the possibility of trouble; so why had they not done anything to stop the mayhem? Mr Syed Azizul Huq, the minister who had come there, was entertained with refreshments in the office so that he could not find out what was going on. He had not been told that while he was being entertained in one part of the mill a riot had erupted in another part. While Mr Huq and the other ministers returned to Dhaka, Mr Mohan Mia and I stayed in the mill premises till 9 p.m. Mr Madani was the commissioner of Dhaka while Hafiz Mohammad Ishak, CSP [Civil Services of Pakistan], was the chief secretary.

When I informed Mr Madani that 500 people had been killed in the riots he did not believe me at first. Mr Madani declared that at best fifty people had been killed. I told him that I had counted the bodies one by one and he should go there himself to verify my figure. Later, he acknowledged that I was right. At nine that night Mohan Mia and I were informed that the mill area had been handed over to the military. Mr Shamsuddoha was the IG of police then. He said to me, 'Good grief! All the military personnel are non-Bengalis.' I could not resist laughing at this reaction and replied, 'What is so surprising about this turn of events? Since you could not keep things under control with your policemen and the EPR, what other option was left except to hand over power to the army?' In those days the EPR was under the control of the provincial government. We would have to go to Dhaka to find out what had really led to this situation. No doubt the chief minister had ordered the army to move in by this time.

We headed straight for the chief minister's house as soon as we reached Dhaka. When we arrived there we were told that he was very worried about me. He was shouting at everyone and blaming them for leaving me behind at the scene of the riot all by myself. When I met him he greeted me very affectionately. He said to me, 'We are going to have our cabinet meeting right now, so please don't go away.'

The cabinet finally met at 10.30 p.m. I could see even before the cabinet meeting had started that Mr Shamsuddoha had managed to win over a couple of ministers. Mr Abdul Latif Biswas (who is no longer alive) was asking angrily why the military had been given the responsibility of controlling the situation. Mr Fazlul Huq entered the meeting at this time. We could also hear the chief secretary, Mr Ishaque, exchanging strong words. I protested against this outburst and said we could deal with these issues later. I told him, 'Let's first find out who are the people responsible for not maintaining law and order at the scene before the trouble started and take punitive action against them since their negligence has led to the death of so many people.' The cabinet meeting now started. We discussed many issues which I am not going to divulge since it is not proper to disclose cabinet proceedings.

By the time the meeting ended and we came out, it was almost 1 a.m. I could see the veteran Muslim League worker Rajab Ali Shet, an admirer of Mr Suhrawardy, and many other non-Bengali leaders standing outside, waiting for us to come out. They told me that I should immediately visit different parts of Dhaka city. Apparently the city was in the grip of a rumour that non-Bengalis were massacring Bengalis everywhere. Non-Bengalis were in danger of being attacked at any moment. Taking Rajab Ali Shet and a few others along with me, I set out immediately. Even at that time of the night street corners were full of people. I got out of the car at intersections, addressed the crowd that had gathered at those spots and tried to calm people down, with some success. By the time I reached home it was 4 a.m. I had not been able to spend even five minutes at home since I had taken oath. Moreover, I had not eaten anything throughout the day. I found Renu waiting silently for me in the house—she too had not taken any food all day.

I have no doubts that these riots were the result of a huge conspiracy aimed at belittling the United Front government and showing it as incompetent in the eyes of the whole world. The conspiracy must have been hatched in Karachi a few days ago and the conspirators must have involved a particular government official and some mill personnel. Capitalists have resorted to this means of inciting riots and creating strife amidst hapless workers over the ages to achieve their own political ends. But I am not so sure if the owner of Adamjee Jute Mill, Malik Gul Mohammad Adamjee, was aware of the conspiracy.

The Central Muslim League under the leadership of Mohammad Ali found in these riots the excuse it was looking for to intervene. Mohammad Ali and his cronies in the Muslim League aided by the West Pakistani industrialists had been attempting to prevent the formation of the United Front but had not succeeded because the Awami League had ultimately become part of it. Now they were resorting to new tactics with the help of their agents to thwart the United Front government's work. This would have been difficult if the United Front had begun with a full-size cabinet from the first day of its existence.

After the United Front won the elections the powerful bureaucrats of the government became alarmed. Many had campaigned publicly on behalf of the Muslim League in the elections. When the Awami League members did not become part of the United Front cabinet initially they had taken heart. But now that we had become part of the cabinet they had become frustrated and were resorting to intrigue. However, Mr Hafiz Mohammad Ishaque, the Chief Secretary, had welcomed our inclusion.

I went to Adamjee Jute Mills the next day and officially instructed everyone to ensure that no workers faced any hardship as far as food and accommodation were concerned. I went to the Secretariat and summoned the Chief Secretary to discuss the situation with him. Meanwhile, negotiations had begun about the distribution of cabinet positions. There too, all sorts of conspiracies were being hatched. Attempts were being made to ensure that the Awami League was deprived of key ministries. It was a pretty difficult situation. Mohan Mia was complicating things after his conversations with Mr Huq. I said to Mr Huq, 'I am fed up with what is going on. If necessary, I'll quit the cabinet and go my own way.'

The next day the ministries were allocated. I was given the Ministry of Cooperatives and Agricultural Development. However, agriculture had been allotted to someone else. Mr Sobhan, CSP, had advised Mohan Mia on the distribution of ministerial posts. I called him and said, 'You don't know me much, so let me tell you not to muddy the water too much.' I went to Mr Huq again and said, 'Grandpa, what's happening? We aren't dying to become ministers. Why have we been asked to join you in this manner if such conspiracies are going to be hatched against us?' He called me to his side and said, 'Let them do what they want to; I'll hand over my portfolio to you. Don't be upset; everything will work out well in the end.' He was a very old man, so what more could I say to him? Besides, he had begun to treat me very affectionately. He would summon me to his side even if there was no real need for anything. He had once said to some assembled journalists, 'I'm an old tree and Mujib is a bark branching out and that's why I am his grandpa and he is my grandson.' I was the youngest of all the cabinet ministers. And he was the oldest member of the cabinet. I would do whatever he wanted me to do. He had a big heart and that is why I had come to respect him. When the conspirators were not all over him he would show his generosity and amiable side. However, because he had become so old he had to depend on them a lot. But the way he was showing his affection for me I was confident that I would be able to rescue him from those people. I went to the office to try to figure out what the work of my ministry amounted to, for I had only a dim idea of what I was supposed to be doing. It was around this time that the ministers moved to their official residences. I too moved into a Minto Road government residence with my wife and children.

A couple of days later Mr Huq said to me, 'I've been informed by the people at Karachi that I have to go there. Ataur Rahman and you will be accompanying me. Nanna, Mohan Mia and Ashrafuddin Chowdhury will also come along; those guys there seem to be up to no good.' I was ready to join him because I wanted to go there for another reason: Mr Suhrawardy was ailing and I wanted to visit him.

We arrived at Karachi. The first thing we did was discuss the situation in East Bengal with the central government. They wanted to know from us what kind of assistance we would want from them. A virulent campaign was going on in West Pakistan to discredit us. They were trying to pin blame on the United Front for the riots that had taken place. I wonder if anyone has ever heard of a government instigating riots to make itself look bad. A government is responsible for maintaining law and order, so why will it risk disrepute by instigating a riot? The riots obviously had been fomented by the losers. They originated from Karachi where the people in charge organized the riots to make the United Front government look bad in the eyes of the world. They were looking hard for an excuse to dismiss the provincial government.

After our talks with the central cabinet, Mohammad Ali of Bogra took us to his room and asked us to sit down. Mr Huq was present too. Mohammad Ali began to talk to him rudely. Just when I thought I couldn't stand his insolence any more, Mohammad Ali turned towards me and said, 'Mujibur Rahman, do you know that I have a huge file against you that is now lying on top of my table?' As he said this, he gesticulated wildly and brought a file from the other side of the room and placed it on the table. I replied, 'Of course you'll have a file on me. It's thanks to you all that I had to be in prison for a long time. But we too have a file against you in our provincial government.' He said, 'What exactly do you mean?' I responded, 'When Khawaja Nazimuddin formed a ministry in 1947 as the prime minister of East Bengal he didn't make you a minister. Do you remember that when we launched our movement on behalf of the Bengali language in 1948 you had secretly contributed 200 taka to us? Many people tend to forget the past too easily.' Mr Huq and Syed Azizul Huq could see things heating up. One of them said, 'Let's go for now; we will resume discussions later.' Before we left I managed to let Mr Ali know that his treatment of Mr Huq had been rude and unmannerly.

I went to visit Mr Suhrawardy, who was quite sick. He wasn't able to lift himself from his bed and was finding it difficult even to talk to us. The physicians had prohibited him from meeting outsiders. But he was very happy to see me. Baby, his daughter, had instructed me not to bring up politics in our conversation. Nevertheless, he slowly brought the conversation around to the topic to learn about the political situation. I said a thing or two in reply and then fell silent. At the end he declared, 'Mohammad Ali and the Muslim League leaders are up to something really devious.'

Mr Huq said to me, 'Governor General Ghulam Muhammad has asked us to meet him.' We therefore went to his official residence. We were taken to the room from which he was running the affairs of the state even though he had to do so from his bed. He was a very sick man and his hands and legs were shaking all the time. His speech was not clear at all. Nevertheless, he entered into a discussion with Mr Huq. He called me by name to find out if I was among those present. Mr Huq pointed at me to indicate that I was. He then asked me to sit by him and asked me, 'People say that you are a communist; is that the truth?' I replied, 'If Mr Suhrawardy is a communist I am one. And if he is something else I am that too.' He smiled and placing his hand affectionately on my forehead said, 'You are still a young man and have a lot to contribute to the country. You have my blessings. I am delighted to have met you.' It was difficult to follow what he was saying since he was not very coherent. His face was partially paralysed. His arms and his legs had shrivelled. But God seemed to have left him with his wits intact and he seemed fully in control of his thoughts.

The next day we heard that talks were going on regarding imposition of Governor's rule in East Bengal and that the cabinet there would be dissolved soon. The central government had ordered the Chief Secretary of the East Pakistan government, Mr Ishaque, to ensure that we didn't return to the province. He was to prevent us from getting plane tickets. But he had refused categorically, saying, 'They are still ministers of the cabinet. Legally, I am bound to listen to them.' He had also been instructed to file a doctored report on our trip. But he had objected to making things up. As a consequence he was later removed from his position and forced to go on long leave. When Mr Ataur Rahman and I came to know of these developments, I told Mr Huq, 'We will return to Dhaka today because if we don't go back immediately we will have to stay here for a while. We won't get any plane tickets afterwards.' When Mr Huq understood the gravity of the situation he called Nanna Mia and said that he too wanted to return to Dhaka. Nanna Mia also agreed to go back with us. However, Mohan Mia and Ashrafuddin Chowdhury decided to stay back in Karachi to find out if they could get any more favours for themselves there.

We booked our tickets and went to see Mr Suhrawardy again. We informed him about some of the goings-on. He was in great pain and told me, 'I'll have to go to Zurich for treatment in a couple of days and need money badly.' I said, 'I'll send some money to Baby as soon as I reach Dhaka.' I felt depressed at the thought that the man who had once distributed thousands among the poor from his earnings had no money for his own treatment now. Such is fate!

It must have been on 29 May that we took the plane back to Dhaka. Our flight was to touch Delhi and Calcutta on the way. With us were Chief Secretary Hafiz Ishaque and Inspector General of Police Shamsuddoha. I had no idea then why and at whose behest Mr Doha had come to Karachi. Later, Mr Huq told me that he had asked him to come along. Just before landing in Calcutta Mr Doha told Mr Huq, 'Sir, I think it is a good idea for you to be in Calcutta tonight. One never knows what might happen because these people are up to no good. Mr Iskander Mirza and N.M. Khan flew to Dhaka on a military plane last night. Something might happen in Dhaka airport. If nothing happens there I'll send an aircraft to fetch you from Calcutta tomorrow.' Fully aware of the gravity of the situation, Mr Huq pointed towards Nanna Mia and me and said, 'Talk to them.' Mr Doha came to us with the same story. I said to him, 'Why will we get down at Calcutta? It is a foreign city now. Let whatever happens to us happen in Dhaka.' Nanna Mia agreed with me. I had no difficulty figuring out why Mr Doha had come up with such unsolicited advice. It was part of a plan that had been hatched in Karachi since the Pakistani rulers wanted to show to the world that what Mr Huq really wanted was to unite the two Bengals—that he was Pakistan's enemy and a traitor. As for us, they wanted to paint us as Mr Huq's accomplices.

As soon as we landed in Calcutta airport journalists surrounded Mr Huq and began asking him all sorts of questions. He put a finger on his lips to indicate that they were sealed but that they could direct their questions at me. The journalists then came towards me. I said to them, 'We have nothing to tell you at this time. If we have anything to say we will say it when we reach Dhaka.' We were delayed for an hour in Calcutta. Mr Doha came to us once more and said, 'I telephoned Dhaka and found out that the whole airport has been surrounded by the military. Think again; what should we do next?' I said, 'Let them do what they want to since it won't affect us. We will go back to Dhaka. We won't stay in another country for a minute longer than we have to'. When we boarded the plane it occurred to me that since Mr Doha worked for the police he considered himself extremely shrewd. He probably felt that since we were politicians we wouldn't be able to see through his plans.

When we reached Dhaka we found that a huge crowd had gathered in the airport to welcome us back. We met everyone and then headed for our homes. We had left Mr Huq's personal assistant, Sajed Ali, in Karachi. He was to inform us by phone of any future developments.

When I reached home I saw that Renu had not yet managed to set up the house properly. I told her, 'I don't think you will have to work on it any longer since they are going to dissolve the ministry and arrest me. Where will you stay in Dhaka then? You will probably have to go back to our village home. You joined me in Dhaka thinking that you will be with me and the children would get a proper education but I guess these things are not going to happen. Also, I have spent whatever money I had.' Renu looked worried. I had a bath, took my lunch and decided to rest for a while. At 3 p.m. someone called to say that the central government had promulgated Section 92(A) and dissolved the provincial cabinet.[31] Major General Iskander Mirza had been made the Governor of East Bengal and N.M. Khan its Chief Secretary.

Getting dressed quickly, I went to Ataur Rahman's house and the two of us headed for Mr Huq's house, where we requested him to call a cabinet meeting. We told him that we should not be obeying the unfair decree imposed on us by the central government and should ignore it. He said he was not sure what he should do next and suggested that we discuss the situation with the others. I talked to Nanna Mia but he seemed baffled by the situation and could say nothing. It seemed that everyone was apprehensive. Mr Ataur Rahman was ready to support me provided the others agreed to do so. We couldn't locate the ministers while Mr Huq confined himself to his upstairs room. I told Mr Ataur Rahman, 'Try and see if you can bring everyone here. Let me go to the Awami League office and remove the documents from it. They might seal the office any time now.'

No sooner had I left the Awami League office with all the relevant documents than the police approached it from another route and surrounded it. When I reached Nanna Mia's house I was told that senior police officials had come in search of me. When I phoned my house I found that they had been there too. I said to Renu, 'If they come looking for me again tell them that I will be coming home soon.' As I left, I told the people present, 'I am headed for prison but let me stress something: you shouldn't obey this unfair decree without protesting against it. You should oppose it openly. The people of the country are ready to do so; all you have to do is lead them. Many of us will land up in jail but it is better to protest and end up there.' When I left Nanna Mia's house I had hoped to meet some of our workers on the way but couldn't find anybody. I left my official car and went home in a rickshaw. A few policemen were guarding my house. But because I came in a rickshaw, they failed to see me go in. Renu asked me to have some food. I did so, got my bed ready and then phoned the district magistrate, Yahiya Khan Chowdhury. I told him, 'The police has been to my house no doubt to arrest me. You will find me there; so send a vehicle for me.' He replied, 'We have to obey orders. I am sending a vehicle, so get ready. They are calling me repeatedly to have you arrested.' I thanked him and hung up. Renu got my things ready, crying as she did so. The children were asleep by then. I told her not to wake them up. I told her, 'What can I say to you? Do what you think is best but staying in Dhaka will be tough for you all. It will be best for you to go to our village home.'

I had requested my friend Yar Mohammad to rent a house for her if Renu decided not to go to our village home. He and the owner of Hotel Al Helal, Haji Helal Uddin, had done so and helped her in my absence. A few days later when Yar Mohammad was bringing Renu to meet me he was arrested at the prison gate. He had been elected MLA from a Dhaka constituency.

Half an hour later a car came to fetch me. There were quite a lot of people in the house then but most fled into the dark of the night fearing arrest. I got into the car and was on my way. A young worker of our party from Gopalganj, Shahidul Islam, was wailing as I was leaving. I got down from the car and said to him affectionately, 'Why are you crying? This is my destined path. I will come out of prison one day but do look after my wife while I am away.'

I was brought to the district magistrate's office. He was waiting for me and said, 'What can I do? The people in Karachi are quite desperate to have you arrested. We knew very well that you would voluntarily turn yourself in as soon as we would send word to you. You have no fear of imprisonment.' His phone was ringing continually and I gauged it didn't make sense to stay in his office room any longer. I said, 'Send me to jail. I am extremely tired and couldn't sleep at all last night in the plane.'

He took me to the next room and made me sit there. Mr Idris was Deputy Inspector General of Police, Dhaka division, then. He came to meet me and behaved very decently with me. He asked if I needed cigarettes or anything else. I said I would be really happy if he sent me to my prison cell immediately. Soon after he left an inspector showed up and began framing an arrest warrant. A case was soon filed against me. It accused me of robbery and attempt to murder, looting and vandalism and of other actions breaking the law. The district magistrate assigned a 'division' for me. It was past midnight when I arrived at the prison gate. I realized I was the only Awami League member to have been brought to the prison. A few minutes later Mirza Golam Hafiz and Syed Abdur Rahim were brought there too. The three of us were kept in the Dewani Ward.

While I was being fetched from the district magistrate's office, Mr Idris had asked me, 'Where does Professor Abdul Hye, Publicity Secretary of the Awami League, live?' I replied, 'Even if I know, I won't say. How do you expect me to tell you such a thing?' In the next ten to fifteen days nearly 3000 workers and supporters of the Awami League were arrested. Only a few workers from other parties, a few hundred students, and about fifty MLAs were arrested. A few MLAs of the Ganatantrik Dal were also among those jailed. Korban Ali, Dewan Mahbub Ali, Bijoy Chatterjee, Khondokar Abdul Hamid, Mirza Golam Hafiz, Yar Mohammad Khan and Mohammad Toaha were brought to the Dewani Ward and seven other cells of the Dhaka central jail. Later, Professor Ajit Guha and Munier Chowdhury were brought to prison too. Mr Fazlul Huq was put under house arrest.

On 6 June Mr Abu Hussein Sarkar called a meeting of the United Front Parliamentary Party at his house. Only a few MLAs showed up. Some ex-ministers also turned up. When the police arrived and imposed a ban on meetings everyone dispersed and went to their homes.

In the speech he gave on the radio imposing Governor's rule in East Bengal, Prime Minister Mohammad Ali attacked Sher-e-Bangla Fazlul Huq as a 'traitor' and labelled me a 'rioter'. Those of our leaders who were outside jail did not think it worth their while to protest against such a statement. The people of our country were looking forward to 6 June and if our leaders had the guts to come up with a programme of action for them, they would have embraced it. Apart from the workers who had been arrested those still outside prison would have sprung into action. The valiant and self-sacrificing workers of the Awami League would have joined them in opposing what had taken place. But they were unable to do anything since they were depending on the so-called leaders of the United Front, who were in fact nothing but opportunists. Many of our workers had successfully courted arrest. If the leaders had called the people to join them in mass action that day we would have witnessed such a massive movement that it would have deterred any conspirators from oppressing Bangladesh in the future. Where 97 per cent of the people had voted for the United Front and were supporting it, they would have been undeterred by whatever carrots or sticks were brandished before them. And to think that the very same people looked on silently at what was going on! Their leaders were keeping totally mum about what needed to be done or what could be done and whether such oppression was to be endured in silence or not.

Only Mr Ataur Rahman Khan came out with a statement against the government a few days later. Maulana Bhasani had gone to England a few days before Section 92(A) was imposed in East Bengal. Mr Suhrawardy was sick and in a Zurich hospital, while I was a prisoner in a cell. When we have an unprincipled leadership at the helm of affairs we may make some progress for a while but such gains will vanish in times of crisis. Of the eighteen or so ministers I was the only one in prison now. If they had only disobeyed the illegal law imposed on us on 6 June and had courted arrest (Mr Huq was an exception since he was already under house arrest) a movement against it would have started spontaneously. Unfortunately, not one man protested against what had happened. As a result it was obvious to the conspirators that no matter how much noise these Bengalis made, and no matter how much popular support they were able to muster, it wouldn't be difficult to suppress them. They would be sure to flee to their burrows if the police flourished their sticks and guns. If they had faced opposition the oppressors would have thought a thousand times before ever daring to take action against Bengalis as a whole.

From this day Bengalis began to face their darkest days. One should never work for national development with unfit leadership, unprincipled leaders and cowardly politicians on one's side. That results in more harm than good for the people of the country. I can't remember exactly when, but it must have been two or three days after I was brought to prison that I was arrested once more under the Public Security Act while still in prison. Those imprisoned under this law can be detained for an indefinite period without trial. The government must have thought that I might be acquitted under the lawsuit initially filed against me, so they opted for the Public Security Act now, hoping to put me behind bars indefinitely. I can't remember what charges they framed against me this time. I had supposedly tried to kill someone or incite some people to acts of vandalism. On inquiry, I found out that the charges against me on this occasion were linked to a recent outbreak of violence in front of the jail gate.

On that day I was in the Awami League office with others, getting ready for iftar. When I was in Dhaka during the month of Ramadan I would usually join others in our office to break the fast. There I got a call informing me that an altercation over a trivial matter outside the Chawk Bazar jail gate had led to prison guards firing on a group of people, killing one man and injuring many others. The Dhaka central jail is located right next to Chawk Bazar. This was when I had not yet joined Mr Huq's provincial ministry. I telephoned Mr Ataur Rahman Khan since his house was very close to Chawk Bazar. He had already been informed of the incident and wanted me to go to his house. The two of us could go from there to Chawk Bazar and then to the prison. As soon I met him we rushed towards Chawk Bazar. Many people had gathered there and the air was thick with excitement. They surrounded us and began to talk excitedly. All of them wanted to talk at the same time and tell us what they had witnessed. When we pleaded with them to narrate their experiences one by one they calmed down a little and told us what they had seen. A warder had apparently got into an argument with a betel nut shopkeeper and this had led to a fight between them. Two to four prison guards then took the warder's side while the people of the locality took up the shopkeeper's cause. In the scuffle that ensued, the prison guards came off worse. They rushed to their barracks to get their guns and fired them. Many in the crowd were injured. Three of the wounded were dragged into the jail. A large crowd had gathered by this time. We asked them to calm down and headed for the jail gate, where we met Syed Azizul Huq aka Nanna Mia (a minister by this time), who had arrived there upon being informed of the incident. Accompanying him was a special government official. All of us approached the jail gate now. There we talked to the jail superintendent and the jailer. By this time a couple of other ministers, the district magistrate and the divisional commissioner had showed up too. Seeing us all as well as the ministers, a crowd began to gather outside the prison gate. Thousands of people were shouting angrily.

Dhaka jail then had an Anglo-Indian sergeant, Mr Godge. I can't vouch for this, but apparently the crowd had started to chant slogans such as 'We want to put Godge on trial' and 'Godge has fired on us'. Godge's house was located across the jail gate. Someone must have pointed to the house to indicate this. The crowd began to storm it. Those who were present, including the ministers, leaders and government officials, requested me to accompany them to Godge's house. Such a major incident had taken place over an hour ago and yet not one armed policeman had appeared on the scene. I went out to tackle the mob. I pushed aside some of the people and tried to control them. With the help of our party workers we drove back the mob from Godge's veranda. From the roof of a car I addressed the mob, asking them to calm down and stop the violence. I assured them that the government would punish the perpetrators. I didn't have a microphone and it was difficult to make myself heard. Meanwhile, the crowd started to mill around Godge's house again. Once more I sped towards Godge's house with our workers and placed ourselves between it and the mob. Many more workers of the Awami League had arrived on the scene by then.

Just when I had managed to placate the crowd and direct them away from the house and towards the jail gate, the IGP, Mr Doha, turned up with some policemen. He grabbed my hand and declared, 'You are under arrest.' I said, 'Great!' The mob began to scream and attempted to snatch me away from him. I tried to calm them down once more. Two or three minutes later Mr Doha resurfaced and said, 'I am sorry I couldn't see you in the dark; I made a mistake. Let's go to the jail gate.' I went with him inside the prison and said, 'Almost two hours have gone by since the disturbances started and you have shown up with the police now. We had to keep things under control. Do what you think is best now. Why do you need me any more? It can't be more than a mile from the jail gate to Lalbagh Police Line and yet it has taken so long for the police force to come to the scene!'

I was exhausted by this time. The crowd had gathered in front of the prison gate once more. We realized that the police was getting ready to fire or charge them with batons. Nobody was trying to calm the mob. The government publicity van had not been summoned although its microphones could have been used to persuade the crowd to disperse. There was no way one could get heard otherwise. I talked to the people sitting in the superintendent's room and left to form a procession with the people outside the jail gate. Many of our workers were amongst the crowd. When I came out I told the people, 'Let's protest against this unjust situation by forming a procession.' I began to lead them. Almost 70 per cent of the people followed me. I led the procession from there to Sadar Ghat, almost one and a half miles away.

When I reached the Awami League office I declared to those present that the next day we would organize a public meeting in Paltan Maidan. What had happened was extremely unjust. Why did the jail warders leave the jail compound and fire on people? Whose permission had they sought to do so? Who had supplied the magazines to them? Aren't warders supposed to have arms with them all the time? I was in the Awami League office discussing these points until almost 10 p.m. We now learned that another round of shooting had taken place in front of the jail gate, killing one person. I didn't feel the need to return to the jail gate. I called Mr Ataur Rahman to inform him of the next day's meeting. He agreed with my decision.

A large public meeting was held in Paltan Maidan the next day. In my speech I demanded that those responsible for the incident should be punished and relatives of those who had died should be compensated. An investigation should also be carried out to find out why the police had failed to arrive on the scene in time. When I joined the cabinet a few days later I tried to initiate discussions on the issue to find out what actions had been taken to resolve it and to determine what was to be done if none had been taken till then.

After our cabinet was dissolved and Governor's rule imposed, I was made an accused in what was labelled the Jail Gate Riot case. The proceedings of this case dragged on till 1955 and were held in the court of Mr Fazle Rabbi, a first-class magistrate. Many false witnesses were summoned to testify against me. Even Mr Godge's daughter was produced in court to testify against me. But they were not able to produce any witness from the public. They did get some of the jail warders to testify on their behalf. Two of them, however, revealed the truth inadvertently when they reported that they had seen me climb on to the roof of a car and speak to the crowd urging them to disperse. But the jail superintendent, Mr Naziruddin Sarkar, did not speak the truth and parroted what the police had told him. The witnesses gave conflicting testimonies. Nevertheless, one of the things they said was that I had asked the mob to be peaceful. So the magistrate concluded that there was no case against me and he acquitted me unconditionally. In his verdict the magistrate said, 'Instead of labelling him a peace-disrupter he should be labelled the preserver of peace.' And yet I had to spend around ten months in prison under the Public Security Act.

While in prison a few incidents depressed me and the other political prisoners. After he had been put under house arrest Sher-e-Bangla Fazlul Huq's supporters managed to make him issue a statement admitting he had been mistaken and express his regret for the action. Since he was the leader of the United Font his statement humiliated us. It is difficult to put into words the extent of our distress at the content of the statement. When we came across it in the newspaper we were startled. He was a very old man then and it was possible that he had become very weak mentally. But what about the people who were outside prison? The people of the country as a whole were behind us. Thousands of our workers were languishing in jail. Those of us who were interned now resolved that we would no longer work with the Krisak Shramik Party. Meanwhile, even in prison we came to know that many leaders of the party who had been expelled from the Muslim League in 1953 were now negotiating secretly with Mohammad Ali to find ways and means of becoming ministers again. If necessary, they were willing to cut themselves loose from the Awami League. Instead of taking action against the government officials responsible for the massive rioting in Adamjee Jute Mills, Mr Iskander Mirza had targeted political workers on becoming the Governor of East Pakistan.

Meanwhile, Muslim League leaders had begun to squabble with each other. Ghulam Muhammad and Mohammad Ali were locked in a battle of minds. Mohammad Ali was no longer the apple of the eye of those in power. He had passed a law in the Constituent Assembly curbing Ghulam Muhammad's power. But Ghulam Muhammad was not the type to let such an act go unchallenged. He, for his part, began to assert himself. He was well aware that the invisible force that had helped him topple Khawaja Nazimuddin from power would back him. It was this invisible force that was once again fomenting trouble. It had now made another move to grab power. When Mohammad Ali passed the legislation in the Constituent Assembly in September snatching away Governor General Ghulam Muhammad's powers, the latter declared a state of emergency in Pakistan and dissolved the Constituent Assembly. It was supposed to be the apex body as far as political power in the country was concerned. Unfortunately, the members of the Constituent Assembly deliberately refrained from giving the country a constitution while they were holding office from 1947 to 1954. The Constituent Assembly had the right to draft a constitution. India and Pakistan became independent at the same time. A Constituent Assembly was formed in both countries then. However, India had got its constitution and held countrywide elections under it in 1952 and was now getting ready for another national election.

Our Constituent Assembly, on the other hand, had come under the grip of a few who had managed to create a coterie within it. Even though they lost the East Bengal Provincial Assembly elections the defeat did not serve as their wake-up call. Instead, they conspired to annul the results of the elections in East Bengal, declared a state of emergency and unleashed a reign of terror there. Mohammad Ali was aware that he did not have the backing of the army and should not have expected its support in any case. The army was bound to support Ghulam Muhammad. Where, then, did he get the courage to take such a foolhardy step? No doubt the invisible force behind all else was goading him on. The Punjabi coterie was ruling Pakistan at this time. They knew that they had made good use of these East Bengali gentlemen as long as they wanted to. Now they had nothing more to offer them. And these gentlemen were putting up more obstacles in their path from time to time. The West Pakistanis had come to realize how vulnerable these people were after the United Front's victory. They were fully aware that these gentlemen did not represent the people of East Bengal.

Mohammad Ali now abandoned his associates, surrendered to Ghulam Muhammad and formed a caretaker government. In the process he became even more of a captive in the hands of Ghulam Muhammad and Chaudhury Muhammad Ali. Although he was the prime minister, it was Chaudhury

Muhammad Ali who really wielded power in Pakistan. Ayub Khan was made the chief of the army and Iskander Mirza a minister and the whole country was thereby delivered to the bureaucrats. Ayub Khan had already begun to harbour ambitions for the highest office. Proof of this can be found in his autobiography, *Friends Not Masters.* He has confessed in this book that on 4 October 1954 he had written down his sentiments about the Pakistani constitution in a London hotel. Why did he write about the constitution then? He was the head of the armed forces of Pakistan and his job was to protect the country from external enemies. It was his responsibility to build up the army accordingly.

Where had Ghulam Muhammad and Chaudhury Muhammad Ali got the courage to cook up these conspiracies? Surely General Ayub Khan was aware of all that was going on behind the scenes but had preferred to remain mum about them. The politicians had begun to belittle each other and the Pakistani people had no confidence in them any more. Taking advantage of this situation, the leaderless and unprincipled men of the Muslim League made another bid to grab power. When the Constituent Assembly was dissolved and a new cabinet formed it was plain that the so-called leaders of the League had transformed themselves into figureheads to decorate ministerial positions. And the leader of the Muslim League Mohammad Ali forgot all about the country after regaining his position as a minister.

When Mohammad Ali of Bogra became the prime minister he tilted Pakistan towards a certain bloc. The world then was divided into two blocs, one Russian and the other American, one socialist and the other democratic/capitalist. Of course Pakistan had been leaning towards the American bloc since the late Liaquat Ali's stewardship of the country. In May 1954 Pakistan signed a military pact with the United States of America. Later, Pakistan joined SEATO [Southeast Asia Treaty Organization] and CENTO [Central Treaty Organization] and signed what was known as the Baghdad Treaty. In the process, the country came totally under American influence. Russia and China assumed that these treaties/pacts were directed against them. It could be said that the treaties had elements that are clearly opposed to communism. The newly created state of Pakistan should have followed a neutral and independent foreign policy. We should not have made enemies of any country. It was our duty to become friends with all countries of the world. It should have been a sin for us to even think of joining any military bloc since we should help maintain peace in the world and since peace is imperative to ensure the economic welfare of the people of a country.

Before I was arrested we had published a statement protesting against the Pakistan–American military pact. The Awami League's policy was to pursue a foreign policy that was independent and neutral. When our statement was published in newspapers the Americans became enraged. An American reporter met Mr Huq and published a report in an American newspaper based on his interview with him. This report was cited by Mohammad Ali in his statement. The reason Mohammad Ali gave so much importance to what an American journalist had reported was of course that both the journalist and Mr Ali were Americans!

Ghulam Muhammad had dissolved the Constituent Assembly unlawfully. Nevertheless, it delighted the people of the country. The members of the assembly may have had the legal right to hold the office but had no moral right to do so any more. People could no longer have any confidence in a body that had been in existence for eight years without giving the country a constitution and that had conspired to dismiss an elected government. Of course, Ghulam Muhammad had acted the way he did, not out of patriotism but out of an instinct for self-preservation and to protect the interests of a coterie representing special agenda. Though I was fully aware that what he had done was wrong I was happy because this Constituent Assembly had no intention of giving the country a constitution. And how could an independent nation progress without a constitution? Even though the members of the Constituent Assembly were not bothered about the issue we were ashamed at their apathy. Most members of the Constituent Assembly belonged to the Muslim League. When the Muslim League leaders were wagging their tails in submission it was only Mr Tamizuddin, (President [Speaker] of the Pakistan Constituent Assembly), who had filed a case against Ghulam Muhammad's action. We were of course in jail at that time and all the information that we could gather came from reading newspaper reports, which we discussed with each other.

Some of our fellow prisoners were released soon afterwards. Now Yar Mohammad Khan, Dewan Mahbub Ali, Bijoy Chatterjee, Professor Ajit Guha, Mohammad Toaha, Korban Ali and I were put in one part of the prison. We were passing time there somehow. Professor Guha took charge of our food requirements. He was a good chef. Although he was unwell he used to do the cooking. After he was released Mr Toaha took up the cooking chores. He wasn't as good a chef as the professor but what he cooked was edible. Every now and then a few of us would tease him about his cooking. He would get so exasperated at this that he would quit cooking and we would plead with him to cook for us again. Fortunately, he was not the type to harbour feelings of resentment for long. It was tough for

Korban Ali to survive in such a situation though, since the food he was served was never enough to satisfy him. He was a big man and had a healthy appetite.

One day they took Korban to the jail gate, saying that he was going to be released. He duly took leave of us and left for the jail gate with his baggage. There he met an IB official who produced a release order and another piece of paper, asking him to sign a bond if he wanted to be freed. If he did not sign the bond, he was told he'd be back in jail. Korban was the stubborn type. He got mad at the man, berated him, returned to the jail and narrated what had happened. Only those who have had the unfortunate experience of getting a release order after languishing in jail for a long time and being taken to the jail gate only to be sent back again will be able to tell you how terrible that experience is. The next day we told the jail authorities that they should not play this trick with us again. If there were any bonds to sign or lawsuits to deal with they should tell us beforehand. If any of us had to come back again after reaching the jail gate with our baggage thinking that we had been freed, we would surely create a ruckus. As political prisoners, we had submitted no applications for our release and there could be no question of us signing any bonds for this purpose.

A few days later another IB official came to meet me. He thought he had worked out a pretty smart way to make me sign the bond. He wasn't going to bring up the subject of signing a bond with me directly. Or perhaps he was feeling embarrassed to do so. I said to him, 'Please don't loiter here. If you really want to talk to me you can stay, but you can take this from me in writing—and you can tell your handlers the same thing too—there can be no question of me signing a bond. What you should do is tell the government to sign a bond promising to play no such trick with me again. And tell them that they shouldn't detain anyone without a trial any more.' The man broke into a smile and said, 'Did I ask you to sign a bond?' I too couldn't help smiling at his disingenuousness.

My days in prison continued somehow. I saw in the newspapers that Ataur Rahman Khan had gone to Zurich to meet Mr Suhrawardy. From there he was scheduled to go to London to talk to Maulana Bhasani. Three Awami League leaders who had accompanied the Maulana to England had not been able to return to the country. They were Professor Mozzaffar Ahmed, Khondokar Mohammad Ilias and Advocate Zamiruddin. This is because they knew they would be arrested the moment they landed in Pakistan. How were they managing to survive in England? Who was supporting them financially? Apparently, the many Bengalis living in that country had managed to find accommodation for them and were helping them in many ways.

In Karachi, Ataur Rahman Khan had a meeting with Ghulam Muhammad. At that time the secretary of the All Pakistan Awami League was Karachi's Mahmudul Huq Osmani. Mr Osmani was with Mr Khan when he went to meet Ghulam Muhammad. When Mr Khan came back to East Bengal he met Manik Mia and many other people. I could understand from his movements that we were in for another round of the politics of conspiracy. It wouldn't be right for the Awami League to get entangled in any of this politicking. But I was a prisoner now and who would get to listen to anything I had to say on the subject?

Apparently Mr Ataur Rahman Khan was going to Zurich to convey a message from Ghulam Muhammad to Mr Suhrawardy. We did a lot of brainstorming to figure out what kind of a message he would be carrying. Surely the first thing Mr Ataur Rahman Khan should have asked for is the release of all political prisoners. If any meetings were going to take place with Mr Ghulam Muhammad and other Muslim League leaders Mr Khan's agenda should have included the question of bringing Maulana Bhasani home and taking steps to release us from prison. Mr Khan returned from Zurich to Dhaka. Mr Ghulam Muhammad also released an itinerary indicating that he too was coming to Dhaka. No doubt it was a good sign that the most powerful man in Pakistan was coming to the city. However, East Pakistan was then under Governor's rule. The previous government had been dismissed. No new government was to be permitted. The MLAs and political workers were all in jail. The Awami League president was in England and the general secretary in prison. Many of its leaders had arrest warrants ready against them. In such a situation, was it right for the Awami League leader to get all worked up about giving Mr Ghulam Muhammad a princely reception? It seemed hard for me to figure out why they were so eager to receive him. I saw in the papers a photograph of Mr Ataur Rahman Khan and Mr Fazlul Huq lined up in Dhaka airport to receive Mr Muhammad with garlands in their hands. To think that both of them had ended up garlanding Mr Ghulam Muhammad!

For some time now the Awami League and the Krisak Shramik Party had been discussing the issue of giving Mr Muhammad a reception. It had already become obvious that the Krisak Shramik Party was not really an organization with any political ideology behind it. The party only existed as a platform for opportunists to ascend by taking advantage of Mr Huq's popularity. This was their only capital and they were going to use it in their bid to become powerful. They had no real principles or any solid footing. They would be willing to garland not only Mr Ghulam Muhammad but even Mohammad Ali of Bogra to achieve their selfish goals. But the

Awami League was a principled organization, and how could its leaders go about garlanding such an undemocratic man? It was difficult for me to comprehend this attitude. My colleagues and I were very troubled by what was happening. We were depressed at the thought of how crazy our leaders had become to get power. They seemed not to understand how a game had begun amongst the two parties forming the United Front. They had contacted the Awami League and the Krisak Shramik Party separately so that Ghulam Muhammad would get a huge reception when he came to East Bengal. And that is exactly what happened when he arrived. But he had already made up his mind about his course of action. He was going to empower Mohammad Ali to split up the United Front. However, I heard later that Ghulam Muhammad had pledged that when Mr Suhrawardy returned from Zurich he would be made the prime minister. The main industrialists of the country and a few bureaucrats did not want the Awami League to come to power at any cost.

In Dhaka Mohammad Ali had managed to come to an understanding with Mr Huq's party that it would be allowed to form a government in East Bengal if they could get rid of the Awami League. To do so they would have to declare that Mr Suhrawardy had nothing to do with the United Front. This was the strategy that they were going to adopt to keep Mr Suhrawardy away from power. Mohammad Ali knew full well that Mr Suhrawardy was the only person who could claim the right to be prime minister. He had achieved much popularity in both East and West Pakistan and the people of both wings of the country wanted to see him in that position. The West Pakistani leaders who were under Chaudhury Muhammad Ali's control knew that if they made peace with Mr Huq's party they would be able to stay in power without giving autonomy to East Pakistan. But the Awami League was not willing to compromise on the issue of autonomy.

When Mr Suhrawardy returned to Karachi after being cured, he was given a huge public reception. Other than Jinnah no one in Pakistan had ever got such a massive reception. Twenty to thirty leaders of East Bengal had gone to Karachi to receive him on his return. Almost everyone, including Mr Ataur Rahman Khan and Mr Abul Mansur Ahmed, had gone to Karachi to receive him. But almost as soon as he was back in Pakistan members of the Krisak Shramik Party began to say that Mr Suhrawardy was nobody to them and that their only leader was Mr Huq. Mr Huq, for his part, supported Mohammad Ali and not Mr Suhrawardy. When it came to the question of forming a cabinet, Mr Ghulam Muhammad told Mr Suhrawardy that there would be no prime minister in the cabinet since its status was that of a caretaker government. Mr Suhrawardy would be made the prime minister soon enough but for the moment his task was to draft a constitution for the country as its law minister. If Mr Suhrawardy was not going to join the cabinet Mr Ghulam Muhammad would be forced to hand over power to the military. Mr Suhrawardy was thus fooled into becoming the law minister. It was only after he had taken the pledge to become the law minister that Mr Abu Hussein Sarkar became a central minister as Mr Huq's nominee. Mr Suhrawardy was entirely ignorant of all these behind-the-scenes manoeuvrings.

I have no idea what kind of advice Mr Suhrawardy got from our leaders but he certainly made a mistake by joining the cabinet without visiting Lahore and Dhaka and without trying to understand the mood of our people. No matter what the leaders of the Krisak Shramik Party had said to him, if he had summoned a meeting of the United Front after coming to Dhaka and had taken his decision after consulting our leaders no one would have cavilled at his decision. The people of the country would have compelled the leaders of the Krisak Shramik Party to do his bidding. Ordinary citizens of the country were seeing darkness descending everywhere. Their one ray of hope was that Mr Suhrawardy would return to the country and lead it towards democracy. In jail we were saddened by the turn of events and a feeling of frustration crept amongst us now. I too could find no excuse for supporting his decision to become the law minister. Indeed, I was quite angry with him for accepting the position. Many people had requested me to telegram him welcoming him back to the country after he had recovered. I told them, 'No way. I am not going to telegram him and there is no reason for me to do so.'

Renu sent me a telegram to inform me that my father was very ill and had little chance of surviving. She was heading for the village with the children to meet him. She had applied to the Chief Secretary, sending him a copy of the application. At that time Mr M.N. Khan was in this position. He had shown his fondness for me even before he had become the Chief Secretary of East Pakistan. At 8 p.m. I heard he had given my release order. I was sad at the thought of having to leave my colleagues behind, especially Yar Mohammad Khan since he had been arrested when he had come to meet me in prison. As I left them, I said, 'Either you will be released or I'll be back in prison with you again.' When I crossed the prison gate I saw that Nuruddin, our party worker from Roy Saheb Bazar, was waiting for me. He said, 'Your wife has just left for your village home since your father is critically ill. She boarded the steamer from Badamtali Ghat. The launch will reach Narayanganj at 11 p.m. If you rush to Narayanganj you should be able to meet up with her there.' I took him along with me to our house. I had not been to this place previously since Renu had rented it on her own while I was in jail. I left most of my luggage there and took only a few things with me as I headed for Narayanganj. In those days getting a taxi was very difficult. I reached Narayanganj only fifteen minutes before the steamer left the dock. Renu was surprised to see me. The children were sleeping. Renu woke them up. Hasina and Kamal embraced me and wouldn't let go of me for a long time. They refused to sleep afterwards and it seemed to me that they had said goodbye to sleep for that night.

However, any feeling of elation I had dissipated soon. This is because the image of my father kept coming to my mind. I could think of only one thing: would I be able to see him alive again? I left the cabin and stood on the deck for a while. The night breeze was blowing against my cheeks after a long time. In jail they always lock you in after dark and you never get to feel it. When the children finally went to sleep Renu and I talked for a long time. I managed to go to sleep just before daybreak. We would have to stay on the steamer the whole day and would reach our village home at night. Nobody knew exactly what shape my father was in. We would have to journey by boat for two miles. No boat from our village home would be at the ghat to receive us. I was tense the whole day.

When we reached our village home at night we found that my father had been taken to Gopalganj since there was no physician who could treat him in our village. This meant a fourteen-mile journey by boat. When I reached Gopalganj at 10 a.m. the next day I was relieved to find that my father was recovering. The attending physicians, Farid Ahmed and Bijiten Babu, reassured me that there was no cause for worry any more. Both were good doctors and seeing me also lifted my father's spirits. The next day I received a telegram from Mr Ataur Rahman Khan informing me that Mr Suhrawardy wanted me to go to Karachi to meet him. But there could be no question of my leaving that very day.

The next day I left for Dhaka via Khulna and Jessore, where I boarded a plane. From Dhaka I headed for Karachi. I still couldn't reconcile myself to what had happened. How could Mr Suhrawardy accept the position of law minister? I did not try to meet Mr Suhrawardy that night. Who knows how things would turn out if I met him in this state of mind? I might even say something offensive to him. I went to meet him the next day at 9 a.m. at Hotel Metropole. He was getting ready to go out. He said, 'I know that you came here last night; why didn't you meet me then?' I said, 'I was tired; besides, you are now Mohammad Ali's law minister!' He said, 'I guess you are angry with me.' I said, 'Sir, I am not mad but I have been wondering if

I made a mistake by thinking of you as my leader all my life.' He replied, 'I guess I know what you mean but say no more. Meet me at 3 p.m. for I will have a lot to tell you then.'

When I went to meet him at three that afternoon he was taking rest. He hadn't recovered completely and was still quite weak. I sat next to him. Soon, he started to talk to me. What he said amounted to this: Ghulam Muhammad had said to him that if he didn't join the cabinet he would hand over power to the military. I said, 'You could have come to East Bengal, discussed the issue with all of us and then made someone else the minister. As far as I can see, he trapped you. I don't see anything good coming out of your decision to join the cabinet; you won't be able to do anything worthwhile. You are on the way to losing whatever popularity you had earned.' He tried to persuade me that he had taken the right decision. He said, 'If I am not able to achieve anything I will quit politics for good; what harm will that do?' I replied, 'You shouldn't have been a party to this politics of conspiracy. You will rue your decision.' He asked me to chalk out a programme for his visit to East Bengal. I said, 'Until Maulana Bhasani is able to come back to the country and until you are able to secure the release of all political prisoners you should not come to Dhaka.' He was angry at me for saying all these things and said, 'In other words, you are telling me that I shouldn't be going to East Bengal at all.' I replied, 'Yes, I am saying something like that.' He shut his eyes and was quiet for a while. Later, he told me that I should come back to see him the next day exactly at 3 p.m. once more.

While I was in Karachi I saw Mr Abu Hussein Sarkar accepting the position of a minister in the central government. Mr Suhrawardy didn't seem to know anything much about what was happening around him. However, now he became more sensitive to what games were being played there.

Mr Huq told the correspondent of a Lahore newspaper that Mr Suhrawardy wielded no real power in the United Front and that I was actually its leader. But it was the Awami League that had a majority in the United Front. Mr Huq was the chief of the Krisak Shramik Party. The combined seats of this party and the Nizam-E-Islami could not match the number of seats we had. How could Mr Huq say such a thing about the leadership of the Awami League? Mr Huq's party had told Mr Ghulam Muhammad that they did not want Mr Suhrawardy to be the prime minister and would like to see Mohammad Ali of Bogra in this position and that is why Mr Suhrawardy was not made the prime minister. Mr Mohammad Ali, for his part, had declared that a government in East

Bengal should be formed by excluding the Awami League from it. I could understand that Mr Mohammad Ali of Bogra was now depending on Mr Huq to prop him up. On the other hand, Chaudhury Muhammad Ali was depending on Mr Suhrawardy's support. Most Krisak Shramik Party leaders were in Karachi at that time. None of them came to meet Mr Suhrawardy.

When I met a couple of Krisak Shramik Party leaders I said to them that they had achieved quite a few things. The agreement we had reached with them previously had stated that Mr Suhrawardy would be the leader of Pakistan and Mr Huq our leader in East Bengal. Now they had come to Karachi and had made the Muslim League leader Mohammad Ali their leader and were backing him. I pointed out to them that they were doing their best to ensure that Mr Suhrawardy was not going to be the prime minister. We, for our part, would be forced to declare that we were not going to follow Mr Huq any more. If necessary the United Front would bring a no-confidence motion against his leadership. We had not empowered Mr Huq to support Mr Mohammad Ali on behalf of the United Front and accept the leader of the Muslim League as our leader. The leaders of the Krisak Shramik Party had been told that they would be given the right to govern East Bengal. A few leaders of the Awami League had also been given such assurance. Even though I had not been able to see eye to eye with Mr Suhrawardy on the issue of his acceptance of a ministerial position in the central government I still found it impossible to see him being insulted by anyone. I said to Mr Suhrawardy, 'Since Mr Huq has openly declared that you are no one in the United Front we are going to have to prove that you are someone special in the Front. We are going to bring a no-confidence motion against Mr Huq. Let Krisak Shramik Party and Nizam-E-Islami stay in the United Front if they want to. You must have the right to speak within it as the leader of the Awami League since the League has an absolute majority in the East Bengal Legislative Assembly.' Mr Suhrawardy replied, 'As long as the Awami League is part of the United Front I am truly no one in it. Mr Huq is the real leader of the United Front and only he can speak on behalf of the Awami League, the Krisak Shramik Party and the Nizam-E-Islami.'

I returned to Dhaka and sat in a meeting with Mr Ataur Rahman Khan, Abul Mansur Ahmed and Manik Bhai and told them everything that had happened in Karachi. I also conveyed to them Mr Suhrawardy's opinion. We had been informed by this time that Maulana Bhasani had arrived in Calcutta but we had no idea where he was staying in the city. Mr Suhrawardy had rung up the Chief Secretary, N.M. Khan, to free all political prisoners.

Many such prisoners were now being freed gradually. The Krisak Shramik Party leaders had not said one word asking for the release of such prisoners since none of their members were in jail. On the other hand, a lot of Awami League MLAs and workers were still in prison and many had arrest warrants being brandished against them.

The five of us discussed the situation at length. On the question of whether a no-confidence motion should be brought against Mr Huq, some of his associates seemed to be much more active than Mr Huq himself. They were for resolving all differences with the Muslim League without bothering about principles or ideals. Who cared about the twenty-one points and the verdict of the people? Three of us initially expressed some reservations about the issue. They had no problems about tabling the no-confidence motion but were wondering if we could push it through. I declared that there was no reason to think we would not succeed in doing so. After all, there is such a thing as acting on one's principles. In the end everyone agreed with me and I summoned a meeting of our working committee. All the members of this committee supported us on the issue except Mr Salam and Mr Hashimuddin. However, they let it be known that they were aware that they were obliged to follow the working committee's decision.

Mr Ataur Rahman Khan and I set to work to get signatures of all MLAs. The question came up about who was going to stand up in front of Mr Huq to bring the no-confidence motion against him. Many expressed their reluctance to do any such thing and I myself felt embarrassed at the idea of doing so. All of us respected him and were even devoted to him. But now he was surrounded by those so-called leaders. We had failed to snatch him away from their clutches despite a hundred attempts to do so. Many of these people had left the Muslim League only a few months before the elections and had been defeated in the struggle for power. In the end it was decided that I would propose the no-confidence motion and Mr Abdul Ghani, Bar-at-Law, would second it. We requested him to call a meeting of the assembly so that we could bring up the no-confidence motion. He agreed to do so and 113 members of the Awami League signed the petition to bring the motion to a vote.[32]

NOTES

1. Huseyn Shaheed Suhrawardy.
2. The notebooks used for the manuscript were examined by the Deputy Inspector General of Prisons, Dhaka Division, Central Jail, Dhaka, on 9 June 1967 and 22 September 1967. The author had been detained at the Dhaka Cantonment since 17 January 1968 on charges of the Agartala Conspiracy case. It may thefore be assumed that the author wrote this autobiography towards the second half of 1967 during his imprisonment at the Central Jail, Dhaka.
3. Now in Bangladesh.
4. An administrative unit consisting of a group of villages. It is governed by a Union Board, a local government body formed by the union's elected representatives.
5. A rupee had 64 poisha in those days.
6. Head clerk/record keeper of a court.
7. The Swadeshi movement originated from the partition of Bengal in 1905 but had run its course by 1908. Of all the nationalist movements which took place and were considered momentous in the pre-Gandhian era, this was thought to be the most successful. The author here was perhaps referring to the nationalist movement led by Mahatma Gandhi against colonization and probably used the word 'swadeshi' to indicate the hard-core followers of the anti-colonial movement.
8. The author seems to have made an error in naming A.K. Fazlul Huq's party. He mentions the Krisak Shramik Party, which was formed in 1953, instead of the Krisak Praja Party, which was launched by him in 1935, and is relevant in the context.
9. Bulbul Academy of Fine Arts (BAFA). This cultural institution was established in 1955 in Dhaka.
10. The Lahore Resolution (1940) demanded the creation of more than one independent state in areas where the Muslims were numerically in the

majority. However, the Delhi convention of 1946 resolved that a single Muslim state to be formed, rather than more than one state. Critics pointed out that as a result of such an arrangement, the Muslim-majority eastern region would be separated from the western Indian Muslim-majority areas by almost 1000 miles of Indian territory. It was obvious that formation of such a state would be rather impractical.

11. An Indian political party which followed the ideals of Netaji Subhas Chandra Bose.
12. The prime minister of Britain, Lord Atlee, had announced general elections for India in January 1946.
13. Written by Alan Campbell-Johnson, press attaché to Lord Mountbatten.
14. A paramilitary civil defence force with duties similar to that of the National Guard.
15. The language movement was a key factor in the demand for autonomy.
16. Tamuddun Majlish was founded immediately after the creation of Pakistan on 1 September 1947, with the aim to promote Pakistani philosophy and culture among the people.
17. Certain areas in the old part of Dhaka city were inhabited by people who spoke a native version of the Urdu language and were subservient to the Urdu-speaking Nawabs and Muslim League leaders.
18. The story relates to Caliph Omar, the second Caliph of Islam. Once during his reign, free cloth was distributed to all the citizens of Madina Manowara, signifying the equality and fairness with which he dealt with people. However, the length of the piece of cloth distributed was short and it was not possible for a man to make a long dress with it. Since the Caliph wore a long dress made from the same material as was given to everyone, ordinary people around him wondered how he was able to get the additional cloth. His son then stood up and explained that he had given his share of the material to his father so that the Caliph could make a long dress for himself.
19. In order to become a primary member of the Muslim League, individuals had to pay a membership subscription. This collection of membership fees was logged in a receipt book. It is this receipt book that is referred to in this text.
20. H.S. Suhrawardy was the lawyer defending the former chief minister of West Punjab, Naqab Iftikhar Husain Mamdot, who was charged under the Public and Representatives Offices (Disqualification) Act [PRODA], 1949. Suhrawardy was unable to have Mamdot completely exonerated but had him cleared of the charges of taking unwarranted compensation.
21. Division status provides the prisoners with extra privileges, that is, better meals, better accommodation, etc.
22. Since renamed as Manufacturing Department.
23. This order was proclaimed on 7 August 1959 during Ayub Khan's regime. The intention of the regime was to disqualify some leading politicians from taking part in any election.

24. The Rawalpindi Conspiracy case was an attempted coup d'état against the government of Liaquat Ali Khan in 1951. The coup was unsuccessful, and was planned mainly by Major General Akbar Khan in conjunction with other military officers and left-wing Pakistani politicians. Eleven military officers and four civilians were accused in this conspiracy. After an eighteen-month trial carried out in secrecy, Major General Khan and poet Faiz Ahmed Faiz were both convicted and sentenced to long-term imprisonment, while some others received varying sentences. When Huseyn Shaheed Suhrawardy later became the prime minister of Pakistan, he was successful in obtaining reprieve for most of the conspirators.
25. No copy of this speech has been found.
26. During this period the terms 'East Pakistan' and 'East Bengal' were used interchangeably. When British India was partitioned on 14 August 1947 the provinces which constituted the western part of Pakistan were Sind, the Punjab, Baluchistan and the North-West Frontier Province (NWFP). The eastern part of Pakistan constituted entirely of a single province—East Bengal. It was only in October 1955 under the 'One Unit' scheme that East Bengal was officially renamed as East Pakistan and the four provinces in the west became West Pakistan.
27. The document was not attached to the manuscript.
28. Those who did not want Sheikh Mujib as general secretary of the Awami League.
29. Results of 1954 Elections (held in March 1954):

Muslim seats 237

United Front	223	(Awami League 140, Krisak Shramik Party 34, Nizam-E-Islami Party 12, Youth League 15, Ganatantrik Dal 10, Communist Party 4, Independent 8)
Muslim League	9	(1 independent joined after the elections)
Khilafat-e-Rabbani	1	
Independent	4	
	237	

General Seats (non-Muslim members) 72

Congress and others 72

Total Seats: 309 (Muslim League 9; United Front and allies 291, others 9).

Source: Rangalal Sen, Political Elites in Bangladesh. Dhaka: UPL, 1986, pp. 123–25.

30. In an address delivered during a visit to West Bengal on 4 May 1954, the then chief minister of East Bengal Sher-e-Bangla A.K. Fazlul Huq made the following speech: 'It is important that the people of two Bengals should realise the fundamental fact that in order to live happily they must render mutual assistance to each other. Politicians had partitioned territories, but

the common mass should ensure that everybody lived peacefully. Language proved to be the most important unifying factor in history and the people of two Bengals, bound together on common language, should forget political divisions and feel themselves to be one.' (Source: *The Morning News*, 5 May 1954. Quoted in Rangalal Sen, *Political Elites in Bangladesh*, Dhaka, UPL, 1986, p. 129.)

31. 'The Governor General of Pakistan had thus added Section 92A to the Government of India Act, 1935 according to which, under certain circumstances, the Governor General could issue a proclamation authorizing the Governor of a province to make laws for that province.' (Source: Hamid Khan, *Constitutional and Political History of Pakistan*, 2nd edition, Oxford, Karachi, 2009, p. 113.)
32. Despite having in hand a 'no-confidence proposal' with the signatures of 133 MLAs, Sheikh Mujib's group failed to bring about the passage of a 'no-confidence motion' against Mr A.K. Fazlul Huq. Thirty-five MLAs from the Awami League under the leadership of Mr Salam Khan opposed the motion. Additionally, quite unexpectedly, the MLAs of Krisak Shramik Party and the Nizam-E-Islami Party MLAs put up a joint front in support of Mr Huq. (Source: S.A. Karim, *Sheikh Mujib: Triumph and Tragedy*, 2nd edition, UPL, Dhaka, 2009, p. 63.)

BIOGRAPHICAL NOTES

Ahmed, Abbasuddin (1909–59) Legendary singer and lyricist. He served as Additional Song Organizer in the Publicity Wing of the East Bengal government. His voice popularized folk music all over Bengal.

Ahmed, Abul Mansur (1898–1979) Man of letters, journalist and politician. He was one of the founding members of the Awami League and was largely responsible for drafting the twenty-one-point programme of the United Front. He served as minister with both the provincial and the federal governments of Pakistan.

Ahmed, Aziz (1906–82) He was a senior non-Bengali member of the Civil Service of Pakistan (CSP). He held the position of Chief Secretary of East Pakistan and prevailed on all-important decisions pertaining to East Pakistan. He served under Ayub Khan, Yahya Khan and subsequently as foreign minister under Z.A. Bhutto.

Ahmed, Dr T., A famous ophthalmologist who practised in Calcutta in the 1930s and 1940s.

Ahmed, Kamruddin (1912–82) Author, politician and diplomat. He was one of the leading members of the All-Party State Language Action Committee in 1948 and 1952. He joined the Awami League in 1954 and was appointed to the central committee of the party. In 1957 he quit politics and became a diplomat. He was one of the ideologues responsible for formulating the ideals of the Bengali nationalist movement that was led by Sheikh Mujibur Rahman in the 1960s.

Ahmed, Kazi Bahauddin (1926–98) From 1948 to 1952 Kazi Bahauddin played a leading role in all the events related to the language movement in Barisal district. In 1954 he was appointed assistant director in the Directorate of Immigration and Passports and was promoted to the position of director general of the department. He was regarded and respected for his role as a cultural activist across Bangladesh.

Ahmed, Khondokar Mahbubuddin (1925–) A senior advocate of the Bangladesh High Court, he was a member of Parliament and a member of presidium of the Bangladesh Nationalist Party (BNP).

Ahmed, Khondokar Mushtaq (1918–96) He was the leader of the rightist elements in the Bangladesh Awami League. He was also the controversial foreign minister of the Bangladesh government-in-exile during the War of Liberation. He tacitly encouraged and assisted the conspirators who assassinated Sheikh Mujibur Rahman on 15 August 1975, and he was rewarded by being made President of Bangladesh the very same day.

Ahmed, Khondokar Shamsuddin Famous lawyer and a member of the legislature of undivided Bengal elected from Gopalganj.

Ahmed, Mohiuddin (1925–97) Eminent politician. He was closely associated with all the major political events in East Bengal. He participated in the Bangladesh War of Liberation. He was imprisoned several times during his political career from the British period to the Bangladesh period for differences in opinion and his non-compromising personality. He served as deputy leader of the opposition from 1979 to 1981.

Ahmed, Mollah Jalaluddin (1926–79) Close associate of Sheikh Mujibur Rahman. He was a founding member of both the Students' League and the Awami League. He was a minister in the cabinet formed by Sheikh Mujibur Rahman. He quit the government for health reasons in 1974. He was Mujib's counsel in the Agartala Conspiracy case.

Ahmed, Nuruddin He was a student leader and worker of the Muslim League based in Calcutta during the 1940s. He was from Pirojpur, Barisal. Subsequently, he became a member of the East Bengal Legislative Assembly.

Ahmed, Tajuddin (1925–75) He was general secretary of the Bangladesh Awami League and Sheikh Mujibur Rahman's able deputy. During the Bangladesh liberation war he was prime minister of the Bangladesh government-in-exile. He was an independent-minded political leader. On 3 November 1975 a rebel group of the army assassinated him and three other senior leaders of the Awami League when they were in Dhaka jail.

Ali, Captain M. Mansur (1919–75) Politician and close associate of Sheikh Mujibur Rahman. He was a minister in the United Front coalition government led by Ataur Rahman Khan from September 1956 to September 1958. He was finance minister in the cabinet formed in Mujibnagar by the Bangladesh government during the War of Liberation and continued as a minister after 1972. In 1975 he was made its prime minister. His contribution in establishing the sovereign country of Bangladesh was immense. A rebel group of the army murdered him when he was in Dhaka jail.

Ali, Chaudhury Muhammad (1905–80) After Partition, he was appointed Secretary General of the Pakistan government and held this position till 1951. In 1951 he was promoted to finance minister. Four years later, in 1955, he was appointed the fourth prime minister of Pakistan.

Ali, Khan Saheb Osman A leading member of the Awami League from Narayanganj. He was also a member of the Legislative Assembly.

Ali, Korban (1924–90) He was elected to the East Bengal Legislative Assembly on a United Front ticket and was also a member of the Bangladesh National Assembly in 1973. He was minister of information and radio in the 1975 cabinet formed by Sheikh Mujibur Rahman. He joined the cabinet of the military government formed by Lieutenant General Ershad on 13 June 1984 and was in charge of various ministries.

Ali, Mohammad (of Bogra) (1900–63) Pakistan's prime minister 1953–55. He was the foreign minister in Ayub Khan's cabinet during 1962–63.

Ali, Syed Nausher (1890–1972) Lawyer and politician, who was elected to the Bengal Legislative Assembly in 1929. He joined Fazlul Huq's cabinet of Bengal in 1937 but resigned due to differences of opinion. He then joined the Indian National Congress. He later became Speaker of the Bengal Legislative Assembly and a member of the Upper House of the Indian Parliament.

Ali, Tafazzal (1905–88) Deputy Speaker, Bengal Legislative Assembly 1945, central commerce minister of Pakistan 1955 and Ambassador to Egypt 1957.

Amin, Nurul (1893–1974) Once the chief minister of East Pakistan. In 1952 he directed the police to fire upon students and the masses during the language movement. This led to the death of many protesters. He also opposed the liberation movement and the independence of Bangladesh. After Bangladesh became independent he became a citizen of Pakistan and was appointed vice-president of that country.

Azad, Maulana Abul Kalam (1888–1958) Prominent leader of the Indian National Congress. He became education minister of India after the country became independent. He played a major part in building modern-day India.

Banu, Lulu Bilkis Daughter of Syed Mahmud Taifur, who authored a famous book on the history of Dhaka. A member of an enlightened and famous family of the region, she also well known for her work as a cultural activist.

Begum, Nadira A prominent woman political activist during the 1940s and the 1950s. She is the sister of professors Kabir Chowdhury and Munier Chowdhury.

Begum, Noorjahan (1925–) Daughter of Mohammad Nasiruddin, the editor of *Saugat*, and herself the editor of *Begum*, a popular weekly for women. In this role she was one of the leaders of the women's movement in her time.

Bhasani, Maulana Abdul Hamid Khan (1880–1976) A politician. Though he was born in Bangladesh, his political career started in Assam. He joined the Indian National Congress in Assam in 1919, participated in the Khilafat and non-cooperation movements and was imprisoned for ten months. In 1926 he initiated the Krisak Praja movement in Assam. In 1937 he joined the Muslim League. He then led a movement in Assam to protest against the atrocities committed against the Bengalis. Subsequently in 1944 Bhasani was elected president of Provincial Muslim League of Assam, and played an active role in the movement for Pakistan.

He was arrested in 1947 in Assam. On being freed in 1948, he returned to East Bengal where he was elected founder president of the East Pakistan Muslim Awami League. In 1957 he left the Awami League and formed the National Awami Party and was elected president of the party. He played leading roles in all the major political events, such as the Partition of 1947, language movement of 1952, mass movement of 1969 and the Bangladesh War of Liberation in 1971. Maulana Bhasani led or participated in all the important peasant and labour movements and fought for the rights of the working people.

Bose, Manoj (1901–87) Famous novelist and publisher.

Bose, Sharat Chandra (1889–1950) Lawyer and politician, and elder brother of Netaji Subhas Chandra Bose. He opposed the partitioning of Bengal when the movement to split India was launched. With Huseyn Shaheed Suhrawardy he attempted to create a sovereign United Bengal.

Bose, Subhas Chandra (1897–1945) This legendary leader of the Indian independence movement formed the Azad Hind Fauj to liberate India from British rule through armed resistance.

Chowdhury, Abu Sayeed (1921–87) A high court judge, Mr Chowdhury was variously the Vice Chancellor of Dhaka University, foreign minister and President of Bangladesh (1972–73).

Chowdhury, Fazlul Quader (1919–73) A student leader of undivided Bengal and subsequently a leader of the Muslim League. He was a member of the East Pakistan Legislative Assembly and became a minister in the Pakistan central government. He was eventually elected Speaker of the Pakistan National Assembly. He opposed the six-point movement launched by Sheikh Mujibur Rahman. He also opposed the Bangladesh liberation war and the movement for independence. He played a key role in the activities of the Razakars (an organization devoted to assisting the Pakistan Army) in Chittagong during the liberation period. He was arrested after the liberation of Bangladesh and charged with being an enemy agent. He died in 1973.

Chowdhury, Habibullah Bahar (1906–66) Writer, journalist, orator, sportsman and health minister of East Pakistan.

Chowdhury, Hamidul Huq (1901–92) Politician, lawyer and newspaper owner. He was a member of the Radcliffe Commission that was given the responsibility of demarcating the Indo-Pakistan border. He became a minister in the East Pakistan government and then foreign minister and finance minister in the Pakistan government. He was one of the men who led the forces that opposed the creation of Bangladesh in East Pakistan.

Chowdhury, Kafiluddin (1899–1972) Lawyer, politician and Awami League minister in the United Front government of East Pakistan. He played a prominent role in 1953 in the formation of the United Front. He began his political career with the Muslim League and then switched to the Krisak Shramik Party before joining the Awami League, where he played an important role. He took active part in the war of liberation as a member of the National Assembly. He is the father of Dr Badruddoza Chowdhury, former President of Bangladesh.

Chowdhury, Moazzem Ahmed (1922–2002) Political activist and businessman. Elected to Pakistan National Assembly 1965 and actively participated in organizing the War of Liberation in 1971.

Chowdhury, Moazzem Hossain, aka Lal Mia (1905–67) A leader of the Muslim League and a member of the Pakistan National Assembly, Moazzem Hossain Chowdhury was popularly known as Lal Mia. He was a central minister and chief whip of the ruling parliamentary party.

Chowdhury, Munier (1925–71) Legendary dramatist, orator, teacher, man of letters and linguist. He was a very popular professor at the Bengali department of the University of Dhaka. He was imprisoned for taking part in the 1952 language movement. At the request of his fellow prisoners, he wrote the famous play *Kabar* (Graveyard) during captivity, and these political prisoners staged the play in prison. He was murdered by the Al-Bader army in the final days of the war of liberation.

Chowdhury, Yusuf Ali, aka Mohan Mia (1905–71) He was elected to the Legislative Assembly of undivided Bengal on a Muslim League ticket. When he was expelled from the Muslim League in 1953 he joined A.K. Fazlul Huq's Krisak Shramik Party. He became a member of Fazlul Huq's cabinet after the United Front won the provincial elections in East Pakistan in 1954. He took part in the movement launched to oppose Ayub Khan and establish democracy. However, he opposed the Bangladesh liberation movement in 1971.

Chowdhury, Zahur Ahmad (1916–74) A politician and labour leader who became a member of the cabinet formed by the Bangladesh government after independence. He made a significant contribution to the movement for autonomy that led to the birth of Bangladesh in 1971.

Chundrigar, I.I. (1899–1960) He was a member of the first cabinet of Pakistan after the country was created in 1947. He replaced Suhrawardy as the prime minister of Pakistan for two months (October–December 1957).

Danesh, Haji Mohammad (1900–86) A famous peasant leader from Dinajpur.

Das, Deshbandhu Chittaranjan (1870–1925) A famous lawyer and politician and the first mayor of the Calcutta Corporation. He was celebrated for playing a key role in bringing Hindus and Muslims together to sign the Bengal Pact of 1923.

Das, Purna A revolutionary college principal of Madaripur. The great poet Nazrul Islam composed the poem 'Purno Abhinandan' (Greetings for Purna Das) on his release from prison. This poem was collected in his *Bhangar Gan*. In it the poet referred to Purna Chandra Das as Madaripur's great hero.

Datta, Dhirendranath (1886–1971) Lawyer and politician. He was elected to the

Bengal Legislative Assembly from the Congress in 1946. After the Partition of India in 1947 he was elected to the Constituent Assembly of Pakistan. He demanded that Bengali be given equal status with Urdu in the Constituent Assembly. This demand was rejected. He was appointed a minister in the cabinet formed by the United Front led by Ataur Rahman Khan in 1954. On 27 March 1971 the Pakistani Occupation Army arrested him from his residence and he has been missing since then.

Faiz, Faiz Ahmed (1911–84) A distinguished intellectual and renowned Urdu poet. He was a member of the All India Progressive Writers' Movement. He had unyielding faith in Marxism. He won the Lenin Peace Prize from the Soviet Union in 1962.

Gauhar, Altaf (1923–2000) A member of the Civil Service of Pakistan. He was the information secretary in Ayub Khan's government.

Ghani, Dr M. Osman Vice Chancellor of Dhaka University from 1963 to 1969.

Ghosh, Prafulla Chandra (1891–1983) The first chief minister of West Bengal, he was re-elected to this position twice.

Guha, Ajit Kumar (1914–69) An academic celebrated for his work on Bengali language and literature. He served for a long time in the Bengali department of Jagannath College and ultimately headed the department. He also taught as adjunct faculty at the University of Dhaka's Bengali department. An intellectual who had an acute sense of politics, he was celebrated as a cultural activist. He was imprisoned for the part he played in the language movement of 1952.

Gurmani, Nawab, aka Mia Mushtaq Ahmed Khan Gurmani (1905–?) A member of the Punjab Legislative Council (1930 and 1932–36) and of the Punjab Legislative Assembly (1937–46). He was Governor of Punjab and later of West Pakistan between 1954 and 1957.

Hafiz, Mirza Golam (1920–2000) A lawyer and pro-Chinese politician who played a leading role in Bhasani's National Awami Party politics. He opposed the independence of Bangladesh. He joined the government of the military dictator Ziaur Rahman, having won a seat in Parliament from the Bangladesh Nationalist Party. He was elected Speaker of the Bangladesh National Assembly.

Hashim, Abul (1905–74) Renowned politician and Islamic thinker. His father, Abul Kashem, was well known as a leader of the Congress party in Burdwan. He attained a law degree from Calcutta University and began practising law in the city. In 1936 he was elected to the Legislative Assembly from Burdwan as an independent candidate. He joined the Muslim League in 1937. He was made general secretary of the Bengal Muslim League in 1943. He adopted a number of measures then to make the Muslim League a modern, democratic and economic- and social-reform-minded political party and undertook schemes to train its workers accordingly. He took steps to publish the weekly *Millat* which propagated the idea of a Muslim League oriented towards the masses. He worked with

Suhrawardy and Sharat Bose for an independent, undivided Bengal. It was at this time that Sheikh Mujibur Rahman became intimate with him. He moved to East Pakistan in 1950. He was jailed for participating in the language movement. However, in 1962 he deviated ideologically and joined the Convention Muslim League headed by Ayub Khan. But he would lend his support to the six-point programme launched by Sheikh Mujibur Rahman later and would oppose the Pakistan government's move to ban Rabindra Sangeet. He was a brilliant orator, scholar and Islamic thinker.

Hossain, Sirajuddin (1929–71) An intellectual and journalist who was martyred in 1971.

Hossain, Tofazzal, aka Manik Mia (1919–69) Renowned journalist and political commentator. A disciple of Huseyn Shaheed Suhrawardy, he promoted democracy and secularism. He made a unique contribution to the creation of Bangladesh through *Ittefaq*, the newspaper he edited. He gave full support to Sheikh Mujibur Rahman's six-point programme through his newspaper and his writing. His pen was active and uncompromising in attacking the Pakistani military administration's role in patronizing communalism and adopting oppressive policies in East Pakistan. The Pakistani government put him behind bars and suspended publication of his newspaper again and again. When in 1964 the Pakistani government fomented Hindu–Muslim riots in Dhaka he took the initiative to publish a joint editorial in leading Dhaka newspapers headlined 'East Pakistan Take a Stand'.

Huda, Mahmud Nurul (1916–96) He was the key man in the founding of the Bengal Muslim Students' League in 1933. He was political secretary of Huseyn Shaheed Suhrawardy from 1943 to 1950. He was also largely responsible for the creation of the Bulbul Academy of Fine Arts.

Huq, A.K. Fazlul (1873–1962) He was elected chief minister of undivided Bengal twice (1937 and 1941) and was legendary for his leadership. He founded the Krisak Praja Party and the Krisak Shramik Party. He became immensely popular by taking the initiative to form the Loans Arbitration Board as chief minister to help farmers extricate themselves from the clutches of moneylenders. Concurrently, he held the portfolio of education minister and implemented policies that would lead to the creation of a middle class among the Muslim peasants of Bengal. He became chief minister of East Pakistan after the formation of Pakistan and later served as the home minister of the country. He was fluent in English, Arabic and Urdu as well as Bengali and had immense charisma. He was popularly known as Sher-e-Bangla.

Huq, Shamsul (1918–65) He was general secretary of the East Pakistan Awami Muslim League. He was imprisoned for taking part in the 1952 language movement. Later he became mentally imbalanced while in prison.

Hussein, Khairat (1924–72) A councillor of the All-India Muslim League from 1937 to 1947. He was nominated to the Bengal Legislative Assembly by the

Muslim League as the representative from Rangpur in 1946. As a protest against the anti-people policies of the Nazimuddin-led government he quit the Pakistan Muslim League in 1948. A founder-member of the Awami League, he gave his support to the language movement. He was elected to the East Bengal Legislative Assembly in 1954 on a United Front ticket.

Iftekharuddin, Mia Muhammad (1908–62) He became a member of the Punjab Legislative Assembly on a Congress ticket in 1937. He joined the Muslim League in 1945. From 1947 to 1954 he was a member of the Pakistan Constituent Assembly. He was the founder of the Azad Pakistan Party (1950–56) and one of the founders and a major figure of the National Awami Party of Pakistan. He also owned the daily *Pakistan Times*.

Ilias, Khondokar Mohammad (1923–95) Writer, cultural activist and politician. Among his books are *Bhasani Jokhon Europe* (When Bhasani was in Europe), *Kato Chabi Kato Gaan* (So many pictures and so much music) and *Mujibbad* (The philosophy of Mujibism).

Islam, Kazi Nazrul (1899–1976) Leading poet in Bengali literature. His popularity as a poet is next only to Rabindranath Tagore's. He wielded the pen against the British Raj in India and was accused of treason and jailed by the British government. He is popularly known as a rebel poet. Nazrul Islam is the National Poet of Bangladesh. Nazrul's short stories, novels, essays and plays are also highly ranked. As a lyricist, music composer and singer he earned outstanding fame among the masses.

Islam, Syed Nazrul (1925–75) A close associate and trusted lieutenant of Sheikh Mujibur Rahman, he was a lawyer and politician. He became acting president in the Bangladeshi government formed in Mujibnagar in 1971. After Bangladesh was liberated he served as minister for industries and then vice-president. He was killed by rebel army men when he was in Dhaka jail.

Jinnah, Muhammad Ali (1876–1948) Founder of Pakistan and the nation's first Governor General.

Kabir, Humayun (1906–69) Famous writer, intellectual and political leader. He was India's minister of scientific research and culture.

Kasuri, Mian Mahmud Ali (1910-?) An eminent lawyer and left-wing politician of Pakistan, a human rights activist and a jurist of standing, he was one of the founders of the National Awami Party. He joined the Pakistan People's Party of Zulfikar Ali Bhutto in 1970 and worked for the adoption of a consensus constitution by the National Assembly of Pakistan in 1973. In 1973 he quit the party in protest against its anti-democratic activities under the dictatorial leadership of Zulfikar Ali Bhutto. He then joined the opposition party Tehriq-e-Istiqlal, under the leadership of Air Vice Marshal Asghar Khan. He was a recipient of the Soviet government's Stalin Prize for Peace.

Khaddar, Abdul Jabbar (1897–1977) He played a key role in setting up the Awami League. After he was refused nomination by the United Front in 1954, he contested as an independent candidate and was elected a member of the Legislative Assembly of East Bengal. Later, he opposed the 1971 War of Liberation. He was also a notable organizer of cooperatives, banks and insurance companies.

Khaliquzzaman, Chaudhury (1889–1973) After Muhammad Ali Jinnah had relinquished the position of president of the Muslim League, Chaudhury Khaliquzzaman became the president of the organization. He then served as the Governor of East Pakistan from 31 March 1950 to 31 March 1953.

Khan, A.Z., aka Akramuzzaman Khan (1888–1933) A very popular sub-divisional officer (SDO) of Gopalganj. He died suddenly and was buried there. A brilliant officer of the Bengal Administrative Service, Mr Khan came from the famous Khan family of Manikganj's Harirampur subdivision's Dadrokhi village.

Khan, Abdul Monem (1899–1971) A Muslim League leader who had been involved in peasant politics but was also active in communal politics. He opposed the language movement in East Pakistan as well as all democratic movements there. He became a cabinet minister of the Pakistani central government. The military dictator General Ayub Khan considered him a trusted lieutenant and appointed him the Governor of East Pakistan. Vehemently opposed to the idea of autonomy for East Pakistan and the six-point programme led by Sheikh Mujibur Rahman, Monem Khan put Sheikh Mujibur behind bars and tortured him on many occasions. He was killed in 1971 when freedom fighters attacked his house.

Khan, Abdus Salam (1906–72) Lawyer and politician. Initially a leader who took an active part in the Pakistan movement and the Muslim League, he broke off from the League because of the Pakistan government's undemocratic and autocratic rule. He joined the Awami League soon after it was founded in 1949. Under the United Front he was appointed to the East Pakistan Legislative Assembly in 1954 and made a minister in its cabinet. In 1955 he quit the Awami League when it decided to drop the word 'Muslim' from its name. He returned to the Awami League later and became a member of the party's central committee. However, he left the party once again to form a pro-Pakistan party called the Pakistan Democratic Party. He was then made the president of this party. He was the chief lawyer for Sheikh Mujibur Rahman during the Agartala Conspiracy trials in 1969.

Khan, Ali Amjad He became a lawyer and practised in Dhaka and Calcutta. He was instrumental in the formation of the Awami Muslim League (later Awami League), and was its founding vice-president. His residence in Dhaka became the meeting place of top leaders and politicians at that time. Due to political differences he resigned from the Awami League. For a while he was associated with some of the minor political parties and later joined the Ayub regime.

Khan, Amiruzzaman (1923–92) Son of Akramuzzaman Khan. He was director general of Bangladesh Television.

Khan, Ataur Rahman (1907–91) Politician and lawyer. He was founding vice-president of the Awami League. He was one of the leading members of the executive committee of the All-Party State Language Action Committee and joint convener of the United Front. He was appointed minister for civil supplies in the East Bengal government headed by A.K. Fazlul Huq. He was chief minister of East Bengal 1956–58. He joined BAKSAL, the party formed by Sheikh Mujibur Rahman in the 1970s. He also was part of the cabinet formed by Lieutenant General Hussein Muhammad Ershad and served as its prime minister for nine months in 1984.

Khan, Hakim Mohammad Azmal (1865–1927) He was a well-known physician of the Unani School, an author and a politician. He was a leader with an all-India following. He gave up the title as well as the gold medal conferred on him by the British government in protest against the Jallianwala Bagh massacre.

Khan, Ibrahim (1894–1978) Renowned writer and educationist. He was principal of Korotia Sadat College, Tangail, and member of the Bengal Legislative Assembly (1946) and the Pakistani National Assembly (1962).

Khan, Khan Abdul Ghaffar (1890–1988) Legendary figure in the subcontinent for his role in the anti-colonial struggle. This great leader also became famous later as the 'Frontier Gandhi' for his work in the North West Frontier Province of Pakistan.

Khan, Khan Abdul Quayyum (1901–81) A major figure in Pakistani politics as well as in the North West Frontier Province.

Khan, Liaquat Ali (1896–1951) Pakistan's first prime minister. He was assassinated on 16 October 1951 in Rawalpindi.

Khan, Maulana Mohammad Akram (1868–1968) Journalist and politician. He was the founding editor of the daily *Azad* and a founding member of the Muslim League. He was president of the East Pakistan Muslim League, vice-president of the All-Pakistan Muslim League and a member of the Pakistan National Assembly. He retired from politics in 1954. He made a significant contribution to the Bengal Muslim Renaissance in pre-partition Bengal. He was also a pioneering journalist of Bengali Muslims.

Khan, Mohammad Ayub (1907–74) Pakistan's President from 1960 to 1969. In 1951 he became the Commander-in-Chief of the Pakistani Army and in 1954–55 he was the defence minister of the country. In October 1958 he became the Chief Martial Law Administrator and took over the complete control of the country through a military coup. Till 1962 he ruled the country through martial law and till 1969 through a political system he had come up with. He attempted to legitimize his rule over Pakistan through a referendum held in 1962.

Khan, Moulvi Tamizuddin (1889–1963) Politician and lawyer. He was imprisoned from 1921 to 1923 during British rule for taking part in the non-cooperation movement. He was nominated by the Congress in 1926 and 1929 to the Bengal Legislative Assembly. He joined the Muslim League in 1930. He was a member of Fazlul Huq's cabinet in the Government of Bengal from 1937 to 1941 and was elected president of the Pakistan Constituent Assembly.

Khan, Mujibur Rahman (1910–84) Editor and man of letters. He edited the monthly *Mohammadi* and was chairman of the editorial board of the daily *Azad*. He wrote the famous book titled *Pakistan*.

Khatun, Anwara (1919–88) One of the founders of the Awami Muslim League. She was married to Mr Ali Amjad Khan. She was active in the political arena, and had worked closely with H.S. Suhrawardy, Maulana Bhasani, Sheikh Mujibur Rahman and others. A lawyer and teacher, she had obtained MA, BT and LLB degrees. She was the first woman to be elected a member of the Bengal Legislative Assembly before the Partition of India and was again elected a member of the East Pakistan Assembly in 1954. She made inspiring speeches to motivate female students during the 1952 language movement.

Khurshid, K.H. (1924–88) Muhammad Ali Jinnah's secretary from 1942 until Jinnah's death. He wrote *Memoirs of Jinnah* (OUP, Karachi, 1990). President of 'Azad Kashmir' under Pakistani control 1949–75, he was dismissed by the Bhutto government.

Kidwai, Rafi Ahmed (1894–1954) A socialist and leader of the Indian independence movement. He led the Muslims in the United Province National Congress. After independence, he was communications minister and then food minister in Nehru's cabinet.

Kitchlu, Dr Saifuddin (1888–1963) A leader of India's freedom struggle, barrister and a leading Muslim nationalist. In 1924 he was elected general secretary of the All India Congress Committee. He was a recipient of the Lenin Peace Prize in 1952.

Lal Mia see Chowdhury, Moazzem Hossain.

Majumdar, Phani Bhushan (1901–81) A staunch follower of Netaji Subhas Bose during the British rule in India. He was leader of the Forward Bloc. He was closely associated with the Awami League from the time of its formation in East Pakistan. He was minister in the Awami League government.

Malek see Malik, Dr Abdul Motaleb.

Malik, Dr Abdul Motaleb, aka Malek (1905–77) Politician, labour leader as well as an ophthalmologist. He was a leader of the Muslim League and was elected both to the Bengal Legislative Assembly and to the Pakistan National Assembly. He served as a provincial minister and was also part of the central government cabinet. During the War of Liberation he was appointed Governor of East Pakistan by the Pakistani military regime. For assisting the Pakistan occupation forces in carrying out genocide he was sentenced to life imprisonment after Bangladesh became independent. Later he was freed in a general amnesty.

Mandol, Jogendra Nath (1906–56) A leader of the Dalits, he was a member of the Pakistan Constituent Assembly and the first law minister of Pakistan. He was the highest-ranking Hindu in any Pakistani cabinet.

Manik Bhai, see Hossain, Tofazzal.

Manik Mia, see Hossain, Tofazzal.

Mia Mushtaq Ahmed Khan Gurmani see Gurmani, Nawab.

Mir, Titu (1782–1831) His real name was Mir Nisar Ali. He came under the influence of the Wahabi doctrine when he went on a pilgrimage to Mecca. On his return to India in 1827 he began a movement for the reform of Islamic practices in the region. He organized weavers and farmers in the Nadia and 24 Parganas districts of West Bengal and launched a movement to oppose the oppressive indigo cultivators and zamindars. His confrontation with the zamindars was eventually transformed into a full-scale war with the British. In 1831 he constructed a bamboo fort in Narkelbaria and launched an independence movement. He was martyred on 19 November 1831 when he was hit by English cannon fire.

Mirza, Iskander (1899–1969) Pakistan's President in 1955–56. In 1954 he was Governor of East Pakistan.

Modabber, Mohammad (1908–84) Journalist and man of letters. He was news editor of the *Daily Azad* for a long time.

Mohammadullah, Mohammad (1921–99) He was the fourth President of the People's Republic of Bangladesh while Sheikh Mujibur Rahman was prime minister. Subsequently, he joined the Bangladesh Nationalist Party and was elected a member of Parliament.

Mohan Mia see Chowdhury, Yusuf Ali.

Moni, Sheikh Fazlul Huq (1939–75) A politician, journalist and writer who was instrumental in giving a socialist dimension to the Awami League's policies. He played a noteworthy role in the creation of independent Bangladesh.

Mookerjee, Shyama Prasad (1901–53) A famous leader of undivided Bengal, an advocate of education and a man committed to social welfare. He was the second son of Sir Ashutosh Mookerjee. He was the finance minister in the cabinet formed in 1941 known as the Bengal Progressive Coalition. He eventually became a minister in the Indian central government. In 1950 he formed the political party devoted to the ideology of Hindutva known as Jana Sangh.

Muhammad, Ghulam (1895–1956) Pakistan's Governor General between 1951 and 1954.

Mullick, Mukunda Bihari A prominent leader of the Dalits of Bengal.

Nandi, Dr Manmatha Nath, A physician renowned in Dhaka for the part he played in progressive movements as well as his selfless care for ordinary people. He was forced to leave Dhaka by the East Pakistan government in the mid 1960s. He then relocated to Jalpaiguri in West Bengal and died there.

Nasiruddin, Mohammad (1888–1994) His crowning achievement was editing and publishing the famous literary monthly *Saugat* from Calcutta but he will be remembered too for being one of the pioneers of the awakening of Bengali Muslims.

Nazimuddin, Khawaja (1894–1964) He was a member of the Dhaka Nawab family. A barrister from London's Middle Temple, he later joined the Muslim League. In 1929 he became the education minister of Bengal. Contesting for elections to the Bengal Legislative Assembly's Patuakhali seat in 1937, he lost to the popular leader A.K. Fazlul Huq. Later, with the help of Huseyn Shaheed Suhrawardy, he stood for, and won, a by-election in Calcutta. He was then elected home minister in the Bengal coalition ministry formed when the Krisak Praja Party and the Muslim League formed an alliance. In 1943 he became the chief minister in the cabinet formed by the Muslim League under his leadership. After the creation of Pakistan he became the first chief minister of East Pakistan. He was one of the leading opponents of the move to establish Bengali as Pakistan's major state language. He later became Governor General and prime minister of Pakistan.

Nehru, Pandit Jawaharlal (1889–1964) A leader of the Indian National Congress and the first prime minister of independent India.

Nishtar, Sardar Abdur Rab (1899–1958) A leading figure of the West Pakistan Muslim League and a front-ranking member of the movement for Pakistan. He became communication minister of Pakistan and was also appointed Governor of the Punjab province.

Nizami, Hamid (1915–62) Eminent journalist of Pakistan and founder-editor of the Urdu daily *Nawa-i-Waqt*.

Patel, Sardar Vallabhbhai (1875–1950) A front-ranking leader of the Indian National Congress. He was deputy prime minister and home minister in Jawaharlal Nehru's cabinet after India achieved independence.

Pir Aminul Hasnat see Sharif, Pir Manki.

Rahman, Azizur A prominent organizer of the Awami League in Mymensingh. He owned the Rubi Press. He was well known as a cultural activist of Mymensingh.

Rahman, Fazlur (1905–66) A leader of the Muslim league and a central minister in the Pakistan government. He was all for making Urdu the only official language of Pakistan and recommended the use of Arabic as the basis of the Bengali script.

Rahman, Hamoodur (1910–75) Dhaka High Court judge (1954–60) and later a Chief Justice of the Pakistan Supreme Court.

Rahman, Mashiur (1920–71) A lawyer and politician who was also well known as a leader of the Awami League. He hailed from Jessore. He was a minister in the United Front cabinet headed by Ataur Rahman Khan in 1954. The Pakistani army murdered him brutally in 1971.

Rahman, Mohammad Zillur (1923–) An advocate by profession; also a close associate of Sheikh Mujibur Rahman. He is at present the President of Bangladesh.

Rahman, Saidur (1909–87) Educationist, philosopher and an intellectual fully committed to advocating the freedom of thought. He was principal of Jagannath College, Dhaka. His memoir is called *Shatabdir Smriti* (Memories of a century).

Rahman, Shah Azizur (1925–87) A politician who opposed the birth of Bangladesh. General Ziaur Rahman made him prime minister of Bangladesh (April 1979–March 1982).

Rashid, Abdur (1912–2003) SDO, Alipur in the 1940's. He was also a football player and secretary of the Calcutta Mohammedan Club. A CSP officer who retired as Federal Secretary, ministry of communication, Government of Pakistan.

Rashid, Begum Zerina (1921–2002) A prominent social activist. Wife of Abdur Rashid, CSP, she led Muslim League women's volunteers for Sylhet Referendum in which Sheikh Mujib also played a part in the men's volunteer group.

Rasmoni, Rani (1793–1861) A well-known zamindar of Bengal during the British period.

Roy, Kiran Shankar (1891–1949) Educationist and politician, an intimate of Netaji Subhas Chandra Bose. He was home minister in the West Bengal cabinet led by Bidhan Chandra Roy.

Sabur, Khan Abdus (1908–82) A politician who served as communications minister for eight years in Ayub Khan's cabinet. He was one of the main opponents of the movement to establish Bangladesh. He was famed for his oratory, parliamentary skills and abilities as a football player.

Saha, R.P. (1896–1971) Ranada Prasad Saha was a philanthropist and social worker. His chief philanthropic achievements include Bharateswari Homes, Kumudini Hospital and Kumudini College in Mirzapur. The Pakistani Army murdered him in 1971.

Sardar, Kader His real name was Mirza Abdul Kader. He was a prominent leader of old Dhaka and a political activist. He was the founder-owner of Lion Cinema.

Sarkar, Abu Hossein (1894–1969) He was elected to the Bengal Legislative Assembly on a Krisak Praja Party ticket. He became a member of the East Bengal Law Federation in 1954. He was appointed the health minister of Pakistan and in 1955 became the chief minister of East Pakistan.

Serniabat, Abdur Rab (1921–75) In his youth he was associated with the left-leaning political organization called the Democratic Party (1952) and with Maulana Bhasani's National Awami Party. He joined the Awami League in 1969. He took active part in the Bangladesh War of Liberation in 1971. After liberation he was given the charge of a number of key ministries. On 15 August 1975 the men who assassinated Sheikh Mujibur Rahman proceeded to his official residence and shot him and his family members. He was married to Sheikh Mujibur Rahman's sister.

Shahabuddin, Khawaja (1899–1977) Younger brother of Khawaja Nazimuddin. A politician, he was a member of the cabinet of undivided Bengal as well as of the central cabinet of Pakistan. As Ayub Khan's information minister, he banned the playing of Tagore songs.

Shamsuddoha, AHM (1901–84) He joined the Indian Police Service in 1924 and held many important positions. In 1952 he was appointed Inspector General of Police of East Pakistan and retired in 1960. In 1965 he became minister for food, agriculture and public works in Ayub Khan's cabinet.

Shariatullah, Haji (1871–1940) He was born in Madaripur district. He was educated in Arabic and Persian in Calcutta, Hooghly and Murshidabad. He went to Mecca when he was eighteen years old and stayed there for sixteen years to learn Arabic and Persian and to gain an Islamic education. He was tutored there by Maulana Murad and a learned divine called Tahir. He later spent two years studying in Cairo's Al-Azhar University where he imbibed Wahabi doctrines. Coming back to his country in 1918, he worked to reform Islamic practices in the region. He launched a movement emphasizing *faraz* or Islamic moral obligations. This was later known as the Faraizi movement. Even though it was initially directed against Hindu zamindars, indigo planters and Islamic heretics, it was later transformed into a movement aimed at overthrowing British rule.

Sharif, Pir Manki, aka Pir Aminul Hasnat (1923–60) He was a religious and yet a progressive leader of North West Frontier Province. He joined the Muslim League in 1945. He was instrumental in helping the North West Frontier Province join Pakistan.

Siddiqui, Justice B.A. He was Chief Justice of the East Pakistan High Court in the final phase of Pakistani rule.

Suhrawardy, Huseyn Shaheed (1892–1963) Sheikh Mujibur Rahman's first political guru. He was a firm believer in western-style democracy. He was famous for his oratorical skills in both Bengali and English. He was the last prime minister of United Bengal (1946) and minister for law and then prime minister of Pakistan.

Suhrawardy, Shahed (1890–1968) Elder brother of Huseyn Shaheed Suhrawardy, a famous educationist and art specialist. He served as ambassador of Pakistan to Spain, Tunisia and Moscow.

Tagore, Rabindranath (1861–1941) Rabindranath Tagore is known as the Bard of Bengali literature. An outstanding genius, he was a poet, playwright, novelist, short story and essay writer, philosopher, lyricist, music composer, singer, painter, actor, social worker and educationist. In 1913 he was awarded the Nobel Prize in Literature.

Tarkabagish, Maulana Abdur Rashid (1900–86) A leader who became prominent because of the part he played in the language movement and as a leader of the Gana Azadi League. Subsequently he became president of the Awami League of East Pakistan.

Toaha, Mohammad (1922–87) A well-known left-wing leader, he was behind the establishment of the Jubo League and played a prominent role in the All-Party State Language Action Committee.

Wahiduzzaman (1912–76) Former leader of the Muslim League and a minister in the central cabinet of Pakistan.

Wasek, Abdul (1909–67) A famous student leader of the 1940s. He had a leading part in the Holwell monument movement. He was elected member of the National Assembly (MNA) for Dhaka-1 seat by the Basic Democrats in 1962.

Zuberi, I.H. Famous educationist and the founder Vice Chancellor of Rajshahi University.

Facsimiles of the jail authority's certifications on notebooks handed over to the author

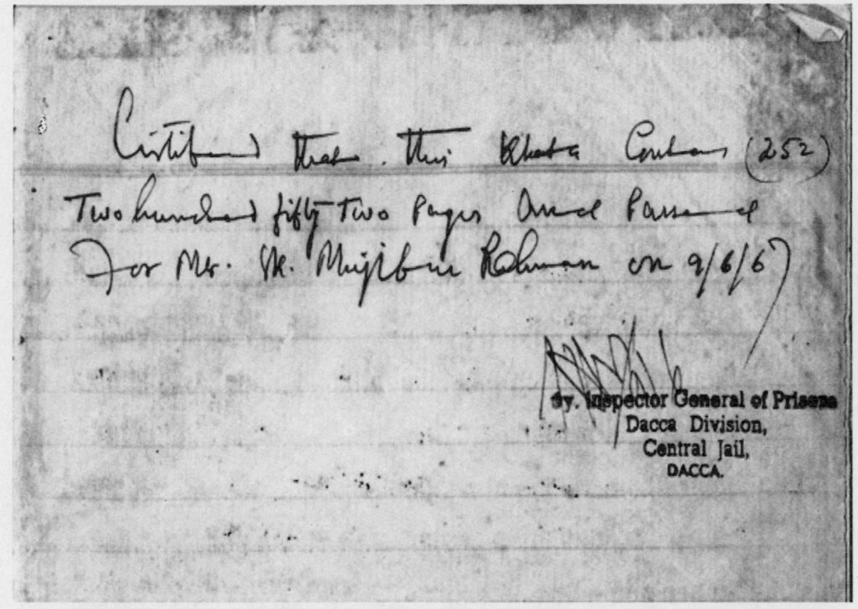

Certified that this Khata Contains (252) Two hundred fifty two Pages and Passed For Mr. Sk. Mujibur Rahman on 9/6/67

Dy. Inspector General of Prisons
Dacca Division,
Central Jail,
DACCA.

Certified that this Khata Contains (220) Two hundred twenty Pages and Passed For Mr. Sk. Mujibur Rahman on 27/9/67

Dy. Inspector General of Prisons
Dacca Division,
Central Jail,
DACCA.

Facsimiles of selected pages from the author's manuscript

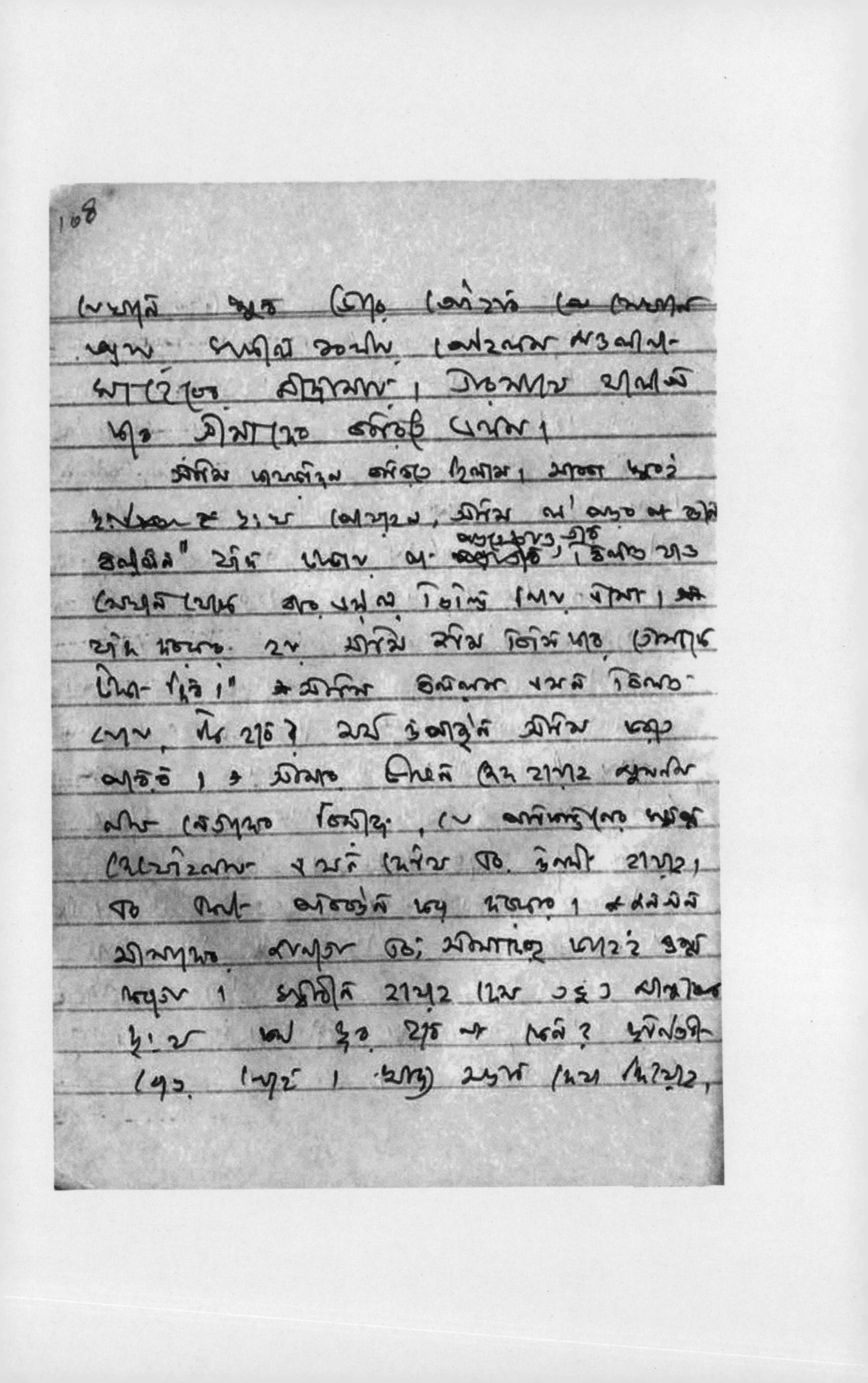

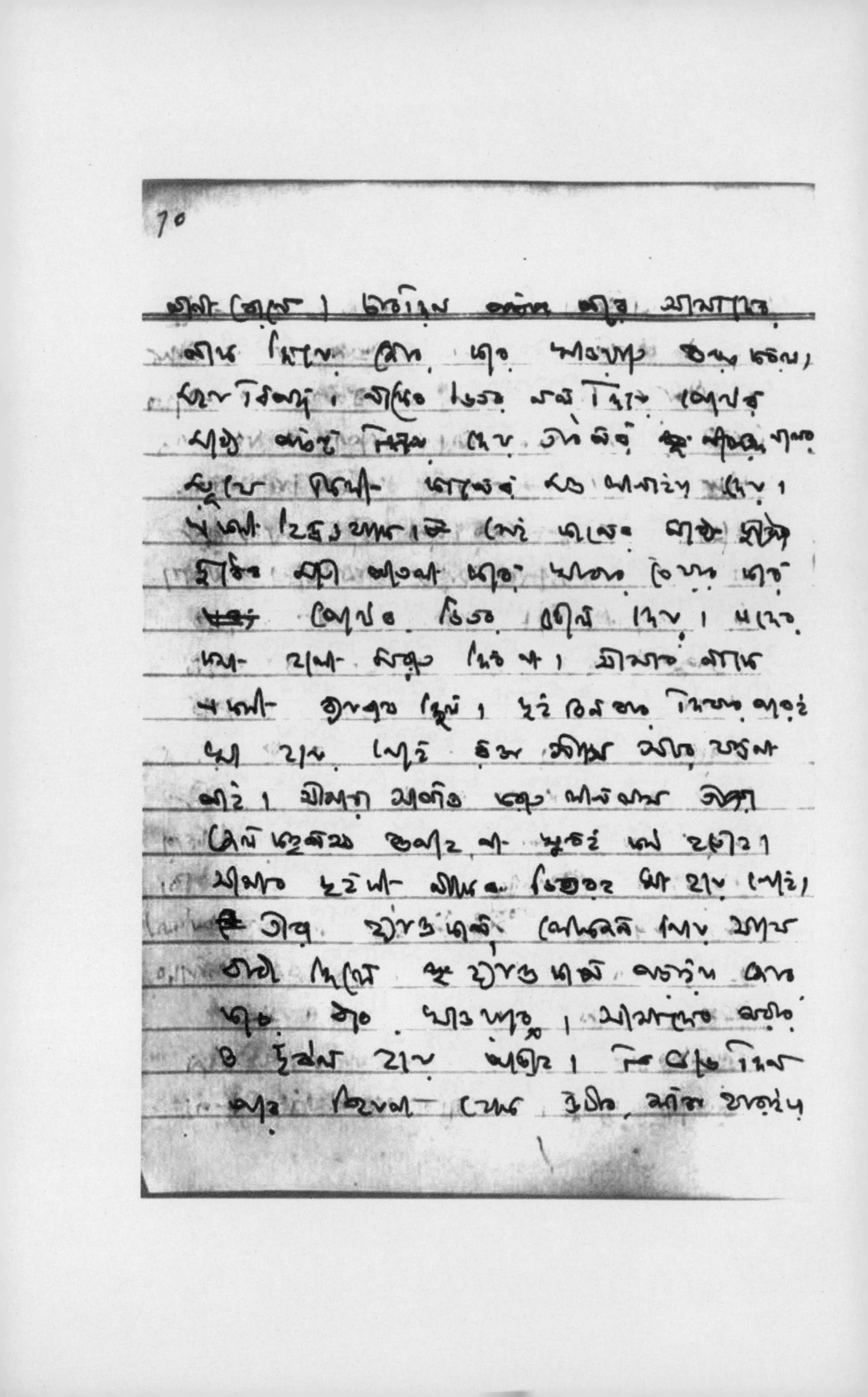

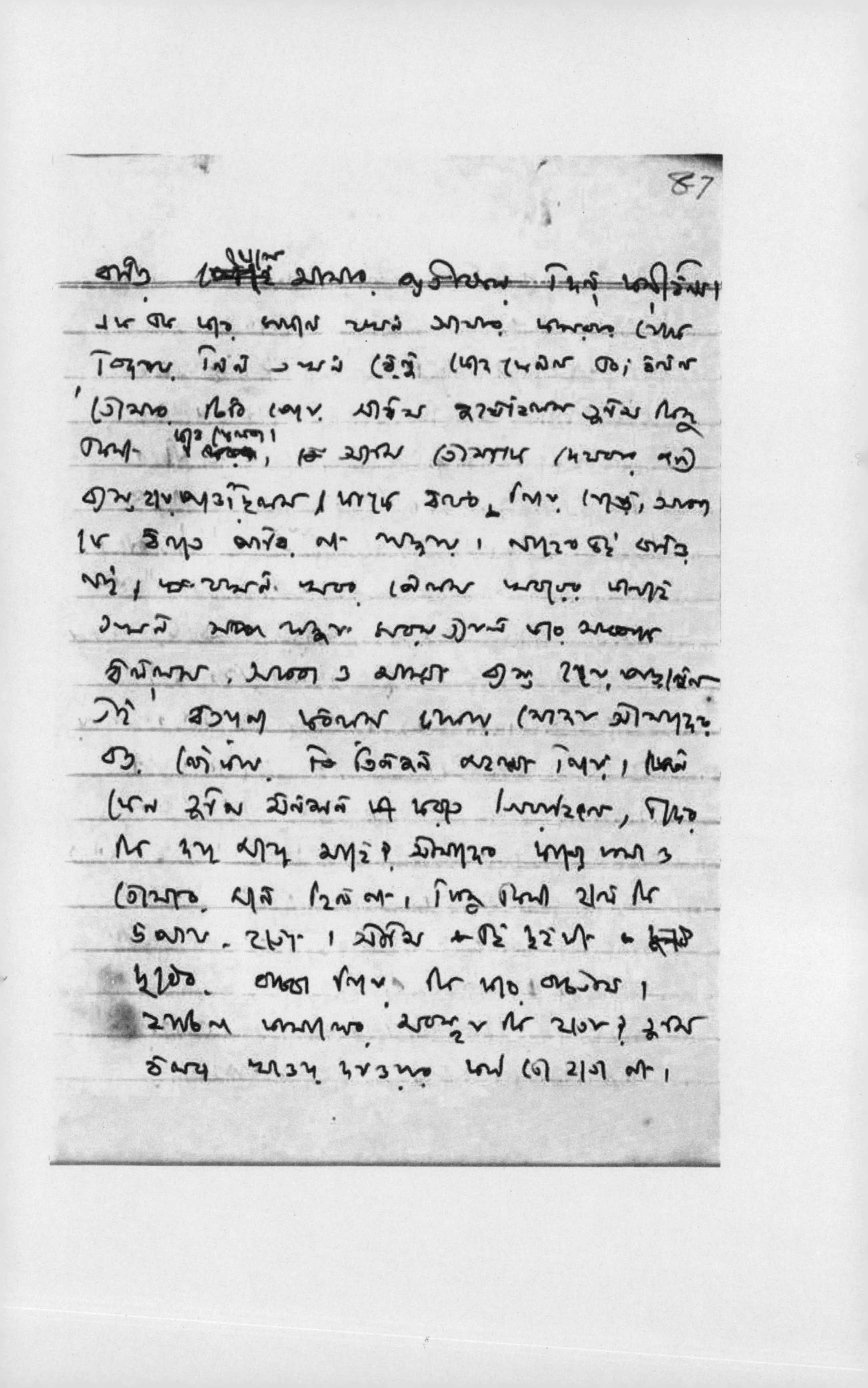

[illegible]

[illegible]

[illegible]

[illegible]

[illegible]

[illegible]

[illegible]

[illegible]

[illegible]

[illegible]

[illegible]

[illegible]

[illegible]

[illegible]

[illegible]

[illegible]

[illegible]

[illegible]

[illegible]

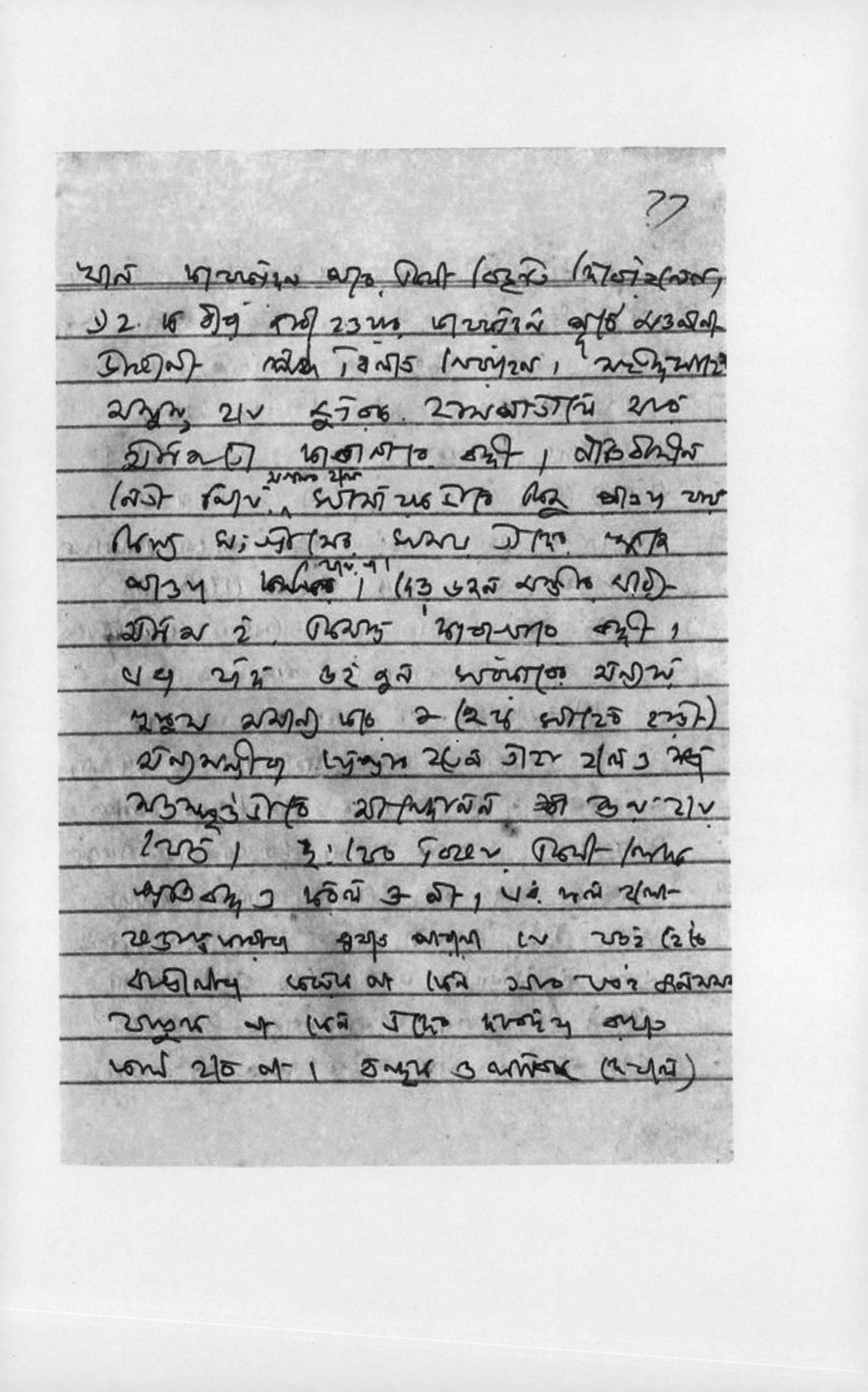

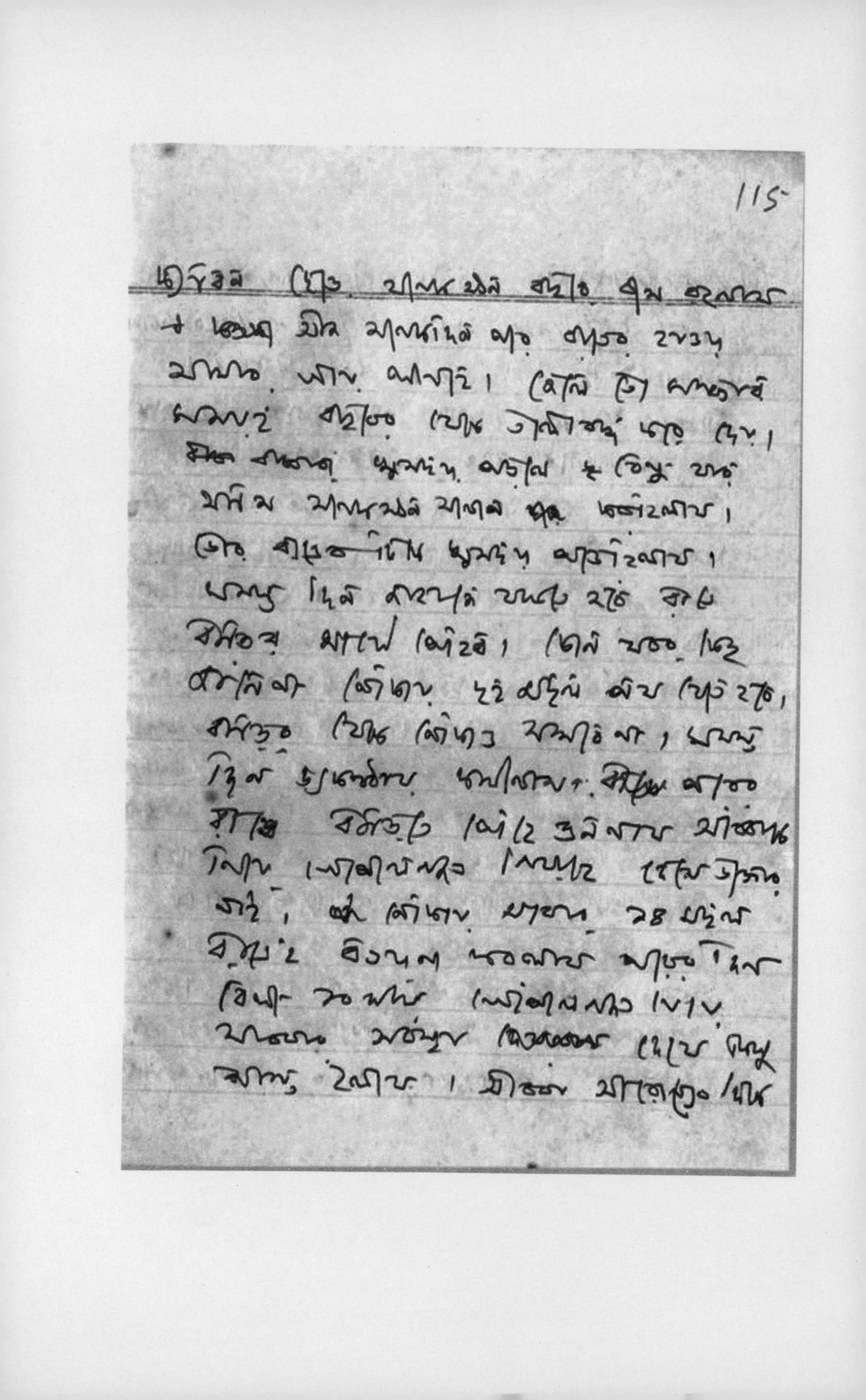

INDEX